T5-AVO-565

THE FIRST AND SECOND DALHOUSIE MANUSCRIPTS

THE FIRST AND SECOND DALHOUSIE MANUSCRIPTS

POEMS AND PROSE BY JOHN DONNE AND OTHERS

A FACSIMILE EDITION

EDITED BY ERNEST W. SULLIVAN, II

UNIVERSITY OF MISSOURI PRESS
COLUMBIA, 1988

University of Missouri Press, Columbia, Missouri 65211
Printed and bound in the United States of America

Library of Congress Cataloging-in-Publication Data

The First and second Dalhousie manuscripts: poems and prose by John Donne and others.

Bibliography: p.
Includes index.
1. English literature—Early modern, 1500–1700
Manuscripts—Facsimiles. 2. Donne, John, 1572–1631
Manuscripts—Facsimiles. 3. British Library. Manuscript. Lansdowne 740 Facsimiles. 4. Trinity College
(Dublin, Ireland). Library. Manuscript. 877
Facsimiles. 5. Manuscripts, English—Facsimiles.
6. English literature—Early modern, 1500–1700.
I. Sullivan, Ernest W.
PR1127.F57 1988 821'.3 87–19126
ISBN 0–8262–0662–X (alk. paper)

∞™ This paper meets the minimum requirements of the American National Standard for Permanence of Paper for Printed Library Materials, Z39.48, 1984.

This book has been brought to publication with the generous assistance of the Publications Program of the National Endowment for the Humanities, an independent federal agency.

FOR ELEANOR

PREFACE

This edition of the Dalhousie I and II manuscripts of the poems and prose of John Donne (1572–1631) and others provides scholars and students with a photographic facsimile and a facing transcription of two of the most important Renaissance verse miscellanies yet discovered. The introduction to the edition discusses the discovery of the Dalhousie manuscripts, describes them, explains how they were compiled and transcribed, and analyzes their textual and literary significance.

The edition revises our knowledge of the genesis and transmission of John Donne's poetic manuscripts by placing the Dalhousie manuscripts very early in the major Donne manuscript traditions. The discussions of the textual and critical significance of the Dalhousie manuscripts establish their importance to Donne textual and critical studies, and the textual apparatus provides the first complete listing of the substantive variants among Donne's seven, seventeenth-century collected editions/issues for the forty-six Dalhousie Donne poems. Further discovery that the Dalhousie I manuscript derives from papers preserved by the Essex family and that the Essex collection became the basis for British Library MS. Lansdowne 740 and, ultimately, Trinity College Dublin MS. 877 suggests that Donne's patrons and poetical coterie, rather than Donne himself, may lie behind the major manuscript collections of his poems; and the deliberate nature of the Dalhousie collections has important implications for the study of Renaissance verse and culture generally. With this publication, the known manuscript locations for the Dalhousie poems are dramatically expanded, making it possible to trace the manuscript circulation of poems by several important Renaissance poets.

Two Texas Tech University Faculty Development Leaves, a Fellowship at the University of Edinburgh Institute for Advanced Studies in the Humanities, an American Council of Learned Societies Grant-in-Aid, a National Endowment for the Humanities Travel to Collections Grant, and the Texas State Organized Research Fund supported the travel and research for the edition.

For permission to examine microfilm of their manuscripts, I am indebted to the Bedfordshire Record Office, Bibliothèque Nationale, Chetham's Library, Derbyshire Record Office, Folger Shakespeare Library, Harvard University Library, Henry E. Huntington Library, Hertfordshire Record Office, University of Illinois Library, John Rylands University Library, University of Kansas Library, Leeds Archives Department, University of Leeds, the United States Air Force Academy, and Yale University Library. For allowing me to examine their manuscripts and for the service of their staffs, I am particularly indebted to Aberdeen University Library; British Library; Bradford District Archives; Cambridge University Library; Emmanuel College Library, Cambridge; St. John's College Library, Cambridge; Magdalene College Library, Cambridge; Trinity College Library, Cambridge; Trinity College Library, Dublin; Edinburgh University Library; London Public Record Office; Leicestershire Record Office; University of Nottingham Library; University of Newcastle upon Tyne Library; New York Public Library; Bodleian Library; All Souls College Library, Oxford; Corpus Christi College Library, Oxford; St. John's College Library, Oxford; Queen's College Library, Oxford; Christ Church College Library, Oxford; Worcester College Library, Oxford; Rutgers University Library; National Library of Scotland; Scottish Record Office; St. Paul's Cathedral Library; Texas A&M University Library; Texas Tech University Library; Victoria and Albert Museum; Westminster Abbey Library; William Andrews Clark Memorial Library; and the National Library of Wales.

The following librarians graciously provided me with manuscript locations of poems: Dr. J. T. D. Hall, University of Edinburgh; Alexander D. Wainwright, Princeton University; H. J. R. Wing, Christ Church, Oxford; Laetitia Yeandle, Folger Shakespeare Library; Norma Aubertin-Potter, All Souls College, Oxford; Judith Wilson, Harvard University; Michael R. Powell, Chetham's Library; Patricia C. Willis, Rosenbach Museum & Library; and Clark Beck, Rutgers University. I particularly thank Timothy Heneage for his hospitality and for granting me access to his manuscript and the Bedford Estates for granting me access to their manuscript.

I am enormously indebted to Drs. Dale Cluff, Ray Janeway, and David Murrah for arranging the purchase of the Dalhousie manuscripts by Texas Tech University Library. I also owe thanks to John Bidwell of the William Andrews Clark Memorial Library, who called my attention to the impending sale of the Dalhousie II manuscript. My colleagues Ted-Larry Pebworth, John T. Shawcross, Gary A. Stringer, and Ed George provided microfilms, important information about poems and authors in the Dalhousie manuscripts, and advice about Renaissance Latin. Jim A. Childress, B.P.H., M. Photog., provided the photography of the Dalhousie manuscripts.

My greatest thanks go to Dr. Peter Beal: he discovered the Dalhousie manuscripts, provided invaluable expertise in helping me locate and purchase the Dalhousie I manuscript, made possible my research with the manuscripts in private hands, lent me xerox and microfilm, and literally wrote the book on the study of English literary manuscripts.

E.W.S.
Lubbock, Texas
August 1, 1987

CONTENTS

DALHOUSIE II TEXT

INTRODUCTION

Modern Provenance of the Dalhousie Manuscripts

In 1977, Peter Beal discovered the Dalhousie I and II manuscripts in the depository of the Dalhousie family at the Scottish Record Office in Edinburgh. Scottish Record Office volume "GD 45 Inventory of Dalhousie Muniments Vol III. Sections 17–26 Pages 648–962," entry 95, p. 947, reads: "[Early 17 cent.] Paper-covered volumes (2), one having the signature of Andrew Ramsay, both containing poems mostly [?all] by John Donne. (One with a few notes in the handwriting of Patrick Maule of Panmure)." Beal lists and describes the Dalhousie I manuscript (Scottish Record Office number GD 45/26/95/1) as Δ11 and the Dalhousie II manuscript (Scottish Record Office number GD 45/26/95/2) as Δ12 and classifies them among the now eight Group II Donne manuscripts in his *Index of English Literary Manuscripts*, vol. 1, pt. 1, p. 251.

The two manuscripts next surfaced at the 21 July 1981 Sotheby's sale in London of "The Property of the Rt. Hon. the Earl of Dalhousie K.T., G.C.V.O., G.B.E., M.C." of Brechin Castle, Scotland. The Dalhousie I manuscript (item 490), the larger of the two manuscripts, was purchased by Virginia Makin, from whom Texas Tech University bought the manuscript on 27 September 1983. The Dalhousie II manuscript (item 491) did not fetch a sufficiently attractive bid and was withdrawn. At a second auction of the muniments of the Earl of Dalhousie at Sotheby's on 15 December 1982, Maggs of London purchased the Dalhousie II manuscript (item 49). Maggs sold the manuscript to Zeitlin and Ver Brugge, a Los Angeles dealer in antiquities, and Texas Tech University purchased the manuscript on 7 March 1983.

Manuscript Descriptions

The Dalhousie I manuscript (henceforth, TT1) evidently suffered no changes between the time of its original cataloging at the Scottish Record Office and its arrival at Texas Tech University. The Scottish Record Office catalog mentions "Paper-covered volumes," an appropriate description for TT1, still bound in very old reinforced paper stitched with very old leather thongs. Neither the binding nor the stitching is original, although the reinforced paper cover and the manuscript leaves show few signs of the wear one would expect around the stitching holes if many rebindings or restitchings had taken place (folios 1–4 do have some minor repair around the bottom hole). The slightly trimmed—there is no loss of text, and the crowded text on some leaves suggests that the copyist recognized that he was nearing the bottom of the leaf—folio leaves measure 293 × 195 mm and have a 63.5 × 14 mm pot watermark with features of watermarks 12701 (1573), 12704 (1542), 12739 (1556), 12765 (1564), and 12805 (1555) in C. M. Briquet, *Les filigranes dictionnaire historique des marques du papier*, 2d ed., and with features of watermarks 466, 469, and 471 in W. A. Churchill, *Watermarks in Paper in Holland, England, France, etc., in the XVII and XVIII Centuries and Their Interconnection.* The sixty-nine-leaf manuscript contains five hands (the following handwriting segments include blank pages up to the succeeding segment): 1A, folios 1–10, 11–20v, 62v–63v; 1B, folios 10v–11; 1C, folios 21–62; 1D, folio 62v; and 1E, folios 64–69v.

TT1 is in excellent physical condition (marred only by very slight water staining and a few worm holes), and the fact that many of its leaves are complete folio sheets rather than loose leaves simplifies determination of its original binding order and relative completeness. Since TT1 has obviously been bound in its current order for a long time, and since its sheets lay unnoticed (and, presumably, undisturbed) for so long, the current order, despite the possibility of lost materials, likely approximates the original. Unfortunately, the presence of only three catchwords (two on rectos and one before a missing leaf!) and of twenty-three blank pages as well as an apparent effort by the copyists to keep poems from spanning more than one leaf prevents certainty in reconstructing the order and contents of the original TT1, particularly for the first twenty-three leaves.

The original order of current folios 1–13 remains particularly problematical: even though only folios 5, 6, and 13 are not full sheets, many of the leaves are blank (folios 3, 4, 7, 8, 12, and 13), two hands (1A and 1B) appear, only three catchwords occur, and only one poem (Sir John Davies's "Unto that sparkling wit, that spirit of fire") occurs from the Dalhousie II manuscript (henceforth, TT2) or from British Library MS. Lansdowne 740 (henceforth, B78), which TT1 closely resembles. Currently, folios 1–4 form a two-sheet quire; folios 5 and 6 are independent leaves; and folios 7–13 form a four-sheet quire with the original folio 7 razored out. I hypothesize an initial, three-sheet quire with sheet 1/4 as the outer sheet, followed by 2/3, and then by a missing sheet containing the remainder of King James's reply to Archbishop Abbot. The catchword "first." on folio 2v of TT1 indicates that something other than the current blank folio 3 followed; and although "first" is not the next word in the *State Trials* version of James's reply, "first" would appropriately continue his reply beyond where the missing leaf in TT1 cuts it off: "I answer, that it may be . . . But leaving this to search, my main Answer is" ("The King's Answer" in "Proceedings between the Lady Frances Howard, Countess of Essex, and Robert Earl of Essex, her Husband, before the King's Delegates, in a Cause of Divorce: 11 James I. A.D. 1613" in T. B. Howell, *A Complete Collection of State Trials*, 2:799). Further, comparing what remains of King James's trial testimony (folio 2r-v) to the complete transcript of his testimony (Howell, 2:798–802) suggests that a single sheet has been lost.[1] A five-sheet quire would have followed: the outer sheet composed of the razored-out original seventh leaf and folio 13, followed by current 7/12, 8/11, 9/10, and current 5/6 as the inner sheet. In this hypothetical quire, only the order of folios 10v–11 (spanned by Sir John Davies's poem) is certain. Current sheet 7/12 is blank and could go nearly anywhere; its tentative position puts its beginning and end in a sequence of blanks. Sir John Davies's poem (folios 10v–11) orders sheets 8/11 and 9/10, though, of course, they need not follow sheet 7/12. Leaves 5 and 6 could have been a single folio sheet: 5 has the watermark, and 6 does not; and they are in hand 1A, which appears only in folios 1–20v and in a brief reply to a Thomas Campion ballad on folio 62v.

The original order of the next group of leaves (folios 14–23) is ambiguous because most of these leaves are not complete sheets and because only a few of the poems in this group appear in either B78 or TT2. Sheet 14/15, which has the inner stitching intact, would seem to be the inner sheet of a nine-sheet quire (folios 14–23) with the first halves of all except sheet 14/15 missing. Working backward from sheet 38/55 (certainly the outer sheet of its quire), one sees that sheet 24/37 must be the outer sheet of the preceding quire; therefore, the fact that Donne's "Satyre IV" spans folios 22–24 means that folio 23 is the final leaf of its quire, must precede folio 24, and must follow folio 22. In turn, folio 21 must precede folio 22 because Donne's "Satyre III" spans folios 21–22. A change from hand 1A to hand 1C places folio 20 before the lengthy sequence beginning with folio 21. Folio 19 precedes folio 20 because an anonymous poem beginning "Some who the speakinge sparke of my first loue did spie" spans 19v–20. Folios 17–19 seem correctly ordered: the poems from 17v to 19 appear as in TT2. No evidence positions folio 16 or sheet 14/15, though folios 15v (15 is blank) to 20 are in hand 1A. The watermarks in these independently bound leaves do not suggest that the matching other half-sheets remain in the manuscript:[2] folios 16–21 have the watermark, and 22–23 do not, but the order of folios 21–23 is known; thus, 22 and 23 cannot match with current folios 16–21.

The seven-sheet quire comprising folios 24–37 is very likely original. Since sheet 38/55 is certainly the outer sheet of the following quire, folio 37 must be the final leaf of this one, and Donne's "Satyre IV" (folios 22–24) establishes that this quire follows folio 23. In addition, since hand 1C covers folios 21–62, the final three quires of TT1 would seem in original order. Sheet 25/36 must follow sheet 24/37 because Donne's "Satyre V" spans folios 24v–25, and sheet 26/35 must follow 25/36 because Donne's "Satyre II" spans folios 25v–26v. Sheet 27/34 must follow 26/35 because the anonymous "Libell agaynst Bashe" spans folios 34–36v. Sheet 28/33 need not follow 27/34, and material could be omitted from between them;[3] however, sheet 28/33 very probably precedes 29/32 because the poems on folios 32 and 32v respectively are headed "*Eligia* 4" and "*Eligia* 5," and that on folio 33 is headed "*Eligia* 6." In the same way, sheet 29/32 probably precedes 30/31 because the poems on folios 30v–31 are headed "*Eligia* 2" and "*Eligia* 3" respectively, and that on folio 32 is "*Eligia* 4." Furthermore, the Overbury "Characters" on folios 29–30 occur in exactly the same order in their only other known manuscript locations (B78, folios 80v–81, and Trinity College, Dublin MS. 877 [henceforth, DT4], folios 141–42v), and folios 29v and 30 share an ink blot near line 12. The presence of material between "*Eligia.* 1" (folio 27r-v) and "*Eligia* 2" need not cause concern because "*Eligia* 2" begins on folio 30v and must follow Sir Thomas Overbury's "The Authours Epitaph. Written by Himselfe" (folio 30).[4]

The nine-sheet quire of folios 38–55 is original. Its outer sheet, 38/55, is linked to the outer sheet of the following quire, 56/69, by Donne's "Communitie" (folios 55v–56); thus, the quire must begin with folio 38. Sheet 39/54 follows 38/55 because Donne's "The Funerall" spans folios 54v–55. Donne's "To Mr. *Rowland Woodward*: 'Like one who'in her third widdowhood'" orders sheets 39/54 and 40/53. Sheet 41/52 follows 40/53 because Francis Beaumont's "To the Countesse of Rutland" spans folios 52v–53. Sheet 42/51 follows 41/52: Donne's "Elegie: 'Oh, let mee not serve so'" spans folios 51v–52. Sir John Roe's "*To Sr Tho. Roe* 1603" orders sheets 42/51 and 43/50; and his "An Elegie. *Reflecting on his passion for his mistrisse*" orders sheets 43/50 and 44/49. Sheet 45/48 follows 44/49: Donne's "Elegie on the Lady Marckham" spans folios 48v–49. Sheet 46/47 follows 45/48: Donne's "Loves diet" spans folios 47v–48.

The final, seven-sheet quire (folios 56–69) almost certainly is original. Its outer sheet, 56/69, must follow 38/55, the outer sheet of the previous quire: Donne's "Communitie" spans folios 55v–56. Sir Walter Ralegh's "The Lie" orders sheets 57/68 and 58/67; Sir Thomas Overbury's translations of Ovid's *Remedia Amoris*, "The Remedy of Loue" and "The second part of the Remedy of Loue," order sheets 58/67, 59/66, 60/65, 61/64, and 62/63. Any possible loss would have to have occurred between sheets 56/69 and 57/68. Interestingly, B78 does have four more Donne poems ("The Dreame," "A Valediction of weeping," "A Feaver," and "The Paradox," folios 125v–27) as well as Sir John Roe's "To Sicknesse" (folio 127v) between the sequence involving Donne's "Womans constancy" (TT1, folio 56; B78, folio 125) and Sir John Harington's "Of the commodities that men haue by their Marriage" (TT1, folio 56v; B78, folio 128); however, since the poems present in B78 could not be omitted between 56 and 56v in TT1 as the result of missing leaves and since the equivalent TT2 manuscript sequence of Donne poems (copied from TT1 at a very early date) also ends with "Womans constancy," the likelihood of leaves

1. James's testimony on folio 2r-v in TT1 corresponds to one and one-half columns in Howell (cols. 798–99); the missing material in TT1, then, corresponds to another two and one-half columns in Howell, or three and one-third folio pages.

2. The only other loose leaves in TT1, folios 5 and 6 (folio 13 is loose but has a substantial remaining stub), contain hand B (folios 15–20 are in hand A) and material unrelated to that found in folios 14–23.

3. TT1 does break with the B78 sequence at folio 28, where TT1 has the anonymous "A Paradoxe of a Painted Face" and B78 has "A Satire: to Sr Nicholas Smith: 1602."

4. Interestingly, B78 has much of the same material between its "Elegie 1" and "Elegia. 2."

containing Donne poems missing between 56/69 and 57/68 seems small.

TT2, on the other hand, underwent some changes between its original cataloging at the Scottish Record Office and its purchase by Texas Tech University. The Scottish Record Office catalog mentions "paper-covered volumes"; however, between the time that Beal saw TT2 at the Scottish Record Office and 21 July 1981, when it was auctioned at Sotheby's, all of its thirty-four leaves had been repaired, mounted on guards, and rebound with a dark blue cloth cover. In addition, its third leaf had been reversed (the earlier, penciled "3" in the same hand as the other modern foliation is still visible on the now verso side; a penciled "3" in a different hand appears on the now recto side). With all traces of the original binding lost and only the modern foliation, the order of the leaves in, and the contents of, the original manuscript remains problematical.

Substantial evidence does suggest, however, that the current state of the manuscript closely approximates the original order of leaves and contents. Catchwords in the hand of the copyist on folios 25v ("her"), 26v ("yett"), and 30v ("striue") establish the sequence of 25–27 and 30–31. Folios 5–6, 7–8, 9–10, 25–26, 26–27, and 30–31 are also ordered by Donne's "Elegie: Loves Progress," which spans folios 5–6; an unidentified poem, "If kinges did heretofore there loues indite," which spans folios 7–8; Donne's "The Will," which spans folios 25v–26; Francis Beaumont's "To the Countesse of Rutland," which spans folios 26–27; and Josuah Sylvester's "The Fruites of a cleere *Conscience*," which spans folios 30v–31. Furthermore, even though they overlap no leaves, poems headed "*Elegia* 3," "*Eligia*. 4," "*Eligia*. 5," and "*Elegia*: 6" sequentially occupy folios 15–17, implying that this unit of pages retains its original order. Finally, Donne's "A Storme" (folio 18r-v) and "A Calme" (folio 19) are in their proper and less obvious sequence. If what are now folios 18 and 19 were in some other sequence when the foliator or binder encountered them, he would not only have had to make a connection between the topics of these two poems but also to have read the first line of "A Calme" ("Our storme is past") to arrange the present order; thus, the foliator or binder very likely found 18 and 19 in their present and traditional order as loose leaves.

Without establishing any specific ordering within the units, handwriting also groups the leaves into larger units that tend to verify the integrity of the above segments. Four hands appear in TT2 (handwriting segments include blank pages up to the succeeding segment): 2A, folio 1; 2B, folios 1v–2v; 2C, folios 3–4v, 21v–34v; and 2D, folios 5–21. These handwriting units support the integrity of the blocks of folios 5–6, 7–8, 9–10, 15–17, 18–19 (all in hand 2D), 25–27, and 30–31.

Watermark occurrences also provide evidence of the original order of TT2. Although no direct evidence identifies any particular folds in any particular sheet, the most complete remaining leaves measure 305 × 195 mm; thus, the leaves were almost certainly originally in folio format, a suggestion supported by the presence of the watermark on almost exactly half of the leaves (sixteen of thirty-four). The watermark, a 67 × 23 mm pot with features of watermarks 12783 (1564–1569) and 12803 (1580–1594) in Briquet and 469 and 471 in Churchill, occurs on folios 3, 5, 8, 12, 14–20, 22, 31–32, and 34. From the previously described evidence of catchwords, poems that span leaves, and poems in labeled or traditional sequences, one can feel reasonably certain that the following watermark pattern matches the original manuscript: yes, no (folios 5–6); no, yes (7–8); no (9–10); yes (15–19); no (25–27); and no, yes (30–31).

Even with the above evidence, the original order of current leaves 1–14 remains extremely ambiguous. Folios 5–14 are in one hand, but the only certain foliation sequence units are 5–6, 7–8, and 9–10, and the order of these units remains uncertain. Folios 1–4 possibly form a two-sheet quire: 1 and 1v have different hands, and 3 and 4 have hand 2C with either three attempts to copy an unidentified poem beginning "My deare and onelie loue tak heede" or three slightly different and partial versions of the poem. These first four leaves would form a two-sheet quire with the watermarks on folios 3 and 4 and the contents not related to any other sequence in the manuscript. Folios 5–14 contain the basis of a seven-sheet quire, particularly if one accepts the present sequence of the 5–6, 7–8, and 9–10 folio units. The innermost sheet would be folio 10 (no) and a missing leaf (yes); expanding outward, one would have 9 (no) and a missing leaf (yes), 8 (yes)/11 (no), 7 (no)/12 (yes), 6 (no)/missing leaf (yes), 5 (yes)/13 (no), and a missing leaf (no)/14 (yes).

The next segment, folios 15–29, likely consists of the inner seven sheets of the original, nine-sheet quire with the leaves in their original order. The innermost sheet would be 21 (no)/22 (yes); expanding outward one would have 20 (yes)/23 (no), 19 (yes)/24 (no), 18 (yes)/25 (no), 17 (yes)/26 (no), 16 (yes)/27 (no), and 15 (yes)/28 (no). The almost certain correctness of the sequence of folios 15–19 (all yes), beginning with "*Elegia* 3," the certitude of the sequence of folios 25–27 (all no), and the exactly matching sequences of watermark occurrences (folios 15–20 yes; 23–28 no) suggest the completeness and correctness of the order of folios 15–28. In fact, it appears that folio 29 (which would complete a unit of Donne poems begun on folio 27) and another leaf immediately preceding or following it originally belonged to the quire of folios 15–28, giving a nine-sheet quire, with only the first two leaves and the leaf adjacent to current folio 29 missing. If the first two missing leaves contained the same material as the identical sequence in TT1 and B78, one of the missing elegies would very likely have been "Elegie: The Comparison" (54 lines), headed "*Eligia* 2" and "Elegia. 2" in TT1 and B78 and immediately preceding "Elegie: The Perfume," the "*Elegia* 3" of TT1, B78, and TT2. TT1 and B78 fill the remainder of these two initial missing leaves with the Overbury "Characters" and "Epitaph."[5] The missing leaf immediately preceding folio 29 would contain "The Funerall" and "Loves Usury" if the sequence parallels that in TT1 and B78.

The final five leaves, folios 30–34, may be the remainder of a three-sheet quire with the second half of the inner sheet missing and lacking the watermark. The catchword "striue" on folio 30v establishes the order of folios 30–31

5. The Elegie 1 of B78 is "Elegie: The Bracelet" (114 lines), which occurs elsewhere in TT1 (folio 27r-v) and TT2 (folios 9–10).

(as well as of 33–34 in the case of a three-sheet quire), and the anonymous poem beginning "Why doe yee giue mee leaue to sip" at the bottom of folio 32v is incomplete.

Transcription and Compilation of the Manuscripts

The entirety of TT1 was undoubtedly transcribed during Donne's lifetime. On the basis of the first and last items in the manuscript—testimony of Archbishop Abbot and King James I concerning the divorce of Lady Frances Howard from Robert Devereux, Third Earl of Essex, on 12 May 1613 and an elegy on Ludovick Stuart, Duke of Richmond, who died 30 July 1624—the Sotheby sales catalog for 21 July 1981 dates TT1 between 1620 and 1625, as does Beal (1:251). Briquet's dates for paper with similar watermarks range from 1542 to 1573.

TT2 was also almost certainly transcribed during Donne's lifetime. It contains two transcriptions of a song "*Carold for new yeeres day* 1624" (folios 21v, 33), its first leaf is dated "the 28th of september the year of our Lord i622," and its final leaf bears "An Epitaph vpon the Duke off Buckinghame" (George Villiers, who died 23 August 1628). Although the Buckingham epitaph could have been transcribed many years afterward from a 1628 original, no source for this epitaph exists in *British Poetry: First and Last Lines* (the index to manuscript poems in the British Library) or in Margaret Crum's *First-Line Index of English Poetry 1500–1800 in Manuscripts of the Bodleian Library Oxford*, suggesting that the TT2 epitaph may be the original.[6] Certainly the uniformity of the paper throughout the manuscript (and folio 34 does have the usual pot watermark) implies that no very great period transpired from the dating of the earliest leaf in the manuscript (28 September 1622) to the transcription of the latest item. Briquet's similar watermarks are dated 1564–1569 and 1580–1594.

Internal evidence suggests, however, that the versions of the texts preserved by TT1 and TT2 may be much earlier than the dated materials at the beginnings and ends of the manuscripts; that at least the main body of poems in hand 1C (folios 21–62, including all but two of the forty-four Donne poems) in TT1 could derive from pre-1609 versions of the Donne poems; and that TT1 to folio 62 was transcribed prior to August 1617. The datable original versions of poems in the sequence are very early indeed: 1595 for the two Davies poems on Richard Fletcher, 1597 for Donne's "The Storme" and "The Calme," and 1602 and 1603 for the Roe poems. John T. Shawcross assigns all the Donne poems in this sequence (indeed, all the Donne poems in TT1 and TT2) dates earlier than July 1611 ("Chronological Schedule of the Poems," *The Complete Poetry of John Donne*, pp. 411–17), and even his July 1611 date for "A Valediction forbidding mourning" depends on Izaak Walton's unsupported account in his *Life of Donne* that Donne wrote the poem when he went abroad with the Druries; the latest certain date for the Donne poems in TT1 and TT2 is 4 August 1609 ("Elegie on Mris. Boulstred"). In addition to the 12 May 1613 date for the divorce proceedings, evidence suggests that the material in TT1 up to folio 62 was transcribed before August 1617. Ted-Larry Pebworth, whose edition of the poems of Henry Wotton is in press, has established that the TT1 version of Sir Henry Wotton's "The Character of a Happy Life" (folio 11) predates the earliest published version (4th impression of Sir Thomas Overbury's *A Wife*, 1614). The Sir Thomas Overbury materials (folios 29–30, 58v–62) must antedate his death on 15 September 1613; yet at least the "Characters" (folios 29–30) postdate the involvement of the Earl of Somerset with Lady Essex (late 1612) if W. J. Paylor is correct in arguing that "A Very Very Woman" and "Her Next Part" specifically attack the behavior of Lady Essex during her divorce (*The Overburian Characters*, pp. 109–11). After the main sequence in hand 1C, hand 1D adds a Thomas Campion song (folio 62v) composed to celebrate the return of James I to Scotland in August 1617 (first published in George Mason and John Earsden, *The Ayres That Were Svng and Played, at Brougham Castle in Westmerland, in the Kings Entertainment* [London, 1618], sig. C1); hand 1A adds a reply to Campion's song (folio 62v); and hand 1E adds two more datable poems of Scottish interest that end the manuscript, "An *Elegie* on the late *Lord William Haward* Baron of Effingham, dead *the tenth of December.* 1615" (actually, 28 November 1615) and "On the Duke of Richmonds fate an Elegie" (d. 30 July 1624); thus, the poems in hand 1C that form the main part of TT1 (folios 21–62) were very likely copied as a unit and taken to Scotland before August 1617. That these seventy poems were together as a unit (suggested by the single hand) is confirmed by the presence of virtually the same unit of poems in B78 (see below).

Obviously, establishing a *terminus ad quem* for copies from the dates of their originals is impossible; however, dating the transcription of the materials to folio 62 in TT1 between the 12 May 1613 divorce proceedings and the return of James I to Scotland in August 1617 would be entirely consistent with the uniform paper, pattern of handwriting segments, early states of the texts (even recognizing that late copies may preserve early textual states), the essentially chronological order of the datable originals represented by the copies, and the switch to poems of particularly Scottish interest at the end of the manuscript. As will appear below, the main poetic sequence in TT2 (folios 5–34) was copied from TT1 in Scotland.

TT1 and TT2 provide a surprising amount of information about their compilation. Both verse miscellanies contain evidence in every gathering and in the work of every copyist that they derive immediately from documents consciously preserved by one or more members of the Essex family. Some of the poems may have been collected from the papers of Robert Devereux, Second Earl of Essex (1565–1601), statesman, soldier, poet,[7] literary patron, and husband of Frances Walsingham, the widow of Sir Philip Sidney.[8] Another possible collector would be

6. Ted-Larry Pebworth, who has identified more than 250 epitaphs on Buckingham, also regards the TT2 epitaph as unique.

7. See Steven W. May, ed., "The Poems of Edward de Vere, Seventeenth Earl of Oxford and of Robert Devereux, Second Earl of Essex."

8. Donne's literary connection to the Sidney family lasted at least

Penelope Devereux (1562–1607), sister to the Second Earl, the Stella of Sir Philip Sidney's *Astrophel and Stella*, literary patroness, and indefatigable defender of her brother's reputation. The collection would have been continued beyond the 1601 and 1607 deaths of the Second Earl and Penelope by the Third Earl (1591–1646), of whom Robert Coddrington wrote: "And if ever any unseverer houres of leisure offered themselves in his study, hee would imploy that time in the perusall of some laboured Poeme, and having great judgment especially in the English Verse, it was his custome to applaud the professors of that Art, as high as their deserts and to reward them above it" (*The Life and Death of the Illvstriovs Robert Earle of Essex* [London, 1646], p. 11), or by Lady Lettice Carey and Mrs. Essex Rich, daughters of Penelope Devereux, to whom Donne wrote "A Letter to the Lady Carey, and Mrs. Essex Riche, From Amyens" in 1611, about the time the collection reached that state in which the Dalhousie manuscripts preserve it.

The most likely copyist or conduit from the court of James to the Dalhousie family would have been Sir John Ramsay, Viscount Haddington and Earl of Holderness (1580–1626). Although the Second Earl of Essex had been executed for treason by order of Queen Elizabeth (25 February 1601), the Essex family was prominent in the court of James I: the Third Earl was restored in blood and honor by act of Parliament in 1604 and his marriage to Frances Howard in 1606 "had been arranged by the King, who was favourably disposed to all who were connected with the late Earl of Essex" (*DNB*, 5:890). Sir John Ramsay would have had an interest in the particular poetry in the collection as well as access to the poetry in circulation through his membership in the Inner Temple (where several of the poets represented in the Dalhousie collection studied law) and as a favored member of the court of James I. Sir John also had a likely connection to the Dalhousies who owned the manuscript—the *DNB* (16:701) identifies him as the second son of James Ramsay of Dalhousie and brother of George Ramsay, First Lord of Dalhousie.[9] Interest in preserving materials associated with the Essex family would have been strong for the Dalhousies: William Ramsay, Second Baron and First Earl of Dalhousie (d. 1674), eldest son of George Ramsay, signed the letter of covenanting lords of 19 April 1639 to the Third Earl of Essex and served with him in the Civil War against Charles I.

The material most obviously linked to the Essex family appears at first glance to be an incomplete letter from George Abbot, Archbishop of Canterbury, to King James I and an apparent incomplete reply of King James regarding the suit of Lady Frances Howard for divorce from Robert Devereux, Third Earl of Essex, on 12 May 1613 (TT1, folios 1–2v). According to the "Proceedings between the Lady Frances Howard, Countess of Essex, and Robert Earl of Essex, her Husband," George Abbot was one of eleven commissioners appointed by James to hear the petition of Lady Frances for divorce on the basis that Robert, despite attempting "very often, again and again" and with the "earnest desire" of Lady Frances, had failed to consummate their nine-year-old marriage (she had been thirteen when they married and he fourteen), even though, according to Lady Frances, he had known other women carnally before and during his marriage to her (Howell, 2:786). The official trial transcripts show that the apparent Abbot "letter" appears as "The Lord Archbishop of Canterbury's Reasons against the nullity" (Howell, 2:794–98) and that the apparent James letter is his immediately following official reply to Abbot's testimony: "To these Arguments of the Archbishop, the king vouchsafed to give an Answer himself, which was as follows" (Howell, 2:798–802). The Dalhousie text closely parallels the official trial record.

The identifiable materials in the second quire (folios 5–13) of TT1 also have links to the Essex family. Edward de Vere, Seventeenth Earl of Oxford (1550–1604), whose poem "My Mind to Me a Kingdom Is"[10] appears on folio 9r-v, as Lord Great Chamberlain oversaw the elevation of Walter Devereux to the earldom of Essex on 4 May 1572. Sir John Davies (1569–1626), whose poem "Unto that sparkling wit, that spirit of fire" appears on folios 10v–11, became Solicitor General for Ireland on 18 September 1603 and surely must have known Essex either through Essex's service as Lord Lieutenant of Ireland from 9 March 1599 to June 1600 or through their mutual Inns of Court acquaintances Sir John Harington, John Hoskyns, and Richard Corbett—all authors present in the Dalhousie manuscripts. Sir Henry Wotton (1568–1639), whose poem "The Character of a Happy Life" appears on folio 11, was secretary to the Second Earl from 1595 to 1601 and accompanied him on the ill-fated expedition to Ireland in 1599 (see Donne's verse letter "*H. W. in Hiber. belligeranti*"). In the second quire, then, the three identifiable authors accounting for three of the four poems have close links to the Second Earl.

Of the thirteen poems in the third gathering (folios 14–23), six of the eight identifiable poems and three of the five authors are connected to the Essex family.[11] John Donne (four poems) served with the Second Earl in the expedition to Cadiz in 1596–1597 and worked for Sir Thomas Egerton the elder, who, as Arthur F. Marotti points out, was "one of the Earl of Essex's most important clients" (*John Donne, Coterie Poet*, p. 116). Alexander B. Grosart prints two letters by the Second Earl from the Bacon papers at Lambeth Library recommending Josuah Sylvester (1563–1618), whose poem "A Caution for Courtly Damsels" appears on folio 17v, for secretarial positions in 1597.[12] Sir John Harington (1560–1612), whose poem "Of a Lady that giues the cheek" appears on folio 18, served the

until his poem "Upon the translation of the Psalmes by Sir Philip Sidney, and the Countesse of Pembroke his Sister," written after the death of the countess on 25 September 1621.

9. G. E. C., *The Complete Peerage* (London: St. Catherine Press, 1916), identifies this John Ramsay as a "distant kinsman" of George Ramsay, rather than as his brother (4:31).

10. This poem has traditionally been assigned to Sir Edward Dyer (1543–1607); however, Stephen W. May's "The Authorship of 'My Mind to Me a Kingdom Is,'" *The Review of English Studies*, n.s. 27 (1975):385–94, argues convincingly for Oxford's authorship.

11. The two identifiable authors unconnected to Essex are the Scottish poet Sir Robert Ayton and Jonathan Richards, a person for whom no record survives but to whom the poem "a songe: 'I die when as I doe not see'" is attributed in British Library Additional MS. 30982.

12. *The Complete Works of Joshuah Sylvester*, 1:xiv.

Second Earl as Commander of the Horse in Ireland and was knighted by him in Ireland on 30 July 1599.

Leaves 24–37 contain eight Donne poems as well as the "Epitaph" and "Characters" (folios 29–30) by Sir Thomas Overbury (1581–1613), who was a close friend of the Third Earl and who was murdered by Lady Frances Howard and her second husband, Robert Carr, Earl of Somerset, for his opposition to their marriage. Of the sixteen poems in the gathering, all twelve identifiable poems by the three identifiable authors (Donne, Overbury, and Davies) have links to the Essex family. Interestingly, the selection of Overburian characters might have had particular relevance for the Third Earl: Paylor argues that these three are very likely by Overbury himself and that "A Very Very Woman" and "Her Next Part" are not only the antitheses of "A Good Woman" but also are a specific attack on Lady Frances Howard (pp. 109–11).

Of the forty poems in the next gathering (folios 38–55), twenty-nine are by Donne, and seven are by Sir John Roe (1581–1608), who served with the Second Earl in Ireland in 1599 and may have been knighted by him: "He chose the career of a soldier and served in Ireland, and probably owes his knighthood to the Earl of Essex, who was somewhat lavish in the bestowal of that honour."[13] Francis Beaumont's "To the Countesse of Rutland" (folios 52v–53) has topical links to the Second Earl: her husband, Roger Manners, First Earl of Rutland (1576–1612), accompanied Essex on the 1599 Irish expedition, was knighted by Essex in Ireland, and participated in the Essex "plot" of 1601 against Queen Elizabeth. John Hoskyns, author of "A Poem upon Absence" and a member of Donne's "coterie" (Marotti, p. 34), knew enough of the Second Earl to use "And the speciale for the perticular, as the Earle is gone into Ireland for E: E" as an example of synecdoche in his "Direccions For Speech and Style."[14]

Of the sixteen poems in the final gathering (folios 56–69), eleven are identifiable, and all six authors have associations with the Second Earl. Two are by Donne; three by Harington; and two by Sylvester. Sir Walter Ralegh, who served with Essex at Cadiz and in the Azores, is the author of "The Lie" (folio 57v); and Thomas Campion (1567–1620), a volunteer in the 1591 Essex expedition to Dieppe, wrote "A Ballad" (folio 62v). "An *Elegie* on the late *Lord William Haward* Baron of Effingham, dead *the tenth of December*. 1615" by Richard Corbett (1582–1635) eulogizes one of the four squadron leaders in the Second Earl's expedition to Cadiz and his companion in the Azores expedition. The final poem, "On the Duke of Richmonds fate an Elegie," mourns the death of Ludovick Stuart, Second Duke of Lennox and Duke of Richmond (1574–1624), who must have known both the Second and Third Earls but may be in the collection for his Scottish connections.

The first gathering of TT2 (folios 1–4) may be incomplete; its only poem is three versions of an ancient Scottish ballad, "My deare and onelie loue tak heede" (later revised and expanded by James Graham, Marquis of Montrose [1612–1650]), which have no link to Essex.

The second gathering (folios 5–14), however, contains fourteen poems, eight identifiable as by five authors (four by Donne, and one each by Davies, Sylvester, Harington, and Richards), with only Richards unconnected to the Essex family.

The third gathering (folios 15–29) contains thirty poems, of which twenty-seven identifiable by four authors (twenty-four by Donne, and one each by Beaumont, Roe, and Francis Bacon) are associated with the Essex family. Francis Bacon (1561–1626), a longtime friend of the Second Earl, later prosecuted him in the 1601 trial for treason against Elizabeth.

In the final gathering (folios 30–34), the six of the eleven poems that are identifiable were written by six authors, four with connections to the Essex family (Donne, Ralegh, Sylvester, and William Herbert).[15] "When my Carliles Chamber was on fire" (folio 32v) by William Herbert, Third Earl of Pembroke (1580–1630), may be linked to the Essex family by both subject and author: "Carlile" may be Lucy Hay, Countess of Carlisle (1599–1660), subject of many poems during the period, and granddaughter of Walter Devereux (1541–76), the First Earl of Essex. Pembroke was a friend of Donne (Donne's son published his poems in 1660), Ralegh, Bacon, Harington, and Daniel, as well as the nephew of Sir Philip Sidney, whose widow, Frances Walsingham, had married the Second Earl in 1601. George Morley's "On the death of King James" is related to the Third Earl by topic (the Third Earl was prominent in the court and military of James I) and author (Morley edited *Excellent contemplations, divine and moral. Written by the magnanimous and truly loyal Arthur lord Capel, Baron of Hadham. Together with some account of his life . . . With his pious advice to his son the late Earl of Essex* [London, 1683]). The anonymous, unique "An Epitaph vpon the Duke off Buckinghame" would have had several links to the Third Earl, who served under George Villiers in the Palatinate and in the 1625 naval assault at Cadiz: Buckingham befriended Archbishop Abbot, opposed the Earl of Somerset, and married Katherine Manners, daughter of the Earl of Rutland.

The handwriting units within the Dalhousie manuscripts also connect the work of each copyist to the Essex family. The ten identifiable poems of the sixteen in the hand of copyist 1A in TT1 (folios 1–10, 11–20v, and 62v–63) are by eight authors (Oxford, Wotton, Ayton, Donne, Sylvester, Harington, Richards, and Campion), with only Ayton and Richards lacking evident links to the Essex family. The only poem in hand 1B is Sir John Davies's "Unto that sparkling wit, that spirit of fire" (folios 10v–11). The majority of the poems (sixty-nine) as well as the three Overburian characters are in hand 1C (folios 21–62): of these, sixty-one are identifiable as by Donne (forty-two), Overbury (three), Davies (two), Roe (seven), Hoskyns, Beaumont, Harington (three), Ralegh, and Sylvester. The one poem in hand 1D is by Thomas Campion (folio 62v). Of the three

13. Sir H. J. C. Grierson, "Note on Sir John Roe," in *The Poems of John Donne* (London: Oxford University Press, 1939), p. lv. Seven of the nine poems that Grierson claims make up the Roe canon appear in TT1.

14. Louise Brown Osborn, *The Life, Letters, and Writings of John Hoskyns, 1566–1638* (New Haven: Yale University Press, 1937), p. 124.

15. Jonathan Richards, "I die when as I doe not see" (folio 31v), has no connection by author to the Essex family.

poems in hand 1E (folios 64–67), the Second Earl is linked by subject to the elegies on Effingham and Richmond. In TT2, hands 2A and 2B appear only on folio 1 and 1v respectively and copy no poems. The thirty-two poems in hand 2C (folios 3–4v, 21v–34v) include twenty-three identifiable (sixteen by Donne and one each by Bacon, Beaumont, Ralegh, Sylvester, Richards, Pembroke, and Morley), with only this second version of Richards's "a songe: 'I die when as I doe not see'" (folio 31v) unrelated by author or content to the Essex family. The segment in hand 2D (folios 5–21) contains twenty-six poems, including thirteen by Donne and one each by Davies, Sylvester, Harington, Richards, and Roe; only "a songe: 'I die when as I doe not see'" by Richards (folio 13v) seems unconnected to the Essex family.

Essentially every part of the Dalhousie manuscripts, whether formed by gatherings or by the workings of various copyists at various times, bears a relatively direct relationship to the Second or Third Earl of Essex. It would seem that the men who had served the earls in civil or military capacities sent their poetry to them in hopes of patronage and preferment and that the poems were then collected (and perhaps arranged) by one of the Essex family. The collection was subsequently copied at least twice, first by someone, perhaps Sir John Ramsy, connected to the Dalhousie family and second into B78 by someone connected to the Cecil family (Penelope Devereux maintained good relations with the Cecil family).[16]

Textual Significance of the Manuscripts

Modern editors of Donne's texts have focused primarily on the seven seventeenth-century collected editions/issues of Donne's *Poems* and on a few major manuscripts that appeared to represent efforts to collect all of Donne's poems. This approach sidesteps the possibility that the collected editions and major manuscript collections of Donne's poems may derive from smaller collections, particularly groups of poems that circulated together, and that the texts of poems in these smaller collections (or even individual poems) of the sort that appear in verse miscellanies might be closer at least chronologically to Donne's originals than are the texts in the larger collections. Although the relationships among the more than two hundred and fifty manuscripts containing Donne's poems need working out before one can establish the precise significance of the Dalhousie manuscripts, these manuscripts do suggest the necessity of postulating a new hypothesis for the genesis and transmission of the texts in what is called the Group II Donne manuscript tradition, and they do suggest the need to reassess the current theory that "Y" (Helen Gardner's hypothetical manuscript behind the Group II tradition) and "X" (her hypothetical manuscript behind the Group I tradition) were collections made by Donne from his own manuscripts.[17]

On the basis of poem sequence, collations, and contents, the Dalhousie manuscripts belong to what Donne's Oxford editors have designated the Group II manuscripts: British Library Additional MS. 18647; Harvard University Library MS. Eng. 966.3; Trinity College, Cambridge MS. R 3 12; DT4; B78; and National Library of Wales Dolau Cothi MS. 6748 (W. Milgate, ed., *John Donne: The Epithalamions, Anniversaries, and Epicedes*, p. lxv). These manuscripts contain a large collection of Donne poems that, according to Helen Gardner, derives from a single manuscript "Y" that was completed around 1625 and that grew by accretion from a smaller collection preserved in B78 (*John Donne: The Elegies and the Songs and Sonnets*, pp. lxvii-lxviii).

The early date and position of B78 in the stemma of the Donne Group II manuscript tradition suggest the potential textual significance of the closely related and even earlier Dalhousie manuscripts (Beal [1:251] assigns B78 to the 1620s). Sir H. J. C. Grierson first recognized the early date of the poems in B78 and its connection with what became the Group II manuscripts: "The Lansdowne MS. 740, in the British Museum, is an interesting collection of Donne's mainly earlier and secular poems, along with several by contemporaries. The text of the *Satyres* connects this collection with *A18* [listed by Grierson, page xcii, as British Library Additional MS. 18646; actually 18647], *N* [Harvard University Library 966.3], *TC* [Trinity College, Cambridge and Trinity College, Dublin MS. 877], but it is probably older, and it contains none of the *Divine Poems* and no poem written later than 1610" (*The Poems of John Donne*, 2:civ-cv). Shawcross assigns all the Donne poems in B78 dates earlier than July 1611 (*Donne*, pp. 411–17), and, as mentioned above, even this July 1611 date for "A Valediction forbidding mourning" is based on Izaak Walton's account in the *Life of John Donne* that Donne wrote the poem when he went abroad with the Druries; the latest certain date is 4 August 1609 for the "Elegie on Mris. Boulstred." Helen Gardner argues that the B78 texts are the earliest of those preserved in the Group II manuscripts: "If we are considering the possibility of 'earlier or later versions' of poems, it is possible that Group II preserves 'earlier versions' in poems that it has in common with *L 74* [Lansdowne 740], and 'later versions' in the poems that the compiler of Y added to make up his very full collection" (p. lxx).

The contents, their sequence, and headings establish the close relationship among B78, TT1, and what remains of the original TT2; the extraordinary parallels among these manuscripts place them securely in the same line of textual transmission. TT1 and B78 have the same seventy-two

16. Materials related to the Essex family probably reached the Marquis of Lansdowne (William Petty, 1737–1805) via the Cecil family papers or via Sir Julius Caesar (1558–1636), one of the commissioners appointed to hear the Lady Frances Howard suit (though Sir Julius is less likely since he sided with Lady Frances): "His [Lansdowne's] valuable collection of manuscripts, which included the original state papers of Lord Burghley, the correspondence of Sir Julius Caesar, and the collections of Bishop White Kennett and Le Neve, were purchased for the British Museum in 1807" (*DNB*, 15:1012).

17. The most recent speculation that "X" derives "from Donne's own collection" appears in Helen Gardner, *John Donne: The Divine Poems*, 2d ed. (Oxford: Clarendon Press, 1978), pp. lxiv-lxv. For the speculation that "Y" comes from a collection sent (along with a manuscript of *Biathanatos*) from Donne to Sir Robert Ker in 1619, see Alan MacColl, "The New Edition of Donne's Love Poems," *Essays in Criticism* 17 (1967):259.

poems (counting the Overburian "Characters," transcribed in both manuscripts as poetry) in the same order in their main poetic sections (folios 21–62 and 58–136 respectively) with few exceptions.[18] TT2 closely parallels the following segments of TT1: Donne's "Elegie: The Perfume" to "The Autumnall" (TT2 folios 15–17v); Donne's "The Storme" to the anonymous "Faire eies do not think scorne to read of Love" (18–21);[19] Donne's "The Legacie" to "A Valediction forbidding mourning" (22v–25);[20] and Donne's "Elegie: 'Oh, let mee not serve so'" to "Womans constancy" (25–29v).[21] With the exception of "Faustus" (folio 57) in the last section of poems by authors other than Donne in TT1 and "Elegie: Loves Progress" in the preliminary section of TT2, the other forty-three Donne poems in TT1 and twenty-eight Donne poems in TT2 appear in B78.

The correspondences among the poem headings and ascriptions in the Lansdowne and Dalhousie manuscripts reinforce the connection implied by the contents and sequence. Of the seventy-two poems contained in both B78 and TT1, forty in TT1 and thirty-nine in B78 have headings in the hands of the original copyists;[22] the thirty-nine headings in B78 are identical to those for the same poems in TT1, but in B78 the heading for Donne's "The Will" has been erased (TT1 and TT2 each have the heading "Loues Legacie"). Sixteen poems in TT2 have headings in the hands of the original copyists; all their headings correspond exactly to those in B78 (except for the erasure of the heading for "The Will") and TT1.

The attributions in the Dalhousie manuscripts are more accurate than those in B78; however, with two exceptions, the same poems bear attributions in the hand of the original copyist in TT1 and B78.[23] These attributions are: Donne's "The Curse" to "*Donne*" in TT1; Donne's "The Autumnall" to "*I D*" in all three manuscripts; Donne's "To Mr. *Rowland Woodward*: 'Like one who'in her third widdowhood'" to "Jo: Roe" in B78 only; Donne's "To Sr. *Henry Wootton*: 'Here's no more newes'" to "*I D*" in both Dalhousies, but to "Jo: Roe" in B78; Sir John Roe's "Song. 'Deare Love, continue nice and chaste'" to "*I R*" in the Dalhousies and to "Sr JR" in B78 (a nonscribal attribution to "J: R:" heads the poem; the attribution in the hand of the original copyist follows the poem and resembles a signature); Sir John Roe's "*An Elegie to Mris Boulstred*: 1602" to "*IR*" (TT1) and "I R" (B78); Donne's "The Legacie" to "*ID*" in TT1 and B78; and Donne's "The broken heart" to "*ID*" (TT1) and "I. D" (B78). The fact that the poems with attributions in the hands of the original copyists all fall within very short segments of the three manuscripts (TT1, folios 17, 33v–44v; TT2, folios 17v–23; B78, folios 86–106v—segments that would reduce to folios 39v–44v, 19v–23, and 99–106v if "The Curse" and "The Autumnall" were not considered) suggests that this sequence of poems (which includes seven of nine extant poems by Sir John Roe) might have circulated as a unit.

Material in TT1 also helps distinguish a subset of manuscripts within Group II and adds evidence that the Essex collection (henceforth, "E") might be the ultimate progenitor of Group II. The presence in the main bodies of TT1, B78, and DT4 of the same three Overburian "Characters" and of Overbury's "Epitaph" in the identical order when, as far as I can determine, the "Characters" and poem do not exist in any other manuscript establishes the certainty of a common progenitor for at least part of these three Group II manuscripts. As mentioned above, Paylor notes that these three characters constitute a specific attack against Lady Frances Howard, who had just divorced the Third Earl of Essex. The fact that the Third Earl would have had a reason for collecting these particular Overburian

18. Where TT1 has the anonymous "A Paradoxe of a Painted Face" (folio 28), B78 has miscellaneous material including Donne's "Satyre I" and Overbury's "The Wife" (folios 68–79v). B78 has a section of blanks and mathematical calculations between the anonymous "Libell agaynst Bashe" and Sir John Davies's "On Bp. Richard Fletcher, Feb. 1594–5" (folios 91v–93v). B78 has Donne's "Elegie: The Anagram" (folio 98) between Donne's "The Calme" and "To Mr. *Rowland Woodward*: 'Like one who'in her third widdowhood,'" while TT1 has "Elegie: The Anagram" in its preliminary materials (folio 16). B78 inserts Donne's "Confined Love" (folio 101) between Sir John Roe's "Song. 'Deare Love, continue nice and chaste" and the anonymous "Wonder of Beautie, Goddesse of my sense"; Sir Thomas Roe's "I can no more resist nor yet subdue" and the anonymous "Yet not despaire and die, and soe accuse" (folio 101v) between the anonymous "Faire eies do not think scorne to read of Love" and Sir John Roe's "*To Ben. Iohnson, 6 Ian.* 1603"; Donne's "The Curse" (folio 108v) between Donne's "The good-morrow" and "Loves Alchymie"; Donne's "To the Countesse of Bedford. 'Reason is our Soules left hand'" (folios 114v–15) between Donne's "Elegie to the Lady Bedford" and "Elegie on Mris. Boulstred"; Donne's "The Dreame," "A Valediction of weeping," "A Feaver," and "The Paradox" as well as the anonymous "*To Sicknes*. 'Whie disease dost thou molest'" (folios 125v–27v) between Donne's "Womans constancy" and Sir John Harington's "Of the commodities that men haue by their Marriage." B78 (folios 129–30) has Sir John Davies's "Unto that sparkling wit, that spirit of fire" (located on folios 10v–11 in TT1) and the anonymous "There hath beene one that Stroue gainst natures powre" where TT1 (folios 57–58) has the anonymous "The famous learned Tullie long agoe," Harington's "Of Women learned in the tongues," Donne's "Faustus," Sir Walter Ralegh's "The Lie," the anonymous "*Emelia* embracing many guifts and loues," and Josuah Sylvester's "The Fruites of a cleere *Conscience*" between Sir John Harington's "Of a Precise Tayler" and Overbury's "The Remedy of Loue."

19. The exception is "Elegie: The Anagram" (folio 31); both Dalhousie manuscripts vary from the B78 sequence for this poem.

20. Eight of thirteen poems, omitting John Hoskyns's "A Poem upon Absence" and Donne's "Twicknam garden," placing "The Curse" on folio 11 (again, both Dalhousie manuscripts break the B78 sequence for this poem), and omitting "Loves Alchymie," "The Sunne Rising," "Lecture Upon the Shadow," and "Image of her whom I love."

21. Nine of eleven poems, omitting Donne's "The Funerall" and "Loves Usury."

22. B78 has twelve headings added in a hand other than that of the original copyist: "Elegie" for "Elegie: The Anagram"; "To mr Rowland Wodward" for "To Mr. *Rowland Woodward*: 'Like one who'in her third widdowhood'"; "To sr Henrie wootton" for "To Sr. *Henry Wootton*: 'Here's no more newes'"; "*The Good Morrow*"; "Alchymy" replacing original copyist's "*Mummy*" for "Loves Alchymie"; "*Breake of Daye*"; "*Sunn Riseing*"; "*Loues lecture vpon the shaddow*"; "*The Triple ffoole*"; "Loues Will" for "The Will"; "*Loues vsurie*"; and "*Womans Constancy*." These additional twelve B78 headings resemble those in the collected editions.

23. The ascriptions in other hands in B78 are the original copyist's ascription to "Jo: Roe" of Donne's "To Mr. *Rowland Woodward*: 'Like one who'in her third widdowhood'" changed to "J: Donne"; the original copyist's "Jo: Roe" for Donne's "To Sr. *Henry Wootton*: 'Here's no more newes'" changed to "J: Donne"; "J. D." for Sir John Roe's "*To Sr Tho. Roe* 1603"; "J D" for Sir John Roe's "An Elegie. *Reflecting on his passion for his mistrisse*." These later attributions, like the additional headings, seem to come from a collected edition.

"Characters" suggests that they might have first been together as a unit in his possession, suggesting in turn that B78 might derive from "E" and that DT4 ultimately derives from "E" as well.

The relationships among the texts in B78, TT1, and TT2 even in the main hands are complicated by nonshared materials as well as by the fact that even the main part of TT2 was not copied all at one time by one person, but it is clear that B78 cannot derive directly from TT1 or TT2 and that TT1 does not descend from TT2. Unless an enormous amount of material is missing from TT1 and TT2 or unless the TT1 and TT2 copyists were very selective even among poems by the same author, TT1 and TT2 cannot have been copied from B78 either. In addition to the extra materials in B78, its earliest foliation (of at least four foliation sequences) indicates that its original folios 32–38 are missing between current folios 73–74 and its original folios 87–100 are missing between current folios 96–97 (interestingly, both TT1 and TT2 break with the B78 sequence at these points). Furthermore, the omission of lines from poems throughout TT1 and TT2 proves that B78 could not derive from TT1 or TT2 even in their original, complete states. The texts of the forty-six Donne poems found in either TT1 or TT2 and B78 (which contains fifty Donne poems) are complete in B78; thus, the omission of lines 14–17 in "Satyre V" (TT1, folio 24v), the second half of line 78 and first half of line 79 in "Satyre IV" (TT1, folio 22), line 89 of "Elegie: The Bracelet" (TT2, folio 9—the present line has been added in a later hand), line 34 of "Elegie: Change" (TT1, folio 32; TT2, folio 16), line 35 of "The Autumnall" (TT1, folio 33v; TT2, folio 17v), line 6 of "Image of her whom I love" (TT1, folio 47v), line 3 of "The Legacie" (TT1, folio 44; TT2, folio 22v), and lines 17–18 in "Loves Usury" (TT1, folio 55) means that B78 cannot derive directly from even the original complete collections of TT1 or TT2. Finally, the omission of line 89 in "Elegie: The Bracelet" in TT2 (folio 9) and its subsequent addition in a later hand with the reading of TT1 as well as the omission of "enowghe" (line 5) and "ffor" (line 56) from "Elegie: The Anagram," "staying" (line 46) from "Elegie: Loves Warre," "he" (line 19) from "The Autumnall," "Sadd" (line 10) from "The Storme," "narrow" (line 6) from "The triple Foole," "itt" (line 13) and "what and" (line 26) from "Loves diet," "and" (line 31) from "Elegie: 'Oh, let mee not serve so,'" "an" (line 18) from "The Will," and "then" (line 3) from "Loves Deitie" from TT2 proves that TT1 did not derive from the original of TT2 and confirms that B78 (in which the words occur) could not have either.

Since B78 and TT1 have such an unusually close relationship, the fact that neither derives from the other implies the existence of a common source, probably "E"; however, TT2 derives from TT1 rather than from "E." The large amount of material missing from TT2, the relative uncertainty of the order of its remaining material, and the presence of two copyists in its main sequence make determining its derivation difficult; nonetheless, the omission of the same lines in the same poems (see above), the presence of eleven poems unique to TT1 and TT2, and the generally very close agreement between their texts of Donne poems (see Textual Apparatus, though the agreement between TT1 and TT2 is much closer for poems in hand 2C than for those in 2D) strongly imply that much of the material in hands 2C and 2D in TT2 derives from TT1 rather than from "E." Further, the contents of the sections of each Dalhousie manuscript that contain most of the Donne poems (TT1, folios 21–62; TT2, folios 5–34) agree closely: the twenty-nine Donne poems in TT2 include only two ("Elegie: Loves Progress" and "The Message") absent from TT1, and TT1, folio 17v, parallels TT2, 13–14; TT1, folios 31–33v, parallels TT2, 15–17v; TT1, folios 38–41, parallels TT2, 18–21; TT1, folios 44–48v, has the poems "The Legacie," "The broken heart," "The good-morrow," "Breake of day," "The triple Foole," "Loves diet," and "A Valediction forbidding mourning" in the same order as they appear in TT2, folios 22v–25, though the materials in these sections are not identical; and TT1, folios 51v–56, parallels TT2, 25–29v, except for the presence of "The Funerall" and "Loves Usury" between "Loves Deitie" and "The Flea." Yet not all of TT2 derives from TT1: not only does TT2 (admittedly in an incomplete state) omit much material from TT1, but it also has eleven poems not found in TT1. Furthermore, the extensive differences between the TT1 and TT2 texts of "Elegie: The Anagram," "The Curse," and "Elegie: The Bracelet" as well as the absence of "The Message" from TT1 prove that the texts in folios 5–11 of TT2, even though they are in the hand of one of the two main copyists of TT2, do not derive from TT1.

Fourteen Donne poems from throughout TT2 have manuscript corrections in a later hand: "Elegie: The Anagram," "The Curse" (extensively corrected), "Elegie: The Bracelet" (extensively corrected), "Elegie: The Perfume," "Elegie: Loves Warre," "Elegie: Going to Bed," "The Storme," "The Calme," "To Mr. *Rowland Woodward*," "To Sr. *Henry Wootton*," "The broken heart," "A Valediction forbidding mourning," "Elegie: 'Oh, let mee not serve so,'" and "The Message." Of these corrections, only those in line 42 of "Elegie: Going to Bed" (imputed *to* imp[ar]ted), line 19 of "A Valediction forbidding mourning" (I'hter *to* I'[c]ht[,]er), line 35 of "Elegie: 'Oh, let mee not serve so'" (mee *to* ~~mee~~ and forgett *to* ~~forgett~~[begett]), and line 24 of "The Message" (now *to* now[e]) are anything other than emendations of TT2 to TT1 readings, and only the changes in "Elegie: 'Oh, let mee not serve so'" are certainly in the direction of printed copy. The single manuscript correction in a later hand in TT1, in line 19 of "A Valediction forbidding mourning" (Inter to In['o]t[h]er), would seem an unfortunate effort by an insensitive reader.

Evidently, "E" continued to grow after its transcription into TT1 and B78, and ultimately its core shows up as folios 13–59 of DT4. DT4 does have "Satyre I" (omitted in TT1 but present in B78) on folios 13–14. However, it also has the same unit of Satyres III, IV, V, II and "Elegie: The Bracelet" (folios 14v–27) as does TT1, as well as the same unit with the verse letters "The Storme," "The Calme," "To Mr. *Rowland Woodward*: 'Like one who'in her third widdowhood,'" "To Sr. *Henry Wootton*: 'Here's no more newes,'" (folios 27v–31v, interrupted by "Elegie: The Anagram" [folios 29v–30] as in B78); the same unit with "Elegie: The Comparison," "Elegie: The Perfume," and

"Elegie: Change" (folios 31v–34); the same Song and Sonnet unit with "Breake of day," "The Sunne Rising," "Lecture upon the Shadow" (folio 36r-v); the same Markham, Bedford, Bulstrode elegies (folios 38–44); and many of the same single poems and pairs of poems. After DT4's folio 60 ("An *Elegie* on the late *Lord William Haward* Baron of Effingham, dead *the tenth of December*. 1615"), DT4 and TT1 share no other material until the Overbury unit (DT4, folios 141–42v, beginning, as in B78, with "A Wife") and Sir John Roe's "An Elegie. *Reflecting on his passion for his mistrisse*" and "Song. 'Deare Love, continue nice and chaste'" (folios 142v–44).

Thus, the steps in the genesis and transmission of what has become the Group II manuscript tradition would seem to be as follows: (1) the existence of an ongoing manuscript collection, "E," made by the Essex family from poems obtained from a coterie of poets associated with the Inns of Court who had some connection to the Essex family; (2) the compilation and/or transcription of this collection between 12 May 1613 and August 1617 as TT1 and its removal to Scotland to the Dalhousie family; (3) the transcription from TT1 in Scotland (many of the spellings, such as "wes" for "was," in TT2 are Scottish) of parts of TT2 including the Donne poems between folios 15 and 31; (4) the transcription from an enlarged "E" of B78, probably in the 1620s (Beal, 1:250–51); (5) the addition of many small collections or another large collection of Donne poems to "E" (with no evidence that Donne, rather than a patron or member of his coterie, collected the necessary manuscripts), creating Gardner's "Y" by the early 1620s; and (6) the transcription in 1623–1625 of DT4 (Beal, 1:251), the largest of the Group II Donne manuscripts with 143 Donne poems. The possibility that Donne did not collect the poems from which Gardner's "Y" derived means that he might not have collected Gardner's "X" either: despite the 1614 letter to Goodyer asking for that "old book" of his poems for the purpose of gathering them for publication (*Letters to Severall Persons of Honour* [London, 1651], pp. 196–97), no evidence exists that Donne ever successfully collected his poems.

Perhaps a note of caution regarding this proposed genesis and transmission of the Group II Donne manuscripts (and Renaissance manuscript texts generally) is in order here. The stemma of "E," TT1, TT2, and B78 only describes certain segments in each ("E," unknown; TT1, folios 21–62; TT2, folios 5–34; and B78, folios 58–136v). Unique poems as well as radically different passages in shared poems exist outside the main sequences; for example, in TT1 lines 14–16 of Donne's "The Curse" (folio 17) read "Or maye he, for her vertue reuerence / Her y^t hates him, only for impotence / And equall traytors be she; and his senc," but in TT2 (folio 11) these lines read "in earely scarcenesse, and longe may he rott / for land, wch had been his, if he had not / himselfe incestuouslie an heire begott." In this case, the TT1 readings belong to the B78 or Group II tradition, while those of TT2 belong to the Cambridge University Library, Additional MS. 5778 and British Library Harley MS. 4955, or Group I tradition. Thus, even though "The Curse" is in the main sequence (hand 2D) of TT2 and not in the main sequence of TT1, its text in TT2, which should derive from "E," B78, or TT1, cannot; and its text in TT1 (outside the main sequence deriving from "E") does derive, if not directly from "E," at least from a manuscript related to "E". The possibility that a manuscript might derive from another that has lost some of its material further complicates the question of textual transmission: the TT2 reading of "crosse" (where most texts read "breake") in line 14 of "The Message," the other Donne poem not contained in TT1, derives from a Group II manuscript; thus, it might have been copied from a now-missing leaf of TT1. The fact that texts of poems from different parts of TT1, TT2, and B78 derive from different manuscript traditions suggests that Renaissance manuscripts should not be thought of or treated as textual units but as collections of smaller groupings of poems or other materials.

Literary Significance of the Manuscripts

The Dalhousie manuscripts, as verse miscellanies, are valuable not only for the study of John Donne's poems but also for the study of Renaissance poetry generally. Peter Beal, who has undertaken the most complete study to date on Renaissance verse miscellanies, describes their potential importance:

> Miscellanies can, however, throw extensive light on the process of textual transmission, on the general practices and assumptions involved in the collecting of verse in this period, on the way contemporaries interpreted texts, and on the nature and provenance of sources. The selection and arrangement of poems by Donne in these MSS, and of accompanying poems by others, are vital clues to the collections from which they derive and to possible reasons for confusion over the canon. Individual texts in miscellanies may, in any case, derive not from large collections at all but from independent early copies of particular poems, and apparent 'corruptions' may, in fact, sometimes represent different versions or states of revision of the text. In short, the potential and far-ranging significance of miscellanies should not be underestimated. (1:248–49)

TT1 contains many of Donne's most frequently written about and taught poems: ten Elegies (including "The Autumnall"), twenty-one Songs and Sonnets, four Satyres, five Verse Letters (including "Elegie to the Lady Bedford"), three Epicedes and Obsequies, and one Epigram, "Faustus." The twenty-nine Donne poems in TT2 include many of those in TT1: ten of the seventeen Elegies (adding "Elegie: Loves Progress," omitting "Elegie: The Comparison"), fifteen Songs and Sonnets (adding "The Message," omitting "Twicknam garden," "The Sunne Rising," "Lecture upon the Shadow," "Image of her whom I love," "The Funerall," and "Loves Usury"), and four of the Verse Letters (omitting "Elegie to the Lady Bedford").

As perhaps the earliest exemplars of an important Donne manuscript tradition, TT1 and TT2 provide authoritative evidence for Donne's canon. TT1 and TT2 are important witnesses for several poems now generally accepted as Donne's but not published in all or any of the seven seventeenth-century editions/issues of Donne's collected *Poems*: "Elegie: The Bracelet" (TT1, 27r-v; TT2, 9–10) was not included until the 1635 second collected edition; lines 29–46 of "Elegie: Loves Warre" were first published anonymously in *The Harmony of the Muses* (1654), pp. 6–

7, and the poem was not published in its entirety as Donne's until F. G. Waldron's *A Collection of Miscellaneous Poetry* (1802), pp. 1–5, and his *The Shakespearean Miscellany* (1802), pp. 1–5; "Elegie: Going to Bed" was first published anonymously in *Harmony* (pp. 2–3) and was not published as Donne's until the seventh collected edition of 1669; "Lecture upon the Shadow" first appeared in the second collected edition (pp. 66–67); and "Elegie: Loves Progress" was first published anonymously in *Harmony* (pp. 36–39) and did not appear as Donne's until the seventh collected edition.

The attributions and groupings in TT1 and TT2 also provide evidence for authorship for some poems mistakenly published as Donne's in the seventeenth-century collected editions/issues or frequently attributed to him in seventeenth-century manuscripts or modern editions.[24] Sir John Roe's "Song. 'Deare Love, continue nice and chaste'" (ascribed to "*IR*" and "*I R*" in TT1 and TT2 respectively), "*To Ben. Iohnson, 6 Ian.* 1603," "*To Ben. Iohnson*, 9. *Novembris*, 1603," "*To Sr Tho. Roe* 1603," and "An Elegie. *Reflecting on his passion for his mistrisse*" (grouped together away from Donne in TT1) appeared as Donne's in the second through the seventh seventeenth-century collected editions. The anonymous "Wonder of Beautie, Goddesse of my sense" and "Faire eies do not think scorne to read of Love" (grouped away from the Donne poems in TT1 and TT2) are frequently ascribed to Donne in seventeenth-century manuscripts. Alexander B. Grosart, *The Complete Poems of John Donne*, and Sir John Simeon, *Miscellanies of the Philobiblon Society*, 3 vols. (London, 1856–1857), accepted Sir John Roe's "*An Elegie to M^ris Boulstred*: 1602" (ascribed to "*IR*" in TT1) as Donne's.

By far the two most problematical poems for the Donne canon among those appearing in TT1 and TT2 are "Elegie: The Expostulation" and "Faustus." Even though "Elegie: The Expostulation" was first published as Donne's in the 1633 collected edition (pp. 300–302), its subsequent publication in the second volume of Ben Jonson's *Workes* (London, 1640), pp. 204–6, sparked a debate over authorship that continues:[25] Gardner's 1965 edition of the elegies lists "Elegie: The Expostulation" as dubia (pp. 94–96). The presence of "Elegie: The Expostulation" in long sequences of poems by Donne in TT1 (twenty-six Donne poems from "The Legacie" on folio 44 to "Womans constancy" on folio 56, broken only by Hoskyns's "A Poem upon Absence" on folio 45 and Beaumont's "To the Countesse of Rutland" on folio 52v) and TT2 (fifteen Donne poems from "The Legacie" on folio 22v to "Womans constancy" on folio 29v, broken only by Beaumont's "To the Countesse of Rutland" on folio 26), manuscripts containing chiefly Donne's poems (and the majority of his elegies) and not containing any of Jonson's, powerfully augments the evidence of the manuscript traditions utilized by Evelyn Simpson to assign authorship to Donne ("Jonson and Donne: A Problem in Authorship," *Review of English Studies* 15 [1939]:274–82).

In 1967, John T. Shawcross first published "Faustus" and, on the basis of its presence amid other Donne poems and its attribution to "JD" in National Library of Scotland MS. 2067, Hawthornden MS. XV (henceforth SN4), assigned its authorship to Donne ("John Donne and Drummond's Manuscripts"). "Faustus" also occurs amid other Donne poems and is attributed to "J D" in National Library of Scotland MS. 6504, Wedderburn MS (henceforth, SN5). Even though TT1 contains primarily Donne poems, its evidence for Donne's authorship of "Faustus" is not as strong as that for Donne's authorship of "Elegie: The Expostulation": "Faustus" is not positioned in a sequence of Donne poems, no other Donne epigrams occur, and three poems by Sir John Harington, Donne's chief competitor for authorship (Shawcross, p. 165n), are nearby ("Of the commodities that men haue by their Marriage," folio 56v; "Of a Precise Tayler," folio 57; and "Of Women learned in the tongues," folio 57). Nonetheless, the appearance of "Faustus" even without attribution in a superior textual version (see below) in an early manuscript in a main Donne textual tradition adds considerably to the evidence for Donne's authorship.

Even though more than 250 manuscripts containing poems by John Donne are now known and most of these manuscripts remain uncollated, TT1 and TT2, as large, and possibly the earliest, exemplars of a major Donne manuscript tradition, will play an important role in establishing the texts of Donne's poems.

Several unique readings in the texts of Donne poems in TT1 deserve serious consideration. TT1's "Surs" for the traditional "sinnes" in line 3 of "Satyre III" ("I must not laugh, nor weepe sinnes, and be wise") is in keeping with the poem as a speech. Line 33 in the TT1 "Satyre III" ("Knowe thy foe the fowle diuell is whom thou") is superior in meter—admittedly an imperfect criterion in a satire—and in sense to the traditional "Know thy foes, the foule Devill h'is, whom thou." Since the dialog in "Satyre IV" concerns linguists (see line 59), TT1's "Linguists" (line 53) makes more sense than does the traditional "linguist" ("For the best linguist? And I seelily").

In other cases, TT1 and TT2 may assist editors in the choice of texts and/or readings. For example, TT1 will provide important evidence for the text of "Faustus." Shawcross uses SN4 as his copy text, emending only the terminal comma to a period: "Faustus keepes his sister and a whore, / Faustus keepes his sister and no more." (p. 165). This version has only nine syllables per line, whereas both SN5 and TT1, which begin each of these two lines with an italic "*Faustinus*" ("*faustinus*" in TT1), have decasyllabic lines. By modern standards, the SN5 version has the superior accidentals ("*Faustinus* keepes his Sister, and a Whore, / *Faustinus* keepes his Sister, and noe more." as opposed to "*faustinus* keepes his sister & a whore / *faustinus* keepes his sister and no more /"). At the least, however, TT1 will serve as an important witness to the "*Faustinus*" reading in preference to the "Faustus" of SN4.

Some other TT1 readings, not clearly superior, that

24. See Grierson, "Appendix B. Poems Which Have Been Attributed to John Donne in the Old Editions and the Principal MS. Collections, Arranged According to Their Probable Authors" (1:401–32) and "Appendix C. A Selection of Poems Which Frequently Accompany Poems by John Donne in Manuscript Collections or Have Been Ascribed to Donne by Modern Editors" (1:433–67).

25. For a review of the arguments, see D. Heywood Brock's "Jonson and Donne: Structural Fingerprinting and the Attribution of Elegies XXXVIII-XLI," *Papers of the Bibliographical Society of America* 72 (1978):519–27.

would become part of the text only if TT1 proved the most authoritative version do have some aesthetic interest. For example, in line 5 of "Elegie: The Anagram," TT1 has "donne," where TT2, collected editions, and all manuscripts read "dimme" ("Though they be dimme, yet she is light enough"). Aside from the amusing pun on Donne's name, "donne" would mean "dull grayish brown"—perhaps a term more appropriate for describing both the "eyes" (line 3) and "teeth" (line 4) than "dimme" would be and every bit as good a contrast with the "light" (line 5) female.

In addition to their value for Donne studies, TT1 and TT2 contain other important Renaissance verse (much of it with significant potential textual authority). TT1 contains an additional forty-seven poems by Sir Robert Ayton, Francis Beaumont, Thomas Campion, Richard Corbett, Sir John Davies (three), Edward de Vere, Sir John Harington (four), John Hoskyns, Sir Thomas Overbury (six, including three of his prose "Characters" transcribed as poems), Sir Walter Ralegh, Jonathan Richards, Sir John Roe (seven), Josuah Sylvester (two), and Sir Henry Wotton. TT1 also contains six anonymous poems that appear in other manuscripts including TT2, one anonymous poem that appears elsewhere only in TT2 ("a songe: 'When my hart seemes most ingaged,'" folio 19), and four unique anonymous poems ("m^r: Lamb: Cookes Epi: to his Bro: Hen:," folio 10; "Some who the speakinge sparke of my first loue did spie," folio 19v; "The famous learned Tullie long agoe," folio 57; and a reply to Thomas Campion's "A Ballad," folio 62v). TT2 contains twenty-four poems by other Renaissance authors (four poems occur more than once: "My deare and onelie loue tak heede," three times; Jonathan Richards's "a songe: 'I die when as I doe not see,'" twice; "Onste and no more, so sayd my loue," twice; and "*Carold for new yeeres day* 1624," twice): Francis Bacon, Francis Beaumont, Sir John Davies, Sir John Harington, William Herbert (Third Earl of Pembroke), George Morley, Sir Walter Ralegh, Jonathan Richards, Sir John Roe, and Josuah Sylvester (two poems). TT2 also contains two anonymous poems appearing in other manuscripts, six anonymous poems appearing in other manuscripts including TT1, one anonymous poem appearing elsewhere only in TT1, and four anonymous unique poems ("If kinges did heretofore there loues indite," folios 7–8; "*Carold for new yeeres day* 1624," folios 21v, 33; "Why doe yee giue mee leaue to sip," folio 32v; and "An Epitaph vpon the Duke off Buckinghame," folio 34v). All told, TT1 and TT2 preserve fifteen heretofore unpublished poems, including ten poems unique to one or both manuscripts.

Given the overwhelming evidence that the main poetic sequences in TT1 and TT2 derive from a collection of poems by a coterie of poets associated with the Essex family and given that TT1 and TT2 may preserve pre-1617 versions of the texts of those poems, many of the texts in TT1 and TT2 have considerable authority for the English poems as well as for the unique Scottish poems. Certainly, the Essex family would have had access to holographs or to very early copies of poems by Sir Henry Wotton, Sir John Roe, Francis Beaumont (at least for "To the Countesse of Rutland"), Sir Walter Ralegh, Sir Thomas Overbury, and Francis Bacon. TT1 and TT2 are particularly critical for the corpus of Sir John Roe's work: with its seven Roe poems, TT1 is second only to B78 (which has eight Roe poems, adding "To Sr Nicholas Smyth," folios 68–69) in number of manuscript Roe poems.[26] Some sense of the superiority of the TT1 readings for Roe's poems can be seen in its reading on folio 43 of "tindes" as opposed to "findes" in Grierson's printing of line 1 of "*An Elegie*" ("True Love findes witt, but he whose witt doth move"): the image system of the entire poem depends on the sparks and fire initiated by love (Bodleian manuscript Rawlinson poet. MS. 31 has "kindles").

Ultimately, the chief literary significance of TT1 and TT2 may lie in the evidence they provide about the way verse circulated and was collected and arranged in the Renaissance. The discovery that verse miscellanies like TT1 and TT2 may not result from random circulation of verse but rather derive from a body of verse by a coterie of authors whose work was intended for the approbation of and deliberately collected by "culture-heroes . . . like Sir Philip Sidney and the [Second] Earl of Essex" (Marotti, p. 33) has profound implications not only for the study of the authorship, dating, manuscript circulation, and texts of Renaissance verse generally but also for our understanding of the function of verse in the aesthetic, social, political, and economic life of the Renaissance.

26. Grierson adds only "*Satyre.* 'Men write that love and reason disagree'" (1:406–7), bringing the total likely Roe canon to nine poems.

DALHOUSIE I

A NOTE ON THE TRANSCRIPTION

The facing transcription of the prose and poetry in the Dalhousie manuscripts attempts, within the limits of modern typography, to reproduce the manuscript text exactly, including all layers of revision by the original and later copyists. Revisions are indicated by the symbol → immediately following the original word and punctuation (if any) and immediately preceding the new word and punctuation (if any). Revisions by later copyist(s) are in square brackets; additions in modern pencil are in braces. When the revision has been made by lining out the original reading, the transcription shows the original reading lined out. Letters lined out so heavily as to render them indecipherable are represented by asterisks. Conjectured readings appear between vertical lines.

The following manuscript abbreviations, used more than once by the various copyists and representable in modern typography, have not been expanded: & *for* and; cōn *for* cion; ¯ and ˜ *for* n or m; m^{t} *for* ment; p *for* par, per, por, pre, and pro; p^{r} *for* pre; q *for* que; q^{d} *for* quod; w^{c}h and w^{ch} *for* which; w^{t}h and wth *for* with; y^{e} *for* the; y^{em} *for* them; y^{ey} *for* they; y^{r} *for* their; and y^{t} *for* that. For unexpanded abbreviations that appear only once, see the Explanatory Notes. The following six manuscript symbols not easily represented by modern typography have been uniformly expanded: (1) "ꝰ" to "^{us}" (e.g. vincibꝰ to vincib^{us} [p. 16, line 60]); (2) "ꝛ" to "^{r}" (e.g. youꝛ to you^{r} [p. 42, line 168]); (3) "ꝯ" to "^{er}" (e.g. euꝯy to eu^{ery} [p. 62, line 40]); (4) "∾" to "st" (e.g. *e*∾ to *e*st [p. 17, line 26]); (5) "ꝭ" to "^{ss}" (e.g. *e*ꝭ*e* to *e*^{ss}*e* [p. 17, line 26]); and (6) "ꞅ" to "es" at the ends of words (e.g. thingꞅ [p. 15, line 2]; the copyists usually employ the more standard "δ" when indicating terminal "s," except in TT2, ff. 3–4v, where copyist 2C used both symbols for the terminal "s"). The manuscript punctuation resembling a modern question mark tilted on its side, which was used by the copyists to represent interrogation and exclamation, has been transcribed as a question or exclamation mark as sense suggests. The various copyists do not indicate italics or distinguish capital letters with perfect consistency; I have italicized and capitalized only when the indication appeared relatively certain.

Italic headings or titles have been added before all items in the manuscripts. The italic numbers at the top left of each page indicate the foliation of the Dalhousie manuscripts.

All manuscript pages were photographed and the photographs developed identically. Leaves that had darkened (particularly at the beginnings and ends of the manuscripts) and leaves on which the ink had faded (generally ink used by the nonprofessional copyists) have been printed slightly darker to make the writing on them more legible.

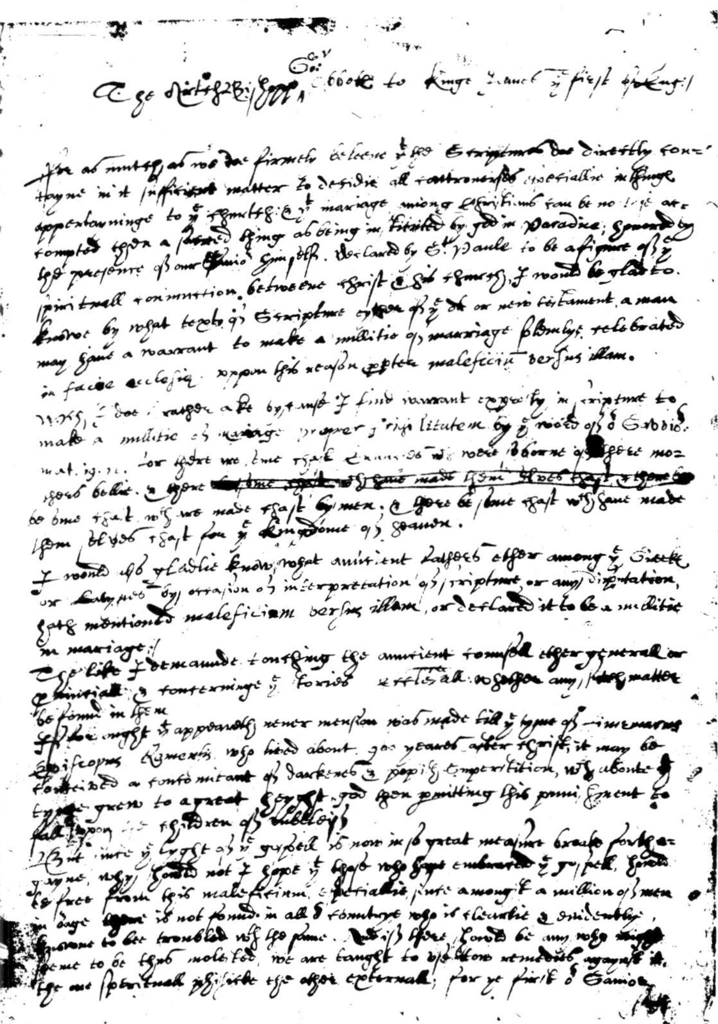

I, 1. Archbishop George Abbot, trial testimony

{1}

The ArtchBishopp Gor: Abbotes to Kinge Iames ye first of Eng:/

ffor as mutch as we doe firmely beleeue yt the Scriptures doe directly con=
tayne in it sufficient matter to decidie all controuersies especiallie in thinges
appertayninge to ye churtch: & yt mariage among Christians can be no lesse ac=
compted then a sacred thing as being instituted by god in *Paradice*; honored by
the presence of our Sauior himself. Declared by St. *Paule* to be a figure of ye
spirituall coniunction betweene christ & his church, I would be glad to
knowe by what text of Scripture eyther of ye old or new testament, a man
may haue a warrant to make a nullitie of marriage pleinlye celebrated
in facie ecclesiae; vppon this reason *ppter maleficiũ versus illam.*
Wch I doe ye rather aske bycause I find warrant expresly in scripture to
make a nullitie of mariage *propter frigi litatem* by ye word of or Savvior:
mat. i9. 12. for there are some chast Eunnches wch were so borne of there mo=
thers bellie. & there ~~be some chast wch haue made them selves chast, & there be~~
be some chast, wch are made chast by men. & there be some chast wch haue made
them selves chast for ye Kingdome of heauen.
I would also gladlie know, what auncient fathers ether among ye Greekes
or Latynes by occasion of interpretation of scripture, or any disputation,
hath mentioned *maleficium versus illam*, or declared it to be a nullitie
in mariage:/
The like I demaunde touching the auncient counsell ether generall or
puinciall, & concerninge ye stories Ecclesticall: whether any sutch matter
be found in them
If, for ought yt appeareth neuer mension was made till ye tyme of *Hinirmarus*
Episcopus *Remensis*, who lived about 900 yeares after christ, it may be
conceived a concomitant of darkenes & popish Superstition, wch aboute yt
tyme grew to a great heyght, god then pmitting this punishment to
fall vpon the children of vnbeleif.
But since ye lyght of ye gospell is now in so great measure broake forth a=
gayne, why showld not I hope yt those who haue embraced ye gospell, showld
be free from this *maleficium*, especiallie, since amongst a million of men
in or age there is not found in all or countrye who is clearlie & euidentlye,
knowne to bee troubled wth the same. And if there showld be any who might
seeme to be thus molested, we are taught to vse tow remedies agaynst it,
the one sperituall phisicke the other externall; for ye first or Sauior.
sayth

I, iv

sayth, *hoc genus demoniorum non eiiciatur, nisi per orationem et ieminiū*:
and S^{t}. Peter speakinge of ye divell sayth *cui resistite firme in fide.* &
the Papistes them selues prescrib almes fastinge & prayer to be
vsed in that case, but y^{t} they ioyne superstitiouslye there exorcismes
there vnto:/ And for corporall phisike to be applied as agaynst a
disease see y^{e} iudgment of o^{r} late Devines, whether they speake of *ma=*
leficium or not:
Now admit the Earle of Essex might be imagined to be troubled wth
maleficiū versus illam. I demaund what Almes hath beene given, what
fasting, hath bene vsed, what prayers haue beene powred oute to
appease the indignation of god towards him or his wife, or what
phisicke hath beine taken or medecines applied for three yeares
togeather.
Not one of these thinges; but the first Stepp must be to p̲nounce
a nullitie in the mariage. of wch declaration we know the
begininge. but no mortall mans witt can foresee the end ether
in his p̲son or in his example:

Iudicium diuersorum de hac materia.

Philippus Melanchton de diuortijs ex impotentia.
Pezelius secunda p̲te explica^{t}*. in exam̃et melanchtonis*
Hem̃ingii Iudiciū.
Hemmingius libello de coniugio repudio et diuorsio.
Polanus lib. de diuorsijs, de repudiis. pag. 9 etc 94.

Six obiections in law made by some of the Iudges deligates.

i The libell to be defective in ye words. *Ar.* 4^{0} *plurib*^{us} *~~ete~~ iteratis vicib*^{us} *tentabit.*
2 The Earles answere to be insufficient, y^{t} he did divers tymes attempt
3 The Earle to ~~ans~~we‸are *cū septi. mar. requise* in law.
4 The Earle to be inspected by *Phisicõns* etc.
5 Doubdted an *impedimentū maleficii precesserit or subsecutū fuerit matrimoniū* notw^{t}hstanding *trienniū cohabitationis elapsū.*
6 Whether notw^{t}hstanding the Tryenniall cohabitation past *nonus terminus cohabitationis arbitrio iudicis*, be not to be assigned for further tryall.

{2}

His ma:ties answere to ye presedent discourse. /

To the first article yt ye scripture directlye or by consequence doth contayne sufficient matter to decide all controversies especiallie in thinges appertayninge to ye church; this in my opinion is *pro= positio erronea*, & on of the puritans grownds, *distinctiō* or *ex= planatiō*: for the orthodoxall pposition is, that ye scripture doth directlie or by consequence contayne in it self a sufficient matter to decide all controversies in poynte of fayth & salvation; of wch sorte a nullitie in mariage cannot be accompted for, one, and therefore your consequence vppon the former pposition must fayle. ffor further satisfaction to your following question, I saie your owne second question doth answere it, for if there be a warrant in scrip= ture for pnouncing a nullitie *propter frigiditatem*, then all the meanes wch makes him *frigidus versus illam*, must be comprehended therein. ffor why doth our churtch iustlye condeme as Incestuous the marriage of a man wth his sisters dawghter, or the mariage of two Sisters, but a *paritate rationis*, for none of them is in *terminis* phibited in scripture, onlie the conclusion is gathered a *paritate ra= tionis*, for if it be not lawfull to marie your fathers wife, because thereby you discouer your fathers shame nor his sister because she is his kinswoman, nor your owne sister bycause thereby you discouer your fathers and mothers shame, it can no more be lawfull to marie your sisters dawghter, for thereby you also discouer your owne shame. As also yt the same reason serues for ascending or descending in poyntes of consanguinitie, *quia par est ratio*, ye like is in this case, for althowgh christ spake onlie of three sortes of Eunches, yett ra= *tio est quia non potest esse copula inter Eunuchum et mulierem.* And therefore S.t *Paule* in ye sixt of the i to ye Corinthians, telleth vs clearlie yt it is not *coniunctio sine copula*. I Conclude therefore *a paritate rationis*, yt christ did comprehend vnder these three sortes of Eunuches all inabilitie, wch did ppetuallie hinder *Copulation versus illam*, whether it were naturall or ac= cedentall; for what difference is betwixt cutting of ye hand and being made impotent thereof. *Amputatio et mutilatio membri*, is all

all one in ciuill law. And it is alike defrawdinge of ye woman, when eyther he who is to be her husband is gelded or when ye vse of yt membr towards her, is by any vnlawfull meanes taken frō her. neither is it any wayes neidfull to craue ye pticuler warrant for *nullities ppter maleficium* out of scripture, no more then there is warrant in yt place for anye nullitie at all. ffor Christ doth not directlie saye yt mariage so made shalbe Null: neither doth he teatch vs what forme of pcesse shalle be vsed in it, neither maketh he mention of a tryniall plation no more then he for biddeth mariage wthin the fourth degree wth oute leaue obtayned of ye bishopp of the diocesse: It is there=fore sufficient to all moderate christians to be taught oute of ye word of god yt mariage is *null sine copula.* & that ye words *quos deus coniunxit* is neuer found in scripture, where yes words doth not preceede, but whether the impediment be not vniversall or *versus illam* only. And whether ye faute thereof hath beene borne wth him, or done to him by violence, of fallen by disease, or disproption or ineptitude betwixt ye parties, or by vnlawfull or vnnaturall practises it is ever *par ratio* for he is *Eunuchus versus illam*, for he owght to be *Eunuchus versus omnes alias*, seing to her onlie was he married, and therefore *a paritate rationis* sutch nullities are grownded, vppon the aforesayd warrant of Scriptures, neither had christ any occation to speake there to ye Iewes concerninge *maleficiū*, for thowgh it be apparant yt god made kinge Abimelech & his familie vnable to abuse Sara Abrahams wife, & so was he made by god him self *Eunuchus versus illam*, & yt it be not vnprobable yt ye diuell beinge gods ape showld imitate gods worke by his filthie witch=crafte by makeinge sutch as god will pmite him vnable *versus illam*. It is pbable yt it was longe after yt tyme before ye deuell put yt trike in vse vppon ye yearth. And to your third & fowrth question, what intention, the fathers & councells make of *maleficium versus illam*,

first.

[I, 3–4v blank] *I, 5. Anonymous, Prayer*

{5}

Conditor celi et terre, rex regum, et dominus dominantium,
qui me de nihilo fecisti, ad imaginem, et similitudinem tuam,
et me ꝑprio tuo sanguine redemisti, quem ego peccator non
sum dignus nominare, nec invocare, nec corde cogitare: Te
suppliciter deprecor, et humiliter exoro, vt clementer, res=
picias me seruum tuum nequam, et miserere mei, qui miser=
tus fuisti mulieri Cananee, et Marie Magdalene, qui
peꝑcisti publicano, et latroni, in cruce pendenti: Tibi con=
fiteor pater piissime, peccata mea, que si volo abscondere
non possum tibi domine; parce mihi christe, quem ego
|nuꝑ| multum offendi, cogitando loquendo, operando, et in
omnibus modis; in quibus ego fragilis homo et peccator
peccare potui: Mea culpa, mea culpa, mea maxima culpa,
ideo domine precor tuam clementiam, qui de celo pro
mea salute descendisti, qui Dauid a peccati lapsu
erexisti; parce mihi domine, parce mihi christe, qui
Petro te negante peꝑcisti, tu es creator meus, et
redemptor meus, dominus meus, et saluator meus
tu es spes mea, et fiducia mea, gubernatio mea, et for=
titudo mea defensio mea, et liberatio mea, vita mea
salus mea, et resurrectio mea flumen meum, et desi=
derium meum, adiutorem meum, et patrocinium meum,
te depricor, et rogo, adiuua me, et saluus ero, guberna
me, et defende me, conforta me et consolare me, confirma
me, et letifica me, illumina me, et visita me suscita
me mortuum, quia factura et opus tuum sum, domine ne
despicias me, quia famulus, et seruus tuus sum, quamuis
malus, quamuis indignus, et peccator, sed qualiscunq sim
siue bonus, siue malus, semꝑ tuus sum: Ad quem ego fugiam

I, 5v

nisi ad te vadam? si tu me eiicis, quis me recipiet? si
tu me despicis, quis me aspiciet? recognosse me ergo
indignum, ad te refugientem, quamuis sim vilis et
immundus, quia si vilis et immundus sum potes me
potes me illuminare si mortuus sim
mundare, si cecus sim ^ *potes me resuscitare, quia*
maior est miserecordia→misericordia tua, quam iniquitas
mea, maior
est pietas tua, quam impietas mea, plus potes de=→di=
mittere, quam ego committere, et plus parcere quā
ego peccator peccare, non e[r]go respicias domine, neq̲
attendas multitudinem iniquitatum mearum, sed
secundum multitudinem miserationum tuarum, mise=
rere mei, et p̱pitius esto mihi maximo peccatori, dic
anime mee salus ~~tuas~~ ego sum: qui dixisti, nolo mor=
tem peccatoris, sed magis vt conuertatur, et viuat:
conuerte me domine ad te, et noli irasci contra me,
deprecor te clementissime pater: propter mise[ri]cor=
diam tuam :/
Q[d] concedat deus vnus essentialiter, et p̱sonaliter
trinus qui est benedictus in secula seculorum Amen:

I, 6. Anonymous, Arms of Christ

{6}

A sheilde of redd a crose of greine
A crovne wrethen, wth thornes keine
A speare, a spounge with nayles three.
A boddie bounden vnto a tree,
Who so this sheilde in harte will take:/
Amongst his enimies; dare he not quake:/

[I, 6v–8v blank] *I, 9. Edward de Vere, My Mind to Me a Kingdom Is*

{9}

My minde to me a kingdome is
sutch pfect ioy therein I finde
that it excelles all other blise
that nature yeildes or comes by kinde.
thowgh mutch I want y^{t} most would haue:
yett still my mind forbids to craue:

No princlye pompe no wealthy store
no force to wine a victorie,
no wyely heade to salve a sore
no shape to please a wanton eye
To none of these I yealde as thrall
for why my minde dothe serve for all:/

I see how plentye surfettes ofte
& hastie clymers sonest fale
I see y^{t} those y^{t} sett alofte
mishape doth threaten most of all
To gett wth toyle and keipe wth feare
sutch cares my minde shall neuer beare:/

Some haue too mutch yett still doe crave
I little haue yett seike no more:
they are but poore thowghe mutch y^{ey} haue
and I am ritch wth little store:
They poore I ritch, they begg I gyve
They lake I leave, the pyne, I lyve:/

I laughe not at an others losse
nor grvdge not at an others gayne,
No worldlye cares my mynde can tosse.
I brovke y^{t} is an others bayne
I feare no foe I force no frend
I lothe no lif: I dread no end:/

I, 9v

Content I lyve wth any staye
& seike no more then may suffice,
I prese to beare no hawtye swaye
looke what I lake my minde supplies:
    Loe how I trivmph like a kinge
    Content wth that my mind doth bringe:/

My wealth is health & quyett ease
my conscienc cleare my cheif defence
I never seike by bribes to please
nor by desertes to give offence
    Thus doe I lyve thus will I die:/
    would all did so as well as I:/

Some weighe there pleasures by there luste
there wisdome by there edge of skill
there treasure too there only truste
and cloaked crafte there store of skill.
    O But all the treasure yt I find
    Is to content; a quiett minde:/ *finis.*

I, 10. Anonymous, m^{r}: Lamb: Cookes Epi: to his Bro: Hen: {10}

m^{r}: Lamb: Cookes Epi: to his Bro: Hen:

What shall I give thee beinge dead y^{t} I
maye bee a brother, & thow better by?
Shall I be dew thy hearse wth teares? why so
they woonte to doe, wch haue least sense of woe
Or shall I thinke wth pompe & funerall fame
to adde ye least of glories to thy name?
Tis bootelese: so are tombes: for we haue seene
Churtches wch weare, & now no chutches beene.
that therefore thow maiste liue, & lyve wth me
loe in my harte thyé monnument shalbe
where thow shalt rest in peace: free from ye thrownge
of rude diseased karkasses amonge,
and wee an Anthem to the hyghest kinge
thow of thy blisse: I of my hopes will singe.
And more Ile vow/ none shall there shrined bee
who doth not match: or mutch resemble thee:/

I, 10v. Sir John Davies, Unto that sparkling wit, that spirit of fire

Vnto that sparklinge witt that spiritt of fier
that diamond like aspect that Eagles eye
whose lightninge makes audactie retier
and yet drawes on respectiue modestie
wth winges of feare and love my spiritt doth fly
and doth therein a flame of fier resemble
w:^{ch} when yt burnes most bright and mounts most high./
then doth yt waver most and most doth tremble./
O that my thoughts were words, O could I speake
the tonge of angelles to express my mynde
for mortall speech is farr to fainte and weake
to vtter passions of soe highe a kinde.
Yo^{w} have a bewtie of such life and light
as yt hath power all wandringe eyes to stay
to move dumbe tonges to speake, lame hands to ‸wright
stayd thoughts to rime, and hard harts to melt away
yet paynters can of this draw everie line
and every wittles p̱sone that hath eyes
can see and Iudge and sweare yt is devine.
for in those outward formes all fooles are wise.
but y^{t} wth my admiringe speritt doth viewe.
(in thought whereof yt would forever dwell.)
eye never saw, the pensell never drew.
pen never could discribe, tonge never tell.
yt is the invisible bewtie of yor minde
yor clere imagination, livelie witt
soe sûnde soe tempored, of such hevenly kinde.
as all mens spiritts are charmed and rapt wth yt.
this life wthin begetts yor livelie looke.
as fier doth make all mettles looke like fier
or yor quicke soule by choyse this bodie tooke.
as angells w:th bright beames there selues attier.

I, 11

{11}

Oh that my brest might ope, and hart might cleave.
that soe yo^{w} might my silent wondringe veiwe.
oh that yo^{w} could my servinge spiritt pseave.
how still wth tremblinge wings yt waites one yo^{w}.
then should[you] see of thought an endles chaine
whose linkes yor bewties and yor vertues bee.
then should yo^{w} see how yor faire forme doth rayne
through all the regions of my phantasie.
then should yo^{w} find, that I am yo^{rs}: as much
as are yor quicke conceites bowroed of none.
or as yor native bewtie, w:^{ch} is such
as all the world will sweare yt is yor owne./
finis

Sir Henry Wotton, The Character of a Happy Life

{⊖} How happie is he borne or tawghte,
that servethe not an others will
whose armor is his honest thowghte
and simple trewth his hyghest skill
whose passions not his maysters are
whose sowle is still prepayred for death
not tyed vnto the world wth care
of princes grace, or vulgar breath;
who envies not whome chance doth rayse
nor vice who never vnderstoode
y^{t} swords makes lesser wownds then prayse
not rvles of state but rweles of good
who god doth late & yearlye pray
more of his grace then goods to lend
and intertaynes ye harmeles day
wth a well chosen booke or frend
that man is free frō servill bands
of hope to rise or feare to falle
Lord of him self thowgh not of landes
& haueinge nothing yett haue all:/

[I, 11v–15 blank] *I, 15v. Sir Robert Ayton, The Sheppherd Thirsis*

[*]

The shippard *Thirsis* longed to die
gaesinge vppon the gracious eye
of her whom he adored & loved
when she whom no lesse passion moued
Thus said o die not yett I pray
Ile die wth thee if thow wilt stay
then *Thirsis* for awhile delayes
the heate he had to end his dayes
but whilst he thus plonged his breath
not dieinge vnto him was death
at last whilst languishinge he layes
and sukes sweit necter from her eyes
the louelye shepperdise who fand
the harvest of her love at hand
wth tremblinge eyes, strayght fell a crieinge
die, Die sweete hart for I am dieinge;
and I the→th[y] swayne did strayght replie
be howld sweete harte wth the I dye
thus spent those happie tow there breath
in sutch a sweite and deathles death
that they retourd in hast[e] agayne
agayne to trie deathes pleasant payne: *finis*

I, 16. John Donne, Elegie: The Anagram

{16}

[*] Marrye: and loue thy *flauia* for she
{ɵ} hath all things wherby others bewtious bee
for thowghe her eyes be smale, her mouth is greate
Thoughe they bee Iuorye, yett her teeth bee Iett
thoughe they bee donne, yett she is light ~~I~~ enowghe
And thoughe her harsh hayre fale, her skinne is rowghe:
What thowghe her ‸~~skinn~~ cheikes bee yeallow, her hayre is reed
give her thyne and shee hath ‸then a mayden head,
These thinges are beavtyes elamentes:/ where these
meite in one, that one ~~ɵ~~ muste as parfeit please.
If reed and white, and each good quallitie
be in the wentch; nere aske wheare it doth lye.
In buyinge things pfumed, we aske if there
bee muske and amber in it, but ~~what~~ not where.
Thowghe all her ptes be not, in the vsuall place
she hath an *Anagram* of a good face
If we might pte the letters but one way
in that leane dearth of words, what coulde we saye
When by the Gam. vt; some musitians make
a pfett sonnge others will vndertake,
By the same gam, vt; changed to equall it
thinges simplye good, can neuer be vnfitt.
She is fayre as any; if albe like her.
and if none bee. then is she singuler.
All loue is wonder; if we Iustly doe
accoumpte he wonderfull; why not louelye too.
Loue builte one beawtye, sone as beawtye dyes
Chose this face charged wth noe deformityes
weomen are like angells, ~~and not~~ they fayre bee
Like those wch fell to worse: but sutch as she
Like to good angells, nothinge can impare.
Tis lesser greif to bee foule, then to haue bein fayre:/

I, 16v

ffor one nights reuelles silke and goulde we chovse
but in longe Iournyes cloth and leather vse:
beawtye is barren oft;/ best hvsbands saye
there is best lande, where is the fovlest waye.
Oh what soveraygne plaster will she bee
If thy past sinnes haue tawght thee ~~Ieasowl~~ Ielowsye
here neids no spyes nor Eweunches; her committ
safe to thy fooes, yee to a marmasett,
When *Belgias* Cittyes, the round Centryes drownd
that durtye fowlnes, gards and armes the towne,
Soe dothe her face gard her, and so for thee
Wch forced by bewsines ofte must absent be
She whose face like Clowds tournes day to nighte
Who mightier then the Sea; makes mores seime white
Whom thowghe vii yeares she in the Stewes had layde
a nunnerye durst receaue and thinke a mayde
and thowgh in childbearth labor she did lye
Midwives, would sweare twere but a Tympanie,
Whom if ^she ~~they~~ accuse I credit lesse
then witches wch impossibles confesse
Whom dildoes, beadstaves and her veluet glase
would be as loth to tutch as Ioseph was
One like none; and likt of none fittest were.
ffor thinges in fassion; euery man will weare:/
finis:/

{17}

A curse:/

Donne
[X]

Whoeve^{r}: guesses, thinkes, or dreames, hee knowes
who is my mistris; wither by this curse.
His only; and only his purse,
may some dull harte; to loue dispose,
and she yealde then to all that are his fooes;
Maye hee be scorned; by one whome all men scorne
fforsweare to others, what to her he hath sworne
ffor feare of missinge; shame of gettinge torne:/

Madnes his sorrow, goute his crampes; may hee
make; by but thinkinge, who hath made him sutch
and may he feele no tutch,
of conscience, but of fame; and be
anguisht, not that t'was sinn, but y^{t} 'twas shee
Or maye he, for her vertue reuerence
Her y^{t} hates him, only for impotence
And equall traytors be she; and his senc,

Maye he dreame treason and beleeve that hee
meant to pforme it, & confesse and dye,
and no recorde tell why,
his sonnes; wch none of his may bee
inherite nothinge but his infamye,
Or may he so longe pasites haue feedd
That he would fayne be theres whome he hath breed
And at the last be circumsiced for bread.

The venim of all stepdames, gamesters gall
what Tyrantes and there subiects interwish
what hearbs, mynes, beasts, fowle, fishe,
can contribute, and all, wch all,
poets or pphetts spoke, and all wch shall
Bee annexd in schedules, vnto this by me
ffall on that man: for if it bee a shee
Nature before hand, hath oute cursed mee:/

finis:

I, 17v. Josuah Sylvester, A Caution for Courtly Damsels

[X] Bewayre fayre Mayd; of musicke courtiers oathes
take heed what gwyftes and fauors you receave,
Lett not the fadinge glose, of silken cloathes
dasell your vertues, or your fame bereave:
ffor loose but once the houlde you haue of grace
Who will regard you^{r} fortune or you^{r} face:/

Eache greidie hande will stryue to catch ye flower
when none regardes the stalke it growes vppon,
Each nature couettes, the frwettes still to devoure
and leaues the tree to faule or stande alone.
Then this advyse fayre creature, take of me
Lett none take fruiçte, vnlesse ye take ye tree:/

Beleive no oathes, nor no ptestinge men
credit no vowes, nor no bewaylinge songe
Lett courtiers sweare, for sweare, & sweare agayne
there harte doth lyve tenn regions from the tongue
ffor when wth o^athes, they make thy harte to treamble
Beleive them leaste for then they most dissemble:/

Beware least Cesor doo corrupt thy minde
or fond ambition,/ sell thye modestie,
Saye thowghe a kinge, thou ever courtious finde
he cannot pdon thy impewritie,
Begyne wth kinge, to subiecte thow wilt falle
ffrom Lord to Laque, ~~and~~^{SO} at last to all:/

finis

Anonymous, On a Maiden-head

~~Lost~~
[X] Lost Iewells may be recouered, virginitye neuer:/
That's lost but once, and once lost, lost for ever:/

I, 18. Sir John Harington, Of a Lady that giues the cheek

{18}

yst for a fauor, or for some dislike
that for your lipp, you tourne to me your cheike
to give you a taste of my vnfayned loue.
your lips and cheikes Ile leaue, and kisse your gloue
but know you why, I make you wth this acquaynted
your gloues be pfumide; your lips & cheikes be paynted:/

Jonathan Richards, a songe: "I die when as I doe not see"

a songe:

I die when as I doe not see
[X] her who is lif & all to me
and when I see her yett I die
in seeinge of her cruelltye:
So y^{t} to me like miserie is wrowght
Both when I see, & when I see her nought→not:

or shall I ~~grive~~ speake, of→or silent gryve
but how can silenc then relieve
& if I speake, I may offend
& speakeinge not my harte will rend
So y^{t} to me I see it is all one
Speake I or speake I not: I am vndone:/

Anonymous, Onste and no more, so sayd my love

Onste and no more, so sayd my love
[X] when in myne armes inchayned.
She vnto me her lips did move
and so my hart, she gayned:

Adew she sayde, be gone I must
for feare of beinge missed
You^{r} hart putts o'er, but in trust
and so agayne she kissed:

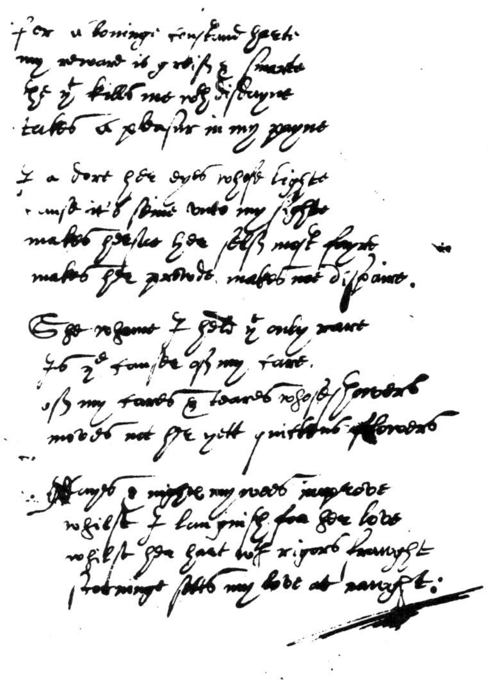

I, 18v. Anonymous, for a louinge constand harte

for a louinge constand harte
my reward is greif & smarte
she y^{t} kills me wth disdayne
takes a pleasur in my payne

I a dore her eyes whose lighte
cause it's seine vnto my sighte
makes her see her self most fayre
makes her prowde makes me dispaire.

She whome I held ye only rare
Is ye causer of my care.
of my cares & teares whose showers
moves not her yett quickens flowers

Dayes & nightes my woes improve
whilst I languish for her love
whilst her hart wth rigors frawght
scorninge setts my love at nawght:

I, 19. Anonymous, a songe: "When my hart seemes most ingaged"

{19}

a songe

X When my hart seemes most ingaged
my love lasts but for a day,
foolish birds that wilbe caged
haueinge meanes to fly away
Loue hath winges & loues to range
I love those, y^{t} love to change

One to hovld & catch at manny
none to trust but all to prove
To coure all not care for any
Is ye wisest course of love,
Love hath: etc

Age affectes a reputation
of a sober steaddie mind.
youth is in ye youthfull fashion
when it wavers like ye winde
Love hath winges etc

Constancie so hyghlye prised
makes a man a slave to one
they are free & well advised
who in louinge all loves none
Love hath winges etc

What are y^{ey} so mutch commended
for a constant louinge harte,
Children, cowards, ill be frended.
fooles vnskilled in lovers arte
Love hath winges etc:

You y^{t} heare my free ꝑfession
and thinke I doe ye world belye
Trie and make a trew confession
you will saye as well as I.
Love hath winges & loves to range
I love those y^{t} loues to change:

I, 19v. Anonymous, Some who the speakinge sparke of my first loue did spie

Some who the speakinge sparke of my first loue did spie
which smother'd vpp in ashes now, not dead (though bvried) lye
They muse y^{t} I not still a lyuinge Idoll prayse
and that my muse (like *Icarus*) flyes what his flyght did rayse
Nor am I so retyred, but yett I one may see
that may (ye center of my thowghts) my fancies obiect bee
I could vnto my self a heauenlye creature shape
by whose excellencie, I could euen grace a second rape.
But only sutch a one could me her captiue call
as I might of my bondage bragge, avoluntarie thrall
No outward beautie now, thowgh nature ioyne wth arte
can draw attendance from my eyes, lesse homage from my harte
Sutch seellie bonds as those, my hart could neuer bind.
I like not *Helens* face so mutch, as I abhorre her mind
whome one might take away, in vayne sought bake an hoste
she ravish'd wth more reason was, then fowghten for, when lost.
Trew worth might force me yett, not coulloures frayle entise
one by my eares, not by my eyes, must now my thoughts surprise
A vertuous creature yett, my fancies might enroule,
wth whome I might (as wth a frend) communicate my soule,
Why might not of y^{t} sex some one thus purchase fame,
as of all virtue capable, and everie way extreame
they what defective is, might to perfection turne
whose vehement affections calm'd, would foster what y^{ey} burne
I wth some of great worth, this wonder would pcure
a vertuous, not voluptuous love, a frenshipp great yett pure
I ~~would~~ for sutch favor would aspire but to prevayle
as might not make a virgin blush, nor matron to loke pale
ffor her to whose praysed partes, I once engag'ed my name
I as a *Phenix* would extoll, to flie over all wth fame

{20}

and her disgrace in ought who did my choyce remayne.
if for nowght els, it could greiue me, as beinge my Iudgments stayne
Thus euen as of my owne, being Iealous of her state,
I what migh honor her ~~might~~ would vrge vrge, what migte dishono^{r} hate
but sutch a loue as this no soddayne fancie founds
but by degrees must stronglie grow, built on eternall grownds
A face first move my eyes, a gesture fix them might
as wch themselves insinuate deseru'dlie in the sight
and then beinge tempted thus what fvrder was to ~~Love~~ prove
a quicke discourse, a vertuous course, by tyme might make me love
Not that externall partes, a stoicke I disdayne
I hold them but as bayts to take, worth y^{t} wch should retayne
when wth a face most fayre, a mind more fayre I find
this angles eyes, y^{t} ankers thoughts, both absolutelie binde
Then doth pfection shine for ~~ye~~ badge which beautie beares
as diamonds enshrin'ed in gold, or starres enstalld in spheares:

{21}

Satire

Kind pittie choakes my spleene braue scorne forbidds
those teares to issue wch swell my eielidds
I must not laugh nor weepe Surs and be wise
Can Railing then cure these worne Maladies
Is not our Mistres faire Religion
As woorthie of all our soules deuotion
As vertue was to the first blinded age
Are not heauens ioyes as valiant to asswage
Lustes as Earths honour was to them Alasse
As wee doe them in meanes shall they surpasse
Vs in the end and shall thy fathers spiritt
Meete blind Philosophers in heauen whose meritt
Of strickt life may be imputed faith and heere
Thee whom he taught so easie waies and neere
To followe damned? Or if thou darest feare this
This feare great courage and hie valour is
Darst thou aid *Mutinous Dutch* & darst thou lay
Thee in Shipps woodden *Sepulchres* a pray
To Leaders Rage to stormes to shott to death
Darst thou diue seas and dungeons of the earth
Hast thou couragious fire to thawe the Ice
Of frozen *North* discoueries and thrice
Colder then *Salamanders* Like deuine
Children in the Ouen ffires of Spaine and the line
Whose Countries Limbecks to our bodies bee
Canst thou for gaine beare? and must euery hee
Which cries not goddesse to thy *Mistris* drawe
Or eat thy poisonous woords courage of strawe
O desperate coward wilt thou seeme bold and
To thy foes and his (who made thee stand
Sentinell in his worldes worlds garison thus yeeld
And for forbidden warres leaue the appointed *field*
Knowe thy foe the fowle diuell is whom thou
Striuest to please for hate not loue would allowe
Thee faine his whole *Realme* to be quitt and as
The worlds all parts wither away and passe
So the worlds selfe thy other loued foe is
In her decrepitt wane and thou louing this
Dost loue a withered and worne strumpett last
fflesh (it selfes death) and ioyes wch flesh can tast
Thou louest and thy faire goodlie soule wch doth
Giue this flesh power to tast ioy thou dost loth
Seeke true *Religion*; O where *Mirreus*
Thinking her vnhows'd here and fledd from vs
Seekes her att *Roome*, there because she doth know
That she was there a thowsand yeares agoe
He loues the Raggs so as wee heere obey
The *statecloth* where the *Prince* sate yesterday
Grants to braue loue will not be inthralld
But loues her onlie who att *Geneua* is calld

I, 21v

Religion plaine simple Sollen yonge
Contemptuous yett vnhandsome as amonge
Lecherous humours there is one that iudges
No wenches wholsome but course country drudges
Grayus staies still att home here and because
Some Preachers (vile ambitious Baudes and lawes
Still new like fashions) biddes him thinke that shee
Which dwells with vs is onlie perfect, hee
Embraceth her whom his godfathers will
Tender to him beeing tender. as wards still
Take such wiues as their *Gardeans* offer or
Pay vallewes. *Carelesse Phrigius* doth abhorre
All because all cannot be good as one
Knowing some women whores dares mary none
Gracchus loues all as one and thinckes that so
As women doe in diuers countries goe
In diuers habitts yett are still one kind
So doth so is *Religion* and this blindnes
Too much light breedes but vnmooued then
Of force must one and forcd but one alowe
And the right, aske thy father which is she
Lett him aske his though truth and falshood bee
Neere twinnes yet truth a little elder is
Be busie to seeke her belieue mee this
He is not of none nor woorst wch seekes the best
To adore to skorne an Image or protest
May all be badd; doubt wiselie in strange way
To stand inquiring right is not to stray
To sleepe or runne wrong is: on a huge hill
Cragged and steepe truth standes and he that will
Reach her must about and about goe
And what the hills soddainnesse resists winne soe
Yett striue so that before age deaths twilight
Thy soule rest for none can woorke in that night
To will implies delay therefore now doe
Hard deedes the bodies paines hard knowledge too
The minds endeuoires reach. and misteries
Are like the sunne dazeling yett plaine to all eies
Keepe the truth which thou hast found men doe not stand
In so ill case here that God hath with his hand
Signed Kinges *Blanck=charters* to kill whom they hate
Nor are they *Vicars* but *Hangmen* to fate
ffoole and wretch wilt thou lett thy soule be tied
To mans lawes by which she shall not be tryed
Att the last day will itt then boote thee
To say a *Phillipp* or a *Gregorie*
A *Harry* or *Martin* taught thee this
Is not this excuse for meere contraries
Equallie stronger? cannot both sides say so
That thou maist rightly obey power her bondes know
Those past her nature and name is changd to bee
Then humble to her is Idolatry

I, 22

{22}

As streames are power is those blest flowers that dwell
Att the rough streames calme head thriue and proove well
But hauing left their Rootes and themselues giuen
To the streames tirannous rage alasse are driuen
Through Mills and Rockes and Woodes and att last almost
Consumed in goinge in the sea are lost
So perish soules which more chuse mens vniust
Powre from god claimed then God himselfe to truste

John Donne, Satyre IV

Well I may now receiue and die my sinne
Indeed is great but I haue beene in
A Purgatorie such as feard *Hell* is
A Recreation and scant *Mappe* of this
My mind neither with prides Itch nor yett hath beene
Poisoined with loue to see or to be seene /
I had no suit there nor newe suit to shewe
Yett went to Court but as *Glare* wch did goe
To a *Masse* in Iest catchd was faine to disburse
The hundred Marckes wch is the Statutes curse
Before he scapd. So it pleased my destinie
Guiltie of my sinne of going) to thinke mee
As prone to all ill and of good as forgettfull
As proud lustfull and as much in debt
As vayne and wittlesse and as false as they
Which dwell att Court, for once going that way
Therefore I suffered this, towardes mee did runne
A thinge more strange then on *Nilus slyme* the *Sunne*
Ere bredd, Or all which into *Noahs Arke* came
A thinge wch would haue posed *Adam* to name
Stranger then seauen *Antiquaries* studies
Then *Affrick monsters Guianaes* rarities
Stranger then strangers one who for a *Dane*
In the *Danes* massacre had sure beene slaine
If he had liued then and without helpe dies
When next pretences against strangers rise
One whom the watch att noone letts scarce goe by
One to whom the Examining Iustice sure would cry
Sir by your Priesthood tell mee what yow are
His Clothes were strange though course and black though bare
Sleeuelesse his Ierkin was and itt had byn
Veluett but t'was now so much ground was seene
Become *Tufftaffata* and our children shall
See itt plaine *Rash* a while then nought att all.
This thing hath trauelld and saith speakes all tongues
And onlie knoweth what to all states belonges
Made of the Accents and best phrase of all these
He speakes strange language if strange meates displease
Art can deceiue or hunger force my taste
But *pedants* motly tonge *soldiours* bombaste

I, 22v

Mountebancks drugg tonge nor the termes of law
Are stronge inough *Preparatiues* to drawe
Mee to beare this yett I must be content
With his tonge in his tonge called complement
In which he can winne widdowes and pay skores
Make men speake treason cosen suttlest whores
Out flatter fauourites or outlie either
Iovius or *Lurius* or both together
He names mee and comes to mee I whisper *God*
How haue I sinned that thy wraths furious rodd
This fellowe chooseth mee he saieth. *Sir*
I loue your iudgement whom doe yow preferre
ffor the best Linguists? and I seelilie
said that I thought *Calepines Dictionary*
Nay but of men most sweet *Sir. Beza* then
Some *Iesuitts* and twoo reuerent men
Of our twoo *Academies* I named; there
He stopt mee and said nay yor *Apostles* were
Good pretty Linguists and so *Panirge* was
Yett a poore gentleman all these may passe
By trauaile then as if he would haue sold
His tonge he praised itt and such woordes told
That I was faine to say If yow had liued Sir
Time inough to be Interpreter
To *Babells Brick Layers* sure the towre had stood
He adds if of Court life yow knowe the good
Yow would leaue lonelines I said not alone
My lonelinesse is but *Spartanes* fashion
To teach by painting *Drunckards* doth not tast
Now *Aretines* pictures haue made fewe chast
No more can Princes Courtes though there be fewe
Better Pictures of vice Teach mee the vertue
He like to a high streatcht *Lutestring* squeakt O sir
'Tis sweete to talke of Kinges *Att Westminster*
Said I the man that keepes the *Abbey Tombes*
And for his price doth with who ever comes
Of all *Sir Harries* and *Sir Edwards* talke
ffrom *Kinge* to *Kinge* naught but *kings* yor eies meet./
Kings only the way to itt is *Kings street*
Hee smackt and cryed hees base *Mechanick coarse*
So are all yor *Englishmen* in their discourse
Are not your french men neat fine as yow see
I haue but one *Frenchman* looke he followes mee
Certes they are neatlie clothd. I of this mind am
Your only wearing is y^{e} *Grogaran*
Not so *Sir* I haue more vnder this Pitch
He would not flie I chafd him but Itch
Scratcht into smart and as blunt Iron ground
Into an Edge hurts woorse (so I foole) found
Crossing hurt me to fitt my sullennesse
He to another key his stile doth dresse

{23}

And askes what newes I tell him of new plaies
He takes my hand and as a still wch stayes
A Sembreefe twixt each dropp he niggardlie
As loth to inrich mee so tells many a lie
More then ten *Hollensheads or Hales or Stowes*
Of triuiall houshold trash he knowes he knowes
When the *Queene* frownd or smild and he knowes what
A subtle states man may gather of that
He knowes who loues whom and who by poison
Hastes to an *Offices Reuersion*
He knowes who hath sold his land and now doth begge
A Licence Old Iron Bootes shoes and Eggeshells
To transport shortly boyes shall not play
Att Spanncounter or blewepoint but shall pay
Tole to some Courtie^{r} and wiser then all vs
He knowes what Ladie is not *painted*, Thus
he with home meates tryes mee I belch spewe spitt
Looke pale and sickly like a *Patient*, yett
He thrusts me more and as if he vndertooke
To say *Gallobelgicus* without booke
Speakes of all states and deedes that haue beene since
The *Spaniards* came to the losse of *Amyens*
Like to a bigg wife att sight of loathed meat
Ready to trauell so I sigh and sweat
To heare his *Macron* talke in vayne for yett
Eeither my humour or his owne to fitt
He like a priuilidged *spie* whom nothing can
Discreditt Libelles now against each great man
He names a price for eu^{ery} Office paid
He saith Our warres thriue ill because delayd
That Offices are intaild and that there are
Perpetuities of them lasting as farre
As the last day and that great Officers
Doe with the *Pirates* share and *Dunkerkers*
Who wasts in meat in clothes in horse he notes
Who loues whores who boyes and who goates
I more amazed then *Circes* prisoners when
They felt themselues turne beasts felt my selfe then
Becomming *Traytor* and me thought I saw
One of our *Gyant Statues* ope his Iawe
To sucke mee in. for hearing him I found
That as burnt venomd *Leachers* doe growe sound
By giuing others their sores I might growe
Guiltie and he free, therefore I did showe
All signes of loathing but since I am in
I must pay mine and my forefathers sinne
To the last farthinge therefore to my power
Toughly and *Stubbernly* I beare the Crosse
But the houre of mercy now was come he tries to bring
Mee to pay a fine to scape his torturinge

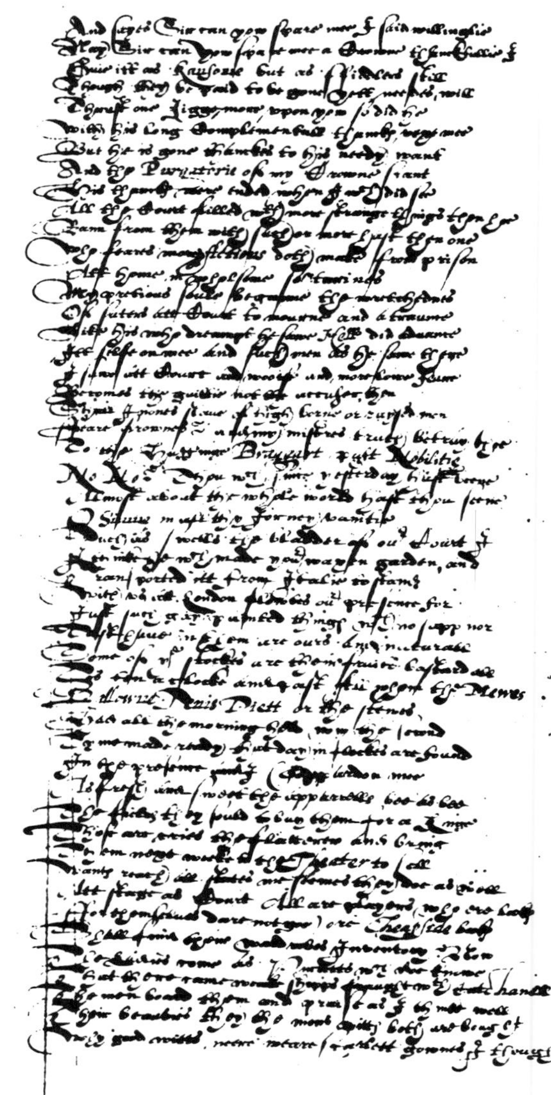

I, 23v

And sayes Sir can yow spare mee I said willinglie
Nay Sir can yow spare mee a Crowne thanckfullie I
Giue itt as *Ransome* but as ffiddlers still
Though they be paid to be gone yett needes will
Thrust one Iigge more vpon yow so did he
With his long Complementall thanckes vexe mee
But he is gone thanckes to his needy want
And the *Purgatorie* of my Crowne scant
His thanckes were ended when I wch did see
All the Court filled wth more strange things then hee
Rann from them with such or more hast then one
Who feares more *Actions* doth make from prison
Att home in wholsome solitarines
My pretious soule beganne the wretchednes
Of suters att Court to mourne and a traunce
Like his who dreampt he sawe *Hell* did aduance
Itt selfe on mee and such men as he sawe there
I sawe att Court and woorse and more lowe feare
Becomes the guiltie not the accuser, then
Shall I nones slaue of high borne or raysed men
ffeare frownes? and my mistres truth betray thee
To the Huffinge *Braggart* puft *Nobilitie*
No No! Thou wch since yesterday hast beene
Almost about the whole world hast thou seene
O *Sunne* in all thy Iorney vanitie
Such as swells the bladder of ou^{r} Court I
I thinke he wch made you^{r} waxen garden, and
Transported itt from Italie to stand
With vs att London flowtes ou^{r} presence for
Iust such gay painted thinges wch no sapp nor
Tast haue in them are ours and naturall
Some of ye stockes are their fruits bastard all
Tis ten a clocke and past All whom the *Mewes*
Ballowne Tenis Diett or the stewes
Had all the morning held now the second
Tyme made ready that day in flockes are found
In the presence and I (God pardon mee
As fresh and sweet the apparrelles bee as bee
The fieldes they sould to buy them for a Kinge
Those are cries the flatterer and bring
Them next weeke to the *Theater* to sell
Wantes reach all states me seemes they doe as well
Att stage as Court All are players who ere lookes
(ffor themselues dare not goe) ore *Cheapside* bookes
Shall find their wardrobes Inventory. Now
The Ladies come as Piratts wch doe knowe
That there came weake shipps fraught wth Cutchanell
The men board them and praise as I thinke well
Their beauties they the mens wittes both are bought
Why good witts neere weare scarlett gownes I thought

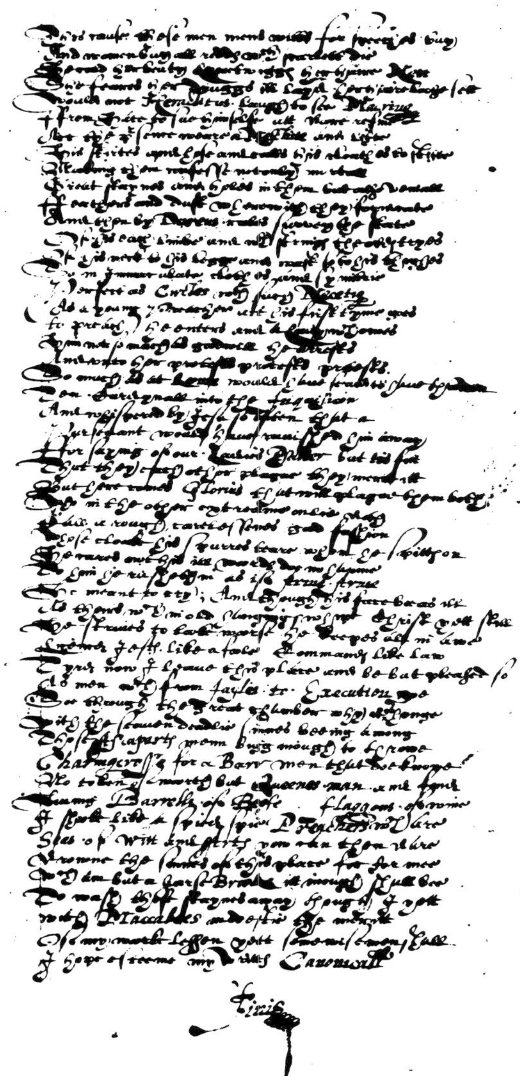

I, 24

{24}

This cause these men mens witts for speeches buy
And women buy all reddes wch scarlett die
He cald her beuty lymetwigges her haire Nett
She feares her druggs ill layd her haire loose sett
Would not *Heraclitus* laugh to see *Macrine*
ffrom Hate to sue himselfe att doore refine
Att the p^{r}sence weare a *Meschite* and lifte
His skirtes and hose and calls his cloathes to stifte
Making them confesse not only mortall
Great staynes and holes in them but also veniall
ffeathers and dust wherewith they fornicate
And then by *Dureus* rules survey the state
Of his each limbe and wth stringes the oddes tryes
Of his neck to his legge and wast so to his thighes
So in Immaculate clothes and symitrie
Perfect as *Circles* wth such *Necetie*
(As a young Preacher att his first tyme goes
to preach) he enters and a Lady wch owes
Him note so much as goodwill he arrests
And vnto her protests protests protests
So much as at *Roome* would haue serud to haue throwen
Ten Cardynall into the *Inquisicon*
And whispered by Iesu so often that a
Purseuant would haue rauished him away
ffor saying of our Ladies *Psalter* but tis fitt
That they each other plague they meritt itt
But here comes *Glorius* that will plague them both
Who in the other extreame onlie doth
Call a rough carelessenes good fashion
Whose cloake his spurres teare whom he spittes on
He cares not his ill woordes doe no harme
To him he rusheth in as if *Arme Arme*
He meant to cry; And though his face bee as ill
As theirs wch in old hanginges whipt Christ yett still
He striues to looke woorse he keepes all in awe
Liciencd Iestes like a foole Commandes like law
Tyrd now I leaue this place and be but pleased so
As men wch from *Iayles* to *Execution* goe
Soe through the great chamber why it $\overset{is}{\wedge}$ honge
With the seauen deadlie sinnes beeing among
Those *Ascapartes* menn bigg inough to throwe
Charingcrosse for a *Barr* men that doe knowe
No token of woorth but *Queenes man* and find
Liuing *Barrells* of *Beefe flaggons* of wine
I shooke like a spied spie *Preachers* wch are
Seas of *Witt* and *Artes* yow can then dare
Drowne the sinnes of this place for for mee
W^{ch} am but a scarse *Brooke* itt inough shall bee
To wash those staynes away though I yett
With *Maccabees* modestie the meritt
Of my woorke lessen yett some wise men shall
I hope esteeme my Writtes *Canonicall*

Finis

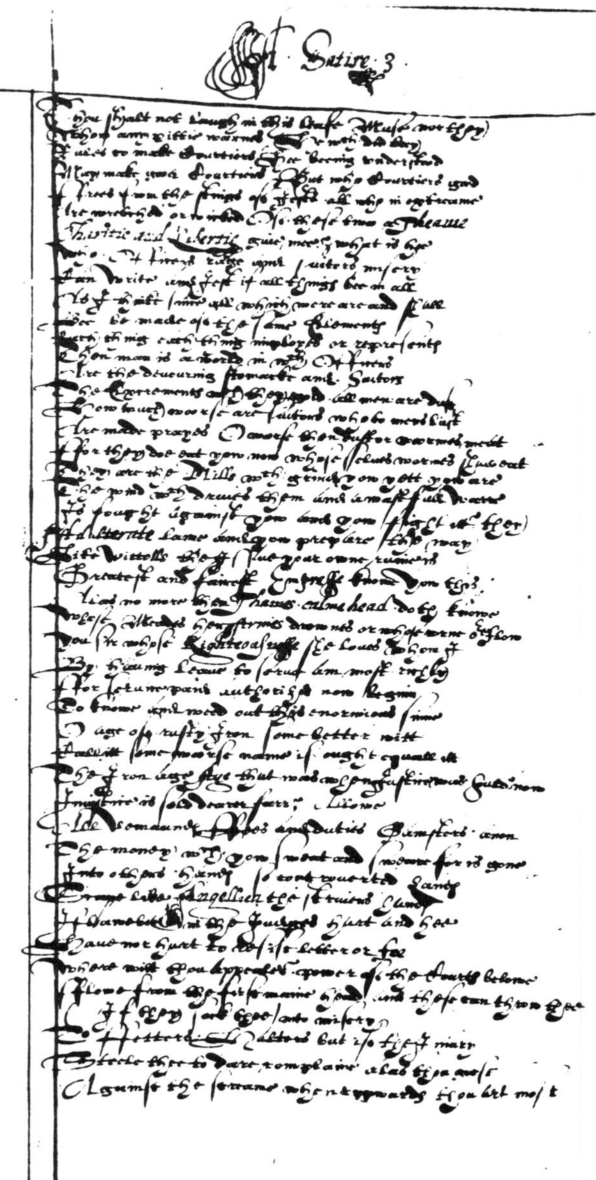

I, 24v. John Donne, Satyre V

A Satire 3

Thou shalt not laugh in this leafe Muse nor they
Whom any pittie warnes He wch did lay
Rules to make Courtiers (Hee beeing vnderstood
May make good Courtiers But who Courtiers good
ffrees from the stings of Iests all who in extreame
Are wretched or wicked Of these twoo a *Theame*
Charitie and Libertie giue mee! what is hee
Who Officers rage and suitors misery
Can Write and Iest if all thinges bee in all
As I thinke since all which were are and shall
Bee be made of the same Elementes
Each thing each thing imployes or representes
Then man is a world in wch Officers
Are the deuouring stomacke and *Suitors*
The Excrementes wch they void. all men are dust
How much woorse are suitors who to mens lust
Are made prayes O woorse then dust or woormes meat
ffor they doe eat yow now whose selues wormes shall eat
They are the *Mills* wch grind yow yett yow are
The wind wch driues them and a wastfull Warre
Is fought against yow and yow fight itt! they
Adulterate lawe and yow prepare the way
Like *Wittolls* the Issue your owne ruine is
Greatest and fairest *Empresse* knowe Yow this
Alas no more then *Thames calme head* doth knowe
Whose Meades her *Armes* drownes or whose corne o^{r}eflow
You sir whose *Righteousnesse* she loues whom I
By hauing leaue to serue am most richly
ffor seruice paid authorizd now beginn
To knowe and weed out this enormious sinne
O age of rusty Iron some better witt
Call itt some woorse name if ought equall itt
The Iron age *Age* that was when Iustice was sould! now
Iniustice is sold dearer farr! Allowe
All Demaundes ffees and duties Gamsters anon
The money wch yow sweat and sweare for is gone
Into others handes so controuerted Landes
Scape like *Angellica* the striuers handes
If lawe bee in the Iudges hart and hee
Haue nor hart to resist letter or *fee*
Where wilt thou appeale? power of the Courtes belowe
fflowe from the first maine head and these can throw thee
(If they suck thee) into misery
To ffetters Halters but if the Iniury
Steele thee to dare complaine alas thou goest
Against the streame when vppwardes thou art most

I, 25

{25}

Heauy and most faint and in these labours they
Gainst whom thou shouldst complayne bee in thy way
Become great *Seas* ore wch when thou shalt bee
fforced to make golden Bridges thou shalt see
That all thy gold was drownd in them before
All thinges followe their likes only who haue may haue
  more
Iudges are Gods he who made and said them so
Ment not men should be fo$^{r}_{\wedge}$cd to them to goe
By meanes of Angells when *Supplications*
Wee send to God to *Dominations*
Powres Cherubins and *Heauens* Courts if wee
Should pay ffees as here! *Dailie Bread* would bee
Scarse to Kinges so it is would itt not anger
A stone A Coward yea a *Martir*
To see a *Purseuant* come in and call
All his Clothes Copes Bookes Primmers and all
His plate *Chalices* and mistake them away
And aske a fee for comminge Oh neare may
ffaire lawes white reuerent name be strumpetted
To warrant *Theftes* she is established
Recorder to destinie on Earth and shee
Speakes fates woordes and tells
Who must be rich who poore who in Chaires who in Iayles
Shee is all faire but yett hath fowle long nayles
With which she scratcheth suitors in bodies of men
Of men so in lawe nayles are the Extremities
So officers stretch to more then lawe can doe
As our Nayles reach what no els part comes too
Why barest thou to yon Officer. ffoole hath hee
Gott those goodes for wch men erst bared to thee
ffoole twice, thrice, thou hast bought wrong and now
  hungerly
Begst right but that dole comes not till these die
Thou haddst much and lawes *Vrim and Thummim* try
Thou wouldst for more and for all hast paper
Inough to cloath all the great *Caricke* pepper
Sell that and by that thou much more shalt leese
Then *Haman* when he sold his Antiquities
O wretch that thy fortunes should moralize
Esops fables and make tales prophesies
Thou art the swimming dogge whom shaddowes cossened
And diuest neere drowninge for what vanished.

Finis

I, 25v. John Donne, Satyre II

Sir though (I ~~god~~ thank god for itt I doe hate
Perfectly all this towne yett there is one state
In all ill things so excellently best
that hate towardes them breedes pitie toward the rest
Though Poetrie indeed be such a sinne
As I thinke that bringes dearths and Spanyardes in
Though like the pestilence and old fashioned loue
Ridlingly it catch men and doth remooue
Neuer till itt be starud out! yett their state
Is poore disarmd like papists not woorth hate
One (like a wretch) wch att barr iudged as dead
Yett promptes him wch standes next and cannot read
And saues his life(giues Ideott Actors meanes
Steruing himselfe) to liue by his laboured *Sceanes*
As in some Organ Puppitts daunce aboue
And bellowes pant belowe wch them doe mooue
One would mooue loue by *Rimes* but Witchcraftes charmes
Bring not now their old feares nor their old harmes. /
Rammes and *Slinges* now are sillie Battery
Pistoletts are thee best *Artillery*
And they that write to Lords rewardes to gett
Are they not like singers att doores for meat
And they that write because all write haue still
That excuse for writinge and for writing ill
But he is woorst who beggarlie doth chaw
Others witts fruites and in his Rauenous maw
rancklie digested doth these thinges out spue
As his owne thinges and they are his owne tis true
ffor if one my meat though it be knowne
The meat was mine the Excrement is his owne
But those doe me no harme nor those wch vse
to out doe Dilldoes and out vsure Iewes
T'out drinke the sea t'out sweare the Letany
Who wth sinnes of all kind as familiar bee
As *Confessours* and for whose sinfull sake
Schoolemen new Tenementes in *Hell* must make
Whose strang sinnes *Canonists* could hardly tell
In wch commandementes large recept they dwell
ffor those punish themselues the insolence
Of *Coscus* only breedes my iust offence
Whom tyme (wch rotts all and makes botches poxe
And plodding on must make a Calfe an Oxe)
Hath made a Lawyer wch was alas of late
But a scarce Poett sollicitor of this state
Then are new *beneficd Ministers* he throwes
Like Netts or limetwigges wheresoere he goes
His Title of *Barrister on euery* wench
And woes in language of the *Pleas and Bench*

{26}

A Motion Lady (speake *Coscus*) I haue beene
in Loue euer since *Tricessimo* of the *Queene*
Continuall Claymes I haue made *Iniunctions* gott
To stay my *Riualls* suit that he should not proceed
Spare me in *Hillary* terme I went
Yow said if I returne next *Assize* in Lent
I should be in *Remitter* of your grace
In the *Interim* my letters should take place
Of *Affidauitts* Woordes woordes wch would teare
The tender Laborinth of a soft maides eare
More More then ten Sclauonians scolding more
Then when windes in our ruind *Abbeyes* rore
When sick wth Poetry and possesst with Muse
Thou wast and madd I hop't but men wch chuse
Lawe practise for meere gaynes bould soule repute
Woorse then Imbrothelld Strumpetts prostitute
Now like an Owlelike watchman he must walke
his hand still att a bill now he must talke
Idlely like Prisoners wch whole moneths will sweare
That only *Suertishipp* hath brought them there
And to euery Suitor lie in euery thinge
Like a Kinges *fauourite* yea like a kinge
Like a wedge in a blocke wring to the *Barr*
Bearing like *Asses* and more harmelesse farr
Lye to the *Graue. Iudge* for Bastardy aboundes
Not in Kings titles nor
Symony or Sodomy in Churchmens liues
As these thinges doe in him by theis he thriues
Shortly as the Sea he will compasse all ou^{r} Land
ffrom *Scots* to *Wight* from *Mount* to *Douer* strand
And spying Heirs melting wth Luxurie
Sathan will not ioy att his sinnes as he
ffor as a thriftie wench scrapes kitchin stuffe
And Barrollinge the droppinges and the snuffe
Of wasting candelles wch in thirtie yeare
Relique like kept perchance buyes wedding geare
Peacemeale he getts landes and spendes as much time
Wringing each acre as men pulling *prime*
In Parchment then large as his fieldes he drawes
Assurances bigg as glosd Ciuill lawes
So huge that men (in our tymes forwardnes
Are fathers of the Church for writing lesse
These he writes not nor for these written payes
Therefore spares no length as in those first dayes
When Luther was professed he did desire
Short *Pater nosters* saying as a ffryer

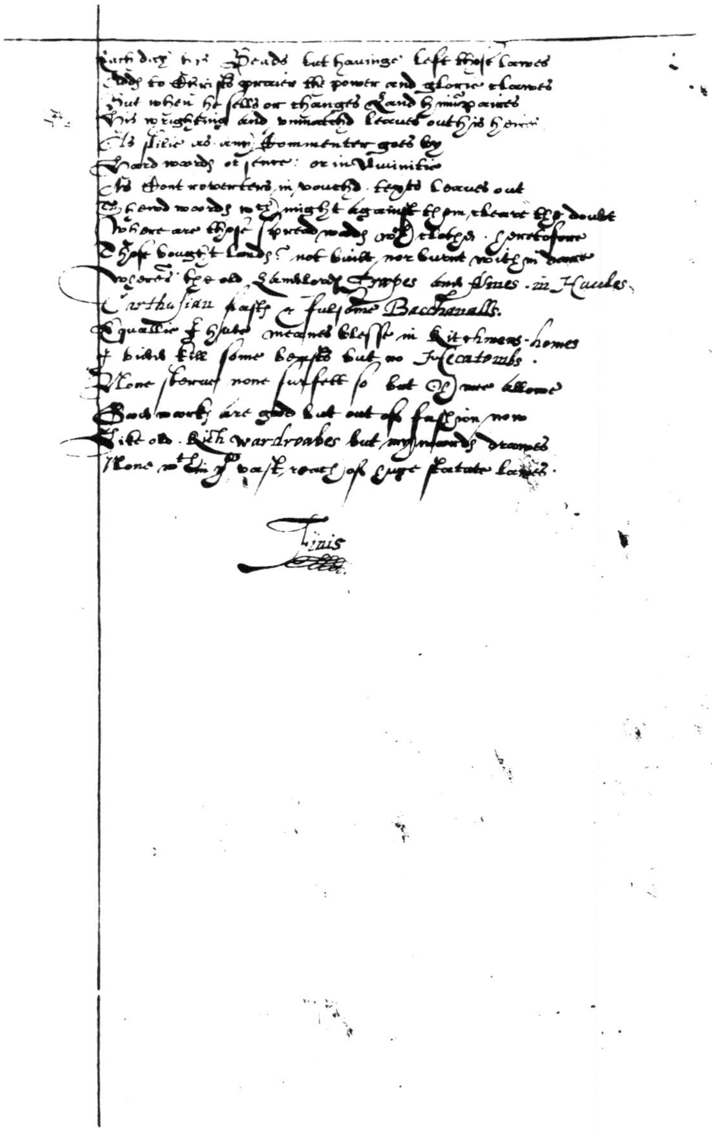

I, 26v

Each day his Beads but hauinge left those lawes
Addes to Christs praier the power and glorie clawes
But when he sells or changes Land h'impaires
His wrighting and vnmatchd leaues out his heires
As slilie as any Commenter goes by
Hard woordes or sence: or in Diuinitie
As Controverters in vouchd texts leaues out
Shewd woordes wch might against them cleare the doubt
Where are those spread woodes wch clothd heretofore
Those bought landes? not built nor burnt within doore
Where's the old Landlordes *Troopes* and *Almes in Haules*
Carthusian fastes & fulsome *Bacchanalls*
Equallie I hate meanes blesse in *Ritchmens homes*
I bidd kill some beasts but no *Hecatombs*
None sterue none surfett so but Oh wee allowe
Good woorkes are good but out of fashion now
Like old *Rich wardroabes* but my woordes drawes
None wthin ye vast reach of huge statute lawes.

Finis

I, 27. *John Donne, Elegie: The Bracelet*

Eligia. 1. {27}

Not that in colour it was like thy haire
[*] for *Arme letts* of that thou mayest lett me weare
Nor that thy hand itt oft embracst and kiste
for so itt had that good wch oft I miste
Nor for that silie old *Morralitie*
That as those linckes were tied our loue should bee
Mourne I that I thy seauen fold chaine haue lost
Nor for the lucke sake but the bigger cost
Oh shall twelue righteous *Angells* wch as yett
No leauen of vile *Soder* did admitt
Nor yett by any fault haue strayed or gone
ffrom the first state of their *Creation*
Angells wch heauen commanded to prouide
All thinges to mee and bee my faithfull guide
To gayne new frendes to appease great enimies
to comfort my soule when I lie or rise
Shall these twelue *Innocents* by thy seuer
Sentence dread Iudge my sinnes great burden beare
Shall they be damnd and in the fornace throwne
And punishd for Offences not their owne
They saue not mee they doe not ease my paines
When in that *Hell* they are burnt and tied in chaynes
Were they but *Crownes* of ffrance I cared not
ffor most of them their naturall Country rott
I thinke possesseth! they come here to vs
So leane so pale so lame so ruinous
And how so ere french *kings* most Christian bee
Their Crownes are circumcisd most Iewishly
Or were they spanish stampes still trauailing
That are become as *Catholique* as their Kinge
Those vnlickd *Bearewhelpes* vnfild *Pistoletts*
That more then cannon shott auailes or letts
W^{ch} negligently left vnrounded looke
Like many Angled figures in the booke
Of some great Coniurer which would inforce
Nature as those doe Iustice from their course
Which as the soule quickens head feet and hart
Of streames like vaynes runnes thorough the earthes eu^{ery} part
Visitt all Countries and haue slilie made
Gorgeous France ruind ragged and decayd
Scotland wch knewe no state proud in one day
And mangled seauenteene headed *Belgia*
Or were itt such gold as that where withall
Almightie *Chimicks* from each *Minerall*
Hauing by subtile fier a soule out pulld
Are durtilie and desperately gulld
I would not spitt to quench the fier they were in
ffor they are guiltie of much hainous sinne
But shall my harmeles *Angells* perish shall
I loose my *Guard* my head my foot my all?
Much hope wch they should nourish wilbe dead
Much of my able youth and *Lustiehead*
Will vanish if thou loue lett them alone
ffor thou wilt loue me lesse when they are gone
Oh be content that some loud squeaking cryer
Well pleasd wth one leane thredd bare groat for hier

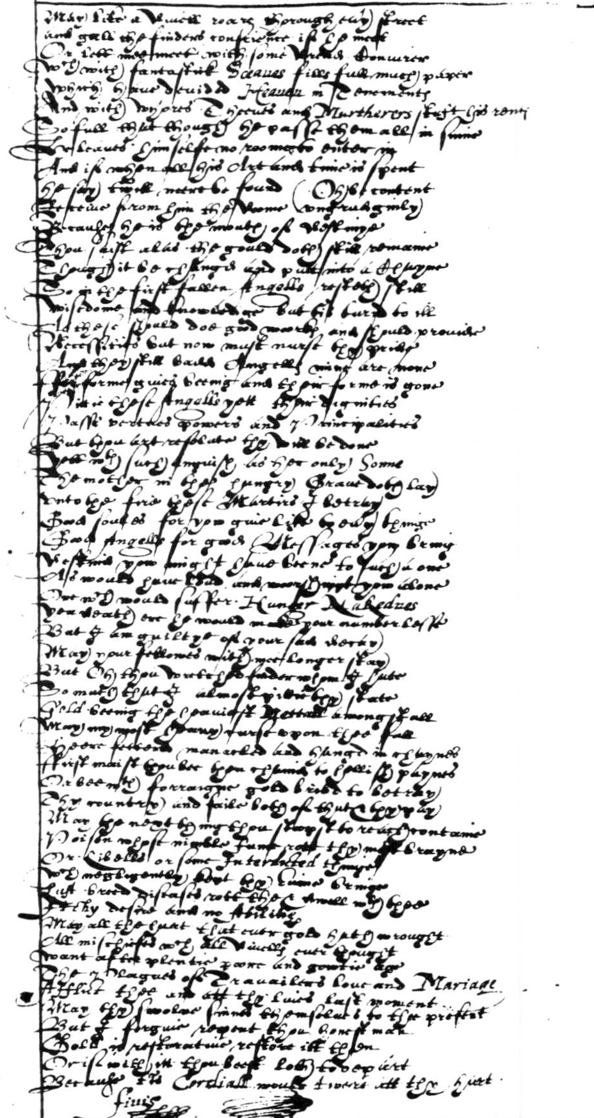

I, 27v

May like a diuell roare thorough eu^ery^ street
and gall the finders conscience if he meet
Or lett mee meet with some dread Coniurer
W^ch^ with fantastick *Sceanes* filles full much paper
Which haue deuided *Heauen* in Tenementes
And with Whores Theeues and *Murtherers* stuft his rentes
So full that though he passe them all in sinne
He leaues himselfe no roome to enter in
And if when all his Art and time is spent
he say t'will neere be found (Oh be content
Receiue from him the doome vngrudginly
Because he is the mouth of Destinye
Thou saist alas the gould doth still remaine
Though it be changd and putt into a chayne
So in the first fallen *Angells* resteth still
Wisedome and knowledge but t'is turnd to ill
As these should doe good woorkes and should prouide
Necessities but now must nurse thy pride
And they still badd Angelles mine are none
ffor forme giues beeing and their forme is gone
Pittie these *Angells* yett their dignities
Passe vertues powers and Principalities
But thou art resolute thy will be done
Yett wth such anguish as her only *Sonne*
The mother in the hungry Graue doth lay
Vnto the fire these Martirs I betray
Good soules for yow giue life to eu^ery^ thinge
Good *Angells* for good Messages yow bring
Destind yow might haue beene to such a one
As would haue loud and woorshippt yow alone
One wch would suffer *Hunger Nakednes*
Yea death ere he would make your number lesse
But I am guiltye of your sad decay
May your fellowes with mee longer stay
But Oh thou wretched finder whom I hate
So much that I almost pittie thy state
Gold beeing the heauiest *Mettall* amongst all
May my most heauy curse vpon thee fall
Heere fetterd manacled and hangd in chaynes
ffirst maist thou bee then chaind to hellish paynes
Or bee wth forraigne gold bribd to betray
Thy country and faile both of that & thy pay
May the next thing thou stoopst to reach containe
Poison whose nimble fume rott thy moist brayne
Or Libells or some *Interdicted* thinge
W^ch^ negligently kept thy ruine bringe
Lust breed diseases rott the & dwell wth thee
Itchy desire and no *Abilitie*
May all the hurt that euer gold hath wrought
All mischiefes wch all diuelles euer thought
Want after plentie poore and gowtie age
The Plagues of Trauailers loue and *Mariage*
*Aff*lict thee and att thy liues last moment
May thy swolne sinnes themselues to thee present
But I forgiue repent thou honest man
Gold is restoratiue restore itt then
Or if with itt thou beest loth to depart
Because t'is *Cordiall* would twere att thy hart

finis

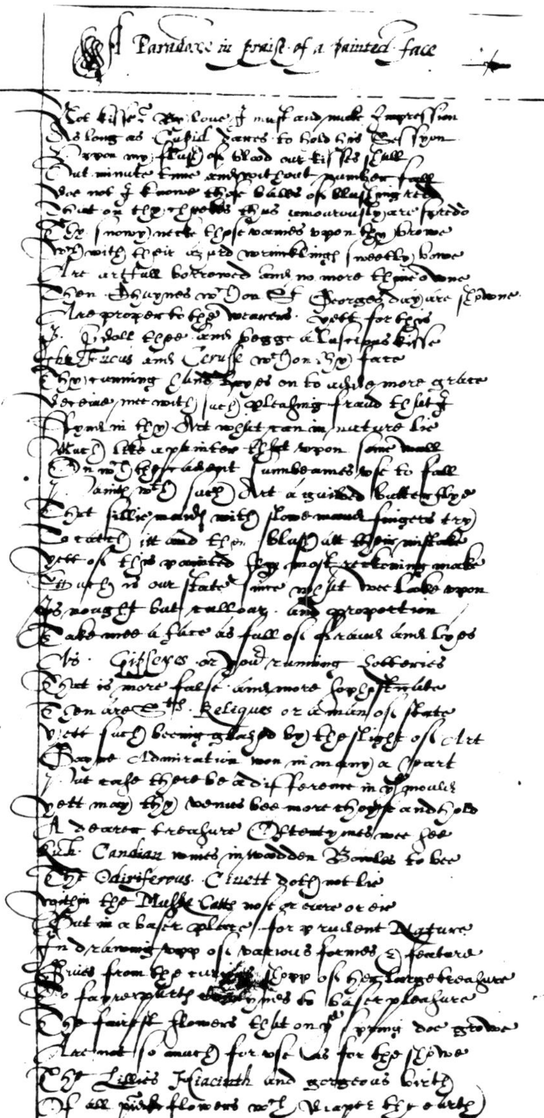

I, 28. Anonymous, A Paradoxe of a Painted Face

{28}

A Paradoxe in praise of a painted face [*]

Not kisse? By loue I must and make Impression
As long as *Cupid* dares to hold his Sessyon
Vppon my flush of blood our kisses shall
Out minute time and without number fall
Doe not I knowe those balls of blushing redd
That on thy cheekes thus amourously are spredd
Thy snowy necke those vaines vpon thy browe
W^{ch} with their azurd wrincklinges sweetly bowe
Are artfull borrowed and no more thine owne
Then Chaynes wch on St Georges day are showne
Are proper to the wearers. yett for this
I Idoll thee and begge a luscious kisse
The *Fucus* and *Cerusse* wch on thy face
Thy cunning hand layes on to adde more grace
Deceiue mee with such pleasing fraud that I
ffynd in thy Art what can in nature lie
Much like a painter that vpon some wall
On wch the cadent sunnbeames vse to fall
Paintes wth such Art a guilded butterflye
That sillie maides with slowe mooud fingers try
To catch itt and then blush att their mistake
Yett of this painted *flye* most reckoning make
Such is our state since what wee looke vpon
Is nought but cullour and proportion /
Take mee a face as full of fraud and lyes
As *Gipseyes* or you^{r} running Lotteries
That is more false and more sophisticate
Then are S^{tes} *Reliques* or a man of state
Yett such beeing glazed by the slight of Art
Gayne Admiration won in many a heart
Put case there be a difference in ye mould
Yett may thy venus bee more choyse and hold
A dearer treasure. Oftentymes wee see
Rich Candian wines in woodden Bowles to bee
The *Odiriferous Ciuett* doth not lie
Within the *Muske Catts* nose or eare or eie
But in a baser place. for prudent Nature
In drawing vpp of various formes & feature
Giues from the curious shopp of her large treasure
To fayre partes comlynes to baser pleasure
The fairest flowers that on y^{e} spring doe growe
Are not so much for vse as for the showe
The Lillies *Hiacinth* and gorgeous birth
Of all pie'd flowers wch diaper the earth

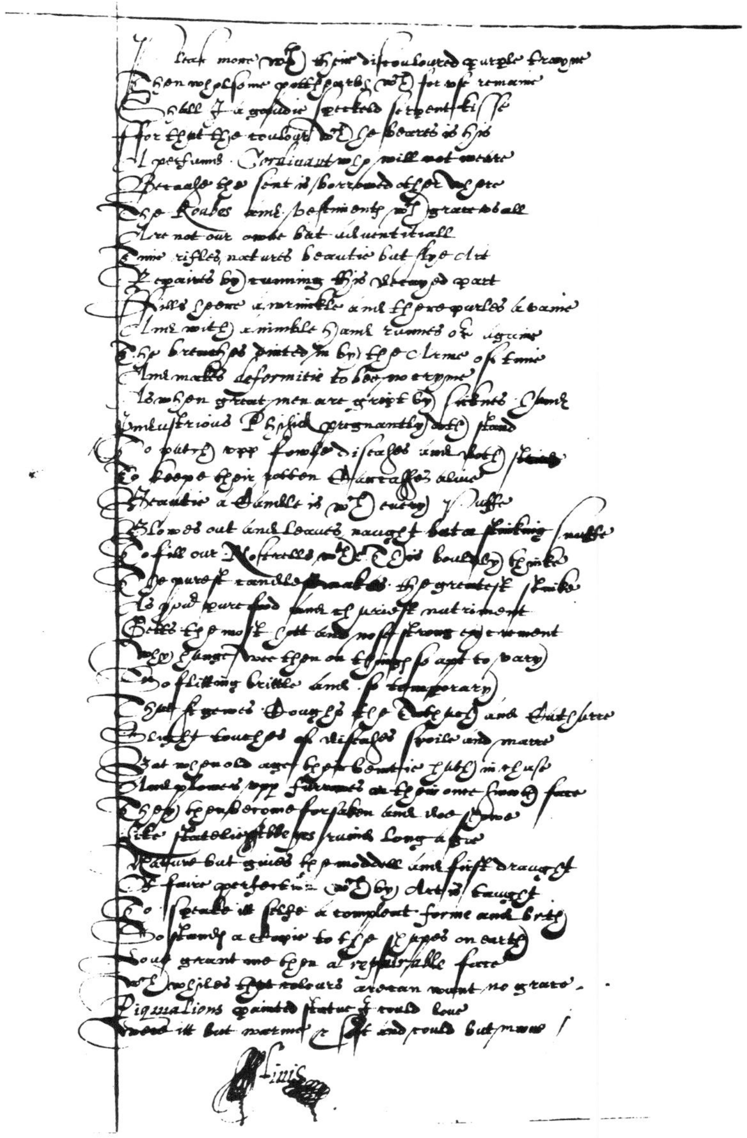

I, 28v

Please more wth their discouloured purple trayne
Then wholsome potthearbes wch for vse remaine
Shall I a gaudie speckeld serpent kisse
ffor that the coulour wch he beares is his
A perfumd *Cordiuant* who will not weare
Because the sent is borrowed other where
The *Roabes* and vestimentes wch grace vs all
Are not our owne but aduentitiall
Time rifles natures beautie but slye Art
Repaires by cunning this decayed part
ffills heere a wrinckle and there purles a vaine
And with a nimble hand runnes o^{re} againe
The breaches dinted in by the Arme of time
And makes *deformitie* to bee no cryme
As when great men are gript by sicknes hand
Industrious *Phisick* pregnantly doth stand
To patch vpp fowle diseases and doth stand→strive
To keepe their rotten Carcasses aliue
Beautie a Candle is wch euery Puffe
Blowes out and leaues naught but a stinking snuffe
To fill our Nostrells wth! This bouldly thinke
The purest candle ~~st~~ makes the greatest stinke
As you^{r} pure food and chariest nutriment
Getts the most hott and nose strong excrement
Why hange wee then on thinges so apt to vary
So flitting brittle and so temporary
That Agewes Coughs the Toothach and Catharre
Slight touches of diseases spoile and marre
But when old age their bewtie hath in chase
And plowes vpp furrowes in their once smooth face
They then become forsaken and doe showe
Like statelie *Abbeyes* ruind long agoe
Nature but giues the moddell and first draught
Of faire perfection wch by Art is taught
To speake itt selfe a compleat *forme* and birth
So standes a copie to the shapes on earth
Loue grant me then a *repairable* face
W^{ch} whiles that colours are can want no grace
Pigmalions painted statue I could loue
Were itt but warme & soft and could but mooue/

finis

I, 29. *Sir Thomas Overbury, A Very Very Woman*

{29}

A Verie woman

Woman is a dowbakd man or shee ment
Well towardes him but fell the two bowes short
Strength and *vnderstanding Her vertue* is
The hedge Modesty that keepes a man from climinge
Ouer into her faultes. Shee simpers as if shee
Had no teeth but lipps and she deuides her eies
And keepes halfe for her selfe and giues the other
To the *Neate* youth Beeing sett downe she casts
Her face into a platt forme wch dureth the meale
And is taken away with the voider Her draught
Reacheth to good manners not to thirst and it is a part
Of their Mistery not to professe *Hunger*
But nature takes her in priuate & stretcheth
Her vpon meat. She is *Mariageable* and *fourteene*
Att once And after she doth not liue butt tarry
Shee reades ouer her face euery morninge
And sometimes blottes out pale & writes redd
Shee thinkes shee is faire though many times her
Opinion goes alone and she loues her glasse
And the *knight* of the *Sunne* for liyng She is hidd
Away all but her face and thates hangd about
With toyes and deuices like the signe of a *Tauerne*
To drawe *Strangers* it is likely she traffiques flesh
And hanges itt out of her shoppwindowes if shee
shewe more she preuentes desier and by too free
Giuing leaues no guift Shee may scape from
the Seruingman but not from the Chambermaid
Shee committes wth her eares for certayne. After
that shee may goe for a maid but she hath beene lyen
With in her vnderstandinge. *Her Philosophy* is a seeming
Neglect of those that bee too good for her
Shees a yonger Brother for her portion but
Not for her portion of witt that comes from her
In a treble wch still is too bigge for itt yett her
Vanitie seldome matches her with one of her owne
Degree for then she will begett another creature
A begger and commonly if she marry better shee
Marries woorse. She getts much by the *Simplicitie*
Of her suitor and for a ieste laughs att him wthout one
Thus she *Dresses* a husband for her selfe and after
Takes him for his patience and the land adioining
Yow may see itt in a seruingmans fresh *Napery*
And his legge stepps into an vnknowne stockinge
I need not speake of his *Garters* the *Tassell shoes*

I, 29v

Itt selfe. *Shee* is *Salamons* cruell creature and
A mans walking consumption euery *Caudle* shee
Giues him is a purge. Her chiefe commendacōn is
she bringes a man to *Repentance*

Sir Thomas Overbury, Her Next Part

Her next part

Her lightnes getts her to swimm att Topp of the Table
Where her wry little finger bewrayes caruing her
Neighbours att the latter end know they are welcome
And for that purpose she quencheth her thirst Shee
Trauailes too and among and so becomes a woman
Of good entertainment for all the folly in ye contry
Comes in cleane linnen to visitt her and she breakes
To them her griefes in sugar cakes and receiues
ffrom them mouths in Exchange many stories
That conclude to no purpose! Her eldest sonne
Is like her howsoever and that dispraiseth him
Best her vtmost drift is to turne him foole: w^{ch}
Commonly she obtaynes att the yeares of discretion shee
Takes a Iourney sometimes to her *Neeces* house but
Neuer thinckes beyond *London* Her *Deuotion* is
Good Clothes. they carie her to Church Expresse
Their stuffe and fashion and are silent if shee bee
More deuout shee liftes vpp a certaine number of
Eies in stead of Prayers and takes the sermon
And measures out a napp by itt iust as longe
She sendes *Religion* afore to *Sixtie* where shee
Neuer ouertakes itt or driues itt before her againe
Her most necessary Instrumentes are a wayting
Gentlewoman and a *chambermaid* she weares her
Gentlewoman still but most often leaues the other
In her chamber windowe shee hath a little *kennell*
In her *Lapp* and shee smelles the sweeter for itt
The vttermost reach of her *Prouidence* is the
ffattnes of a *Capon* and her greatest Envie is
The next *Gentlewomans* better *Gowne Her*
Most commendable skill is to make her husbandes
fustian beare her veluett. This she doth many
Times ouer and then is deliuered to old age
And a *Chaire* where $eu^{er}y$ body leaues her

finis

I, 30. Sir Thomas Overbury, A Good Woman

{30}

A good woman

A good woman is a comfort like a man Shee lackes
Of him nothing but heat. Thence is her sweetnes of
Disposition wch meetes his sweetnes more pleasantly so
Wooll meetes *Iron* easier then Iron Her greatest
Learning is *Religion* and her thoughts are on her
Owne sexe or on men without casting the difference
Dishonesty neuer comes neerer then her eares and then
Wonder stopps itt out and saues vertue the labour
She leaues the neat youth telling his Lushious
Tales and putts back the seruing mans putting forward
With a frowne yett her kindnes is free inough to
Bee seene for itt hath no guilt about itt and her mirth
Is cleare that yow may looke thorough itt
Into vertue; but not beyond. She hath not
Behauiour att a certaine but makes itt to her
Occasion: She hath so much knowledge as to loue
Itt and if shee haue itt not att home she will
ffetch itt for this sometymes in a pleasant discontent
She dares chide her *sexe* though she vse itt
Neuer the woorse: Shee is much within and frames
Outward thinges to her mind not her mind to them *Shee*
Weares good clothes but never better for she findes
No degree beyond *Decency*: *She* hath a content
Of her owne and so seekes not a husband but
ffindes him. *Shee* is indeed most but not much to
Description for she is direct and one and hath not
The varietie of ill! Now she is giuen fresh
And aliue to a *Husband* and shee doth nothing more
Then loue him for shee takes him to that purpose
After this her chiefest vertue is a good husband
for Shee is Hee./ *Finis*

Sir Thomas Overbury, The Authours Epitaph. Written by Himselfe

The Epitaph to Mr Ouerbu: wife

The spann of my daies measured here I rest
That is my bodie but my soule his guest
Is hence discended whither neither tyme
Nor faith nor hope but only loue can clime
Where beeing now enlightened she doth knowe
The truth of all men ergo of one belowe
Onlie this dust doth here in pawne remaine
That when the world dissolues she come againe

finis

I, 30v. John Donne, Elegie: The Comparison

Eligia 2

As the sweet sweat of Roses in a still
As that wch from chafd Muskattes pores doth trill
As the almightie Balme of the earlie East
Such are the sweat dropps on my Mistres breast
And on her necke her skinn such lustre setts
They seeme no sweat dropps but pearle Coronetts
Rancke sweatie froth thy Mistres browe defiles
Like spermatique issue of ripe monstrous biles
Or like that skumm wch by needes lawlesse law
Enforcd *Sanserraes* starued men did drawe
ffrom parboyld shoes and bootes & all the rest
W^{ch} were wth any soueraigne fatnes blest
And like vile liyng stones in saffrond tinn
Or wartes or Wheales they hung vpon her skinn
Round as the World's her head on eu^{ery} side
Like to that fatall Ball wch fell on *Ide*
Or that whereof God had such Iealousie
As for the rauishing thereof wee die
Thy head is like a rough statue of Ieat
Where Marckes for Eyes nose mouth are yett scarce sett
Like the first Chaos or flatt seeming face
Of *Cinthia* when the earths shadowes her embrace
Like *Proserpines* white beautie keeping chest
Or Ioues best fortunes vrne is her faire brest
Thine like worme eaten Trunckes cloathd in *seales* skinns
Or graue thates durt w^{t}hout and stinch within
And like that slender stalke att whose end standes
The Woodbine quiuering are her armes and handes
Like rough barckd Elmeboughs or the russett skin
Of men late scourgd for madnes or for sinn
Like sunn parchd quarters on ye citie gate
Such is thy tannd skins lamentable state
And like a bunch of ragged carretts stand
The short swolne fingers of thy gowtie hand
Then like the *Chimicks* masculine equall fire
W^{ch} in the Lymbeckes warme Wombe doth inspire
Into the earths woorthlesse durt a soule of gold
Such cherishing heat her best loued part doth hold
Thines like the dread mouth of a fired gun|ne|
Or like hott liquid mettalles newlie runne
Into clay mouldes or like that *AEtna*
where round about the grasse is burnd away

I, 31

{31}

Are not your kisses then as filthy and more
As a worme sucking an invenom'd sore
Doth not thy fearfull hand in feeling quake
As one wch gatheringe flowers still feard a snake
Is not your last Act harsh and violent
As when a Plough a stony ground doth rent
So kisse good Turtles so deuoutlie nice
Are Priests in handlinge reuerent sacrifice
And such in searching woundes the surgeon is
As wee when wee embrace or touch or kisse
Leaue her and I will leaue comparing thus
She & *comparisons* are odious

Finis

John Donne, Elegie: The Perfume

Elegia 3.

Once and but once found in thy company
All thy supposde escapes are laid on mee
And as a Thiefe att Barr is questioned there
By all the men that haue beene robd that yeare
So am I (by this traiterous meanes supprisde)
By thy *Hidroptique* father catechisde
Though he had woont to search wth glazed eies
As though he came to kill a *Cocatrice*
Though he haue oft sworne that he would remooue
Thy beauties beautie and food of ou^{r} loue
Hope of his goodes; if I with thee were seene
Yett close and secrett as our soules ^we^ haue beene
Though thy *Immortall* mother wch doth lie
Still buried in her bedd yett will not die
Take this aduantage to sleepe out day light
And watch thy entries and returnes all night
And when she takes thy hand and would seeme kind
Doth search what *Ringes* and *Armeletts* she can find
And kissing notes the colour of thy face
And fearing least thou art swolne doth thee embrace
And to try if thou long doth name strange meates
And notes thy palenes blushinges sighes & sweats
And politiquely will vnto thee confesse
The sinnes of her owne youths ranck lustinesse
Yett loue these sorceries did remooue and mooue
Thee to gull thy mother for my Loue
Thy little brethren wch like *fairy* spirittes
Oft skipt into our chamber those sweet nights
And kist and ingled on thy fathers knee
were bribd next day to tell what they did see
The grim eight=foot=high Ironbound=seruingman
That oft names god in Oathes and only then
He that to barr the first gate doth as wide
As the great *Rhodian Colossus* stride

I, 31v

Which if in *Hell* no other paines there were
Makes mee feare *Hell* because he must be there
Though by thy father he were hir'd for this
Could neuer witnesse any touch or kisse
But of twoo common Ill: I brought wth mee
That wch betrayd mee to mine enimie
A lowd perfume wch att mine entrance cride
Euen att thy fathers nose so wee were spide
When like a Tirant King that in his bedd
Smelt Gunnpowder the pale wretch shiuered
Had itt beene some badd smell he would haue thought
That his owne feet or breath that smell had wrought
But as wee in our Ile imprisonned
Where cattell only and diuers dogges are bredd
The Pretious Vnicornes strange monsters call
So thought he good *strange* that had none att all
I taught my silkes their whistling to forbeare
Euen my opprest shoes dumbe and speechles were
Onlie thou bitter sweet whom I had laid
Next mee$^{mee}_{\wedge}$ traiterously hast betrayd
And vnsuspected hast invisiblie
Att once fledd vnto him and staid wth mee
Base excrement of earth wch dost confound
Sence from distinguishing the sick from sound
By thee the seelie Amorous suckes his death
by drawinge in a leprous harlotts breath
By thee the greatest stayne to mans estate
ffall's on vs to be called effeminate
Though thou be much lou'd in the *Princes Hall*
There thinges that seeme exceed substantiall
Godes when yee fum'd on *Altars* were pleased well
Because yow were burnt not that they lik^{d} your smell
Yow are loath some all beeing taken simple alone
Shall wee loue all thinges ioynd & hate each one
If yow were good your good doth soone decay
And yow are rare that takes the good away
All my perfumes I giue most willingly
To embalme thy fathers coarse! what will he die /

finis

I, 32. *John Donne, Elegie: Change*

{32}

Eligia 4.

Although thy hand and faith and good woorkes too
X Haue sealed thy loue wch nothing should vndoe
Yea though thou fall back that *Apostasie*
Confirmes thy loue Yett much in much I feare thee
Women are like the Arts forc'd vnto none
Open to all searchers vnprizd if vnknowne
If I haue caught a bird and lett him flie
Another fowler seeing those meanes as I
May catch the same bird and as those thinges bee
Women are made for man not him nor mee
Foxes and goates all beasts change when they please
Shall women more hott wilie wild then these
Be bound to one man? and did nature then
Idlely make them apter to endure then men
They are our clogges not their owne if a man bee
Chaind to a *galley* yett the *galley* is free
Who hath a plowd land casts all his seed corne there
And yett allowes his ground more corne should beare
Though *Danvoy* into the sea must flowe
The sea receiues *Rhene Volga and Poe*
By nature wch gaue itt this libertie
Thou lou'st but oh canst thou loue itt and mee
Likenesse glewes Loue then if so thou doe
To make vs like and loue must I change too.
More then thy hate I hate itt rather lett mee
Allowe her charge then change oftner then shee
And so not teach but force my opinion
To loue not any one nor eu^{er}y one
To liue in one land is captiuitie
To runn all countryes a wild *Roguery*
Waters stinke soone if in one place they bide
And in the vast sea are woorse putrifide
But when they kisse one banck & leauing this
Then are they purest change is the ioy & nursery
Of musique life ioy and eternitie

Finis

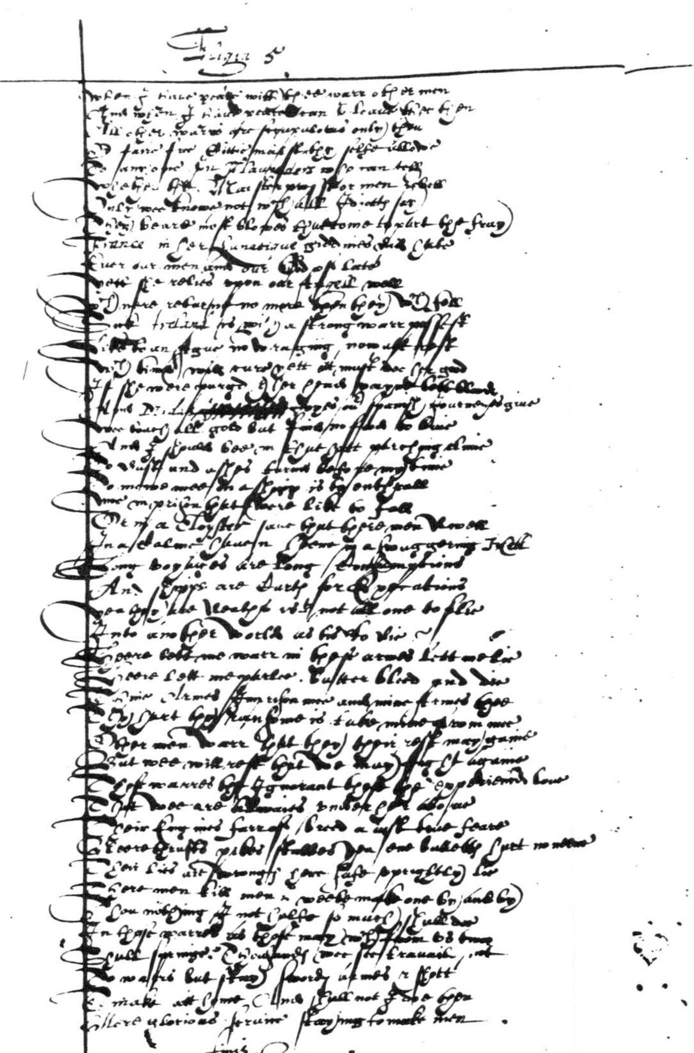

I, 32v. John Donne, Elegie: Loves Warre

Eligia 5

When I haue peace with thee warr other men
And when I haue peace can I leaue thee then
All other warrs are scrupulous only thou
O faire free cittie maist thy selfe allowe
To anyone In *Flaundders* who can tell
Whether the Maister presse or men rebell
Only wee knowe not wch all Idiottes say
They beare most blowes that come to part the fray
France in her *Lunatique* giddines did hate
Euer our men and our God of late
Yett she relies vpon our *Angell* well
W^{ch} nere returne no more then they wch fell
Sick *Ireland* is with a strong warr possest
Like to an *Ague* now raging now att rest
W^{ch} time will cure yett itt must doe her good
If she were purgd & her head vayne lett blood
And *Midas* ~~Iourneyes~~ Ioyes ou^{r} spanish Iourneyes giue
Wee touch all gold but find no food to liue
And I should bee in that hott parching clime
To dust and ashes turnd before my time
To mewe mee in a shipp is to enthrall
Mee in prison that were like to fall
Or in a *Cloyster* saue that there men dwell
In a calme hauen heere in a swaggering *Hell*
Long voyages are long consumptions
And shippes are cartes for Executions
Yea they are deaths is't not all one to flie
Into another world as tis to die?
Heere lett me warr in these armes lett me lie
Heere lett me parlee batter bleed and die
Thine Armes Imprison mee and mine Armes thee
Thy hart thy ransome is take mine from mee
Other men warr that they their rest may gaine
But wee will rest that we may fight againe
Those warres the Ignorant these the experienc'd loue
That wee are alwaies vnder her aboue
Their Engines farr of breed a iust true feare
Neere thrusts pikes stabbes yea ene bullettes hurt no neere
Their lies are wronges here safe vprightly lie
There men kill men! weele make one by and by
Thou nothing I not halfe so much shall doe
In those warres as those may wch from vs twoo
Shall springe! Thousandes wee see trauaile not
To warrs but stay swordes armes & shott
To make att home And shall not I doe then
More glorious seruice staying to make men

finis

{33}

Elegia 6

X Come Madame come all rest my powers defie
Vntill I labour I in labour lie
The foe ofttymes hauing the foe in sight
Is tired wth standing though they neue^{r} fight
Of with that girdle like heauens *zones* glisteringe
But a farre fairer world encompassinge
Vnpinn that spangled brest plate wch you weare
That th eies of busie fooles may be stopt there
vnlase your selfe for that harmonious chim
Tells me from you that now is your bedd time
Of with that happie buske whom I envie
That still can bee and still can stand so nigh
Your Gownes going of such beautious state reueales
As when from flowry *Meades* the *Hill* shadowe steales
Of with you^{r} wiery coronett and showe
The hairy diadem wch on yow doth growe
Now off with those shoes and then softly tread
In this loues *hallowed Temple* this soft bedd
In such white Roabes heauens *Angells* vse to bee
Receiued by men: Thou'*Angells* bringst wth thee
A heauen like *Mahametts* paradise And though
Ill *spiritts* walke in white wee easilie knowe
By this those *Angells* from an euill spiright
They sett our haires butt these the flesh vpright
Licence my roauing handes and lett them goe
Behind before betweene aboue belowe
O my *America* my new found land
My *Kingdome* safe when wth one man mand
My *Mine* of Pretious stones my *Emperie*
How blest am I in thus discouering thee
To enter in those bondes is to be free
Then where my hand is sett my seale shall bee
full Nakednes all Ioies are due to thee
As soules vnbodied bodies vncloathd must bee
To tast whole Ioyes *Iems* wch you women vse
Are as *Atlantaes Balles* cast in mens viewes
That when a soules eie lighteth on a *Gemm*
His earthlie soule may couett theirs not them
Like Pictures or like bookes gay *Couerings* made
for lay men are all women thus arayed
Themselues are *Mistique* bookes wch onlie wee
Whom their imputed *grace* will dignifie
Must be reueald. Then since I may know
As liberallie as to a Middwife showe
Thy selfe cast all yea this white linnen hence
Here is no *Pennaunce* much lesse Innocence
To teach thee I am naked first why then
What needest thou haue more *Couering* then a man /

finis

I, 33v. John Donne, The Autumnall

Widdowe Her

I D No spring nor summer beautie hath such grace
\+ As I haue seene in one *Autumnall* face
Yong beauties force your loue and thats a rape
This doth but councell yett yow cannot scape
If it were a shame to loue here twere no shame
Affection here takes reuerence his name
Wher her first yeares the golden age? thats true
But now shees gold oft tried but neuer new
That was her Torridd and inflaming time
This is her habitable *Tropique* clyme
ffaire eies who askes more heat then comes from hence
Hee in a feauer wishes pestilence
Call not those wrinckles graues; if graues they were
They were loues graues for els he is no where
Yett lies not loue dead heere but heere doth sitt
vowed to this trench like an Anchoritt
And here till her wch must bee his death come
He doth nott digg a graue but build a Tombe
Here dwells hee though he soiourne every where
In progresse yett his standing house is heere
Heere where still euening is not noone nor night
Where no voluptuousnes but all delight
In all her woordes vnto all hearers fitt
Yow may att Reuells yea att Councell sitt
This is loues Tymber youth her vnderwood
There hee as wine in Iune enrages blood
Which then comes seasonablest when our tast
And apetite to other thinges is past
Zerzes strange Lydian loue the *Platan* tree
Was loud for age none beeing so large as shee
Or because beeing yong nature did blesse
Her youth wth ages glorie *Barennesse*
If wee loue thinges long sought Age is a thing
W^{ch} wee are fifty yeares in compassinge
Age must be loueliest att the latest day
But name not winter faces whose skinns slack
Lanck as an vnthrifts purse but a soules sack
Whose eies seeke light within for all here is shade
Whose mouthes are holes rather worne out then made
Whose eu^{ery} tooth to a seuerall place is gone
To vexe their soules att the Resurrectyon
Name not these liuing deaths heades vnto mee
ffor these not ancient but Antiques bee
I hate extreames yett I had rather stay
With tombes then cradles to weare out a day
Since such loues naturall lation is may still
My loue discend and iourney downe the hill
Not pantinge after groning beauties soe
I shall ebbe on wth them that homeward goe

Finis

I, 34. Anonymous, Libell agaynst Bashe

{34}

[X]

I knowe not how it comes to passe
But sure it is not as itt was
My pen is sett on riming now
And if you aske I know not how
fforsooth my witts are growen so rash
That I must board wth Mr Bash
And though I leape beyond my lash
To play the knaue a little *Crash*
It is but *Rime* and *Reuell* dash
ffor why my libertie is large
I am not tied by any charge
To call a spade a spa=va=vade
Nor yett to count a Curtall Iade
To bee a Iennett bredd in Spayne
My witts are dull my speech is plaine
ffor I must call a knaue a knaue
And though he thinke I raile and raue
Yett when I speake of such a slaue
Lett him be sure I will not spare
To rime a little out of square
But will you know w^{ch} *Bash* I meane
Or els it were not woorth a beane
It is not *Bash* the Millers man
nor *Bash* the *Bruer* of the *Swann*
nor *Bash* the *Butcher* though he bee
As Butcherlike a knaue as he
But this is *Bash* the new made *squire*
Of *Stansteed* towne in *Hartfordshire*
Duke of *Albeefe* nam'd for the nones
And *Marques* of y^{e} *Marrowbones*
Countie of *Calues heads* by like degree
And *Vicount Neates tongues* this is hee
But shall I spend a little tyme
To blaze his name in riding ryme
Then will I doe the best I can
To paint you foorth a proper man
ffirst of his name of great renowne
This *Bash* was borne in *Worcester* towne
Perhapps yow take my woordes as skornes
But there his *Sire* made shooing hornes
As for his youth he spent itt well
Not where his father wont to dwell
But wandring through here and there
In many a towne and sundry *sheere*
To seeke the fortune of his happ
Butt att the last he caught a clapp
In *Beuer* castle in ye vale
As some men say marke well my tale
Neither for better nor for worse
But euen for cutting of a purse
Well that passe his luck was good
To scape that scowring by the Rood

I, 34v

ffrom whence he came (but wott yee what
That country after was too hott
And so he went to London walles
Where after sundry climinge falls
He fell in *Consanguinitie*
And linked in *Affinitie*
With Bauds & Brothells whores and *knaues*
Cutthroates: Enchanters Banckrupt slaues
Clippers Coyners and Conveyers
Priuie=Takers and Pilferers
Bribers and false Extortioners
Of euery wicked fashion
With all abhomination
Thatt att the last he scrapt so much mucke
and grewe so rich by *Cuckolds* lucke
That now he gan for to disdaine
The name of *Purveyour* it was to plaine
And on the ground he might not tread
for ioulting of his *Heauie head*
Well lett itt bee as bee it might
This scabby *Squire this Dunghill knight*
Gan now on horsebacke for to ride
Along the street in pompe and pride
But ere he lett his office slipp
He gaue poore *Elliott* such a tripp
That he was faine to crack twoo pointes
for nought but hempe could hold his iointes
Well *Elliott* once was *Purveyour*
and *Bash* became a noble *Seigneur*
The walles of *Stansteed* were too lowe
And vpp in hast then must they goe
Much like the *Towre* of *Babilon*
Wch fell to great confusion
And so shall his att last I hope
ffor though this *Bash* did scape the *Rope*
And bee as stout as *Turke or Pope*
Yett if you give mee leaue to grope
Within the lining of a *Cope*
Then of his house this needes must hitt
That either fire must perish itt
Vell rapto alter habebit
And why? foorsooth because it is
Variis constructa rapinis
Bee as may bee is no banninge
A knaues life is not worth scanninge
ffor if it were I could you tell
That he hath spent his talent well
And never hidd itt in ye ground
why should he to one stocke be bound
for I dare lay you twenty pound
there was no strumpett to be found

{35}

Were she sore or were she sound
But he would broach her barrell loe
Beshrewe mee then if I say soe
But lett that passe amongst the rest
Vox populi vox dei est
Alas but little might he doe
To putt on his owne brothers shoe
With such a shooing horne or twoe
And were his brother not vnkind
But of an honest thanckfull mind
Surelie he would take the paine
to send him home his hornes againe
And so to lett him haue as good
In token of their brotherhood
ffor though he then might spare them well
While he was yong and bare the bell
Yett now forsooth I can yow tell
That he hath woorke enough att home
Abroad hee need not for to rome
He hath a yong wife hath he caught her
Nor that she was a wisemans daughter
Nor that that was a wise mans part
But sure poore wench itt pincht her hart
Of wch the Lord soone send her ease
Although and if itt might her please
I could assure her now and than
A prettie morsell of a man
That should be proper sweet and good
Better then *Neates tongues* by the *Rood*
Alas alas itt fretts my blood
ffor why of late I haue hurd say
Shee was deliuered this other day
Of a knaue child both faire and fatt
W^{ch} was good luck but wott yow whatt
How much the better had itt beene
If she had beene deliuered cleane
Of the knaue himselfe and all
Oh there had beene a festiuall
ffor then some lustie *Reueller*
Would haue beene glad to haue maried her
And so to haue done him good *Almes deedes*
And first to helpe her att her needes
And then to sett a broach the Tunne
Of poundes and pence so lewdlie wonne
But sith that now I haue begunne
I will assay not for to misse
To tell yow plainlie what he is
ffirst of his shape itt doth appeare
Much like a Tunne of double beere
And he that well doth marke his nose
W^{ch} is as redd as any Rose

I, 35v

Then out of doubt he will suppose
That *Bash* loues double beere full well
Or if a man the truth should tell
ffirst if his body were sett vppright
And his necke were cutt of quite
A man that had good lust to shite
Might sitt att ease vpon his necke
And downe his throat without all checke
The durt would fall into his gutts
And then itt might be tried by rutts
Whether the durt that downe did fall
Or that wch was there first of all
Be putrifide best of twaine
This is a question that is plaine
Or if itt bee as I haue heard
Whether his filthy feltred beard
Be fitter for a dizard
Or for a Masker on his vizard
Another question doth arise
Whether the twinckling of his eies
Bee all of drinck or ought of sleepe
Or when he smileth like a sheepe
What faith or troth he meanes to keepe
Now some there be that make a doubt
Whether his *Turkie* coloured snout
Be bigger then his mouth about
Loe thus they dally wth the lout
But this I boldly dare avowe
That he is wasted like a cowe
And like a bull in brest & browe
And somewhat snowted like a sowe
Eid like a ferritt when he winckes
Mouth like a Mattock when he drinkes
Breathd like a polecatt when he stinckes
And may not such a man as this
Thinck him selfe woorthy to kisse
A *Councellours* daughter where she pisse
Yes indeed and so he shall
With lippes wth tongue and mouth and all
But of his shape a little more
Or els itt should offend him sore
Sett him on foote and he goes then→than
Reeling and rowling like a *Swann*
Sett him on horsebacke out of doubt
he rideth like a demie lout
Or if I doe not forgett the foole
Like a Toad on a washing stoole
But hang him vpp and so tis best
And lett his face hang East or West
And on his shoulders wilbe spread
The plaine signe of ye *Saracens head*

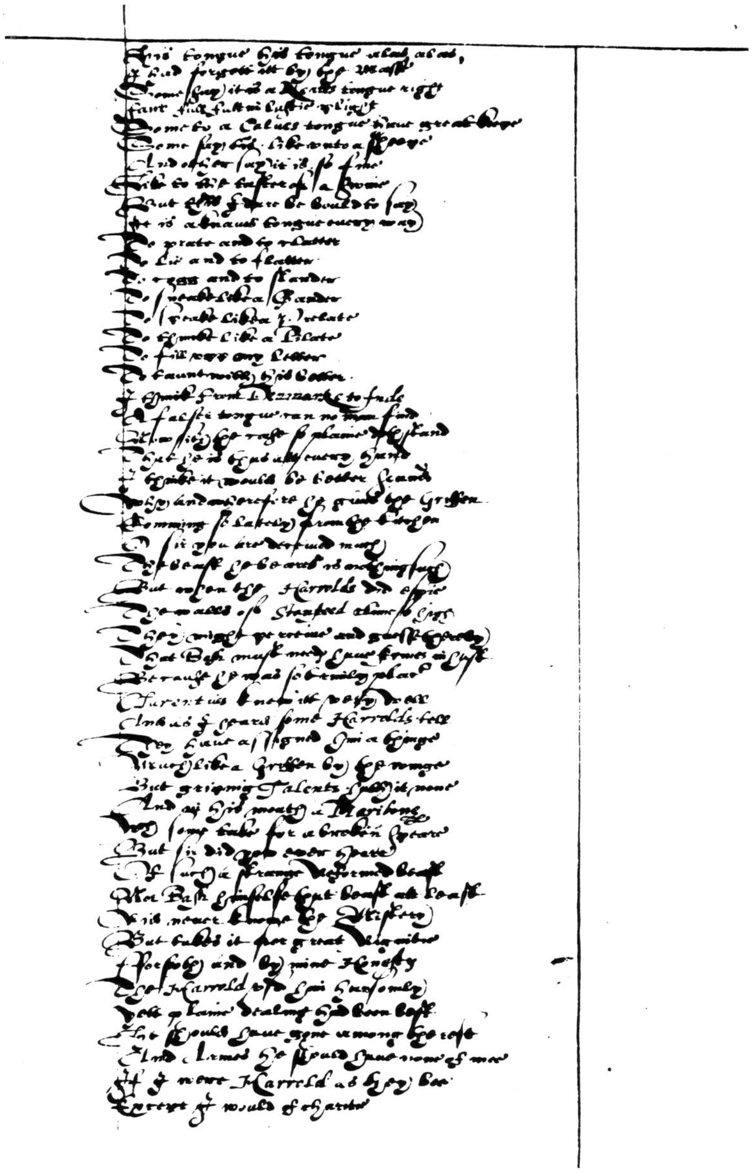

{36}

His tongue his tongue alas, alas,
I had forgott itt by the Masse
Some say it is a *Neates* tongue right
faire full fatt in lustie plight
Some to a *Calues* tongue haue great keepe
Some say t'is like vnto a sheepe
And other say it is so fine
Like to the taster of a swine
But this I dare be bould to say
It is a knaues tongue euery way
To prate and to clatter
To lie and to flatter
To cogg and to slander
To sneake like a Gander
To speake like a Prelate
To thincke like a Pilate
To fill vpp my letter
To taunt with his better
I thinck from *Denmarke* to *Inde*
A falser tongue can no man find
Now sith the case so plaine doth stand
That he is thus att euery hand
I thinke it would be better scan'd
Why and wherefore he giues the *Griffen*
Comming so lately from the kitchen
O sir you are deceiued much
The beast he beares is nothing such
But when the *Harrolds* did espie
The walls of *Stansteed* clime so high
They might perceiue and guesse thereby
That *Bash* must needes haue *Armes* in hast
Because he was so trimly plac't
Clarentius knew itt very well
And as I heard some *Harrolds* tell
They haue assigned him a thinge
Much like a *Griffen* by the winge
But griping *Talents* hath it none
And in his mouth a *Maribone*
Wch some take for a broken speare
But sir did yow ever heare
Of such a strange deformed beast
Nor *Bash* himselfe that beast att least
Did neuer knowe the Mistery
But takes it for great dignitie
fforsooth and by mine *Honesty*
The *Harrold* vsd him hansomly
Yett plaine dealing had been best
He should haue gone among the rest
And Armes he should haue none of mee
If I were *Harrold* as they bee
Except I would of charitie

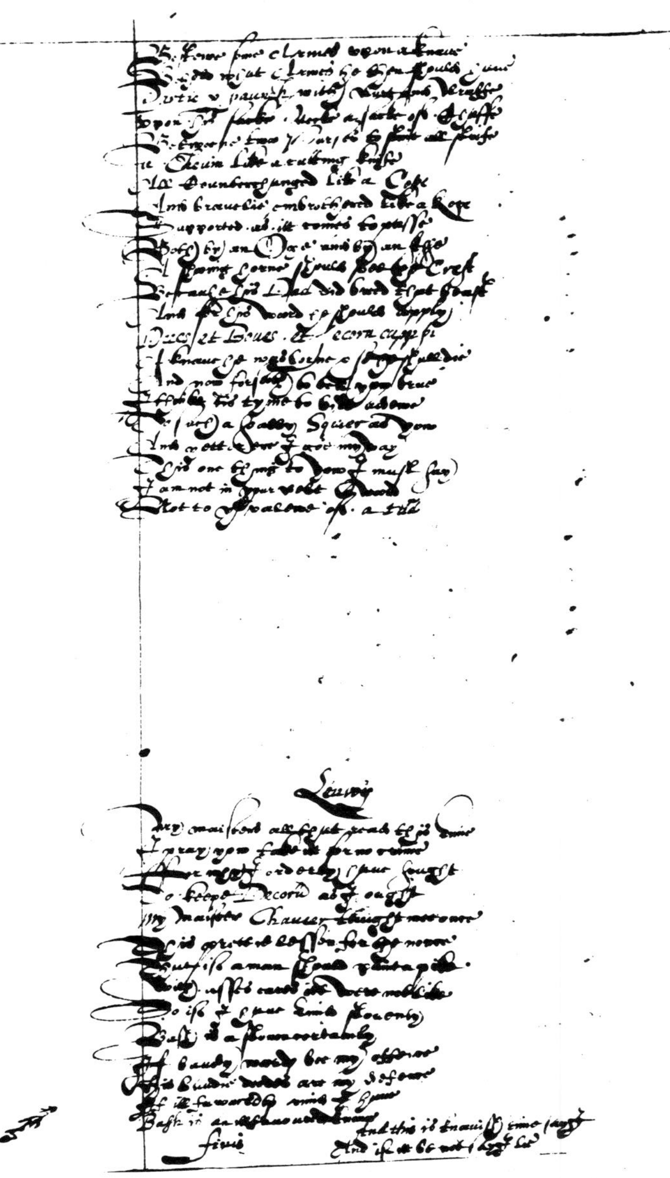

I, 36v

Bestowe some Armes vpon a knaue
Behold what Armes he then should haue
Partie p̲ paunch with Durt and Draffe
Vpon his ~~sacke~~ Necke a sacke of Chaffe
Betweene twoo Purses to stint all strife
a *Cheuin* like a cutting knife
All counterchanged like a *Cope*
And brauelie embrothered like a *Rope*
Supported as itt comes to passe
Both by an Oxe and by an *Asse*
A shooing horne should bee the *Crest*
Because his *Dad* did breed that beast
And for his woord he should apply
Oues et Boues et pecora campi
A knaue he was borne & so he shall die
And now forsooth to tell yow true
I thinke tis tyme to bidd adewe
To such a scabby *Squier* as yow
And yett or ere I goe my way
This one thing to yow I must say
I am not in your debt a woord
Not to ye valewe of a *tu^{r}d*

Anonymous, Lenvoy

Lenvoy

My maisters all that read this rime
I pray yow take itt for no crime
ffor why I orderly haue sought
To keepe *Decorũ* as I ought
My maister *Chaucer* taught mee once
This prettie lesson for the nonce
That if a man should paint a pike
With asses eares itt were not like
So if I haue rimd slouenly
Bash is a slouen certainly
If baudy woordes bee my offence
His baudie deedes are my defence
If ill fauouredly rimd I haue
Bash is an ill fauoured knaue
And this is knauish rime say I
finis
And if itt be not say I lie

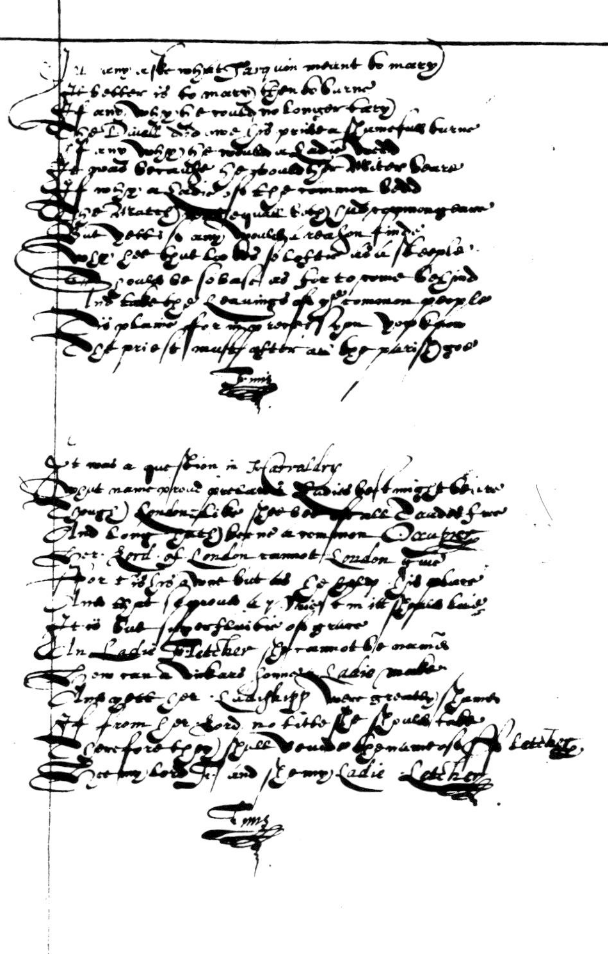

I, 37. Sir John Davies, On Bp. Richard Fletcher, Feb. 1594–5

{37}

If any aske what *Tarquin* meant to mary
It better is to mary then to burne
If any why he could no longer tary
The *Diuell* did owe his pride a shamefull turne
If any why he would a Ladie wedd
It was because he would her Miter beare
If why a Ladie of the common bedd
The Match was equall both had common geare
But yett if any would a reason finde
Why hee that lookes so loftie as a steeple
Should be so base as for to come behind
And take the Leauings of y^e common people
Tis plaine for in precessyon yow know
The priest must after all the parish goe

Finis

Sir John Davies, In Londenensem Episcopum iampridem Dominae et scortae nuptias 1595

It was a question in *Harroldry*
What name proud prelates Ladies best might beare
Though *London*=like shee bee of all Trades free
And long hath beene a common *Occupier*
Her *Lord* of *London* cannot *London* giue
ffor t'is his owne but as he holdes his place
And that so proud a Priest in itt should liue
It is but superfluitie of grace
An *Ladie Fletcher* she cannot be nam'd
How can a vickars sonne a *Ladie* make
And yet her *Ladishipp* were greatly shamd
If from her Lord no title she should take
Therefore they shall deuide the name of *ffletcher*
Hee my Lord *F* and she my *Ladie Letcher*

Finis

I, 37v. Anonymous, Mris Attorney scorning long to brooke

\+ Mris Attorney scorning long to brooke
The Insolency of her proud master *Cooke*
Hath caught him now and turnd him to the place
Where first he learnd to plead a *Clients* case
And more then that its said she telles him plaine
Sheele putt him to his hornebooke once againe
He harbours now where once the Ancient Iewes
To pray and offer sacrifice did vse
One of those Trumpettes him to Commons calles
That *Iosua* had to pull downe *Iericho* walles
The senate sees his plaguie horned plight
And yett he liues *vir* mande of any wight
Saue of one Malt horse=headed smoke drid Asse
Att the signe of *viderit vtilitas*
Instead of *Reuells Mummings Masques* and plaies
He must sing *Heigh ho* all these hollidaies
Banning his state who such misfortune *seeles→feeles*
The heauiest heades possesse the lightest heeles
A ladd that lay with *Doctour Burcots* wife
By *Burcotts* Phisick neere had lost his life
This great wordmonger he likewise by woordes
To his Corriuall the like death affoordes
But wott yow why poore *Robin* is distrest
It was for breeding in the *Cuckoes* nest
Who ere sawe garden so well walld about
That it could keepe a *Robin Redbreast* out
Thoughtst thou that nature framde so braue a wench
To carie a pack of paltrie pedlars french
No Mris Attorney scornes vnto the death
A seruile swaine that selles vnsauoury breath

Finis

I, 38. *John Donne, The Storme*

{38}

A Storme

X Thou wch art I (tis nothing to be soe
Thou wch art thy selfe by these shalt knowe
Part of our passage and a hand or eie
By *Hilliard* drawne is woorth an history
By a woorse painter made; And without pride
When by thy Iudgement they are dignified
My lines are such t'is the Preheminence
Of frendshipp only to impute Excellence
England, to whom wee owe what wee bee and haue
Sadd that her sonnes should seeke a foraigne graue
(ffor fates or *fortunes drifts* none can sooth say
Honour & misery haue one face and way)
ffrom out her pregnant entrailes sighd a wind
W^{ch} att th'ayers middle=marble-roome did find
Such strong *Resistance* that itt selfe itt threwe
Downeward againe and so when it did viewe
How in the *Port* our *Fleet* deare time did leese
Withering like Prisoners wch lye but for ffees
Mildly itt kist our sailes and fresh and sweet
As to a stomack steru'd whose insides meete
Meat comes, itt came, and swole ou^{r} sailes when wee
So Ioyd as *Sara her swelling* ioyd to see
But t'was so kind as our *Contrymen*
W^{ch} bring frendes one dayes way and leaue them then
Then like twoo Mightie Kinges wch dwelling farr
asunder; meet against a third to warr.
The *South* and *West windes* ioynd and as they blewe
Waues like a Rowling Trench before them threwe
Sooner then yow read this line did the gale
Like shott not feard till felt our sayles assaile
And what att first was calld a gust the same
Hath now a stormes anon a *Tempests* name
Ionas I pittie thee and curse those menn
Who when the storme raged most did wake thee then
Sleepe is paines easiest salue and doth fulfill
All offices of death except to kill
But when I wak.^{d} I saw that I sawe not
I and the sunne wch should teach mee had forgott
East, *West*, *Day Night* and I could but say
If the world had lasted now itt had beene day
Thousandes our noises neere yett wee amongst all
Could none by his right name but *Thunder* call
Lightening was all our light and itt raynd more
Then if the Sunne had druncke the sea before
Some cofind in their cabines lie! *Equallie*
Greeud that they are not dead and yett must die

I, 38v

And as sin burthened soules from graues will creepe
Att the last day some foorth their cabbins peepe
And tremblinglie aske newes and do heare soe
Like *Iealous Husbands* what they would not knowe
Some sitting on the *Hatches* would seeme there
With hideous gazing to feare away feare
There note they the shippes sicknesses the *Mast*
Shakd with this Ague and the *Hould and Wast*
With a salt dropsie clogd and all ou^{r} Tacklinges
Snapping like to high stretchd treble stringes
And from our Tatterd sayles ragges dropp downe soe
As from one hangd in chaynes a yeere agoe
Euen ou^{r} Ordinance placd for our defence
Striue to breake loose and scape away from thence
Pumping hath tird our men and what's the gaine
Seas into Seas throwne wee such→sucke in againe
Hearing hath deafd our sailours and if they
Knewe how to heare theere's none knewe what to say
Compard to these stormes death is but a qualme
Hell somewhat lightsome and the *Bermuda calme*
Darkenes lights elder brother his birthright
Claymes o^{re} this world and to heauen hath chasd light
All thinges are one and that one none can bee
Since all formes vniforme deformitie
Doth couer. So that wee except god say
Another *Fiat* shall haue no more day
So violent yett long these furies bee
That though thine absence sterue mee I wish not thee

Finis

I, 39. *John Donne, The Calme*

{39}

A Calme

X Our storme is past and that stormes tirannous rage
A stupid calme but nothing itt doth swage
The fable is inverted and farr more
A Blocke afflictes now then a storke before
Stormes chafe and soone were out themselues or vs
In *Calmes Heauen* laughes to see ^{vs}~~thus~~ languish thvs
As steddie as I can wish that my thoughts were
Smooth as thy Mistres glasse or what shines there
The sea is nowe And as those Isles wch wee
Seeke when wee can mooue our shippes rooted bee
As water did in stormes now pitch runnes out
As lead when a fir'd church becomes one spout
And all our beautie and our trime decayes
Like courtes remoouing or like ended playes
The *fightings* place now seamens ragges supplie
And all the *Tackling* is but *Frippery*
No vse of Lanthornes and in one place lay
ffeathers and dust today and yesterday
Earths hollownesses wch the worldes lunges are
Haue no more wind then the vpper vault of thayre
Wee can nor left ffrendes nor sought foes recouer
But *Meteorlike* saue that wee mooue not houer
Only the *Calenture* together drawes
Deare frendes wch meet dead in great fishes iawes
And on the *Hatches* as on Altars lies
Each one his owne Priest and owne sacrifice
Who liue that Miracle doe multiplie
Where walkers in hott Ouens doe not lie
If in despite of this wee swimm that hath
No more refreshing then the *Brimstone Bath*
But from the Sea into the Shipp wee turne
Like Parboyld wretches on the coales to burne
Like *Baiazet* encag'd the shepheardes scoffe
Or like slack sinewed *Sampson* his haire of
Languish our shippes Now as a *Miriade*
Of Ants durst the Emperou^{r}s lou'd snake invade
The crawling Galleyes sea *Gaoles* ffinny chippes
Might braue our *Venices* now beddridd shippes
Whether a rotten state and hope of gaine
Or to diffuse mee from the queasy paine
Of beeing belou'^{d} and louing; or the thirst
Of *Honour* or faire death out pushd mee first
I loose my end for heere as well as I
A desperate may liue and a coward die
Stagge dogge and all wch from or towardes flies
Is payd wth life or pray or doeing dies

I, 39v

ffate grudgeth vs all and doth subtilie lay
A scourge against wch wee all forgett to pray
Hee that att sea praies for more wind may as well
Vnder the *Poles* begge cold or heat in *Hell*
What are wee then how little more alas
Is man now then before he was hee was
Nothing for vs we are for nothing fitt
Chance or ou^{r} selues still disproportion itt
Wee haue no will no power no sence! I lie
I should not then thus feele this misery

Finis

John Donne, To Mr. Rowland Woodward*: "Like one who'in her third widdowhood"*

Like one who in her third widdowhood doth professe
Her selfe a Nunn tir'd to a retirednesse
So affectes my muse now a chast fallownesse

Since shee to fewe yett to too many hath showne
How loue song woordes weedes and satirique thornes are growne
Where seedes of better Artes were earlie sowne

Though to vse and loue *Poetry* to mee
Bethrothd to no one Art be no Adultery
Omissions of good Ill as Ill deedes bee

ffor though to vs itt seeme and be light and thin
Yet in those faithfull skales where god throwes in
Mens woorkes vanitie waighes as much as sin

If our soules haue staind their first white yett wee
May cloath them with faith and deare honesty
W^{ch} god imputes as Natiue puritie

There is no vertue but Religion
Wise valiant sober iust are names wch none
Want wch want not vice=covering discretion

Seeke wee then our selues in ou^{r} selues for as
Men force the sunne wth much more force to passe
By gathering his beames wth a christall glasse

So wee if wee into our selues will turne
Blowing the sparkes of vertue may outburne
The strawe wch doth about our hartes soiourne

You know *Phisicians* when they would enfuse
Into any oile the soule of simples vse
Places where they may lie still warme to chuse

{40}

So woorkes retiredness in vs to rome
Giddilie and to be euery where but att home
Such freedome doth a banishment become

Wee are but farmers of our selues yett may
If wee can stock our selues vpp lay
Much much deare treasure for the great rent day

Manure thy selfe then to thy selfe be approued
And with vaine outward thinges bee no more mooued
But to knowe that I loue thee & would be beloued

Finis

John Donne, To Sr. Henry Wootton: *"Here's no more newes"*

ID Here is no more newes then vertue I may as well
Tell yow *Callis* or St *Michaells* tale for newes as tell
That vice doth here habituallie dwell

Yett as to gett stomackes we walke vpp and downe
And toyle to sweeter rest so may god frowne
If but to loath both I haunt Court or Towne

ffor here no one is free from the extremitie
Of vice by any other reason free
But that the next to him is still woorse then hee

In this worldes warrfare they whom Ragged fate
(Godes Commissary) doth so thoroughly hate
As in the Courtes squadron to marshall their state

If they stand arm'd wth seelie honestie
With wishing prayers & neat integritie
Like *Indians* against spanish hostes they bee

Suspicious boldnes to this place belonges
And to haue as many eares as all haue tonges
Tender to knowe loath to acknowledge wronges

Beleeue mee Sir in my youths giddiest dayes
When to be like the Court was a plaies praise
Playes were not so like Courtes as Courtes are like plaies

Then lett vs att these *Mimick Antique* Iests
Whose deepest proiectes and egregious gests
Are but dull *Moralls* of a game att *Chests*

But now t'is incongruitie to smile
Therefore I end and bidd farewell a while
Att *Court* though from Court were the better stile

Finis

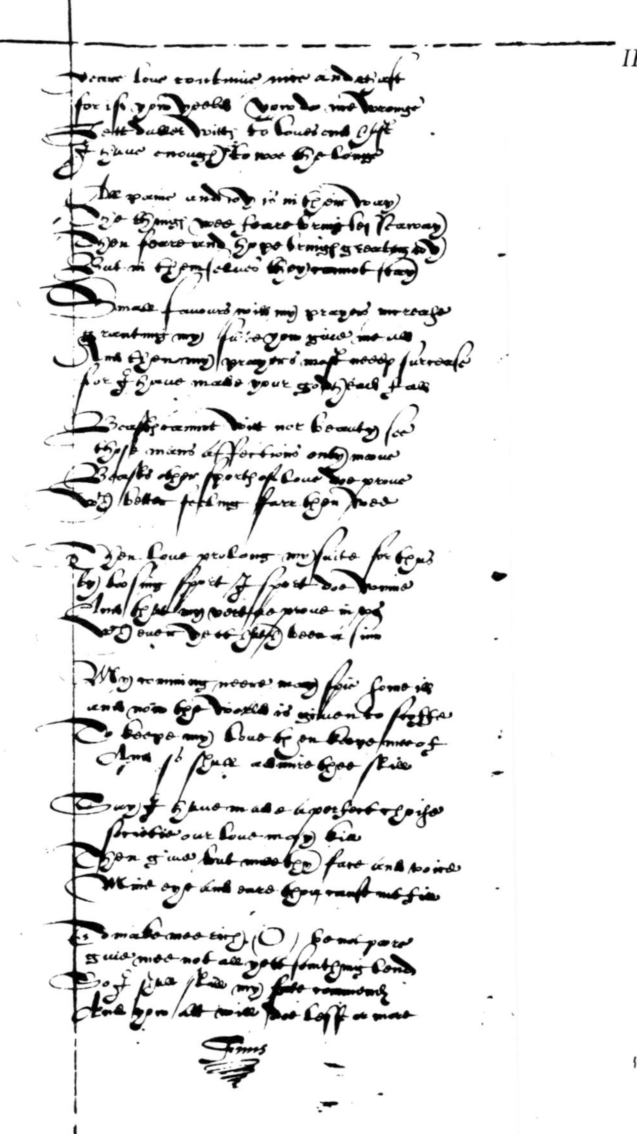

I, 40v. Sir John Roe, Song. "Deare Love, continue nice and chaste"

Deare loue continue nice and chast
for if yow yeeld yow doo me wronge
Lett duller wittes to loues end hast
I haue enough to woe the longe

All paine and ioy is in their way
The thinges wee feare bring lesse away
Then feare and hope bringes greater ioy
But in themselues they cannot stay

Small fauours will my prayers increase
granting my suite yow giue me all
And then my prayers must needes surcease
for I haue made your godhead fall

Beastes cannot witt nor beauty see
those mans affections only mooue
Beasts other sportes of loue doe proue
W^th^ better feeling farr then wee

Then loue prolong my suite for thus
by loosing sport I sport doe winne
And that my vertue proue in vs
W^ch^ euer yett hath been a sinn

My comming neere may spie some ill
and now the world is giuen to scoffe
To keepe my loue then keepe mee of
And so shall admire thee still

Say I haue made a perfect choise
societie our loue may kill
Then giue but mee thy face and voice
Mine eye and eare thou canst not fill

To make mee rich (O) be not poore
giue mee not all yett somthing lend
So I shall still my fate commend
And yow att will doe lesse or more

Finis

I, 41. Anonymous, Wonder of Beautie, Goddesse of my sense

{41}

Wonder of Beautie Goddesse of my sence
Yow that haue taught my soule to loue aright
Yow in whose limbes are natures chiefe expence
ffit instrument to serue your matchles spiright

If euer yow haue felt the Misery
Of beeing banisht from your best desier
By absence tyme or fortunes tirany
Striuing for cold and yett denied the feir

Deare Mistres pittie then the like effectes
The wch in mee your absence makes to flowe
And hast their ebbe by your diuine aspect
In which the pleasure of my life doth growe
Stay not too Long for though it seeme a wonder
Yow keepe my body & my soule asunder

Finis

Anonymous, Faire eies do not think scorne to read of Love

ffaire Eies doe not thinke scorne to read of loue
That to your Eies durst never yett presume
Since absence those sweet wonders doo reemooue
That nourish thoughts yett sence & woordes consume

This makes my penn more hardie then my tongue
ffree from my feare yett feeling my desire
To vtter that I haue concealed so long
By doing what yow did you^{r} selfe requier

Beleeue not him whom loue hath left so wise
as to haue power his owne tale for to tell
ffor childrens griefes doe yeeld the loudest cryes
and cold desires may be expressed well

In well tould loue most often falshood lies
But pittie him that only sighes and dyes

Finis

I, 41v. Sir John Roe, To Ben. Iohnson, 6 Ian. 1603

An Epistle to Mr Ben: Iohnson Ian 6 1603 /

The state and mens affaires are the best plaies
Next yours t'is no more nor lesse then due praise
Wright but touch not the much descending race
Of Lordes houses so settled in woorthes place
As but themselues none thincke them vsurpers
It is no fault in thee to suffer theirs
If the Queene Maske or King a hunting goe
Though all the court followe lett'hem wee knowe
Like them in goodnes that court nere will bee
ffor that were vertue and not flattery
fforgett we were thrust out, It is but thus
God threatens Kinges, Kinges Lordes as Lordes doe vs
Iudge of strangers trust and beleeue your frend
And so mee And when I true frendshipp end
With guiltie conscience lett mee be worse stunge
Then with *Pophans* sentence. Theeues, or *Cookes* tongue,
Traytours are! ffrendes are our selues This I thee tell
As my frend and to my selfe as counsell
Lett for a while the tymes vnthriftie rout
Contemne learning and all your studies flout
Lett them scorne *Hell* They will a *Serieant* feare
But creditors will not Lett them increase
In Riott and excesse as their meanes cease
Lett them scorne him that made them and still shunn
His grace, but loue the whore who hath vndone
Them and their soules But that they that allowe
but one God should haue religions ynow
ffor the Queenes Masque and their husbandes for more
Then all the Gentiles knewe or Atlas bore
Well lett all passe and trust him who nor crackes
the bruised reed nor quencheth smoaking flaxe

Finis

I, 42. *Sir John Roe,* To Ben. Iohnson, 9. Novembris, *1603*

{42}

Another Epistle to Mr Ben: Iohnson Nov 9 1603

If great men wrong mee I will spare my selfe
If meane I will spare them I know that pelfe
Wch is ill gott the owner doth vpbraid
Itt may corrupt a Iudge make mee afraid
And a *Iurie* but twill reuenge in this
That though himselfe be Iudge he guiltie is
What care I of weaknes if men taxe mee
I had rather sufferer then doer bee
That I did trust it was my natures praise
ffor breach of woord I knew but as a phrase
That Iudgement is that surely can comprise
the world in preceptes) most happie and most wise
What though though lesse yett some of both haue wee
Who haue learnd itt by vse and misery
Poore I whom euery petty crosse doth trouble
Who apprehend each hurt that is don me double
And of this, (though it should sincke mee carelesse
it would but force mee to a stricter goodnes
They haue great oddes of mee who gaine do winne
(If such gaine be not losse) from euery sinne
The standing of great mens liues would affoord
A prettie summe if god would sell his Woord
He cannot they can theirs and breake them too
How like are they that they are likened too
Yett I conclude they are amidst my euilles
If god, like godes, the naught are so like deuilles

Finis

Sir John Roe, An Elegie to Mris Boulstred: 1602

An Eligie to Mrs Boulstredd

IR Shall I goe force an Eligie abuse
My witt and breake the *Hymen* of my Muse
for one poore houres loue? deserues it such
Wch serues not mee to doe on her so much
Or if itt would? I would that fortune shunn
Who would be rich to bee so soone vndone
The beggar's best his wealth he doth not knowe
And but to shewe itt him increaseth woe
But wee may enioy an houre when neuer
itt returnes who'ld haue a losse for euer
Nor can so short a loue if true but bring
A halfe houres feare with the thought of loosing
Before itt all houres were hope and all are
that shall come after itt yeares of dispaire

I, 42v

This Ioy bringes the doubt whether it were more
To haue enioy'd itt or haue died before
T'is a lost Paradice a fall from Grace
Wch I thinke Adam felt more then his race
Nor need those Angells any other *Hell*
It is enough for them from heauen they fell
Besides conquest in loue is all in all
That when I list shee vnder mee may fall
And for this turne both for delight and viewe
Ile haue *succuba* as good as yow
But when these toyes are past and hott blood endes
the blest enioying is, wee still are frendes
Loue can but bee frendshippes outside their two
Beauties differ as myndes and bodies doe
Thus I this great good still would bee to take
vnlesse one hower another happie
Or that I might forgett itt instantly
Or in that blessed estate that I might die
But why doe I thus trauell in ye skill
Of despisd Poetry and pchance spill
My fortunes, or vndoe my selfe in sport
By hauing but that dangerous name in Court
Ile leaue and since I do your poett proue
Keepe yow my lines as secrett as my loue

Finis

Sir John Roe, To Sr Tho. Roe *1603*

An Eligie to Sr Thomas Roe 1603

Tell her if shee to hired seruantes shewe
Dislike, before they take their leaue they goe
When nobler spiritts startes att no disgrace
ffor who hath butt one mind hath but one face
If then why I tooke not my leaue she aske
Aske her againe why she did not vnmaske
Was she or proud? or cruell? or knewe shee
T'would make my losse more felt & pitied mee?
Or did she feare one kisse might stay for moe
Or els was she vnwillinge I should goe
I thincke the best and loue so faithfullie
I cannot chuse butt thinke that she loues mee
If this proues not my faith then lett her try
How in her seruice it will fructifie
Ladies haue boldly loud bidd her nenewe
That decayd woorth & proue the times past true

{43}

Then he whose witt and verse now goes thus lame
With songes to her will the wild Irish tame
How ere Ile weare the blacke & white ribband
White for her fortunes? blacke for mine shall stand
I doe esteeme her fauours not their stuffe
If what I haue was giuen I haue inough
And all's well for had shee lou^{d} I had had
All my frendes hate for not departinge sadd
~~All my~~ I feell~~e~~ not that; yett as the racke the gout
Cures so has this woorse griefe that putt out
My first disease naught but that woorse cureth
Which I dare foresee naught cureth but death
Tell her all this before I am forgott
That not too late she greve she lou^{d} mee not
Burthen'd with itt I was to depart lesse
Willing then those which die and not confesse

Finis

Sir John Roe, An Elegie. *"True Love findes witt, but he whose witt doth move"*

Elegia /

True loue tindes witt but he whose witt doth mooue
Him to loue confesseth he doth not loue
And from his witt passions and true desier
Are forcd as hard as from the flint is fier
My loue is all fier whose flames my soule doe nurse
Whose smoakes are sighes whose euery sparks a verse
Doth measure winne women then I know why
Most of our Ladies with the Scotts doe lie
A Scottes measured in each sillable terse
And smooth as a verse and like that smooth verse
Is shallowe and wantes matter but in his handes
> And they are rugged Her state better standes
[^° And if that linth of misorie be hir lott]
Å In briefe shees out of measure lost so gott
Greene sicknes wenches (not needes must) but may
Looke pale breath short att court none so long stay
Good witt neere dispaird there or (*Ay me*) said
ffor neuer wench att court was rauished
And she but cheates on heauen whom so you winne
thincking to share the sport but not the sinne

Finis

I, 43v. Sir John Roe, An Elegie. Reflecting on his passion for his mistrisse

An Elegie

Come ffooles I feare you not all whom I owe
Are paid but yow. then rest mee ere I goe
But chance from yow all soueraigntie hath gott
Loue woundeth none but those whom death dares not
Els if yow were and iust in equitie
I should haue vanquishd her as yow did mee
Els louers should not braue deaths paines and liue
But tis a rule death comes not to relieue
Or pale and wann deaths terrours are they laid
So deepe in louers they make death afraid
Or (the least comfort) haue I company
Ore=came shee fates Loue death as well as mee
Yeas, fates doe silke vnto her distaffe pay
for their ransome wch taxe on vs they lay
Loue giues her youth wch is the cause why
Youth's for her sake some wither and some die
Poore death can nothing giue yett for her sake
Still in her turne he doth a Louer take
And if death should prooue false shee feares him not
Our *Muses* to redeeme her she hath gott
That last fatall night wee kist I thus prai'd
Or rather thus dispair'd I should haue said
Kisses and yett despaire the forbidd tree
Did promise and deceiue more then shee
Like Lambes that see their teates and must eat hay
A foode whose tast hath made me pine away
Diues when thou sawst blisse and crauedst to touch
A small little dropp thy paynes were such
Here griefe wantes a fresh witt for mine beeing spent
And my sighes weary groanes are all my rent
Vnable longer to endure the payne
They breake like thunder and doe bringe downe rayne
Thus till dried teares sodder mine eies I weepe
And then I dreame how yow securelie sleepe
And in your dreames doe laugh att mee I hate
And pray loue all may he pitties my state
X But sayes therein I no reuenge should find
The Sunn would shine though all the world were blind
Yett to try my hate Loue shewd mee your teare
And I had died had not you^r^ smile beene there
Your frowne vndoes mee you^r^ smile is my wealth
And as yow please to looke I haue my health
Mee thought loue pittiyng mee when he saw this
Gaue me your handes their backes and palmes to kisse
That cur'd me not but to beare payne gaue strengh
And what it lost in force itt tooke in length

I, 44

{44}

I calld in Loue againe who feard yow soe
That his compassion still prou'd greater woe
ffor then I dreampt I was in bedd wth yow
X But durst not feele for feare't should not proue true
This merritt not your anger had itt beene
The *Queene* of *Chastitie* was naked seene
And in bedd not to feele the payne I tooke
Was more then for *Actaeon* not to looke
And that breast wch lay ope I did not know
But for the clearnes from a Lumpe of snowe

Finis

John Donne, The Legacie

Elegie

ID When I died last and deare I die
X As often as from thee I goe)
And louers houres bee full eternitie
I can remember yett that I
Something did say and something did bestowe
Though I be dead wch sent mee I should bee
Mine owne Executor and Legacy

I heard me say tell her anon
That my selfe (thats yow not I)
Didd kill mee and when I felt me die
I bidd mee send my hart when I was gone
But I alasse could there find none
When I had ript and searchd where hartes should bee
Itt killd mee againe that I who still was true
In life in my last will should coozen yow

Yett I found something like a Hart
But cullours itt and corners had
It was not good itt was not badd
Itt was entire to none and fewe had part
As good as could be made by Art
Itt seemd and therefore for our losses sadd
I thought to send that hart in stead of mine
But oh no man could hold it for t'was thine

Finis

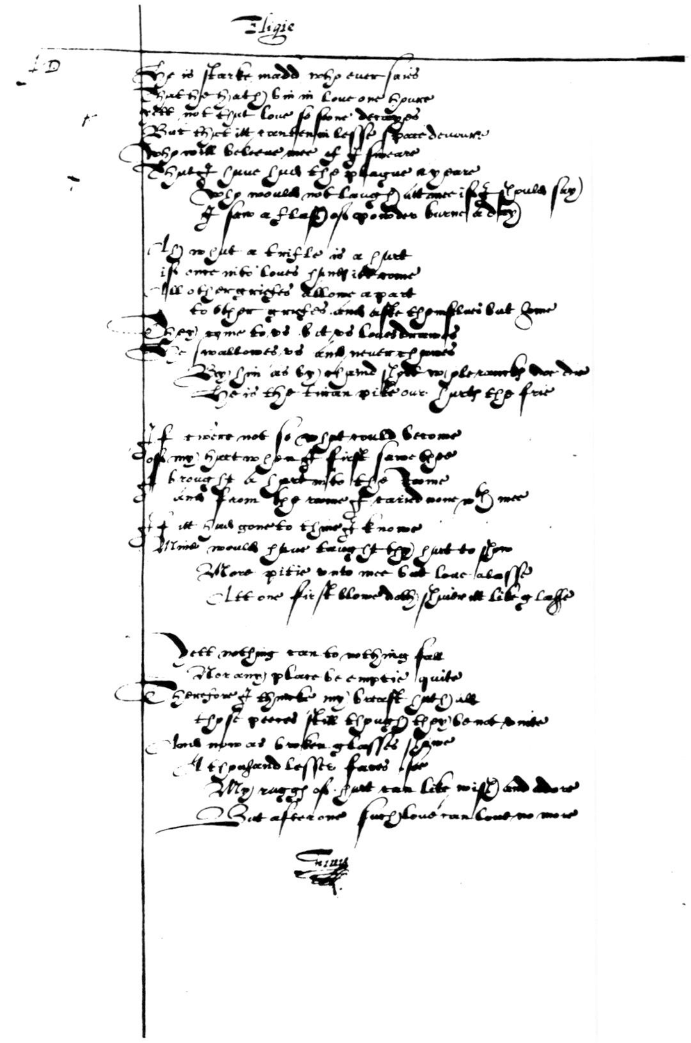

I, 44v. John Donne, The broken heart

Eligie

ID He is starke madd who euer saies
That he hath bin in loue one houre
* yett not that loue so soone decayes
But that itt can ten in lesse space deuoure
Who will beleeue mee if I sweare
X That I haue had the plague a yeare
Who would not laugh att mee if I should say
I saw a flash of powder burne a day

Ah what a trifle is a hart
if once into loues handes itt come
All other griefes allowe a part
to other griefes and aske themselues but some
They come to vs but vs loues drawes
He swallowes vs and neuer chawes
By him as by chaind shott whole ranckes doe die
He is the tiran pike our hartes the frie

If t'were not so what could become
of my hart when I first sawe thee
I brought a hart into the Roome
and from the roome I caried none wth mee
If itt had gone to thine I knowe
Mine would haue taught thy hart to show
More pitie vnto mee but loue alasse
Att one first blowe doth shiuer itt like glasse

Yett nothing can to nothing fall
Nor any place be emptie quite
Therefore I thincke my breast hath all
those peeces still though they be not vnite
And now as broken glasses showe
A thousand lesser faces soe
My ragges of hart can like wish and adore
But after one such loue can loue no more

Finis

I, 45. John Hoskyns, A Poem upon Absence

{45}

X Absence heare thou my protestation
Against thy strength
Distance and length
Doe what thou maist for alteration
ffor hartes of truest mettall
Absence doth ioyne and Time doth settle

Who loues a Mistres of such qualitie
His mind hath found
Affections ground
Beyond time place and all mortalitie
To harts that cannot vary
Absence is present Time doth tarry

My sences want their outward motion
which now within
reason doth winn
Redoubled by her secrett notion
Like rich men that take pleasure
in hiding more then handling treasure

* By *Absence* this good meanes I gaine
that I can catch her
where none can watch her
In some close corner of my braine
There I embrace her and there kisse her
and so enioy her and so misse her

Finis

John Donne, Twicknam garden

Twittnam Garden

Blasted with sighes and svrrounded wth teares
Hether I came to seeke the springe
And att mine eies and att mine eares
Receiue such balmes as els cures euery thinge
But oh selfe traitor I doe bringe
The spider loue wch transubstantiates all
and can convert *Manna* to gall
And that this place may thoroughlie be thought
True paradise I haue the serpent brought

T'were holsommer for mee that winter did
Benight the glorie of this place
and that a graue frost would forbidd
These trees to laugh and mocke mee in my face
But I may not this disgrace
Endure nor leaue the garden loue lett mee
some senceles part of this place bee
Make mee a Mandrake so I may grone heare
Or a stone fountaine weeping out the yeare/

I, 45v

Hether with Christall Vialls Louers come
And take my teares wch are Loues wyne
And try your Mistres teares att home
ffor all are false wch tast not iust like mine
Alasse harts doe not in eies shine
Nor can you more iudge womans thoughtes by teares
then by her shaddowe what she weares
Oh peruerse *Sexe* where none is true but shee
Who is therefore true because her truth kills mee /

Finis

John Donne, The good-morrow

X

I wonder by my troth what thou and I
did till wee lov'd were wee not weaned till then
But suck'd our childish pleasures seelilie
Or slumbred wee in the seauen sleepers den
T'was so but as all pleasures fancies bee
If euer any beutie I did see
Which I desierd and gott t'was but a dreame of thee/

And now good morrow to our waking soules
which watch not one another out of feare
But loue; all loue of other sights controules
and makes a little roome an euery where
Lett sea discoverours to new worldes haue gon
Lett *Mapps* to other Worldes one worldes haue
Lett vs possesse our world each hath one and is one

My face in thine eye thine in mine appeares
and plaine true hartes doe in the faces rest
Where can wee find two fitter *Hemispheares*
Without sharpe *North* without declining West
What euer dies is not mixt equallie
If both our loues be one or thou and I
Loue iust alike in all none of these loues can die

Finis

I, 46. John Donne, Loves Alchymie

{46}

Mummy

Some that haue deeper diggd Loues mine then I
say where his *Centrique* happines doth lie
I haue lov'^{d} and gott and told
But should I loue gett; tell till I were olde
I should not find that hiddenn mistery
Oh t'is imposture all
And as no *Chimick* yett the *Elixir* gott
but glorifies his pregnant pott
I If by the way to him befall
Some odoriferous thinge or Medecinall
So louers dreame a rich and long delight
but gett a winter seeming sommers night

Our ease and thrift our honou^{r} and our day
shall wee for this vaine bubbles shaddowe pay
Endes loue in this? that my man
can be as happie as I can? if he can
Endure the short scorne of a bridegroomes play
That louing wretch that sweares
T'is not the bodies marry but the mindes
wch he in her *Angelique* findes
would sweare as iustly that he heares
In that daies rude hoarse *Minstralsie* the Spheares
Hope not for mind in woman att their best
sweetnes and witt they are but *Mummy* possest

finis

John Donne, Breake of day

T'is true t'is day what though itt bee
Wilt thou therefore rise from mee
Why should we rise because t'is light?
Did wee lie downe because t'was night
Loue that in despite of darknes brought vs hither
should in despight of light hold vs together

Light hath no tongue but is all eie
if it could speake as well as spy
This is the woorst that it could say
that beeing well I faine would stay
And that I loue my hart and louer so
That I would not from him wch hath them goe
Must buisines thee from hence remooue
Oh thats the woorst disease of loue
The poore the foole the false loue can
Admitt but not the buisied man
He that hath buisines and makes loue doth doe
such wrong as if a maried man should woe

Finis

I, 46v. John Donne, The Sunne Rising

Busie old foole vnrulie Sunn
Why dost thou thus
Through windowes and thorough curtaynes call on vs
Must to thy Motions louers seasons runn
Saucy pedantique wretch goe chide
Late schoole boyes and soure prentises
Goe tell court huntsmen that the king doth ride
Call contry Antes to haruest Offices
Loue all alike no season knowes nor clyme
Nor houres dayes moneths wch are the ragges of tyme

Thy beames so reverenc'd and strong
Whie shouldst thou thincke
I could eclipse and cloud them wth a wincke
but that I would not loose her sight so long
If her eies haue not blinded thine
Looke and to morrow late tell mee
Whither both Indies of spyce and Myne
be there thou lefts them or lie here with mee
Aske for those kinges whom thow sawst yesterday
And thou shalt heare all heere in one bedd lay

Shee is all states and all *Princes* I
nothing els is
Princes do but play vs compard to this
All honours *Mimique* All wealth *Alchymy*
Thou sunn art halfe as happy as wee
In that the worlds contracted thus
Thine age askes ease and since thy duties bee
to warme the world that don in warming vs
Shine here to vs and thou art eu^{ery} where
This bedd thy center is these walles thy sphere

Finis

John Donne, Lecture upon the Shadow

Stand still and I will read to thee
a Lecture loue in loues Philosophy
These three houres that wee haue spent
walking heere two shaddowes went
Along wth vs wch wee our selues produc'd
But now the sunn is iust aboue our head
we doe these shaddowes tred
and to braue cleernes all thinges are $reduc^{d}$
So whilst our Infant loues did growe
Disguises did and shaddowes flowe
from vs and our cares but now t'is not soe

{47}

That loue hath not attaynd the highest degree
Which is still diligent least others see
    Except our loues att this noone stay
    wee shall new shaddowes make the other way
As the first wee→were made to blinde
others these wch come behinde
        will woorke vpon our selues and blind ou^{r} eyes
        if our loues faint and westwardly decline /
To mee thou falslie thine
And I to thee to mine actions shall disguise
    The morning shaddowes weare away
    but these growe longer all the day
    but (oh) loues day is short if loue decay
Loue is a growing or full constant light
And his first minute after noone is night

Finis

John Donne, The triple Foole

I am two fooles I knowe
for louing and for saying so
    In whineing Poetry
But wheere's that wise man that would not bee I   +
        if shee would not deny
Then as the earths inward narrow crooked lanes
Do purge sea waters frettfull salt away
        I thought if I could drawe my paines
Through Rimes vexation I should then allay
Griefe brought to Numbers cannott be so fierce
ffor he tames itt that fetters itt in verse

But when I haue done soe
some man his Act and voyce to show
        doth sitt and singe my paine
And by delighting many frees againe
    Griefe wch verse did restrayne
To Loue and griefe tribute of verse belonges
but not of such as pleases when t'is red
        both are increased by such songes
ffor both their Triumphes so are published
And I wch twoo fooles doe soe growe three
    Whoe are a little wise the best fooles bee /

Finis

I, 47v. John Donne, Image of her whom I love

Elegie

Image of her whom I loue more then shee
Whose faire impressyon in my faithfull hart
Makes mee her Mettall and makes her loue mee
As Kinges doe coynes to wch their stamps impart
The valewe, Goe, and take my hart from hence
Honours opresse weake spirittes and our sence
Strong obiectes dull the more the lesse wee see
When you are gone and reason gone wth you
Then fantasie is Queene and soule and all
Shee can present ioyes meaner then yow doe
Convenient and more proportionall
So if I dreame I haue yow I haue yow
for all our ioyes are but Phantasticall
And so I scape the paine for paine is true
And sleepe wch lockes vpp sence doth lock out all
After a such fruition I shall wake
and butt the wakeing nothing shall repent
And shall to loue more thanckfull *sonnetts* make
then if more honour teares & paynes were spent
But dearest hart and dearer Image stay
alasse true Ioyes att best are dreame inough
Though yow stay heere yow passe to fast away
for euen att first lifes taper is a snuffe
ffilld wth her loue may I bee rather growne
Madd wth much hart then Idiott wth none

Finis

John Donne, Loves diet

Loues Diett

To what a cumbersome vnwildines
X and burthenous corpulence my loue had growne
But that I did to make itt lesse
and keepe itt in proportion
Giue itt a diett made itt feed vpon
That wch loue woorst endures, discretion/

Aboue one sigh a day I allowed him not
of wch my fortune and my faultes had part
And if sometymes by stealth hee gott
a shee sigh from my M^{ris} hart
And though to feast on that I lett him see
t'was neither very sound nor meant to mee

{48}

If he wrung from me a teare I brined itt too
  With scorne or shame that him itt nourisht not
If he suk'd hers I lett him knowe
  t'was not a teare wch he had gott
His drinke was counterfait as was his meat
for eyes wch roule towardes all weepe not but sweat

Whatsoever he would distaste I write that
and burnt my lies when shee writt to mee
    And that that fauour made him fatt
    I said if any title bee
Convai'd by this (ah) what doth itt auaile
to bee the fortieth name in an entayle

Thus I reclaimd my buzzard loue to flie
att what and when and how & where I choose
        Now negligent of sport I lie
        and now as other falkners vse
I spring a Mistris sweare write sigh and weepe
and the game killd or lost goe talke and sleepe

Finis

John Donne, A Valediction forbidding mourning

Elegie

As vertuous men passe mildlie away
  and whisper to their soules to goe
And some of their sadd frendes doe say
  the breath goes now and some sayes no
So lett vs melt and make no noyse
  No teare floudes nor sigh tempestes mooue
T'were prophanation of our ioyes
  to tell the *Laiety* of our Loue
Moouing of the earth bringh→brings harmes & feares
  men reckon what itt did and ment
But tripidation of the spheres
  though greater farr is Innocent
Dull sublunarye Louers Loue
  (whose soule is sence) cannott admitt
Absence because it doth remooue
  those thinges wch elemented itte
But wee by a loue so much refind
  that our selues know not what itt is
Itter→Inter→In['o]t[h]er assured of the mind
  careles eyes lippes and handes to misse

I, 48v

Our twoo soules therefore wch are one
though I must goe endure not yett
A Breach but an expansion
Like gold to ayerie thinnes beat
If they be twoo they are twoo soe
as stiffe twin=compasses are two
Thy soule the fixed foot maketh no showe
to move, but doth if thother doe
And though itt in the *Center* sitt
Yett when the other farre doth come
Itt leanes and harkens after itt
and growes direct as itt comes home
Such wilt thou bee to mee who must
Like thother foote obliquely runne
Thy firmnes makes my circle iust
and makes mee end where I begunn .

Finis

John Donne, Elegie on the Lady Marckham

An Eligie vpon the death of the La: Markham

Man is the world and death the Ocean
to which god giues the lower partes of man
The sea invirons all and though as yett
god hath sett markes and boundes twixt vs and itt
Yett doth itt roare and gnawe and still pretend
and breake our banck when ere itt takes a freind
Then our Land waters (teares of passion) vent
our waters then aboue our firmament
Teares wch our soule doth for her sinne lett fall
take all a brackish tast and funerall
And euen those teares wch should wash sinn are sinne
Wee after Godes *Noe* drowne the world againe
Nothing but man of all invenomb'd thinges
doth woorke vpon itt wthin borne stinges
Teares are false spectacles: wee cannot see
thorough passions mistes what wee are nor what shee
In her this sea of death hath made no breach
but as the tide doth wash the slimy beach
And leaues imbrothered woorkes vpon the sand
so is her flesh refind by deaths cold hand
As men of *China* after an ages stay
Doe take vpp purslane where they buried clay

{49}

So att this Graue her Lymbeck wch refines
the Diamondes Rubies saphires pearles and mines
(Of wch this flesh was) her soule shall inspire
fflesh of such stuffe as God when his last fire
Annulls the world to recompence itt shall
Make, and name then the *Elixir* of this all
They say when the Sea gaines itt looseth too
If carnall death the yonger brother doe
Vsurpe the bodie our soule wch subiect is
to the elder death by sinne is freed by this
They perish both when they attempt the Iust
for graues our *Trophees* are and both deaths Dust
not subiect to danger So vnobnoxious now shee hath buried both
for none to death sinnes wch to sinne are loth
Nor doe they die wch are not loth to die
so shee hath this and that *Virginitie*
Grace was in her extreamlie diligent
that kept her from sinne yett made her repent
Of whatt small spotts pure white complaines! alasse
how little poison breakes a christall glasse
Shee sinnd but iust enough to lett vs see
That Godes Woord must bee true. All sinners bee
So much did zeale her conscience rarifie
That extreame truth lackd little of a lie
Making Omissions, Actes, layeing the tuch
of sin on thinges wch sometimes may be such
As *Moses Cherubims*, whose natures doe
surpasse all speed by him are wronged too
So would her soule already in heauen seeme then
to clime by teares the common staires of men
How fitt she was for god I am content
to speake, that death his vaine hast may repent
How fitt for vs how euen and how sweete
how good in all her titles and how meet!
To haue reform'd this forward heresy
that women can not partes of frendshipp bee
How morall how Deuine shall not be told
least they that heare her vertues thinck her old
And least wee take deaths part and make him glad
of such a pray and to his triumph adde

Finis

I, 49v. John Donne, Elegie to the Lady Bedford

An Elegie to the La: Bedford

Yow that shee and yow thats double shee
  in her dead face halfe of your selfe shall see
Shee was the other part for so they doe
  wch build them frendshipps become one of twoo
So twoo, but that themselues no third can fitt
  which were to be so when they were not yett
Twinnes though their birth: *Cusco & Musco* take
  as diuers starres one constellation make
Paird like two eyes haue equall motion so
  both but one meanes to see and way to goe
Had yow died first a carkasse she had beene
  and wee your rich tombe in her face had seene
Shee like the soule is gone and yow heere stay
  not a liue frend but th'other halfe of clay
And since yow act that part as men say here
  Lies such a *Prince* when but one part is there
And doe all honour and deuotion due
  vnto the whole so wee all reuerence yow
ffor such a frendshipp who would not adore
  in yow who are all what both was before
Not all as if some perished by this
  but so that in yow all contracted is
As of this all though many partes decay
  the pure wch elemented them shall stay
And though diffus'd and spredd in infinite
  shall recollect and in one all vnite
So Madam as her soule to heauen is fledd
  her flesh rests in the earth as in a bedd
Her vertues due as to their proper *spheere*
  returne to dwell wth yow of whom yow were
As perfect Motions are all circular
  so they to you their sea whose lesse streames are/
Shee was all spices you all *Mettalls* soe
  in yow twoo wee did both rich *Indies* knowe
And as no *fire* nor rust can spend or waste
  one dramme of gold but what was first shall last
Though it be forc't in water earthe, salt, aire,
  expansd in infinite none will impaire
So to your selfe you may Additions take
  but nothing can yow lesse or changed make
Seeke not in seeking new to seeme to doubt
  that yow can match her or not be wthout
Butt lett some faithfull booke in her roome bee
  yett but of *Iudith* no such booke as shee

Finis

I, 50. John Donne, Elegie on Mris. Boulstred

{50}

An Eligie vpon the death of M^{ris} Boulstredd

Death I recant and say vnsaid by mee
what ere hath slipt that may diminish thee
Spirituall Treason *Atheisme* t'is to say
that any can thy summons disobey
The earths face is but thy table and thy meat
Plants, *Cattell*, *men*, dished for death to eat
In a rude hunger now he millions drawes
Into his bloodie or plaguie or staru'd iawes
Now he will seeme to spare and doth more wast
Eating the best fruites well preseru^{d} to tast
Now wantonly he spoiles and eats vs not
but breakes of frendes and letts vs peacemeale rott
Nor will the earth serue him he sinckes the Deepe
Where harmeles fish *Monastique* silence keepe
Who were (death dead) by Rowes of liuing sand
might spunge that Element and make itt Land
He roundes the Ayre and breakes the Himique noates
In birdes *Heauens Quiristers organique* throats
Which if they did not die might seeme to bee
a tenth ranke in the heauenlie *Hierarchie*
O strong and long liu'd death how camst thou in?
and how without creation didst beginn
Thou hast and shalt see dead befo~~u~~re thou diest
All the fower *Monarchies & Antichrist*
How could I thinke thee nothing that see now
In all this all nothing els tis butt thou
Our birthes and lifes vices and vertues bee
wastfull consumptions and degrees of thee
ffor wee to liue, our bellowes were and breath
Nor are wee mortall diyng dead but death
And though thou bee'st (O mightie bird of pray
so much reclaymd of god that thou maist lay
All that thou kill'st att his feet yett doth hee
Reserue but fewe and leaues the most to thee
And of those fewe now thou hast ouerthrowne
One whom thy blowe makes not ours Nor thine owne
Shee was more stories hie! hopelesse to come
to her soule thou hast offered att her lower Roome
Her soule and body was a Kinge and Court
but thou hast both of Captaine miste and fort
As houses fall not though the king reemooue
Bodies of Saintes rests for their soules aboue
Death getts twixt soules & bodies such a place
As sinn insinuates twixt iust men and grace

I, 50v

Both woorkes a seperation no diuorce
  Her soule is gone to vsher vpp the coarse
Wch shalbe almost another soule for there
  Bodies are purer then best soules are heere
Because in her her vertues did outgoe
  Her yeares. Ô emulous death wouldst thou doe ~~say~~
And kill her yonge to thie losse? must the cost
  Of beautie and witt apt to doe harme be lost
What though thou foundst her proofe 'gainst sins of youth
  On euery age a diuers sin pursueth
Thou shouldst haue staid and taken better hold
  Shortly ambitious couetous when old
She might haue prou'd and such Deuotion
  might once haue straid to supersticon
If all her vertues must haue growne yett might
  Abundant vertue haue bredd a proud delight
Had she preserued iust there would haue beene
  some what would sinn misthinking she did sinn
Such as would call her frendshipp loue, and faine
  to sociablenesse a name prophane
Or sin by tempting or not daring that
  by wishing though they never had her whatt
Thus might thou haue slaine more soules had'st thou not crost
  Thy selfe and to triumph thy army lost
Yett though theis wayes be lost thou hast left one
  Wch is immoderate griefe that she is gon
But wee may scape that sin yett weepe as much
  our teares are due because wee are not such
Some teares that knott of frendes her death must cost
  because the Chaine is broke though no lincke lost

Finis

I, 51. John Donne, Elegie: Death

{51}

Another Eligie vpon the death of M^{ris} Boulstred

Language thou art to narrow and too weake
  to ease vs now great sorrowe cannot speake
If wee could sigh our accentes and weepe woordes
  Griefe weares and lessens that teares breath affoordes
Sadd hartes they lesse doe seeme the more they are
  (so guiltiest menn stand mutest att the barr)
Not that they know not feele not their estate
  But extreame sence hath made them desperate
Sorrowe to whom wee owe all that wee bee
  Tirant in the fift and greatest *Monarchie*
Wast that she did possesse all hartes before
  Thou hast killd her to make thine *Empire* more
Knewst thou some would that knewe her not lament
  As in a deluge perish the Innocent
Wast not inough to haue that pallace won
  But thou must race itt too that was vndon
Hadst thou staid there and lookt out att her eyes
  All had adored thee that now from thee flies
ffor they lett out more light then they tooke in
  They tould not when but did they day begin
Shee was too *Saphirine* and cleere for thee
  Clay fflint and Iett now thy fitt dwellinges bee
Alas she was to pure but not to weake
  Who ere saw christall Ordinance but t'would breake
And if wee by→bee thy conquest by her fall
  thou'st lost thy end for in her perish all
Or if wee liue wee liue but to rebell
  they know her better now that knew her well
If wee should vapour out or pine or die
  since the first went that were not misery
She changd our world wth hers: now she is gon
  Mirth and prosperitie is oppression
ffor of all Morall vertues she was all
  the *Ethicks* speake of vertues *Cardinall*
Her soule was *Paradice* the *Cherubin*
  sett to keepe itt was grace that kept out sin
She had no more that lett in death for wee
  all reape consumption from one fruitfull tree
God tooke her hence least some of vs should loue
  Her like the plant him and his lawes aboue
And when wee teares he mercy shedd in this
  to raise our mindes to heauen where now she is
Where if her vertues would haue lett her stay
  Wee had had a Saint now a holliday

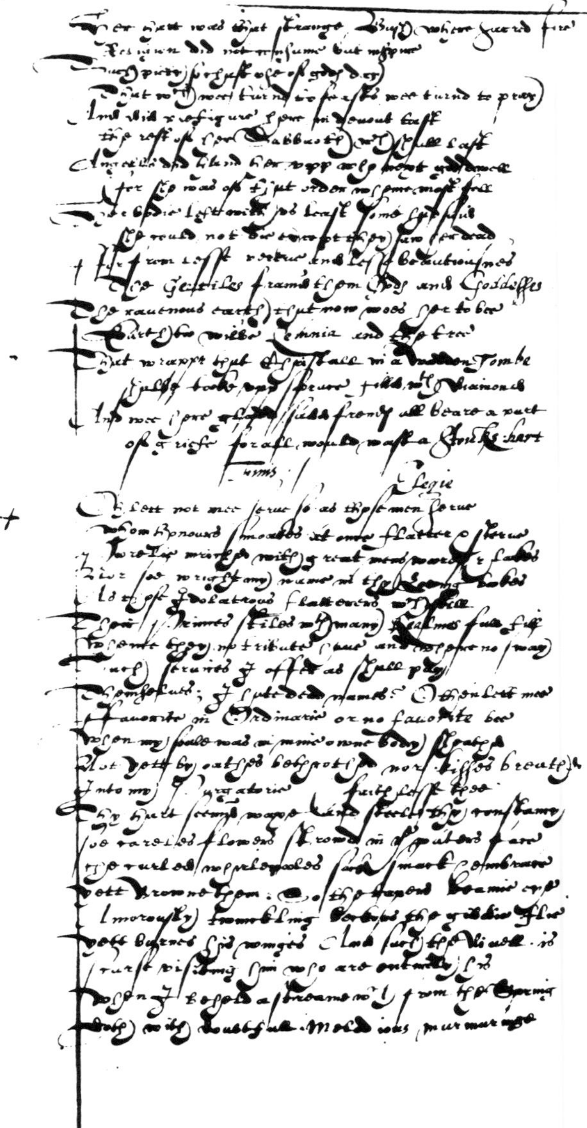

I, 51v

Her hart was that strange Bush where sacred fire
  Religion did not consume but inspire
Such piety so chast vse of godes day
  That wch wee turnd to feasts wee turnd to pray
And did prefigure here in deuout tast
  the rest of her Sabbaoth wch shall last
Angells did hand her vpp who next god dwell
  (for she was of that order whence most fell
Her bodie left with vs least some had said
  she could not die except they saw her dead
ffor from lesse vertue and lesse beautiousnes
  The *Gentiles* fram'd them Godes and *Goddesses*
The rauenous earth that now woes her to bee
  Earth too wilbe *Lemnia* and the tree
That wrappr that Christall in a woodden *Tombe*
  shalbe tooke vpp spruce filld wth Diamond
And wee here gladd sadd frendes all beare a part
  of griefe for all would wast a *stoicks hart*

Finis /

John Donne, Elegie: "Oh, let mee not serve so"

Elegie

Oh lett not mee serue so as those men serue
  whom honours smoakes at once flatter & sterue
Poorelie inrichd with great mens woordes & lookes
Nor soe wright my name in thy Loving bookes
As those Idolatrous flatterers wch still
Their Princes stiles wth many *Realmes* full fill
Whence they no tribute haue and where no sway
Such seruices I offer as shall pay
Themselues; I hate dead names! O then lett mee
ffauorite in Ordinarie or no *fauorite* bee
When my soule was in mine owne body sheathd
Not yett by oathes bethrothed nor kisses breathd
Into my Purgatorie (faithlesse thee
Thy hart seem'd waxe and steele thy constancy
soe careles flowers strowd in ye waters face
the curled whirlepooles suck smack & embrace
Yett drowne them. So the tapers beamie eye
Amorously twinckling beckons the giddie flie
Yett burnes his winges And such the diuell is
scarse visiting him who are entirely his
When I beheld a streame wch from the Spring
Doth with doubtfull Melodious murmuringe

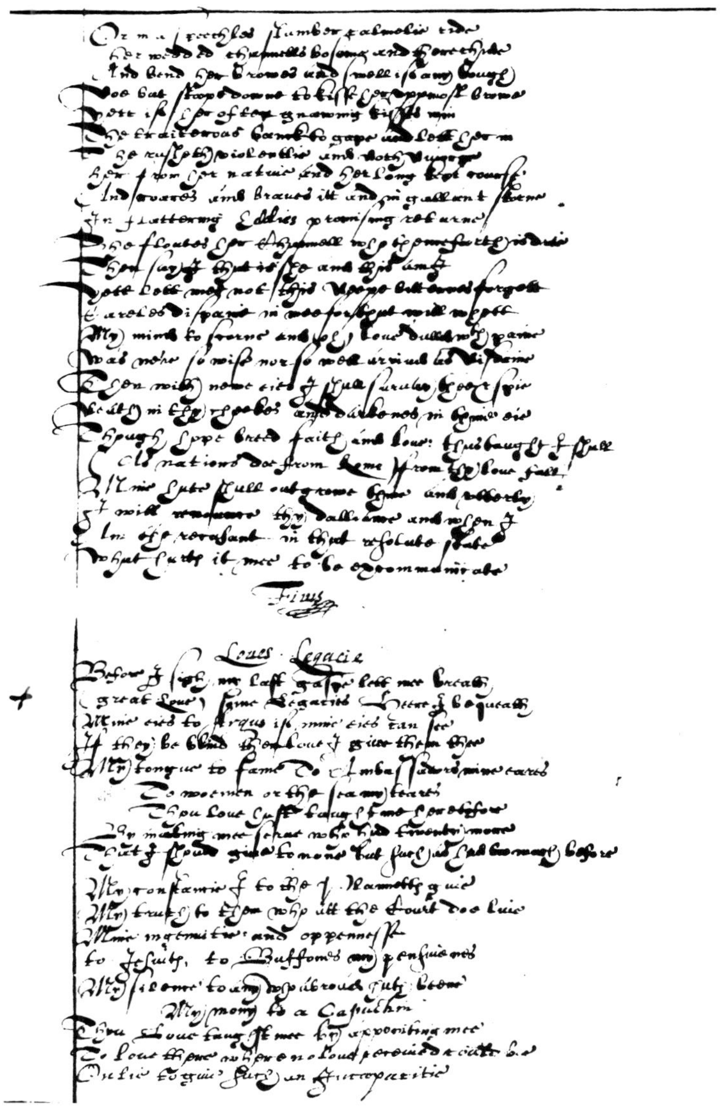

{52}

Or in a speechles slumber calmelie ride
  her wedded channells bosome and there chide
And bend her browes and swell if any bough
Doe but stoope downe to kisse her vppmost browe
Yett if her often gnawing kisses win
The traiterous banck to gape and lett her in
She rusheth violentlie and doth diuorce
her from her natiue and her long kept course
And roares and braues itt and in gallant skorne
In flattering *Eddies* promising returne
She floutes her channell who thencefoorth is drie
Then say I that is she and this am I
Yett lett mee not this deepe bitternes forgett
Careles dispaire in mee for that will whett
My mind to scorne and (oh) loue dulld wth paine
Was ne're so wise nor so well arriud as disdaine
Then with newe eies I shall suruay thee & spie
Death in thy cheekes and darkenes in thine eie
Though hope breed faith and loue: thus taught I shall
(As nations doe from *Rome*) from thy loue fall
Mine hate shall outgrowe thine and vtterly
I will renounce thy dalliance and when I
Am the recusant in that resolute state
What hurtes it mee to be excommunicate

Finis

John Donne, The Will

Loues Legacie

Before I sigh my last gaspe lett mee breath
\+ (great Loue) some Legacies Heere I bequeath
Mine eies to *Argus* if mine eies can see
If they be blind then loue I giue them thee
My tongue to fame. To Ambassadors mine eares
    To woemen or the sea my teares
    Thou loue hast taught me heretofore
  By making mee serue who had twenty more
That I should giue to none but such as had too much before

My constancie I to the Plannettes giue
My truth to them who att the court doe liue
Mine ingenuitie and oppennesse
to Iesuites, to Buffones my pensiuenes
My silence to any who abroad hath beene
      My mony to a *Capuchin*
Thou Loue taughst mee by appointing mee
To loue there where no loue receiued could bee
Onlie to giue such an Incapacitie

I, 52v

I giue my reputation to those
Wᶜʰ were my frendes mine industry to foes
To schoolemen I bequeath my doubtfullnes
My sicknes to Phisicians or excesse
To nature all that I in rime haue writt
        And to my company my witt
        Thou loue by making mee adore
  her: who begott this loue in mee before
Taughst mee to make as though I gaue when I did but restore

To him for whom the passing bell next tolles
I giue my Phisick bookes my written Rolles
Of Morall counsell I to Bedlam giue
My brazen Meddalles vnto them wᶜʰ liue
In want of bread; To them wᶜʰ passe among
All forrainers: mine English tongue
        Though loue by making mee loue one
        Who thinckes her frendshipp a fitt portion
for yonger Louers dost my guiftes thus disproportion

Therefore Ile giue no more But Ile vndoe
The world by dying because loue dies too
Then all your beauties will be no more woorth
Then gold in *Mines* where none doe drawe itt foorth
And all your Graces no more vse shall haue
        Then a *Sun=Diall* in a graue
        Thou loue taughst mee by making mee
  Loue her who doth neglect both thee & mee
To invent and practise this one way to adnihilate all three

Finis

Francis Beaumont, To the Countesse of Rutland

To the Countesse of Rutland

Madam

X So may my verses pleasing bee
so may you laugh att them and not att mee
Tis something to yow I would gladlie say
but how to doe it cannot find the way
I would auoid the common trodden waies
  to Ladies vsd wᶜʰ bee or loue or praise
As for the first that little witt I haue
  is not yett growne so neere vnto the graue
But that I can by that dime fading light
  perceiue of what and vnto whom I wright
Lett such as in a hopeles wittles rage
  can sigh a quier and reade itt to a Page

{53}

(Such as can make tenn sonnetts ere they rest
When each is but a great blott att the best
Such as can backes of bookes and windowes fill
  with their two furious diamond and quill
Such as are mortified that they can liue
  Laught att by all the world and yett forgiue)
Write loue to you; I would not willinglie
  Be pointed att in every company
As was the little Taylour who till death
  Was hott in loue w^th^ *Queene Elizabeth*
And for the last in all my idle daies
  I never did yett liuing woman praise
In verse or prose and when I doe beginn
  Ile pick some woman out as full of sinn
As you are full of vertue, with a soule
  As black as yours is white, a face as fowle
As yours is beautifull for itt shalbe
  Out of the rules of *Phisiognomy*
So farr that I doe feare I must displace
  The art a little to lett in the face
Itt shall att least four places→faces be belowe
  the diuelles; and her parched corpes shall showe
In her loose skinn as if some spiritt she were
  Kept in a bagg by some great *Coniurer*
Her breath shalbe as horrible and vild
  As euery woord yow speake is sweet and mild
Itt shalbe such a one as will not bee
  Couered with any Art or Pollicie
But lett her take all waters fumes and drincke
  she shall make nothing but a dearer stincke
She shall haue such a foot and such a nose
  As will not stand in any thing but prose
If I bestowe my praises vpon such
  t'is charitie and I shall meritt much
My praise will come to her like a full bowle
  bestow'd att most need on a thirstie soule
Where if I singe your praises in my rime
  I loose my Incke my paper and my time
Adde nothing to your overflowing store
  and tell you naught but what yow knew before
Nor doe the vertuous minded (wch I sweare)
Madam I thinke you are) indure to heare
Their owne perfections into question brought
  But stopp their eares att them for if I thought
You tooke a pride to haue your vertues knowne
  (*Pardon me Madam*) I should thinke them none
But if your braue thoughts (wch I must respect
  aboue your glorious titles) I shall accept
These harsh disordered lines I shall ere long
  dresse vpp your vertues new in a new song
Yett farr from all base praise or flattery
  although I knowe what ere my verses bee
They will like the most seruile flattery show
  if I write truth and make my subiect yow./

finis

I, 53v. John Donne, Elegie: The Expostulation

Elegie

To make the doubt more cleare that no womans true
  was itt my fate to proue itt strong in you
Thought I, but one, had breathed purest ayre
  and must shee needes be false because shees faire
Is itt your beauties marke or of your youth
  Or of your perfection not to studdy truth
Or thinke you heauen is deafe or hath no eies
  Or those she hath smile att your periuries
Are vowes so cheape wth women at→or the matter
  Where of they are made that they are writt in water
And blowne away with wind? or doth they breath
  (both hott and cold) att once make life and death
Who could haue thought so many accentes sweet
  fform'd into woordes so many sighes should meet
As from our hartes so many oathes and teares
  sprinckled (among all sweeter by your feares
And the deuine impression of stolne kisses
  (that seald the rest) should now proue emptie blisses
Did yow drawe bondes to forfeyt Signe to breake
  Or must wee read yow quite from what yow speake
And find the truth out the wrong way? or must
  The first desier you false would wish you Iust
O I prophane Though most woemen bee
  This kind of beast; My thought shall accept thee
My dearest loue. ffroward Iealousie
  With circumstance might vrge thy Inconstancy
Sooner Ile thinke the Sunn will cease to cheare
  The teeming earth! and that forgett to beare
Sooner that Riuers will runne backe or Thames
  With Ribbes of Ice in Iune would bind his streames
Or nature by whose strength the world endures
  Would change her course before you alter yours
But Ô that trecherous breast to whom weake yow
  Did trust our counselles and wee both may rue
Hauing his falshood found too late t'was hee
  That made yow cast your guiltie and yow mee
Whilst he black wretch betrayed each simple woord
  Wee spake vnto the cunning of a third
Curst may he bee that so our loue hath slaine
  and wander on the Earth wretched as *Cayne*
Wretched as hee and not deserue least pittie
  In plagueing him lett misery be wittie
Lett all eies shunn him and he shunn each eie
  till he be noysome as his infamy
May he without remorce deny god thrice
  And not be trusted more on his soules price
And after all selfe torment when he dies
  May woolues teare out his hart *vultures* his eies

{54}

Swine eat his bowells and his falser tongue
  that vttered all be to some Rauen flonge
And lett his carion coarse be a longer feast
  To the kinges dogges then any other beast
Now I haue curst lett vs our loue reuiue
  In mee the flame was never more aliue
I could begin againe to court and praise
  And in that pleasure lengthen the short daies
Of my liues lease Like Painters that doo take
  Delight, not in the made woorke but whilst they make
I could renewe these times when first I sawe
  Loue in your eies that gaue my tongue the lawe
To like what yow lik'd and att Masques and plaies
  Commend the selfe same Actours the same wayes
Aske how yow did and often with intent
  Of beeing Officious be impertinent
All wch were such soft pastimes as in these
  Loue was as subtle catchd as a disease
But beeing gott it is a treasure sweet
  Wch to defend is harder then to gett
And ought not be prophan'd on either part
  ffor though t'is gott by chance t'is kept by art

Finis

X

John Donne, Song: "Goe, and catche a falling starre"

A song

Goe and catch a falling starr
  gett with child a Mandrake roote
tell mee where all past yeares are
  or who cleft the diuells foot
Teach mee to heare *Mermaides* singing
  Or to keepe of envies stinging
      And find
      what wind
Serues to aduance an honest mind

If thou beest borne to strange sights
  thinges invisible see
Ride ten thousand daies and nights
  till age snowe white haires on thee
This→Then when thou returnst will't tell mee
All strange wonders that befell thee
      And swere
      No where
Liues a woman true and faire

If thou findst one lett mee know
such a pilgrimage were sweet
Yett do not I would not goe
  though att next doore we might meet
Though she were true when you mett her
And last till yow write your letter
      Yett shee
      wilbee
false ere I come to ~~th~~ two or three

finis

I, 54v. John Donne, Loves Deitie

Loues Deitie

I long to talke wth some old louers ghost
Who died before the God of loue was borne
I cannot thincke that he who then loued most
suncke so lowe as to loue one wch did skorne
But since this God producd a destinie
And that vice=nature Custome letts itt bee
I must loue her that loues not mee

Sure they wch made him God meant not so much
nor he in his yong godhead practisd itt
But when an ever flame twoo hartes did touch
his office was indulgentlie to fitt
Actiues to Passiues: correspondency
Onlie his subiect was itt cannot be
Loue till I loue her that loues mee

But euery Moderne God will now extend
his vast prerogatiue as farr as *Ioue*
To rage to lust to write to to commend
all is the purlewe of ye god of loue
Oh were wee weakned by this Tiranny
To vngod this child againe it would not be
that I should loue who loues not mee

Rebell & Atheist too why murmure I
as though I felt the worst that loue can doe
Loue might make mee leaue louing or might trie
A deeper plague to make her loue mee too
W^{ch} since she loues before I am loath to see
ffalshood is woorse then hate and that must bee
If shee whom I loue should loue mee

Finis

John Donne, The Funerall

The Funerall

Who euer com**es to shrowd mee doe not harme
nor question much
That subtile wreath of haire wch crownes mine arme
The mistery the signe you must not touch
for tis my outward soule
ViceRoy to that wch then to heauen beeing gon
Will leaue this to controwle
And keepe these limmes her Prouinces from dissolution

{55}

ffor if the sinnewie thredd my braine lettes fall
through euery part
Can tie those partes and make mee one of all
These haires wch vppward grewe and strength and art
haue from a better braine
Can better doe itt, except she meant that I
by this should know my paine
As prisoners then are manacled when they are condemnd to die

What ere she ment by itt burie itt with mee
for since I am
Loues Martir it might breed Idolatrie
if into anothers handes these reliques came
and t'was humilitie
To affoord itt ^all ~~loue~~ wch a soule can doe
So tis some brauery
That since yow would saue none of mee I bury some of you

Finis

John Donne, Loves Usury

ffor euery houre that thou wilt spare me now
I will allowe
(Vsurious God of loue twenty to thee)
When wth my browne my gray haires equall bee
Till then loue lett my bodie raigne and lett
Mee trauaile soiourne snatch plott haue forgett
Resume my last yeares Relique. Thincke that yett
Wee had never mett

Lett mee thinke my Riualls letter mine
att att next Nine
Keepe middnightes promise mistake by the way
the maid and tell the ladie of that delay
Onlie lett mee loue none no not the sport
ffrom country grasse to comfitures att court
or citties *Quelque choses* lett report
My mind transport

If thine owne honour or my shame or paine
thou couett most att that age thou shalt gaine
Doe thy will then Then subiect and degree
And fruit of loue Loue I submitt to thee
Spare mee till then Ile beare itt though she be
one that loues mee.

Finis

I, 55v. John Donne, The Flea

Marke butt this flea and marke in this
how little that wch thou deniest mee is
Mee it suck'd first and now suckes thee
And in this flea our twoo bloodes mingled bee
Confesse itt this cannot be said
A sin, or shame or losse of maydenhead
Yett this enioyes before itt woe
and pamperd swelles wth one blood made of twoo
and this alasse is more then wee could doe

Oh stay three liues in one flea spare
Where wee almost ~~the~~ nay more then maried are
This flea is yow and I and this
our mariage bedd and mariage Temple is

Though Parentes grudge and yow wee are mett
and cloystered in these liuing walls of Iett
Though vse make thee apt to kill mee
Lett not to thy selfe murther added bee
and sacriledge three sinnes in killing three

Cruell and suddaine hast thou since
Purpled thy naile in blood of Innocence
In what could this flea guiltie bee
except in that dropp wch itt suckt from thee
Yett thou triumphst and saist that thou
findst not thy selfe nor mee the weaker now
T'is true then learne how false feares bee
Iust so much honour when thou yeeldst to mee
Will wast as this fleas death tooke life from thee

Finis

John Donne, Communitie

Good wee must loue and must hate ill
ffor ill is *ill* and good good still
but there are thinges indifferent
W^{ch} wee may neither hate nor loue
but one and then another proue
as wee shall find our fancy bent

If then att first wise nature hadd
made women either good or badd
then some wee might hate & some wee might chuse
but since she did them so create
That wee may neither loue nor hate
Onlie this rests *All*, All may vse

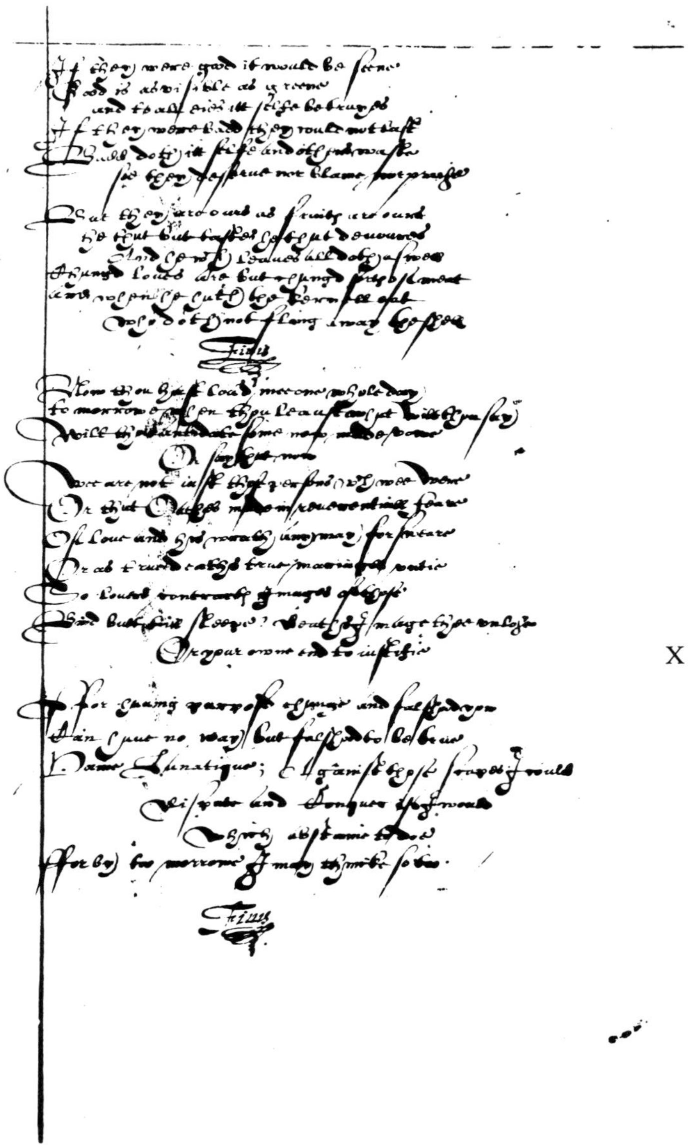

{56}

If they were good it would be seene
Good is as visible as greene
  and to all eies itt selfe betrayes
If they were badd they could not last
Badd doth itt selfe and others waste
  soe they deserue nor blame nor praise

But they are ours as fruites are ours
 he that but tastes he that deuoures
  And he wch leaues all doth as well
Changd loues are but changd sortes of meat
and when he hath the kernell eat
  Who doth not fling away the shell

Finis

John Donne, Womans constancy

Now thou hast lou'd mee one whole day
X to morrowe when thou leaust what wilt thou say
Wilt thou antidate some new made vowe
  Or say that now
Wee are not iust those persons wch wee were
Or that Oathes made in reuerentiall feare
Of loue and his wrath any may forsweare
Or as true deaths true mariages vntie
So louers contractes Images of those
Bind butt till sleepe? Deaths Image thee vnlose
  Or your owne end to iustifie

ffor hauing purposd change and falshood yow
Can haue no way but falshood to be true
Vaine Lunatique; Against those scapes I could
  Dispute and conquer if I would
  Which abstaine to doe
ffor by too morrowe I may thincke so too. /

Finis

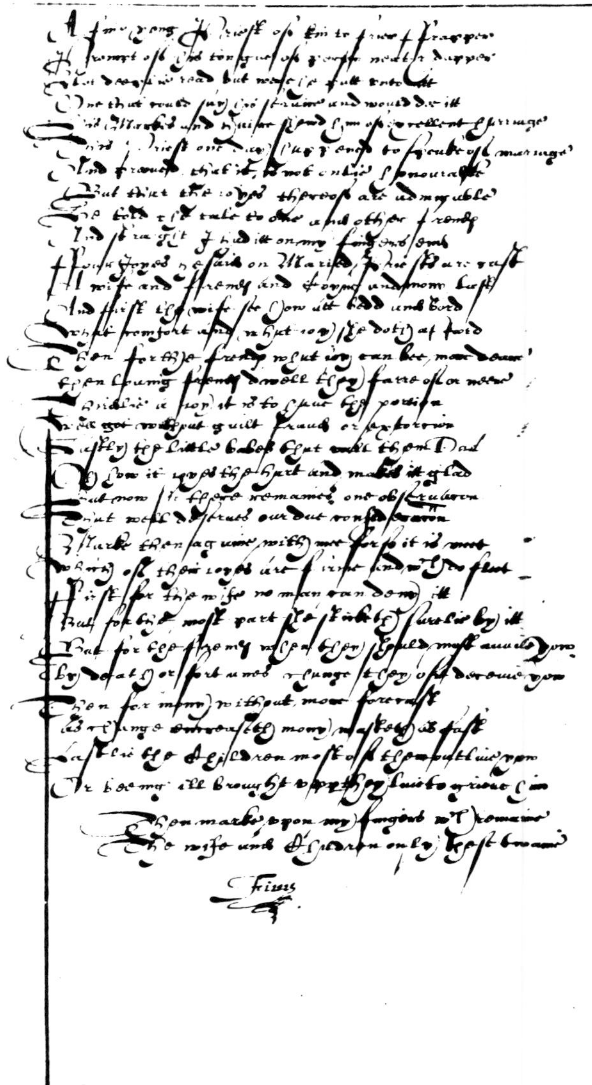

I, 56v. Sir John Harington, Of the commodities that men haue by their Marriage

A fine yong Priest of kin to frier ffrapper
Prompt of his tongue of person neat & dapper
Not deeplie read but were he putt vnto itt
One that could say his seruice and would doe itt
His Markes and haire shewd him of excellent harriage
This Priest one day happened to speake of mariage
And prooued that it is not onlie honourable
But that the ioyes thereof are admirable
He told the tale to one and other frendes
And straight I had itt on my fingers end
ffour Ioyes he said on Maried Priests are cast
A wife and frendes and coyne and mony last
And first the wife see how att bedd and bord
What comfort and what ioy she doth affoord
Then for the frendes what ioy can bee more deare
then louing frendes dwell they farre of or neere
Thirdlie a ioy it is to haue the portion
Well got without guilt fraud or extorcion
Lastly the little babes that call them *Dad*
Oh how it ioyes the hart and makes itt glad
But now sir there remaines one obseruacon
That well deserues our due consideracon
Marke then againe with mee for so it is meet
Which of their ioyes are firme and wch do fleet
ffirst for the wife no man can deny itt
But for the most part she sticketh surelie by itt
But for the frendes when they should most auaile yow
by death or fortunes change they oft deceiue yow
Then for mony without more forecast
as change encreaseth mony wasteth as fast
Lastlie the children most of them outliue yow
Or beeing ill brought vpp they liue to grieue him
Then marke vpon my fingers wch remaine
The wife and children only these twaine

Finis

I, 57. Sir John Harington, Of a Precise Tayler

{57}

A Taylour thought a man of vpright dealing
True but for liyng honest but for stealinge
ffalling one day extreamlie sicke by chance
Was on a sodaine in a wondrous trance
The fiendes of *Hell* mustering in fearfull manner
Of sundry coloured silkes displayd a banner
That he had stole and wishd as they did tell
That one day he might find itt all in *Hell*
The man affrighted with this apparition
Vpon Recouerie grewe a great precisian
He bought a bible of the new translation
and in his life he shewd great reformation
He walked mannerlie and talked meekelie
He heard 3 sermons & 2 Lectures weekelie
He vowed to shunn all company vnrulie
And in his speach he vsd no oath but trulie
And zealouslie to keepe the Sabbaoths rest
His meat for that day on the Eue was drest
And least the custome that he had to steale
Might cause him sometimes to forgett his zeale
He giues his Iourney man a speciall charge
that if the stuffes allowance beeing large
He found his fingers were to filch inclinde
Badd him haue then the banner in his mind
This done I scant can tell the rest for laughter
A captaine of a shipp brought 3 daies after
3 yardes of 3 pile veluett and 3 quarters
to make venetian hose belowe the garters
Hee that precisely knewe what was enough
soone slipt away 3 quarters of ye stuffe
His man that sawe itt said in derision
Remember master how you sawe the vision
Peace knaue q^{d} he I did not see a ragge
Of such a coloured silke in all the flagge

Finis

Anonymous, The famous learned Tullie long agoe

The famous learned Tullie long agoe
spake in a spleenefull moode a lustie woord
None thinking then that now it should be so
Rome saith he for the gowne before the sword
Itt seemes the man in spiritt did foresee
The Ladies of this age wch now preferr
ffor Riches and for titles of degree
the man of wealth before the man of warr
And well itt fittes that so for wise respectes
Their youthfull greennesse should wth grauenes meet
Saue only this that age in his defectes
Comming to bedd wth cold & frozen feet
The Ladie findes her bargaine but affoordes
ffaint doinges for a few well spoken woordes

Finis

Sir John Harington, Of Women learned in the tongues

You wished me to take a wife faire rich & yong
that had the lattin french & spanish tongue
I thanckt & told yow I desird no such
I feard one language might be tongue to much
Then loue I not the learned? yes as my life
A learned mistris but not a learned wife

finis

John Donne, Faustus

X *faustinus* keepes his sister & a whore
faustinus keepes his sister and no more /

I, 57v. Sir Walter Ralegh, The Lie

Goe soule the bodies guest
+ vpon a thanckles errant
ffeare not to touch the best
the truth shalbe thy warrant
Goe since I needes must die
And giue them all the lie

Say to the Court it glowes
and shines like rotten wood
saie to the Church it shoes
what's good but doth no good
If Court and Church replie
Giue Court & Church the lie

Tell men of high condition
that rules affaires of state
Their purpose is Ambition
their practise onlie hate
And if they do reply
feare not to giue the lie

Tell Potentates they liue
acting but others actions
Not lou'd vnlesse they giue
not strong but by their factions
If Potentates reply
Giue Potentates the lie

Tell those that bragges it most
they begge for more by spending
And in their greatest cost
seeke nothing butt commendinge

Tell witt how much it wrangles
in tickle pointes of *finenesse*
Tell wisdome she intangles
in pointes of ouernicenes

Tell zeale it wantes devotion
tell loue it is but lust
tell time it is but motion
tell flesh it is but dust

Tell age it dailie wasteth
Tell honour how itt alters
Tell beautie that she blasteth
tell fauour that she faulters

Tell Phisicke of her boldnes
tell skill it is preuention
Tell Charitie of coldnes
tell Loue it is contention

Tell fortune of her blindnes
tell nature of decay
Tell frendshipp of vnkindnes
tell Iustice of delay

{58}

Tell Artes they haue no scandalles
but varie by esteeming
Tell schooles they want profoundnes
and stand too much on seeming

Tell faith t'is fledd the Citie
tell how the Contry erreth
Tell man‸he shakes of pittie
say vertue least preferreth

So when thou hast as I
Commanded thee done babbling
Although to giue the lie
Deserues no lesse then stabbing

Stabb att thy soule who will
No stabbe thy soule can kill

Finis

Anonymous, Emelia *embraceing many guifts and loues*

Emelia embraceing many guifts and loues
the honester she is the woorse she proues
Lais giues pleasure for the guiftes she takes
But she a filthie game of vertue makes
A modest maid should haue chast handes chast eies
not thinke that chastitie in one part lies
To smile on all and to drawe on all louers
Bee she vntoucht an vnchast mind discouers

Finis

Josuah Sylvester, The Fruites of a cleere Conscience

The fruites of a good conscience

To shine in silke and glister all in gold
\+ [no:] To shewe in wealth and feed on daintie fare
To build vs houses statelie to behold
the Princes fauour and the peoples care
Although theis guifts be great and very rare
the groaning gout the collicke & the stone
Will marre their mirth & turne itt all to moane
But bee itt that the bodie subiect bee
to no such sicknes or the like annoy
Yett if the conscience be not firme & free
Riches is trash and honour butt a toy
The peace of conscience is that perfect ioy
Wherewith godes children in this life be blest
to want the wch better want the rest
The want of this made *Adam* hide his head
The want of this made *Cain* to waile & weepe
The want of this makes many goe to bedd
When they god wott haue little lust to sleepe
Striue Striue therefore to entertaine & keepe
So rich a Iewell and so rare a guest
Wch beeing had a rush for all the rest

Finis

I, 58v. Sir Thomas Overbury, The Remedy of Loue

The Remedy of Loue

When Loue did read the title of my booke
He feard least some had armes against mee tooke
Suspect mee not for such a wicked thought
Vnder thy cullours wch so oft haue fought
Some youths are oft in loue but I am ever
and now to doe the same I doe perseuer
I meane not to blott out what I haue taught
Nor to vnwinde the webb that I haue wrought
If any loue and is with loue repaide
Blest be his state he needeth not my aide
But if he reape scorne where he loue hath sowne
of such it is that I take charge alone
Why should loue any vnto hanging force
When as (euen) hate can driue them to no woorse
Why with their owne handes should itt cause men perish
When it is peace alone that loue doth cherish
Ile ease yow now wch taught to loue before
the same hand wch did wound shall ease the sore
The same earth poisoned flowers & loathsome breedes
The rose is often neighbour vnto weedes
To men and women both I Phisick giue
Or els I should but halfe the sick world relieue
If any for that sexe vnfitting are
Yett they by mens examples may beware
Had wicked *Scylla* this my counsell redd
the golden haire had stucke to *Nisus* head
[++] Take heed when thou dost first to like begin [+]
thrust not loue out but lett him not come in
By running farr; brookes runne wth greater force
tis easier to hold then to stopp the horse
Delay addes strength and faster hold impartes
Delay the blades of corne to eares convertes
The tree wch now is father to a shade
and often head against the wind hath made
I could att first haue pluckt vpp wth mine hand
though the sunnes prospect now it dares withstand
Then passions ere they fortifie remooue
In short time liking groweth to bee loue
Be prouident and so preuent thy sorrowe
Who will not doo't to day cannot to morrowe
The riuer wch now multiplied doth swell
Is in his cradle but a little well
Oft that wch when t'is done is but a scarr
becomes a wound whilest wee the cure diferr
But in thine hart if loue be firmlie seated
and hath such root as cannot be defeated

{59}

Although in hand att first itt did not take you
att point of death t'were cruell to forsake you
That fier wch no water can asswage
for want of stuffe att length must end his rage
Whiles Loue is in his furious heat giue place
What councell cannot delay bringes to passe
Att first his mind impatient and sore
Doth Phisick more then disease abhorre
Who but a foole a mother will forbidd
her sonne new dead some teares to shedd
When she a while hath spoke her griefe in teares
Wth patience, then if patience she heares
Out of due season who so Phisick giues
Though it cause health yett hath he done amisse
And frendlie counsell vrged out of date
doth frett the sore and cause the hearers hate
But when loues anger seemeth to appease
by all meanes labour to shunn Idlenes
This bringes him first this stayes him and no other
thisis to *Cupid* both his nurse and mother
Barr Idlenes loues arrowes blunt will turne
and the vnflameing fire want power to burne
Loue neare doth better entertainment finde
then in a dissolute and empty mind
Sloth is loues bawde if thow wilt then leaue wooing
Lett still thy bodie or thy mind be dooinge
ffull happines neere stopt wth rubbe of chance
Ease vncontroul'd long sleepes and dalliance
Doe wound the mind though neuer pierce the skin
and thorough that wound loue slily creepeth in
Then either vnto bookes goe make thy mone
so shalt thou haue most company alone
Or els vnto the doubtfull warrs goe range
Redie this life for honour to exchange
The *Parthian* that valiant *Runnaway*
to yeeld new cause of *Triumph* doth assay
Ægistus a letcher and why so
The cause was he had nothing els to doe
When all the youth's of Greece for *Troy* was bound
and wth a wall of men inclos'd itt round
Ægistus would not from his home remooue
where he did nothing but that nothing loue
If theis faile to the country then repaire
for any care extinguisheth this care
There maist thou see the Oxe the yoke obey
and thorough the earth plowes eating thorough their way

I, 59v

To whom thou maist sett corne to vse & see
(for euery corne) spring vpp a little tree
The sunn beeing midwife thou shalt oft find there
Trees bearing farr more fruit then they can beare
And how the siluer brookes in riding post
Till they in some Riuer themselues haue lost
There maist thou see the goates scale hiest hill
That they their bellies and their duggs may fill
And harmeles sheepe to whom was no defence
By nature ever giuen but Innocence
There maist thou learne to graft and then note how
the old tree nurseth the adopted bowe
And of his sapp doth some allowance rate
though his fruit from him do degenerate
There maist thou see the hare tread many a ring
the houndes into a Laborinth to bringe
Vntill he (hauing long his life delay'd
by his owne stepps be to the dogges betrayed
Or fishing vse so thou the fish shalt see
punishd to death for their credulitie
Doe this that thou maist weary bee att night
so sleepe in spight of thoughts shall close thy sight
Lett not thy memory thinges past repeat
t'is easier to learne then to forgett
Therefore keepe distance and thy loue forsake
this to effect some Iourney vndertake
I know thou wilt wish raine and faine delay
and oft thy doubtfull foot stand att a stay
But how much more itt grieves thee to be gon
so much the more remember to goe on
Name not the miles nor once looke backward home
the *Parthians* by flight doe ouercome [+]
Some say my rules are hard I doe confesse itt
I must needes hurt the wound because I dresse itt [+]
Wilt thou bide for thy bodies health vexation
W^{ch} straight decayes wthout foodes reparation
And will not doe this thie mind to mend
the better halfe wch did from heauen discend
ffor your owne comfort this one proofe I say
t'is harder farr to part then stay away
ffor custome wth the hardest thinges that are
Will make vs in short time familiar
If thou be once abroad there long abide
Least comming home thou in relapse doe slide

{60}

Then will thine absence bring thee to woorse plight
as fasting breedes a greater appetite
Thincke not by witchcraft to fright loue away
ffor Pluto himselfe was in loue they say
Circes vsd this the wandering knight to stirr
Yett many miles were twixt his loue and her
But he that is so vext that would esteeme
All paines but cheape his freedome to redeeme
Lett him alone summe vpp his M^{ris} crimes
Thinck how much she hath cost thee many times
Thincke how she vsd to sweare and kindlie speake
and faithles straight her woord and oath to breake
And thincke the same night that shee the denies
That greedie, wth some seruingman she lies
Vrge this thy matter neuer wilbe spent
for sorrowe will make any eloquent
I was in loue my selfe the other day
And shee vngratefullie would not loue repay
Then grewe I the Phisician and the sicke
and did my selfe recouer by this tricke
I said she was not faire when I did eie her
Yett to confesse the truth I did belie her
yett I att length for many times I said itt
Gainst mine owne knowledge to my selfe gaue creditt
Still neere to vertue vices bordering lie
for on both sides of her they seated bee
Then the good partes thou in thy M^{ris} knowest
to one of those twoo vices see thou bowest
Accompt the fatt as swolne the browne turn'd black
If she be slender say she flesh doth lack
If she be merry sweare that she is light
If modest thinck it is for lacke of witt
This done thy Mistris bee shee not to coy
Wherein she hath no guift nor grace to employ
If she sing harsh intreat her still to singe
Hath shee fatt fingers then a lute her bringe
If she stride wide then gett her foorth to walke
Or speake shee ill then giue her cause of talke
If she dance hobling lett her not sitt still
and make her laugh if that her teeth be ill
Sometimes into her chamber earlie presse
Before att all pintes→pointes she her selfe can dresse
That which is *Venus* Image now t'is done
was (whilest it was a making) ragged stone

I, 60v

With clothes and Tires our iudgementes bribed bee
and woman is least of what wee see
But least thou too much trust this rule beware
for many like truth fairest naked are
Yett venture in for there is often found
the stuffe whereof their painting is compound
And boxes wch vnto their cheekes giues colour
and water wch doth wash their faces fowler/

Finis i. partis

Sir Thomas Overbury, The second part of the Remedy of Loue

The second part of the Remedy of Loue.

Hitherto haue I breathd now will I bring
My ranging course into a shorter Ringe
When that night comes wch manny hath lost thee
and much sweet bitter expectation cost thee
Whiles thou art heauy and thy spirittes downe
and foolishly wise by repentance growne
Then lett thine eies her body note till they
Doe something find amisse and thereon stay
Some may perchance theis prcepts trifles call
Who is not help't by any may by all
ffor all I cannot fitt Instructions find
because wee twoo are like in face and mind
The same that one doth not mislike att all
A great deformitie some others call
As that nice youth that did his loue withdraw
because his Mris hee att Priuie sawe
They loue in iest that so can whole become
When Cupid shootes att such he drawes not home
Striue thou to bee in loue wth twoo together
so shall thy loue be violent in neither
ffor when thy mind by halfes doth doubtfull stray
One loue doth take the other force away
The selfe same strength vnited is more stronge
then when to twoo it pain→parted doth belong
Great riuers beeing peace meale oft deuided
Doe shrinke att length to brookes that may be strided
This trick hath many helpt therefore wee see
Women for spite terme itt Inconstancy
The old loue by succession out is droue
In *Helen Paris* lost *Oenones* loue
She wch hath manie sonnes makes not such mone
as she wch looseth all her sonnes in one
The falsest loue a second loue vndoes
for in a crosse way loue doth himselfe loose

{61}

Although thy hart with fier like *Ætna* flame
Lett not thy M^{ris} once perceiue the same
Smother thy passions and lett not thy face
tell thy mindes secrettes while she is in place
Thy hart beeing stormy lett thy face be cleare
Nor lett loues fier by smoake of sighes appeare
Dissemble tonge till thy dissembling breed
Such vse as thou art out of loue in deed
I haue from drinking so my selfe to keepe
Laid on a bedd and winckt my selfe asleepe
Oft haue I seene youths faine them selues in loue
till taken att their woordes they so did proue
If shee appoint thee any night to come
and comming thither findst her not att home
Doe not make sonnetts att her chamber dore
Nor thy repulse as a mischance before→deplore
Nor to her when thou meetest her againe
Of thy owne wronges or thy vntruth complaine
for to be patient time will easilie make itt
if thou haue patience but to vndertake itt
Hee that from farr his m^{ris} doth admire
and dares not hope of hauing his desire
His mind a care incurable will proue
for that wee thincke forbidden most wee loue
Distrust not then till thou heare her reply
Who asketh faintlie teacheth to deny
Say if all theis faile this next will helpe impart
and loue of others to selfe loue convert
ffor thoughts of loue no longer vs possesse
then whiles wee liue in health and happines
Lett him that is indebted thincke alone
That whiles he thinckes his day drawes neerer on
Whom a hard father from his will doth lett
Lett him before him still his father sett
Lett him wch will a wife wth nothing take
Thinke that from preferrment she will keepe him backe
None need this Phisick of *Phisicians* borrowe
for none but hath some cause of feare & sorrowe
Lett him that deepelie loues and is farre gone
(Like an ill doer) feare to be alone
Vse not to silent groaues aside to shrincke
Nothing loue more vpholdeth then to thincke
Then will thy mind thy M^{ris} Picture take
for Memory all thinges past doth present make
Then like *Pigmalion* wee an Image frame
And fall in loue deuoutlie with the same
Therefore then night lesse dangerous is the day
Because then thoughts new borne talke sendes away

I, 61v

Then shalt thou find how much a frend is woorth
Into whose breast thou maist thy griefe powre foorth
Phillis alone frequented riuers side
Clouded with shade of teares till there she di'de
Who loues must louers company refuse
ffor loue is as infectious as newes
By looking on sore eies wee sore eies gett
and fier doth alwaies on the next house sett
Did not infection to the next neighbour flie
Diseases would with their first owners die
A wound new healed will soone breake out againe
therefore from seeing of thy loue refraine
Nor will this serue but thou must shunn her kin
and euen the house wch she abideth in
Lett not her nurse nor chambermaid once mooue thee
though they protest how much their M^{ris} loues thee
Nor into any question of her breake
Nor of her talke (though thou against her speake)
He that saies oft that he is not in loue
by repetition doth himselfe disproue
I would not wish thy loue in hatred end
Lett her that was thy loue be still thy frend
But when yee needes must meet then shew thy spiritt
thincke how she loues some fellowe of lesse meritt
Make not thy selfe against thou seest her fine
for this is doubtles of some loue a signe
The reason is as I my selfe haue tride
why many men so long in loue abide
Because if they some kinder looke obteyne
they foorth with thincke they are belou'd againe
To our owne flatteries creditt wee do giue
and what wee would haue true we soone belieue
So they like gamsters leese on more and more
least they should loose that little lost before
But trust not thou their woordes and though they sweare
Yett womens Oathes are Othes of *Atheists* heere
Nor as a signe of griefe their weeping take
But thinke their eies vse soluble doth make
Be still and sullen beare a grudge in mind
Nor tell the cause least she excuses find
He that beginneth with his loue to chide
that man is willing to be satisfied
Beautie is nothing woorth for if wee loue
the fowlest in our iudgement faire will proue
Therefore the only meanes by wch to try them
is then to iudge when fairer doe stand by them
Conferre their faces and with all their mind
Who seeth onlie with his eies is blind

I, 62

{62}

Comparison the touch stone is whereby
wee from the good the better doe descry
T'is but a trifle wch I meane to speake
and yett loues strength this trifle oft doth breake
All letters written from thy Mistris burne
such *Reliques* louers mindes doe backwardes turne
Though thou canst not behould them while they flame
  thy loues funerall fier thincke the same
Take heed least thou into the place resort
  which by accessarie to your sport
Stirr not the ashes wch doe fire conceale
  nor touch the wound wch is about to heale
Loue cannot be maintaind with pouerty
  his riott doth with riches best agree
Honour and titles though not felt nor seene
  the chiefest cause of loue to some hath beene
ffrequent not plaies for whiles wee others loue
see acted wee our selues doe parties proue
Vpon my proofe *Musique* and dauncing flie
  for musicke trees and stones did mollifie
And fishes too though they tsemselues→themselues be dumbe
  to heare *Arions* voyce did gladlie come
And dauncing some more passions doth raise
Then reason pacifies in many daies
These melt the mind and soft our hartes doe make
  and thereby loues impression apt to take
Touch not the *Poets* wch of loue doe sing
  they vs to loue by imitation bringe
Whilest wee in them doe others loue behold
  change but the names the tale of vs is told
What man (but some stiffe clowne) but soone will prooue
  by reading in such bookes in loue with loue
Barr them I say for that in them is found
a certaine *Musique* and a wanton sound
vnles I by *Apollo* be misled
t'is a mutation wch most loue hath bredd
Much easines doth cloy and most wee sett
by that which wee with doubt from others gett
Then frame thy selfe but surmise
  that cold in middle of her bedd she lies
Atrides could be dull by *Helens* side
And was content att *Creet* from her to bide
Vntill by *Paris* she from him was rented
then was his loue by others loue augmented
Lastlie I must some meates forbidd the sick
  that I in all may be Phisician like
Vse not on sweet and iuicy meates to feed
for fullnes of such doth lusts hunger breed
And stuff'd with such wee any doe admire
When all their beautie lies in our desire
But wine is more prouoking farr then meat
This heates our blood and itt on rage doth sett
This drownes our mindes and makes it sence obey
Loues winges beeing wett he cannot flie away

Finis

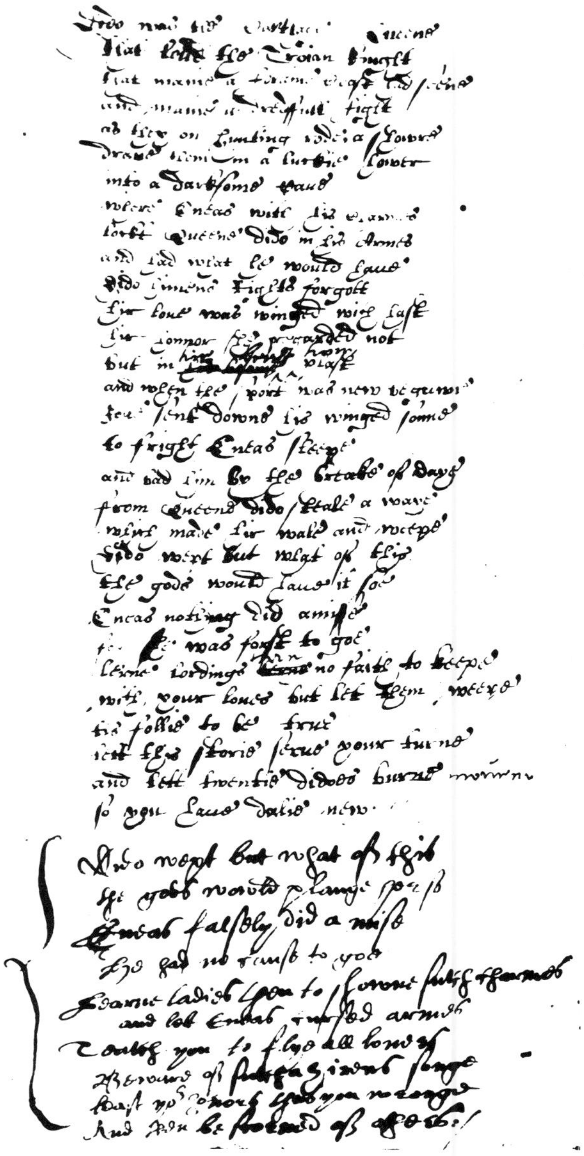

I, 62v. Thomas Campion, A Ballad

Dido was the Carthage Queene
  that lou'd the Troian knight
  that manie a foraine coast had seene
  and manie a dredffull fight
  as they on Hunting rode, a showre
  draue them in a luckie hower
  into a darksome caue
  where Eneas with his charmes
  lockt Queene dido in his Armes
  and had what he would haue
  Dido himens Rights forgott
  hir loue was winged with hast
  hir honnor she regarded not
  but in [hir]~~his~~ ~~bosome~~[breest]‸‸[him]plast
  and when the sport was new begunne
  Ioue sent downe his winged sonne
  to fright Eneas sleepe
  and bad him by the breake of daye
  ffrom Queene dido steale a waye
  which made hir wale and weepe
  Dido wept but what of this
  the gods would haue it soe
  Eneas nothing did amisse
  for ~~s~~he was forst to goe
  lerne lordings[then]~~lerne~~ no faith to keepe
  with your loues but let them weepe
  tis follie to be true
  lett this storie serue your turne
  and lett twentie didoes ~~burne~~ [mourne]
  so you haue dalie new. //

Anonymous answer to Campion

Dido wept but what of this
  the gods wowld plauge her so
Eneas falsely did a mise
  He had no cause to goe
Learne ladies then to showne sutch charmes
    and lett Eneas cursed armes
Teatch you to flye all louers
  Beware of sutch a Sirens songe
  least yor honors thus you wronge
  And then be scorned of others:/

I, 63. Anonymous, On a Cobler

{63}

An epitath:

Heire lyes an honest cobler whom curst fate
perceiving neere worne out, wowld needs transslate
twas a trew poore soule, & tyme hath beine
He wowld well lickard goe throw thick & thynne,
Death put a trick vppon him & what waste
He called for his nall, death browght him his laste.
Twas not vprightly done to cut his thread
who mended more & more till he was dead
But being gone, this only can be sayed
Honest Iohn Cobled→Cobler lyes heire vnderlayde:/

[I, 63v blank] *I, 64. Richard Corbett, An* Elegie *on the late* Lord William Haward *Baron of Effingham, dead* the tenth of December. *1615*

{64}

An Elegie upon the death of the
Late Lord Howard Baron of Effing=
=ham dead, the 10. Dec: 1615.

I did not know the lord, nor doe I striue
To win accesse, and grace with Lords aliue.
The dead, I serue: from whom nor faction, can
Moue mee nor fauour, nor a greater man
To whom no uice Commends me, no bribe sent
From whom no pennance warnes, nor portion spent
To these I dedicate as much of me
As I can spare from mine owne husbandrye
And till ghosts walke, as they weer wont to doe
I trade for some, and doe their errands too
But first I doe enquire, and am assur'd
what tryalls in their iourneyes they endur'd
what certenties of Hono^{r} *and of worth*
Their most uncertaine lifetimes haue brought forth.
And who so did least hurt, of this small store
He is my patron be hee rich, or poore.
First I will know of fame (after his peace
when flattery, and enuie both do cease)
who ruled his actions, vertue? or my lord?
did the whole man relye upon a word?
A badge, a title? or aboue all chance
seem'd hee as Ancient as his Cognizance?
What did hee? acts of mercy? and refraine
Oppression in himselfe, and in his trayne
was his essentiall table full as free
As boasts, and inuitations use to bee?
(where if his russet frend did chance to dine)
whither his satten man would fill him wine?
Did hee thinke periury as loud a sin
Himselfe forsworne as if his slaue had been?
did hee seeke regular pleasures? was he knowne
Iust husband to one wife, and shee his owne?
Did hee giue freely without pause, or doubt?
And read petitions ere they were worne out?
Or should his well deseruing client aske
would hee bestow a tilting, or a Masque
To keepe need vertuous and that done not feare
what lady damn'd him for his absence theire?

I, 64v

Did hee attend the court for no mans fall?
wore hee the ruine of no Hospitall?
And when hee did his rich apparrell don?
put hee no widdow, nor no orphan on?
did hee loue simply? vertue for the thing?
The king for no respect but for the king?
But aboue all, did his Religion waite
upon gods Throne? or on the chaire of state?
hee that is guilty of no quaere heere
Outlasts his Epitaph, outliues his heyre
But their is none such, none so litle bad
who but the negatiue vertues euer had
of such a lord we may expect the birth
hees rather in the wombe then in the earth
and ~~th~~ twere a crime in such a publique fate
For one to liue well, and degenerate./
and theirefore I am angry when a name
Comes to upbraid the world as Effingham
Nor was it modest in thee to depart
ere thy approach was ready, and to dye
ere custome had prepar'd thy calumny.
Eight dayes are past since thou hast paid thy debt
to sin and not a libell stirring yet
Courtiers (who scoffe by patent) silent sitte
And haue no use of slander, nor of witt.
But which is monstrous thought against the tide
The water=men haue neither rayl'd, nor lide
of good and bad theire no distinction knowne
for in thy praise the good, and bad are owne
it seemes wee all are couetous of Fame
And heire→heari^ngwhat a purchase of good name
Thou lately madest, are carefull to encrease
our litle by the holding of some lease
From thee our landlord, and theirefore the whole crew
speakes now like tenants ready to renew.
It were to sad to tell thy pedigree
Death hath disordered all misplacing thee
whilst now the Herauld ~~with~~in his line of heyres
Blots out thy name and fill the place with teares

I, 65

{65}

And thus hath cunning death or nature rather
Made thee praeposterous Ancient to thy father
who greiues hee is so: but like a glorious light
shines ore thy heart. He theirefore who^would ~~will~~ write
And blaze thee throughly may at once say all
Heere lyes the Anchor of the Admirall.

Let others write for glory, or reward
Truth is well paid when shee is sung and heard./

I, 65v. Anonymous, On the Duke of Richmonds fate an Elegie

On the Duke of Richmonds
fate an Elegie:/

It was the morne that ushered that blest day
whereon great Brittaines hopes and fortunes lay
which, heauen (enamored on this Isle) hath sent
To Auspicate one happy parliament
When, great with publique cares our sacred Herua
pleased to giue ishue to his mind minerua
In a solicitous muse as then hee sate
these faire conceptions how to propogate
A bird of night about his chamber flutters
And skriching thrice these fatall accents utters
The Duke is dead which Duke the amas'd king cryes
Indefinite feares doubling his Agonies
For thought in eithers fate hee should haue found
his Diademe missed a rich Diamond.
yet since that might (heauen knowes) haue been the man
that brought our hopes on shore, his Buckingham
whom equall fame doing faith, and vertue right
hath stil'd the Kings, and peoples fauorite
whose zeale to truth to strong to bee seduced
Blew up the mines of hell and thence reduced
Our loue led Thesus from the inchanting twines
of wealth and beauty Ro[mi]~~in~~es two Proserpines
It was a question primely pertinent
To know which Duke the rigid Herald meant
and thankes to heauen in euills so extreme
Theire were choise) death hath obseru'd a meane
Twas but the Neptune of the Northen maine
But, quoth the King, at whom sterne death made ayme
The Duke hath destin'd god and you to freind
To waft your Tropheis to the extreamest Inde
Your all admired Admirall suruiues
And Castors death, a Pollux life reuiues
Is this your meane the king replies in wroth
I lost in Richmond a rich world of worth
hee was to mee noe lesse then th'Articke pole
to heauen, hee bore the halfe up of my soule.

66 I, 66

{66}

Hee was to mee nearer in loue then blood
I stiled him great, but heauen Install'd him good
The solid councellor the steward Iust
the faithfull Patriott in him kisse the dust
Teste me ipso. and with that a spring
of pearly teares confus'd the Oceans King
And euery drop distill'd from sou^{r}aignes eyes
of vulgar teares doth Hecatombes comprise
Thinke there was cause for sorrow to goe deepe
when hee that ioyes all harts enioyes to weepe.
Thinke theire was cause greifes billowes should goe hight
when princely sighes fain'd tempests from the Skye
Thinke theire was cause to mourne. seen, and allow'd
when the uniuersall eye affects a cloud
when on a day of Ioy so generall
A Iubile so panted for of all
The king by such a sad adiournem^{t} somons
To fill the scene of sorrow. Peeres, and Commons
But harke me thinkes that Crittricke inquisition
the Parlam: of Paules (which by commission
Censures the occurrents of the time, whose witty
Speaker, and those other midle Isles committy
passe upon all the world) demands a reason
why Richmond disappear'd so out of Season
why such a prince the pillar of a state
should vanish and no starre denounce his fate
why leauing such fare fortunes undisposed
hee was so on the suddaine discomposed
why mute upon a day of parlaiment
why quitt such flesh being licensed to breake Lent
with many a curious why without a wherefore
to which I spare to shape an Answer theirefore
yet giue me leaue (a litle will suffice
Duke Humphryes' guest) to satisfy, some whyes
what need a commet brandish'd from the skie
indigitate a vertuous prince to dye
when blazing pride, and lustfull blandishment
are growne fixt stars in the court firmam^{t}
Twas Cesars wish a death free from deaths feares
Tis there rapt motion dignifies the spheares.

I, 66v

suppose his death precipitate. yet twere hard
To censure who liu'd well, who dy'd unprepar'd
Death is a Don that on aduantage lies
and glories in defeates giuen by surprize
Trust him not Princes: his false Ambuseadoes
haue prou'd more dangerous then his grand Armadoes
Had hee by faire assaults this prince assaid
Nature, and art had both reenforc'd their aid
Religion too the season being wholly
would haue dispacth for rescue many a volly
of feruent prayers: many a pale faced fast
and happely obtain'd some truce at last
Meane time twas happy since fate could not stay
Death hurried him to heauen the priuy way
hath hee the common rode of nature trod
and by dease been driuen to arriue ad→at god
Lord what a hell of torment, and temptation
must hee haue past during heauens visitation
heere emptie vissits, and frothy complements
clogging the soules winge in her passing hence
as if to condole, and congratulate
were all the essentialls of a great mans state
There sholes of Montebanks assuring ease
when hope lyes Iawfalne. and to earne theire fees
In th'article of death, and dissolusion
vexing the soule with fond irresolution
heire a learned lawyer with his knotty pate
distracts the mind to setle the estate
and yet be thinking after much a doe
hees sworne to the law leaues that unsetled too
Theire an unpensioned troope of fle‸w followers crying
To see theire vast hope in theire lords death dying
heire (Iudged to stale virginity) an heard
of chambermaides and women unpreferd
But of the Dutches spiritt of bitternesse
To haue seen her violate that golden tresse
which had so oft in blisse enchaind his eye
had been enought to haue maide him dye
his soule to hers in Adamantine ties
was linkt. and death that grand obseruer wise

I, 67

{67}

To cut a Gordion that hee could not loose
without exasperating both their woes
Thus what they witte call suddenly to dye
hee found the shortest cut to Eternitie
And for the season heauen could not haue sent
to mortifie the flesh more fit then Lent
A Parliamt that might redintegrate
The breaches Gondamur had trencht ith state
and rectifie the members which→with the head
was such a wisht that millions would haue blest
to effect it. Richmond seeing now this was
by heauens accomodation brought to passe
his Ioyes surcharg'd the spirit breakes forth and sings
A nunc demittis to the king of kings
heauen takes him at his word and so hee dyes
Ioy hath as well, as greife her Extasies
Thus what in him the world can most deplore
was a wisht rapture to the Elizian shore
They say it is found in Merlins leaues inrould
two English Dukes the senate could not hould
And seeing it so concernes the present state
that the one must their the affaires of spaine relate
and heauens decrees admit no alteration
the other undertooke this transmigration
To gratulate with Ioue the safe arriuing
of our long long'd for Prince from spanish wiuing
Oh may that match be crown'd with consum̄ation
when hee returnes from this negotiation. /

[I, 67v–69v blank]

DALHOUSIE II

II, 1. Anonymous [Patrick Maule?], Notations

Sett in the kitching gardine; the 28th of september
the year of our Lord 1622. {1}
Apricok stones three scor
of peich and neckteriens stones a hunderith
and four,

II, iv. Andrew Ramsay, Prayer

In my defenc god me defend and bring
my soull to ane good end guhen I am sick and
Lyk to ye father of heauens heauie mynd amene
andreae RAmsey Andrae RAmsey finis amene
god
seaue and defend thy |chosen| flok
floke which now

[II, 2r-v blank] *II, 3. Anonymous, My deare and onelie loue tak heede*

{3}

My deare and onelie loue tak heede, least fame a fault descry.
If thou now longing louers feede; vponne thy wandring eye
Noe Marble wall can hearts restraine wch truth and trust deceiue
If thyne steall out, myne stayes in paine, I loue and cannot leaue

If louers oathes shoute thorough thy heart, that maks noe breach in myne
Thy scaled walles pleades my desert, wch noe plottes vndermine
If my fire me not loue consume, though thine in smoake remoue
True vertue cannot corne→[torne] consume→[to sume], nor can I leave to loue

O lett thy vertue trueth prolong, which feares noe faults surprise
My loue shall man the wall. so stronge, too force the seadge to rise
But if the ruler rule so ill, a commonwealth too proue
Yet my scale shall keep the Monarch still, I cannot leaue to loue

If thy close fraud or open ~~powe~~r[thou] my wounded heart betray
Noe trumpet shall sound vp my woes, I'le silent march away
And foulde myne armes like ensignes vp.→vp[;] my colours none shall reaue
Though nevir more I tast thy Cupp[,] I loue and cannot leaue

I'le shune that cruell neroes name that burnt his Empires pryde
I will releiue thy broken fame[,] thy shame[none]shall [~~none~~] deride
Thy spiret pouer makes myne more braue, my skorne shall pitie proue
My teares my greues shall grace thy graue I cannot leaue to loue

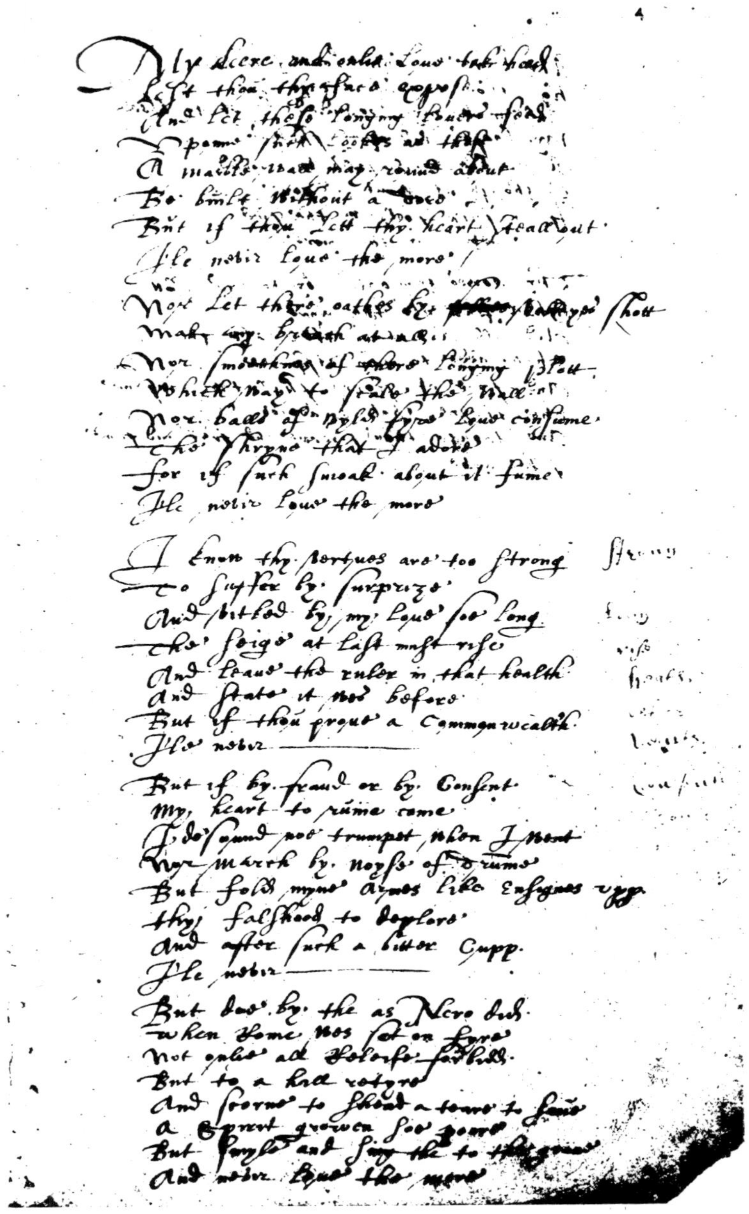

[II, 3v blank] *II, 4. Anonymous, My deere and onlie loue tak heed*

{4}

My deere and onlie loue tak heed
Lest thou thye face expose
And let these longing louers feed
Vponne such lookes as these
A marble wall may round about
Be built without a dore
But if thou lett thy heart steall out
I'le nevir loue the more/

Nor let there oathes by ~~follies~~ volleyes shott
Mak any breach at all
Nor smoothnes of there longing plott
Which way to scale the wall
Nor balls of wyld fyre loue consume
The shryne that I adore
for if such smoak about it fume
I'le nevir loue the more

I know thy vertues are too strong [strong]
To suffer by surprize
And vitled by my loue soe long [long]
The seige at last must rise [rise]
And leaue the ruler in that health [heath]
And state it wes before [befor]
But if thou proue a Commonwealth [wealth]
I'le nevir ____________

But if by fraud or by Consent [Consentt]
My heart to ruine come [come]
Ide sound noe trumpet when I went
Nor march by noyse of drum̃e
But fold myne Armes like Ensignes vpp.
thy falshood to deplore
And after such a bitter Cupp.
I'le nevir ____________

But doe by the as Nero did.
when Rome wes set on fyre
Not onlie all Releife forbidd.
But to a hill retyre
And scorne to shead a teare to saue
A Spirit growen soe poore
But smyle and sing the to the graue
And nevir loue the more

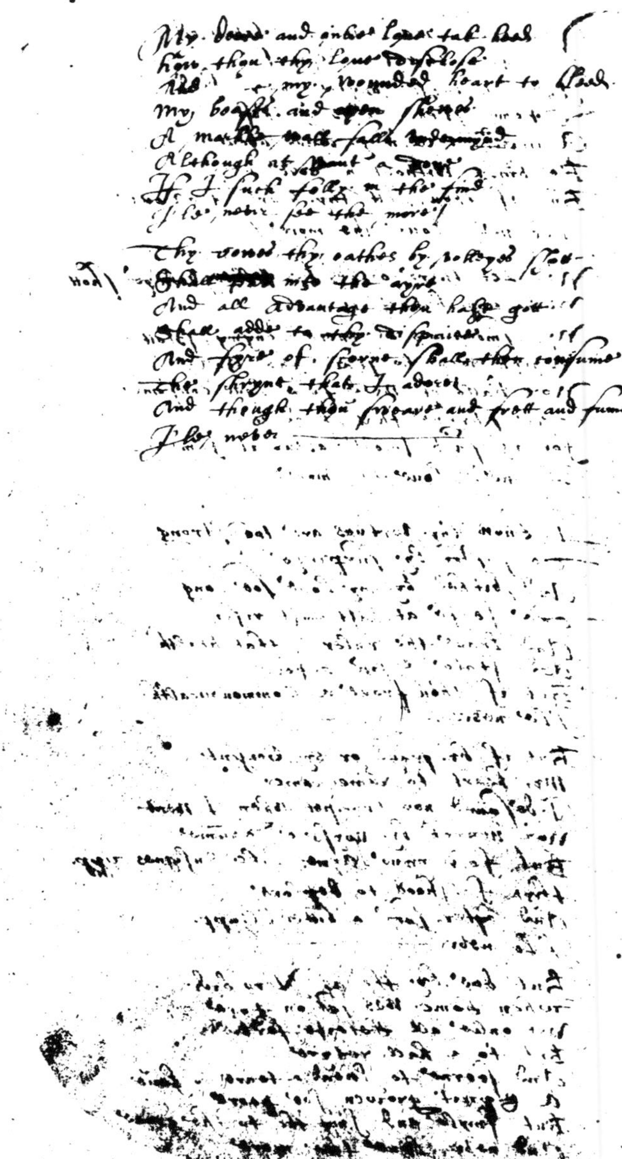

II, 4v. Anonymous, My deere and onlie loue tak heed

My deere and onlie loue tak heed
how thou thy loue disclose
And mak my wounded heart to bleed
My boasts and open shewes
A marble wall falls vndermynd
Although it want a dore
If I such folly in the find
I'le nevir see the more/

Thy vowes thy oathes by volleyes shott
Shall pas into the ayre
And all advantage thou hast gott
Shall adde to thy dispaire
And fyre of scorne shall then consume
The shryne that I adore
And though thou sweare and frett and fume
I'le nevir ____________

II, 5. John Donne, *Elegie: Loves Progress*

{5}

Who ever loues, if he doe not propose
The righte true endes of loue: He is one wch goes
To sea for nothinge but to make him sick
And loues a beare whelpe borne: if wee ouer lick
Our loue, and force new strange shapes to take
Wee err and of loue a monster make
Were not a calfe a monster, that were growne
facde like a man though better then his owne?
Perfec$\overline{\text{on}}$ is in vnitie: preferr
One woman first, and then one thinge in her
I when I vallew Gould may thinke vpon
The ductilnes, the Applica$\overline{\text{con}}$,
The wholesomnes, the Ingenuitie,
from rust from soyle from fire ever free:
But if I loue it tis because tis made
By our new *Naturs vse*, the soule of Trade.
All this in women we might thinke vpon,
(if women had them) but yet loue but one
Can men more Iniure women then to say
They loue them for that, by wch they are not they?
Maks vertue woman? Must I coole my blood
Till I both be, and finde one wise and good
May barren Angells loue soe: but if wee
Make love to woman virtue is not shee
As beautie is not nor welth: He that strange→stryes thus
from her to hers, noe more Adultrous
Then if he tooke her maide. search every spheare
And firmam^{t} o^{r} *Cupid* is not there:
Hees an Infernall Godes and vnder ground
Which→With *Pluto* dwells where Gould and fire
  aboundes
Men to such Godes theire sacraficeinge coales
Did not in Alters lay but pittes and hoales
Although we see *Celestyall* bodies moue
Aboue the earth; the earth wee till and love:
soe wee her Ayres contemplate; wordes and hart
[+] And virtues, but we love the *Centrique* part
Nor is the soule more worthie, or mor fitt
for love then this, as Infinit as it.

II, 5v

But in attaininge this desert place
How much they stray that sett out at face
The hayre a forrgst is of Ambushes
Of springes, snares, fetters, and Mannackles.
The brow becalmes vs when tis smouth and plaine
And when tis wrincled shipwrackes vs againe
Smouth tis A parradice where wee would have
Immortall stay and wrinck[l]ed is our grave.
The Nose like to the first Meridian
Not twixt an Easte and Weste, but twixt two sonnes.
It leaves A rosie cheeke *Hemispheare*
On either side, and then direct vs where
Vpon the Islandes fortunate we fall
(Not fainte *Canarie* but *Ambrosiall*)
Her swellinge lippes: to wch when we are com
Wee Anchor there, and thinkes or selves at home:
ffor they seeme all: There siren songe and there
wise *Delphigue* Oracles
Then in a creeke where chosen *Pearles* doe swell
The *Remora* her cleauinge tonge doeth dwell
These and the gloryous *Promontory* her
Orepast: and the straight *Hellesponte* betweene
The sestos and *Abidos* of her brestes
Not of two lovers, but two loues yr nestes
Sucseedes a boundles sea, but that thine Eie
Some Ieslandes Moles may scatteredes there discry
And saylinge towardes hir India, in that way.
Shall at her faire *Atlantique Nauell* stay.
though thence the currannt be thy Pilott made
Yet ere thou be where thou wouldst be imbayed
Thou shalt vpon another forrest sett
Where some doe shipwrack, and noe further gett
When thou art there consider what this chace
Mispent, by thy beginige at the fface
Rather sett out belowe, practice my Arte:
some *symetrie* the foote hath with that part
Wch thou doste seeke, and is the Mapp for that
louely enough to stop, but not stay at
Eeach subiect to disguise, and change yt is
Men say the Devell never can change his
It is the Embleme wch hath figured
ffirmenes: Tis the first pte that comes to beldl

II, 6

{6}

Ciuility we soe refindes, the kiss
W^{ch} at the face began trasplanted is
Since to the handes, since to the inperiall knee
Now at the papall foot delightes to be:
If kinges thinke that the neerer way and doe
kisse from the foote, lovers may doe soe too.
ffor as free spheares moue faster far then can
Birdes whome the ayre resites, soe may that man
W^{ch} goes this emptie and etheryall way,
Then if at beauties Elem^{tes} he stay
Rich Nature hath in woman wisely made
Two purses and there mouths auersly laid,
They then wch to the lover tribute owe,
That way wch that Exchequer lookes must goe:
Hee wch doth not, his Error is as greate
As who by *Clister* gave the stomache meate.

[II, 6v blank] *II, 7. Anonymous, If kinges did heretofore there loues indite*

{7}

[X]

If kinges did heretofore there loues indite
as they now personate, those kinges doe write,
Then why not I; by heaven he loved no~~t~~ more
then I doe thee, were he an Emperor:
well in extarnall toyes, he might expresse
In larger guiftes, and such like amplenesse
More then I can: but for that better part
the inward meani~~es~~^{nge} truely for a hart
that my Angellike M^{rs} thates the thinge
that in loves listes soundes greater then a kinge
and such is myne! knowest thou who I am
(   ) thy devouted servant princely dame
he that by wordes of mouth, at that blest shrinne
and moste angell ~~est~~ like portrature of thine
have offered vp soe many othe~~r~~s to moue
comes now by writinge to implore thy love
All his meanes left for never till I die
will I leave begginge love if you denie
doe not devinest buetie then make boaste
of holdinge for a tyme what must be loste
Tyme that does maister all, makes vassalls kinges
at laste orecomes e'ne the vnlikest thinges
thinke that→[w]hat delay hath bred alreadie love
and lett that thought my worthie M^{rs} moue
hadst thou when first of all, that I did woe thee
and truely proffered love and service to the
accepted them: I had not then been left
to this poore straight of writinge seldome spedinge shift
I had not then bene banished, the wch vse
and too much seene resortinge to thy house
at last procured for where they both consent
seldome does eye perceive or power prevent
for one still studyinge, for bringinge to passe
what dessignd lately by the other was
as pde→Ide imbrace the love, yet none should see
thou sendes me word, when such a tyme should be
wch then adventringe, wantinge thy love to instruct me
my passions often, did a misse conduckt me
Oh guide me yet, and though some tyme be loste
wele spend the pleasure cominge wth more coste
Each kisse weed had before anothers greetinge,
shall now be tripled, at our tymes of meetinges:
put case tis held that sometyme to denye
and not at first to grant is modestie
wch error may restraine my M^{rs} yet
all thinges, have limites feaire→fayre you knowe, then lett

II, 7v

You will have likewise limites too, and yeeld,
honor as much to him, that leaves the feild
ofte tymes belonges, as he that keepes it still
and bouldly bides the venture of all ill
It is not vnto our wills to constant be
but vnto reasone, thates the dignitie:
Reasone requires the loved, to love againe
retayninge worth still, you must love me than
And though the world perhaps may vainely tell
how I have here and there, and theire been ill:
and I grant it the more miraculus
My M^{rs} is, that can reduce me thus.
wthin her selfe, wch heretofore was led
and had desires all vnlimitted;
yet not miraculus to her: tis knowne
shee is each perfectyon in her selfe a lone
ffor he were vaine, weede say seekes dyuers fayres
when he in one may have all sortes of wayres
sutinge wth his desires: choyse and good,
witt spirritt, person, beautie fame, and blood,
All wch you are, and beeinge you are thus
you beeinge a lone enough are populus
I could deare M^{rs} never covitt more
you beeinge wth me I had women store
And soe could live, lockt vp, and never see
nor yet be seene of any onely thee
wth whome Ide spend more varyinge delightes
then freedome, and a broad suites appetites
would I desire orations to be made me!
speake thou and thousandes could not more pswaid me
or wish for musick doe thou onely singe
and never better, was expressed on a stringe
would I desire warres, what warres could be
more pleasinges then the combates had wth thee
Beleeve me fare, thou beinge once enioyed
there could be noethinge wantinge nothinge voyd,
wth me, wch now wantes all, ~~if~~ debarred of her
beeinge obtayned the worldes not ampler
I can but wonder much, that he whome lawes
hath tyed thee to; can spend in other cause
Then what is you; or prostitude himselfe
In the world else exposed worthlesse pelfe:
Sith if he did consider, or had sence
you are the extract, of all excellence:
or if he did consider or did knowe
and did apply himselfe vnto you beinge soe

II, 8

{8}

Then that you should haueinge that worthynesse
that you can discerne betweene the greate and lesse
and knowe the Treasure y^{t} your selfe contayne
too greate for one sole subiect to retaine
yet that you two beeinge parrallelld by none
should stricktly thus confine your selfe in one;
O thinke of that, perhaps you will reply,
why hees my husband S^{r}·/ and till he die
I must not love another. o vaine thinge
and from the wiues of owld, how differinge
he is your husband soe was his Mother too
wife to his ffather, aske what shee did doe
if shee had never loue, then have thou none
but ile assure the Deare that shee had one
And if shee thought shee well might chalinge two
what may my M^{rs} thinke then is her due
followe her steps, the answer will be good
to dash thy husband, if it be vnderstood
for it were vnfitt in sonnes to thinke of more
then what there ffathers mirritted before
deare my love do it tis nothinge by this Inke
besides the com̄on, and y^{e} world does thinke
That we are what, you may vnderstand me
let not deceive it, then so pray com̄end me

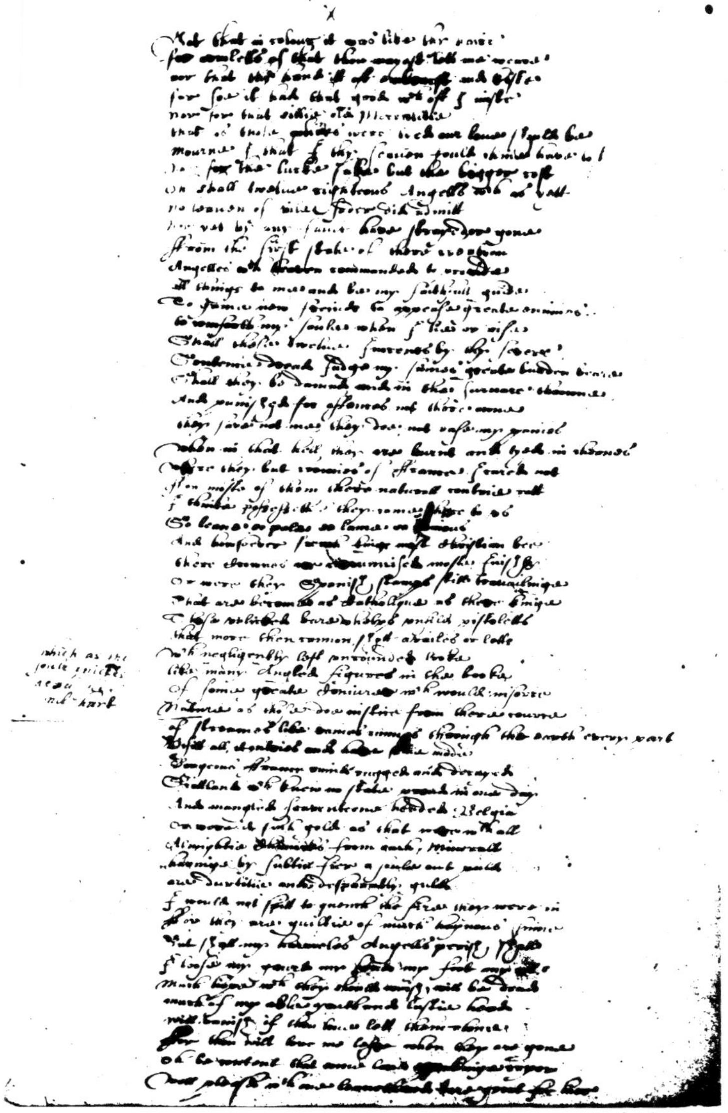

{9}

X

Not that in colour it was like thy haire
for armletts of that thou mayest lett me weare
nor that thy hand itt oft embrace→embrac~~e~~t and kiste
for soe it had that good wch oft I miste
nor for that sillie old Morralitie
that as those ~~p~~li^{n}nks were tyed our loue should be
Mourne I that I thy seauen fould chine have lost
Nor for the lucke sake but the bigger cost
Oh shall twelue righteous Angells wch as yett
No leauen of vile soder did admitt
Nor yet by any fault have strayed, or gone
ffrom the first state of there creatyon
Angelles wch heaven commanded to provide
all thinges to me and be my faithfull guide
To gaine new freindes to appease greate enimies
to comforth my soule when I lie or rise
Shall these twelue Inocents by thy severe
Sentence dread Iudge my sinnes greate burden beare
Shall they be damnd, and in the furnace throwne
And punished for offences not there owne
they save not me, they doe not ease my paines
When in that hell, they are burnt and tyed in cheanes
where→w[a]ere they but crownes of ffrance I cared not
ffor moste of them there naturall contrie rott
I thinke possesseth! they come [~~t~~]here to vs
So leane so pale so lame so [r]*‸[u]ainous
And howsoever french kinges most christian bee
there crownes are circumcised moste Iuishly
Or were they Spanish stamps still trauailinge
That are become as catholique as there kinge
Those vnlicked bare whelps vnfild pistoletts
that more then cannon shott availes or lettes
wch negligently left vnrounded looke
like many Angled figures in the booke
Of some greate coniurer wch would insorce
Nature as these doe iustice from there cource

which as the soule quickes head feet and hart

of streames like vaines runnes through the earth every part
Visitt all contries and have slilie made
Gorgeous ffrance ruined rugged and decayed
Scottland wch knew no state proud in one day
And mangled seaventeene headed Belgia
Or were it such gold as that we[a]re wthall
Almightie chimicks from each Minerall
havinge by subtill fier a soule out puld
are durtilie and desparatly guld
I would not spitt to quench the fire they were in
ffor they are guiltie of much haynous sinne
But shall my harmeles Angells perish shall
I loose my gaurd my head my foot my all?
Much hope wch they should norish will be dead
much of my able youth and lustie head
will vanish if thou loue lett them alone
ffor thou wilt love me lesse when they are gone
Oh be content that some loud speakinge→squakinge cryer
Well pleasd wth one leane thred bare groat for hier

II, 9v

May like a deuell rore through every street
and gall the fingers→finders conscience if he meet
Or lett me meete wth some dread coniurer
wch wth fantasticke Sceanes fills full much paper
W^{ch} haue deuided Heauen in tenementes
And wth whores theaues and Murtherers stuft his rentes
So full that though he passe them all in sinne
he leaues himselfe no roome to enter in
And if when all his art and tyme is spent
he say twill neere be found (oh be content
Receive from him the doome vngrudgingly
Because he is the mouth of destinye
Thou saist alas the gould doth still remaine
though it be chainged and put into a cheane
Soe in the first fallen Angells resteth still
Wisdome and knowledge but tis turned to ill
As these should doe good workes and should provide
Necessaties but now must nurse thy pride
And they still bad Angelles mine are none
ffor forme giues beeinge and there forme is gone
Pittie these Angells yet there dignities
passe vertues powers and principallities
But thou art resolute thy will be done
yet wth such anguish as her onely sonne
The Mother in the hungrie grave doth lay
vnto the frier these Martirs I betray
good soules for you give lite→li[f]e to every thinge
good Angelles for good messages you bringe
desdaind→des[t]ind you might have been to such a one
As would have loved and worshippt you alone
One wch would suffer hunger Nakednes
Yea death ere he would make your number lesse
[but I am gultie of your sade decay,]
{⊖} ‸May your fellowes wth me longer stay
But oh thou wreched finder whome I hate
So much that I almoste pittie thy estate
Gould beinge the heauiest mettell amongst all
May my moste heauie course vpon the fall
Here fettred manacled and hanged in cheanes
first maiste thou be then chaind to hellish paines
or be wth forraigne gould bribd to betray
thy conterie and faile boath of that and thy pay
May the next thinge thou stopot→sto$\overset{\circ}{\wedge}$pst to reach contayne
poyson whose nimble fume rott thy moyste brane
Or lybells or some interdicted thinge
wch negligently kept thy ruine bringe
Lust breedes deseases rott the, and dwell wth thee
If→I[tchie]~~thy~~ desire and noe abilletie
May all the hurt that ever gould hat[h] wrongt
All mischeifes wch all duells→d[i]u[i]lls ever thought
want after plentie poore, and goutie age
The plages of trauellers loue and Marriage
Afflict thee, and at thy liues last moment
May thy swolne sinnes themselves to the present
But I forgive repent thou honest man
gould is restorytive restore it then

II, *10*

Or if wth it thou beest loath to departe
Because tis cordiall would twere at thy hart

ffinis./

Sir John Davies, Unto that sparkling wit, that spirit of fire

X

Vnto that sparklinge witt that spirritt of fire
That diamond like aspeck, that eagles eie,
Whose lightninge makes audacitie retyere,
and yet drawes on respective modestie,
wth winges of feare and loue my spiritt, doth flye
and doth therein a flame of fire resemble
wch when it burnes moste bright, and mountes moste high
then doth it wauer moste, and moste doth tremble
Oh that my thoughtes were wordes: o could I speake
the tonge of Angells to expresse my mynde,
ffor mortall speach is far too faint and weake
to vtter passions of soe high a kinde
You haue a beautie of such life and light,
as it hath power all wandringe eies to stay
to moue dome thoughtes to speake, lame handes to write,
stayed thoughtes to runne, hard hartes to melt away,
Yet painters can of this drawe every lyme→lyne,
and every wittles person that hath eies,
can see and Iudge and sweare it is deuine
for in those outward formes all fooles are wise;
But that wth my admireinge sperritt doth vieue
in thought whereof it would for ever dwell
Eie never sawe the pensell never drue
pen never could describe tonge never tell
It is the inuisable beautie of your mynde
your cleare Imagination lively witt
so tund so temperate→tempored of such heavenly kinde
as all men['s] spirrittes are charmed and rapt wth it./
this life w^th^in begettes your liuely looke
as fire doth make all mettles like→lo^o^ke like fire,
or your quick soule, by choyce this bodie tooke,
as Angells wth bright beames themselves attire
o that my brest might ope, and hart might cleave,
that soe you might my silent wondringe viewe
o that you could my servinge spirritt perceive
how still wth trimblinge winges it wates on you
then should you see ^of thoughtes^ ~~how youres~~ and endlesse chaine
whose linkes your beauties and your vertues be
then should you see how your fare forme doth raine→raigne
through all the regions of my phantasie
then should you finde that, I am yo^rs^ as much
as are your quicke conceites, borrowed of none
or as your nature→natiue beautie wch is such
as all the world will sweare it is your owne

{11}

The Cursse

X

Who ever guesses, thinkes, or dreames he knowes
who is my M^{rs}, whither by this Cursse
his onely and ^[onely] his ~~onely~~ purpose→[purs]
may some dull hart to loue dispose
And shee yeeld then to all that are his foes
^May he be scorned by one, whome all ~~else~~[men] scorne
forsweare~~wthfeare~~^of~~and~~ missinge, shame of gettinge torne

for sweare to others what to her he hath sworne^

Madnesse his sorrowe, goute his crampe may he
make, by but thinkinge who hath made him such
and may he feele noe tuch
of contyence→con[c]yence, but of fame, & be,
Anguished, not that twas sinne, but that twas shee
in earely scarcenesse, and longe may he rott
for land, wch had been his, if he had not
himselfe incestuouslie an heire begott

May he dreame treason, and beleeve that he
ment to performe it, and confesse, and die
And noe record tell why
his sonnes wch none of his may be
Inhirrett noethinge but his infamie
or may^he so longe parasites haue fed
that he would faine be theires, whome he hath bred
and at the last he→[b]e cercumcisd for bread

The venin of owld stepdames, gamsters gall
what tyrantes and there subiectes interwish
what ~~plantes~~,[hearbs] myne[s], beastes, foule, fish,
Can ~~subi~~ contribute, all ill wth→wch all
prophetes, or poetes speake and all w^{ch} ~~all~~ shall
be anexd in scedules vnto this by [the]~~ty~~^me
fall on that man, for if it be a shee
nature before hand, hath out cursed me

II, 11v. John Donne, The Message

Song

[X] Send home my longe strayed eies to me[e]
wch oh! too longe have dwelt on the[e]
yett since there they have learned such ill
such forcd fassions
and false passions
that they be[e]
made by thee
fitt for noe good sight keepe them still

Send home my harmlesse hart againe
wch noe vnworthy thought could staine
wch if it be taught by thyne
to make Iestinges
of protestinges
and crosse both
word and oath
keepe it, for then tis none of myne

Yet send me back my hart and eies
that I may~~might~~ knowe and see thy lyes
and may laugh when that thou
art in anguishe
and dost languish
for some one
that will none
or proue as false as thou art now[e]

II, 12. Anonymous, A Paradoxe of a Painted Face

{12}

[X]

Not kisse? by loue I must and make Impression
As longe as Cupid dares to hold his Session
vpon my flush of blood our kisses shall
out minitt tyme and wthout number fall
doe not I knowe those balls of blushinges redd
that on thy cheekes thus Amoruslye are spred
Thy snowey neck those vaines vpon thy browe
wch wth there Azur'd wrinklings sweely bowe
Ar artefull borrowed and noe more tyine→t[h]ine owne
then cheanes that ~~are~~ on St Georges daie are showne
are proper to the wearers, yet for this
I Idoll the and begge a luscious kisse
The fucus and cerusse wch on thy face
thy cunninge hand layes on to ad more grace
deceaue me wth such pleaseinge fraud that I
finde in thy art what can in nature lye
Much like a painter that vpon some wall
on wch the cadent Sunne beames vse to fall
Paintes wth such art a guilded butter flye
that sillie mades wth slowe moued fingers trye
to catch it and then blush at there mistake
yet at this painted flye moste reckoninge make.
such is our state sence what wee looke vpon
Is nought but color, and proportyon
Take me a face as full of fraud and lyes
as Gipseyes, or your runinge lotteries
That is more false and more Sophisticute
then are S$^{t[s]}$ Reliques or a man of state
Yet such beeinge glazed by the slight of art
Gaine Admiracon won in many a hart
Put case therebe a difference in the mould
Yet may thy venus be more choyse and hold
A deearer treasure, Often tymes we see
Rich, Cundian vines in wodden bowles to bee
The Odiriferous. Ciuett doth not lie
Wthin the Muske Cattes nose or eare or eie
But in a baser place, for prudent Nature
In drawinge vp of varyous formes and feature
gives from the curyous shopp of her large treasure
The fayre partes comlynes to beaser pleasure
The fairest flowers wch on the springe doe growe
Are noe→no[t] soe much for vse as for the showe
The lillies Hiacinth and gorgeous birth
Of all pi'dd flowers wch diaper the earth
please more wth there discouloured purple traine
then wholesome potthearbs wch for vse remaine
Shall I a gaudie speckled serpent kisse
for that the color w^{ch} ~~is~~ he beares is his
A perfumed Cordiuant who will not weare
Because the sent is borrowed other where

II, 12v

The Roubes and vestimentes wch grace vs all
ard→are not our owne but aduentitiall.
Tyme ryfles natures beautie but slye art
repayers by cunninge this decayed part
ffills here a wrinkle and there purles a vaine
And wth a nimble hand runnes or againe
The breaches dinted in by the arme of tyme
and ‸[makes]deformatie to be noe crime
As when greate men are gript by sicknesse handes
Industrious Phisick pregnatly doth stand
to pach vp fowle deases and doth strive
To keepe there rotton carcasses alive
beautie a candle is, wch every puffe
blowes out and leaues nought but a stinking snuffe
To fill our nostrells wth! this bouldly thinke
the purest candle makes the greatest stinke
As your pure food and chariest nutriment
‸getes the most hott and nosestronge excrement
Why hange we then on thinges so apt to vary
Soe flittinge brittle and so temporary
that Agewes Coughs the toothach and Catharre
Slight touches of deseases spoyle and marre
But when old age there beatie hath in chase
and plowes vp forrowes in there once smooth face
They then become forsaken and doe showe
Like stately Abbyes ruind longe a goe
Nature but gives the Moddell and first draught
of faire perfectyon wch by art is taught
To speake it selfe a compleate forme and birth
So standes a coppie to the shaps on earth
Loue grant me then a repairable face
Wch whiles that colours are can want noe grace
Pigmalions painted statur[i]e I could love
Were it but warme and soft and could ~~not~~‸[but] moue./

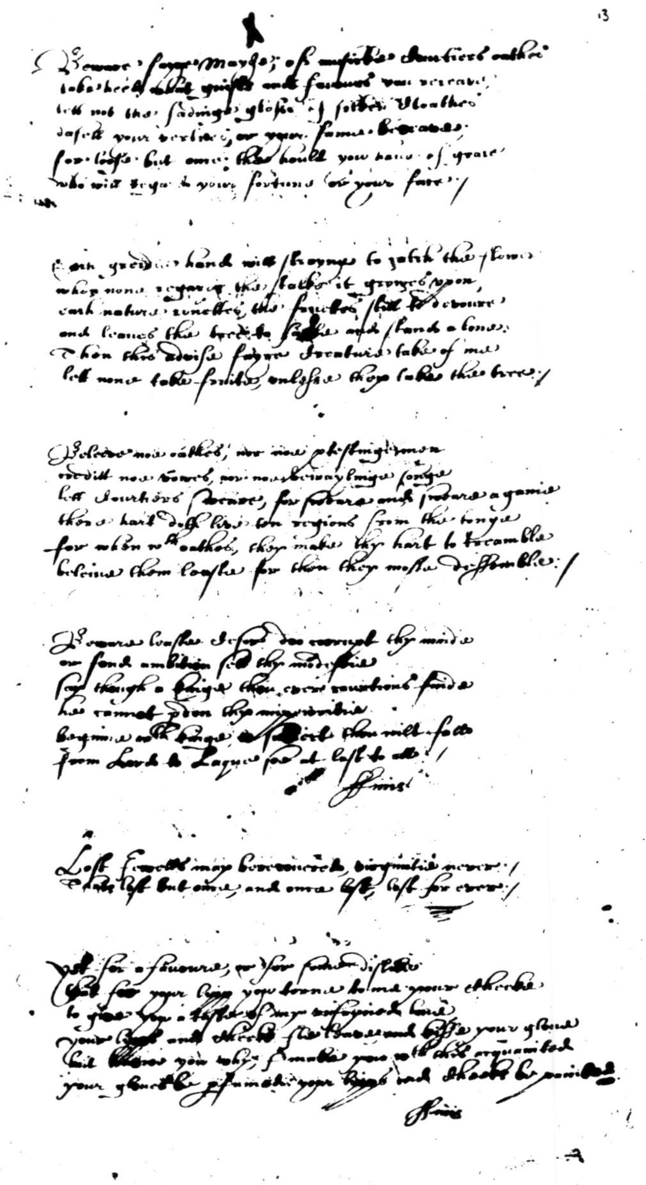

II, 13. Josuah Sylvester, A Caution for Courtly Damsels

{13}

[X]

Beware fayre Mayde; of musicke courtiers oathes
take heed what guiftes and fauours you receave,
lett not the fadinge glosse, of silken cloathes
dasell your vertues, or your fame bereave;
for loose but once the hould you haue of grace
Who will regard your fortune or your face./

Each greidie hand will strayne to catch the flower
when none regardes the stalke it growes vpon,
each nature couettes, the fruettes still to devoure
and leaues the tree to faule→falle and stand alone.
Then this advise fayre creature take of me
lett none take fruite, vnlesse they take the tree:/

Beleeve noe oathes, nor noe p̱testinge men
creditt noe vowes, nor noe bewaylinge songe
lett courtiers sweare, for sweare and sweare againe
there hart doth live ten regions from the tonge
for when wth oathes, they make thy hart to treamble
beleiue them leaste for then they moste dessemble:/

Beware leaste Cesor doo corrupt thy minde
or fond ambition sell thy modestie
say though a kinge thou ever courtious finde
he cannot p̱don thy impewritie
beginne wth kinge, to subiect thou wilt fall
from Lord to Laque soe at last to all:/

ffinis

Anonymous, On a Maiden-head

Lost Iewells may be recouered, virginitie never:/
Thates lost but once, and once lost, lost for ever:/

Sir John Harington, Of a Lady that giues the cheek

Yst for a fauoure, or for some dislike
that for your lipp you torne to me your cheeke
to give you a taste of my vnfayned loue,
your lipps and cheekes Ile leave, and kisse your gloue
but knowe you why, I make you wth this acquainted
your gloues be p̱fumed: your lipps and cheekes be painted

ffinis

II, 13v. Jonathan Richards, a songe: "I die when as I doe not see"

A songe

I die when as I doe not see
her who is life and all to me
[X] and when I see her yett I die
in seeinge of her cruelltie:
So that to me like miserie is wrought
boath when I see, and when I see her not→no[ught]
or shall I speake, or silent crave→[g]r[ee]ve
but hou can silence then releeve
And if I speake I may offend
and speakeinge not my hart will rend
so that to me I see it is all one
speake I, or speake[‸I]not: I am vndone:/

Anonymous, Onste and no more, so sayd my loue

Onste and no more, so sayd my loue
When in my armes inchayned,
shee vnto me her lips did move
and soe my hart, shee gayned:

Adue shee said, be gone I muste
for feare of beeinge missed
Your hant puttes over, but in trust
and soe againe shee kissed

Anonymous, ffor a louinge constant hart

ffor a louinge constant hart
my reward is greefe and smart
shee that kills me wth disdayne
takes a pleasure in my paine

I adore her eies whose lighte
cause ites seene vnto my sight
makes her see her selfe moste faire
makes her prowde, makes me dispare.

She whome I held the onely rare
Is the causer of my care
of my cares and teares whose showers
moves not her yet quicknes flowers

Dayes and Nightes my woes improue
whilst I languish for her loue
Whilst her hart wth rigors fraught
scorninge settes my loue at naught

II, 14. Anonymous, A songe: "When my hart seemes moste ingaged"

{14}

[X] A songe

When my hart seemes moste ingaged
my loue lastes but for a day
foolish birdes that wilbe caged
haueinge meanes to fly away
Loue hath winges and loues to range
I loue those that loue to change

One to hold and catth at many
none to trust but all to prove
to courte all not care for any
is the wisest course of loue
Loue hath: &c

Age affecttes a reputation
of a sober steddie mind,
youth is in the youthfull fassion
when it wavers like the winde
Loue hath: &c

Constancie so highly prised
makes a man a slaue to one
they are free and well advised
who in louinge all loues none
Loue hath: &c

What are they soe much commended
for a constant louinge hart
children, cowardes, ill befrended
fooles vnskilled in louers arte
Loue hath: &c

You that heare my free profession
and thinke I doe the world belye
try and make a true confession
you will say as well as I.
Loue hath winges and loues to range
I loue those that loues to change

[II, 14v blank] *II, 15. John Donne, Elegie: The Perfume*

{15}

Elegia 3.

Once and but once found in thy company
All thy supposed escapes are laid on me
And as a Thiefe att Barr is questioned there
By all the men that have beene robd that yeare
So am I (by this traterous meanes supprised)
By thy *Hidroptique* father catechisde
Though he had woont to search with glazed eies
As though he came to kill a *Cocatrice*
Though he have ofte sworne that he would remooue
Thy beauties beautie and food of [of]^{or} loue
Hope of his goodes; if I wth thee were seene
Yet close and secrett as our soules wee have beene
Though thy ymmortall Mother wch doth lie
Still buryed in her bedd yet will not die
Take this advantage to sleepe out day light
And watch thy entries and returnes all night
And when shee takes thy hand and would seeme kinde
Doth search what Ringes and Armelettes shee can finde
And kissinge notes the colour of thy face
And feareinge leaste thou arte swolne doth thee imbrace
And to try if thou longe doth name strange meates
And notes thy palenes, blushinges, sightes→sighes and sweates
And politiquely will vnto thee confesse
The sinnes of her owne youths rancke lustinesse
Yet loue these sorcerers did remooue and mooue
Thee to gull thy Mother for my loue
Thy little Bretheren wch like fairy spirittes
Oft skipt into our chamber those sweete nightes
And kist and ingled on thy ffathers knee
Were bribd next day to tell what they did see
The *Grim* eight=foot=high Ironbound=seruingman
That oft names god in Oathes and onely then
He that to barr the first gate doth as wide
As the greate *Rhodian Colossus* stride
Which if in *Hell* noe other paines there were
Makes me feare *Hell* because he must be there
Though by thy ffather he were hired for this
Could never wittnesse, any touch or kisse
But of two common Ill: I brought wth me
That wch betrayed me to myne enimie
A lowd perfume wch at myne entrance cried
Even at thy ffathers nose soe wee were spide
When like a Tirant Kinge that in his bedd
Smelt Gunnpowder the pale wrech shivered
Had it been some bad smell he would have thought
That his owne feet or breath that smell hat wrought
But as wee in our Ile impresoned
Where cattell onely and diuers dodgges are bred
The pretious Vnycornes strainge monsters call
Soe thought he good, strange, thad had none att all
I taught my silkes there whistlinges to forbeare
Even my opprest shoes dumbe and speachles were

II, 15v

Onely thou bitter sweet whome I had laid
Next mee, me, traiterously haste betrayed
And vnsuspected haste invisiblie
Att once fled vnto him and stayed wth me
Basse excrement of earth wch doste confound
Scence from distinguishinge the sick from sound
By thee, the seelie Amorous suckes his death
by drawinge in a leaprous harlottes breath
By thee, the greatest staine to manes estate
ffalls on vs to be called effeminate
Though thou be much loued in the *Princes Hall*
There thinges that seeme exceed substantiall
Godes when yee fum'd on *Altars* were pleased well
Because you were burnt not that they liked your smell
You are loathsome all beeinge taken simple alone
Shall wee loue all thinges ioyned and hate each one
If you were good your good doth soone decay
And you are rare that takes the good away
All my perfumes I give moste willingly
To embalme thy ffathers coarse! what will he die

ffinis

{16}

Eligia. 4.

Although thy hand and faith and good workes too
Haue sealed thy loue wch noethinge should vndoe
Yea though thou fall back~~st~~ thatst *postasie*
Confirmes thy loue yett much in much I feare thee
Women are like the Arts. forcd vnto none
Open to all searchers vnprized if vnknowne
If I have caught a bird and lett him flie
Another fowler seeinge those meanes as I
May cath the same bird and as those thinges be
Women are made for man not him nor mee
Foxes and *Goates* all beastes change when they please
Shall women more hott wilie wild then these
Be bound to one man and did nature then
Idlely make them apter to endure then men
They are our clogges not there owne if a man be
Chained to a *Galley* yet the *Galley* is free
Who hath a plowed land castes all his seed corne there
And yet allowes his grownd more corne should beare
Though *Danrvy* into the sea must flowe
The sea receaues *Rhene Volga* and *Poe*
By nature wch gave it this libertie
Thou lou'st but oh canst thou loue it and me
Likenesse glewes Loue then if soe thou doe
To make vs like and loue must I change too.
More then thy hate I hate it rather lett me
Allowe her change then change oftener then shee
And soe not teach but force my opinion
To loue not any one nor every one
To live in one land is captiuitie
To runn all cuntryes a wild *Roguery*
Waters stinkes seone→ssone if in one place they bide
And in the vast sea are worse putrified
But when they kisse one banke and leauinge this
Then are they purest change is the ioy and misery
Of musique life ioy and eternitie

ffinis

II, 16v. John Donne, Elegie: Loves Warre

Eligia. 5.

When I have peace wth thee warr other men
And when I have peace can I leave thee then
All other Warrs are scrupulous onely thou
O faire free cittie maist thy selfe allowe
To any one In *fflannders* who can tell
Whither the Maister presse or men rebell
Onely wee knowe not wch all Idiottes say
They beare moste blowes that comes to parte the fray
ffrance in her Lunatique giddines did hate
Ever our men and our God of late
Yet shee relyes vpon [our] *Angell* well
W^{ch} neere returne noe more then they wch fell
Sick Ireland is wth a stronge warr possest
Like to an *Ague* nowe rageinge now at rest
W^{ch} tyme will cure yet it must doe her good
If shee weere purgd and her head vaine lett blood
And *Midas* Ioyes our spanish Iourneyes gives
We touch all gould but finde noe foud to live
And I should be in that hott parchinge clime
To dust and ashes turned before my tyme
To mewe me in a shipp is to enthrall
Me in preson that were like to fall
Or in a *Cloyster* save that there men dwell
In a calme hauen here in a swaggeringe hell
Longe voyages are longe consumptyons
And shipps are cartes for Executyons
Yea they are deaths is't not all one to fly
Into another world as tis to die
Heere lett me warr in these armes lett me lye
Heere lett me parlie. better bleed and die
Thine armes Impresone me and my armes thee
Thy hart thy ransome is, take myne from me
Other men warr that they there rest may gaine
But wee will rest that wee may fight againe
Those warres the Ignorant these the experience loue
That wee are alwayes vnder her aboue
There engines farr of breed a iust true feare
Neere thrustes pikes stabbes Yea ene bullettes hurt noe neere
Theire lies are wronges here safe vprightly lie
There men kill men! weele make one by and by
Thou nothinge I not halfe soe much shall doe
In those warres as those may wch from vs two
Shall springe! Thousandes wee see trauaile not
To warres but stay swordes armes and shott
To make at home And shall not I doe then
More gloryous seruice to make men

ffinis

{17}

Elegia: 6.

Come Maddame come all rest my powers defie
vntill I labour I in labour[,] lie
The foe oftymes hauinge the foe in sight
Is tyred wth standinge though they never fight
Of wth that girdle like heauens *zones* glistringe
But a farr fairer world encompassinge
vnpin that spangled brestplate wch you weare
That thee eies of busie fobles may be stopt there
vnlase your selfe for that *harmonious* chim
Tells me from you that nowe is your bedd tyme
Of wth that happie buske whome I envie
That still can bee and still can stand so nigh
Your gownes goeinge of such beautyous state reveales
As when from flowr~~e~~y *Meades* the *Hill* shadowe steales
Of with your wearie coronett and showe
The harie diadem wch on you doth growe
Now of wth those shoes and then softly tread
In this loues *hallowed Temple* this soft bedd
In such white Robes heauens *Angells* vse to bee
Received by men: Thou'*Angells*: bringst wth thee
A heauen like *Mahametts* paradise And though
Ill spirrittes walk in whide wee easely knowe
By this those *Angelles* from an evill spiright
They sett our haires but these the flesh vpright
Licence my rouainge handes and lett them goe
Behinde. before. betweene. aboue, belowe:
O my *America* my new found land
My kingdome safe when wth one man mand
My *mine* of Pretyous stones my *Emperie*
How blest am I in thus discoueringe thee
To enter in these bondes is to be free
Then were→[wher]e my hand is sett my seale shall bee
full Nakednes. all Ioyes are due to thee
As soules vnbodied bodies vncloathe must be
To taste whole Ioyes. *Iems* wch you women vse
Are as *Atlantaes Balles* cast in mens viewes
That when a soules eie lighteth on a *Gemm*
His earthly soule may couett theires ‸not~~on~~ them
Like Pictoures or like bookes gay coueringes made
for lay men are all women thus arayed
Themselves are *Mistique* bookes wch onely wee
Whome their impa[r]ted *grace* will dignifie
Must be reueald Then since I may knowe
As liberally: as to a Middwife showe
Thy self cast all yea this white linnen hence
Here is noe *Pennannce* much lesse Innocence
To teach thee I am naked first why then
What needest thou haue more coueringe then a man./

ffinis

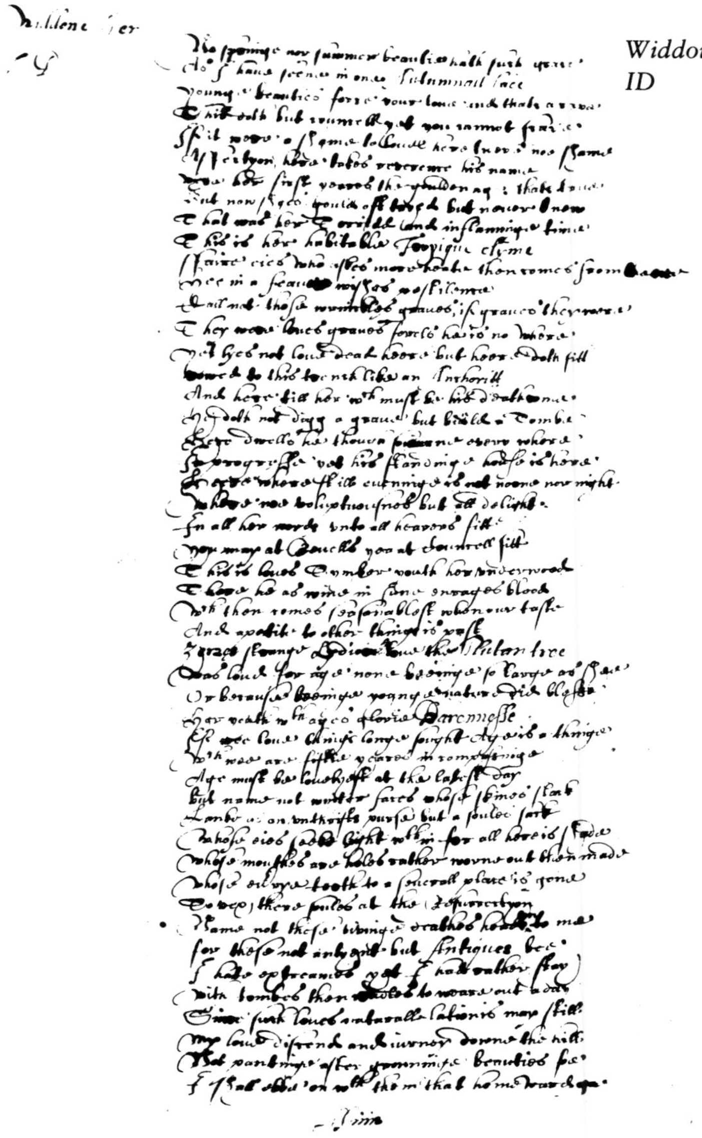

II, *17v. John Donne, The Autumnall*

Widdowe Her ID

No springe nor summer beautie hath such grace
As I haue seene in one *Autumnall face*
Younge beauties force your loue and thates a rape
This doth but councell yet you cannot scape
If it were a shame to loue here twere noe shame
Affectyon here takes reverence his name
Where her first yeares the goulden age? thates true
But now shees gould oft tryed but neuer ŧ new
That was her Torridd and inflaminge time
This is her habitable *Tropique clyme*
ffaire eies who askes more heate then comes from theere→hence
Hee in a feauer wishes pestilence
Call not those wrinckles graues, if graues they were
They were loues graues forels he is no where
Yet lyes not loue dead heere but heere doth sitt
vowed to this trench like an *Anchoritt*
And here till her wch must be his death come
He doth not digg a graue but build a Tombe
Here dwells he though soiourne every where
In progresse yet his standinge house is here
Heere where still eueninge is not noone nor night
Where noe voluptuousnes but all delight
In all her wordes vnto all hearers fitt
You may at Reuells yea at Councell sitt
This is loues Tymber youth her vnderwood
There he as wine in Iune enrages blood
W^{ch} then comes seasonablest when our taste
And apetite to other thinges is past
Zerzes strange Lydion loue the *Plutan tree*
Was loud for age none beeinge so large as shee
Or because beeinge younge nature did blesse
Her youth wth ages glorie *Barennesse*
If wee loue thinges longe sought Age is a thinge
W^{ch} wee are fiftie yeares in compassinge
Age must be louelyest at the latest day
but name not winter faces whose skines slack
Lanke as an vnthriftes purse but a soules sack
Whose eies seeke light wthin for all here is shade
Whose mouthes are holes rather worne out then made
Whose eu^{er}rye tooth to a seuerall place is gone
To vex there soules at the Resurrectyon
Name not these livinge deathes heads y^{n}to me
for these not antyent but *Antiques* bee
I hate extreames yet I had rather stay
With tombes then cradles to weare out a day
Since such loues natarall lation is may still
My loue discend and iurney downe the hill
Not pantinge after growninge beauties foe
I shall ebbe on wth them that homeward goe

ffinis

II, 18. John Donne, *The Storme*

{18}

A Storme

Thou wch art I (tis nothing to be soe
Thou wch arte thy selfe by these ~~thou~~ shalt knowe
Parte of our passage and a hand or eie
By *Hilliard* drawne is worth an history
By a worse painter made; And wthout pride
When by thy Iudgment they are dignyfied
My lynes are such tis the Preheminence
Of freindshipp onely to impute Excellence
England, to whome we owe what wee be and have
that her sonnes should seeke a foraigne grave
ffor fates or fortunes driftes none can sooth say
Honour and misery have one face and way
ffrom out her pregnant entrailes sighd ~~and~~ wind
W^{ch} at the ayers middle=marble-roome did find
Such stronge resistance that it selfe it threwe
Downeward againe and soe when it did viewe
How in the port or fleet deare tyme did lease
Witheringe like Prisoners wch lye but for fees
Myldly it kist our sayles and fresh and sweet
As to a stomake starv'd whose insides meetes
Meate comes, itt came, and swole our sailes when wee
Soe Ioyd as, *Sara her swellinge* ioyd to see
But twas soe kinde as our cuntrymen
W^{ch} bringe freindes one dayes way and leave them then
Then like two Mightie kinges ~~he~~ wch dwellinge farr
a sunder, meete against a third to warr
The *South* and *West* windes ioynd and as they blew
Wayues→[Wa]ues like a kowlinge→Rowlinge Trench before
them threwe
Sooner then you read this lyne did the gale
Like shott not feard till felt our sayles assaile
And what at feirst was calld a gust the same
Hath now a stormes, anon a *Tempests* name
Ionas I pittie thee and curse those men
Who when the storme raiged moste did wake the then
Sleepe is paines easiest salue and doth fullfill
All officies of death except to kill
But when I wak'd I saw: that I saw not
I and the sunne wch should teach me had forgott
East, *West*, *Day Night* and I could but say
If the world had ~~but~~ lasted now it had been day
Thousandes our noises weer yet wee amongst all
Could none by his right ~~hand~~ name but *Thunder call*
Lightninge was all our light and it rained more
Then if the *Sunne* had dranck the sea before
Some cofind in theire cabins lie! *Equallie*
Greeud that they are not dead and yett must die
And as sin burthened soules from graues will creepe
Att the last day some foorth there cabbins peepe
And tremblingly aske newes and doe heare soe
Like *Iealious Husbands* what they would not knowe
Some sittinge on the Hatches would seeme there
Wth *Hidious* gazinge to feare away feare

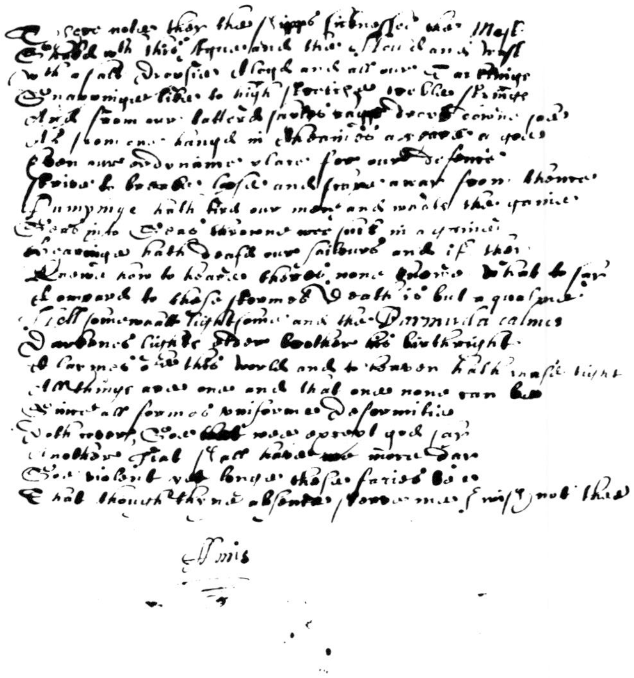

II, 18v

There note they the shipps sicknesses the Mast
Shakd wth this *Ague* and the *Hould* and wast
Wth a salt dropsie clogd and all our Tacklinges
Snappinge like to high stretche treble stringes
And from our tatterd sayles ragges drops→dropp downe soe
As from one hangd in cheaines a yeare a goe
Even our ordynance place for our defence
strive to breake loose and scape away from thence
Pumpinge hath tird our men and whates the gaine
Seas into Seas throwne wee suck in againe
Hearinge hath deafd our sailours and if they
Knewe how to heare theres none knewe what to say
Compard to these stormes Death is but a qualme
Hell somewhatt lightsome and the *Barmuda calmes*
Darkenes lightes elder brother his birthright
Claymes ore this world and to heaven hath chas'd light
All thinges are one and that one none can be
Since all formes vniforme deformitie
Doth cover, Soe that wee except god say
Another Fiat shall have noe more day
Soe violent yet longe these faries bee
That though thyne absence sterve me I wish not thee

ffinis

II, 19. *John Donne, The Calme*

{19}

A Calme

Our storme is past and that stormes tirannous rage
A stupid calme but noethinge it doth swage
The fable is inverted and farr more
A blocke afflictes now then a stock before
Stormes chafe and soone were out themselves or vs
In Calmes *Heaven* laughes to see vs languish thus
As steddie as I can wish that my thoughtes were
Smooth as thy Mistres glasse or what shines there
The sea is now And as those Tsles→Isles wch you→[wee]
Seeke when we can moove our shipps rooted bee
As water did in stormes now pitch runnes out
As lead when a fird church becomes one spout
And all our beautie and our traine decayes
Like courtes remooving or like ended playes
The fightinge place now seamens ragges supplie
And all the Tacklinge is but *Frippery*
Noe vse of Lanchornes→Lan[t]hornes and in one place lay
ffeathers and dust to day and yesterday
Earths hollownes wch the worldes lunges are
Have noe more wind then the vpper valt of th'ayre
Wee can nor left ffreindes nor sought foes recouer
But Meteortie→Meteorlike save that wee moove not hone
Onely the Calenture together drawes
Deere freindes wch meet dead in great fishes iawes
And on the haches as on Alters lyes
Each one his owne Preist and owne sacrafice
Who live that Miracle doe Multyplie
Where walkers in hott Ouens doe not lye
If in dispite of this we swimm that hath
Noe more refreshinge then the *Brimstone Bath*
But from the sea into the shipp we turne
Like pareboyld wretches on the coales doe→to burne
Like *Baiazet* encagd the shepheardes scoffe
Or like slack sinewed *Sampson* his haire of
Languish or→o[ur] shipps Now as a *Miriade*
Of Antes durst the Emperours lou'd snake invaide
The crawlinge Galleyes sea goates ffinny chipps
Might brave our *Venices* now beddridd shipps
Whether a rotten state or hope of gaine
Or to dessuse me from the qu'esy paine
Of beeinge beloud; and louinge, or the thirst
Of honour or ~~f~~fraire death out past→p[u]s[h'‸d] me first
I loose my end for heere as well as I
A desperate may live and a coward die
Stagge dogge and all wch from or towardes flyes
Is paid wth life or pray or doeinge dies
ffate grudgeth vs all and doth subtilie lay
A scourge against wch wee all forgett to pray
He that at sea prayes for more wind may as well
Vnder the Poules begg cold or heate in *Hell*
What are we then, how little more alasse
As→Is man now then before he was he was
Nothinge for vs we are for noethinge fitt
Chance or ~~ever~~‸[our] selues still disproportyon itt
We have noe will noe power noe sence; I lie
I should not then ‸thusfeele this misery. / *ffinis*

II, 19v. John Donne, To Mr. Rowland Woodward: *"Like one who'in her third widdowhood"*

Like one who in her third widdowhood doth professe
Her selfe a Nunn tir'd to a retirednesse
Soe affectes my muse now a chast fallownesse

Since shee to fewe yet to too many hath showne
How loue songe wordes weedes and satirique thornes are growne
Where seedes of better Artes were earely sowne

Though to vse and loue *Poetry* to me
Bethrothe to noe one Arte be noe Adultery
Omissions of good Ill as Ill deedes be

ffor though to vs itt seeme and delight→[b]elight and thin
yet in those faithfull skales where god thrownes→throw[s] ~~is~~ in
Mens woorkes vanitie waighes as much as sin

If our soules have stayned their feirst white yet wee
May cloath them wth faith and deere honestie
W^{ch} god Imputes as Nature→Natiue puritie

There is noe vertue but Religion
Wise valyant sober iust are names wch none
Want wch want not vice=coveringe discression

Seeke wee then our selves in our selves for als
Men force the sunne, wch much more force to passe
By gatheringe his beames wth a christall glasse

Soe wee if wee into our selves will turne
Blowinge the sparkes of vertue may outburne
The straw wch doth aboute our hartes soiourne

You knowe Phisuians when they would enfuse
Into any oyle the soule of scimples vse
Places where they may lye still warme to chuse

Soe woorkes retirednes in vs to rome
Giddilie and to be every where but at home
Such freedome doth a banishment become

Wee are but farmers of our selves yett may
If we can stock our selves vpp lay
Much much ‸^{deere}treasure for the great rent day

Nature thy selfe then to thy selfe be approued
And wth vaine outward thinges bee noe more moued
But to knowe that I loue thee and would be beloued

Finis

II, 20. *John Donne, To Sr.* Henry Wootton: *"Here's no more newes"*

{20}

I D Here is no more newes then vertue I may as well
Tell you *Callis* or St *Michaell* tale for newes as tell
That vice doth here habituallie dwell./

Yett as to gett stomackes wee walke vpp and downe
And toyle to sweeter rest so may god frowne
If but to loath boath I hant Courte and→or Towne

ffor where none is free from the extremitie
of vice by any other reasone free
But that the next to him is still woorse then hee

sin→[I]n this worldes warrfare they whome Ragged fate
Godes Comnissary doth soe throughly hate
As in the Courtes squadron to marshall there estate

If they stand arm'd wth seely honestie
Wth wishinge praires and neate integritie
Like *Indians* against spanish hostes they bee

Suspitions boldnes to this place belonges
And I→to have as many eares as all have tonges
Tender to knowe loath to acknowledge wronges

Beleeve me S^{r} in my youths giddiest dayes
When to be like the Courte was a plaies praise
Playes were not so like Courtes as Courtes are like playes

Then lett vs att these *M[i]mick Antique* Iests
Whose deepest proiectes and egredious gestes
Are but dull *Moralls* of a game at *chests*

But now t'is incongruitie to smile
Therefore I end and bidd farewell a while
Att Court though from Courte were the better stile

ffinis

I R

II, 20v. Sir John Roe, Song. "Deare Love, continue nice and chaste"

Deere loue contynue nice and chaste
for if you yeeld you doe me wronge
Lett duller wittes to loues end hast
I have enough to woe the longe

All paine and ioy is in theire way
the thinges wee feare bringes→bringe lesse away
Then feare and hope bringes greater ioy
But in themselves they cannot stay

Smale fauoures will my prayers increase
grantinge my suite you give me all
And then my prayers must needes surcease
for I have made yor godhead fall./

Beastes cannot witt nor beautie see
those mans affectyons onely moue
Beastes other sportes of loue doe proue
Wth better feelinge farr then wee

Then loue prolonge my suite for thus
by loosing sporte I sporte doe winne
And that ~~by~~^[may] vertue proue in vs
Wch ever yett hath been a sin

My com̄inge neere may spy some ill
and now the world is given to scoffe
To keepe my loue then keepe me of
And soe^[I]shall admire thee still

Say I had→haue made a p̱fect choyce
societie our loue may kill
Then give but me thy face and voyce
Myne eie and eare thou canst not fill

To make me rich (O) be not poore
give me not all yett ~~yett~~ somethinge lend
Soe I shall still my fate com̄end
And you att will doe lesse or more

ffinis

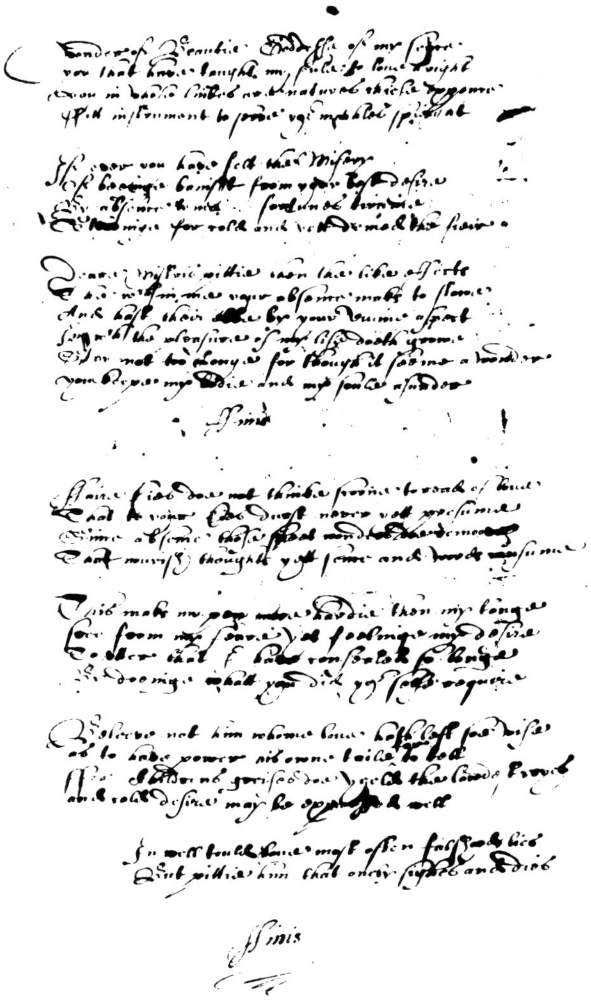

II, 21. Anonymous, Wonder of Beautie, Goddesse of my sense

{21}

Wonder of Beautie Goddesse of my sence
you that have taught my soule to loue a right
You in whose linbes are natures chiefe expence
ffitt instrument to serve yor matchles spieght→spiright

If ever you have felt the Misery
Of beeinge banisht from your best desire
By absence tyme or fortunes tiranie
Stervinge for cold and yett denied the fieir

Deare Mistris pittie then the like effectes
The wch in me your absence makes to flowe
And hast their ebbe by your diuine aspect
Im→In wch the pleasure of my life doeth growe
Stay not too Longe for though it seeme a wonder
you keepe my bodie and my soule asunder

ffinis

Anonymous, Faire eies do not think scorne to read of Love

ffaire Eies doe not thinke scorne to read of loue
That to your Eies durst never yett presume
Since absence those speet→s[u]eet wonders doe remoove
That nourish thoughtes yett sence and wordes consume

This makes my pen more hardie then my tonge
free from my feare yet feelinge my desire
To vtter that I have consealed so longe
By doeinge whatt you did yor selfe require

Beleeve not him whome loue hath left soe wise
as to have power his owne taile ‸for to tell
ffor childrens greifes doe yeeld the lowdest cryes
and cold desire may be expressed well

In well tould loue most often falshood lies
But pittie him that onely sighes and dies

ffinis

II, 21v. Anonymous, Carold for new yeeres day *1624*

Carold for new yeeres day 1624

Tymes have there seasons and doe comprehend
Mens severall actionns and produce there end
One day another tellis and everie yeere
To th' mazed world strange thingis doe still apperre
Vers.j The world turnes round as whether Cock in wind
Man turnes as oft, yet care and thought dothe find
Still doe wee hope a new yeeris bringis us ~~h~~ rest
And yet poore soules wee find our Cares encreast

Gymill Is truethe and worthe of thingis now whollie gone
Must all ^[bee] caried by opinione
Can nothing pleise but y[t] ~~at~~ wche schee esteemes
And nothing good but yat wche onlie seemes

Chorus Flie soule on wyngis of faithe to heaven aboue
Bidd worldlie joyes adewe there fixe they love
Heire Pilgrime lyk thow liuest in wretched Case
Earthe but thy Inne, heaven is thy mansione place

Tyme wears out all thingis withe his *Chariott* wheele
The flint the adamant, the treysse→t[w]ysse heat stile
Vers.2 The statlie stagge; the Eagle, and the Oake
All bend and bow vnder tymes heavie yoake
All freindlie guests and favores of the yeere
Are cleane forgott as thoughe they nevir were
There is nothing yeare→[h]eare, but godis grace lastethe sure
And this in spight of tyme shall still endure

II, 22. Francis Bacon, The worlds a bubble, and the life of man

{22}

The worlds['s] a buble, and the lyfe of man
Lesse then a spann;
In his conceptione wretched from the wombe
Soe to the tombe
Nurst from the cradle, and brought vp to yeeris
with teares→[c]eares and feares
Who then to fraile mortalitie shall trust
But limns the water or but wreats in dust
2 *Yet whilst with sorrowe heere wee liue opprest*
what lyf is best
Courts are but onlie superficiall schooles
to dandle fooles
The rurall pairtis are turned into a den
of savage men
And wher~~a~~s that citty from fowlle vice so frie
But may be termed the worse of all the thrie
3 *Domesticke cares afflicts the husbands bedd*
or paines his head
They that liue single tak it for a curse
or doe thingis worse
They wold haue children those y[t] ~~at~~ haue them none
or wish them gone
What is it then to haue or haue no wife
But single thraldome or a double strife
4 *Our owin affections still at home to please*
is a disease
To crosse the seas to any forraigne soyle
perrill and toyle
Warres with the noyse affrights vs, when they cease
wee are worst in peace
What then remains, but that wee[still] sould ~~still~~ cry
Not to be borne ore being borne to die→dye

finis

II, 22v. John Donne, The Legacie

Elegie

When I died last and deare I die
As often as from the I goe
And lovers houres bee full Eternitie
I can remember yett that I
Something did say, and something did bestowe
Though I be dead wch sent mee I should bee
Mine owne executor and legacie

I heard me say tell her anone
That my self (thats yow not I)
Did kill mee and when I felt me die
I bidd mee send my heart when I wes gone
But I alace cwold there find none
When I hade ript and searchd where harts should bee
It killd mee againe that I who still wes true
In lyfe in my last will should coozen yow

Yett I found something lyke a hart
Butt cullours itt and corners hade
It wes not good, itt wes not badd
It wes entire to none and few hade part
As good as could be made by Art
It seemd and therefore for our losses sadd
I thought to send that heart in stead of myne
But oh no man could hold it for, t'wes thyne

finis

II, 23. John Donne, The broken heart

{23}

Elegie

Hee is stark madd who ever sayes
That hee hath beene in love one houre
Yett not that love so soone decayes
Butt that it can ten in less space devoure
Who will beleive mee iff I sweare
That I have hade the plague a yeare
    Who wold not laugh ~~h~~ att ~~once~~^[mee] if I should say
    I saw a flashe of powder burne a day

Ah whatt a trifle is a hart
if once into loves hands it come
All other greifs allow a part
    To other greifes, and ask themselues but home→some
They come to vs, but vs loves drawes
Hee swallowes ws and nevir Chawes
    By him as by chaind shott wholle rankis doe die
    Hee is the Tyran Pike our hartes the frie

If t'were not so what could become
Of my hart when I first saw thee
I brought a hart into the Roome
And from the Roome I caryed none wth mee
If itt hade gone to thyne I knowe
Myne wold have taught thy heart to shew
    More Pittie vnto me, but love alace
    Att one first blow dothe shiver it like glasse

Yett nothing can ~~to~~ to nothing fall
Nor anie place be emptie quite
Therefor I think my breast hathe all
    Those peeces ~~all~~ still thoughe they be not vnite
And now as broken glasses showe
A Thousand lesser faces soe
    My raggis of heart can lyk wishe and adore
    But after one suche love can love no more

finis

II, 23v. John Donne, The good-morrow

I wonder by my trothe what thow and I
Did till wee loved, were wee not weaned till then
But suck our childishe pleasures seelilie
Or slummerd wee in the seaven sleepers den
T'wes so but as all pleasures fancies bee
If ever any beautie I did sie
Wch I desyrd and gott t'wes but a dreame of the

And now good morrow to our waking soules
Wch watche not one another out of feare
But love, all ~~other~~ love of other sightes controulles
And makes a littill roome an everie where
Lett sea discoverers to new worlds have gone
Let mapps to other worlds one worlds have shone
Lett ws posses our world each hathe one and is one

My face in thyne eye, thyne in myne appears
And plaine true hartes doe in the faces rest
Where can wee find two fitter hemisphers
Without sharp North wthout declynīg west
What ever dyes is not mixd aequallie
If both our loves be one or thow and I
Love just alyk in all none of these loves can dye

finis

John Donne, Breake of day

T'is true t'is day what though it bee
Wilt thow therfore rise from mee
Why should wee ryse becaus t'is light
Did wee lye downe becaus t'is→t'wes night
Loue that in despyt of darknes brought ws hither
Should in despight of light hold vs together

Light ~~is~~hath no tounge but is all eye
If it could speak as well as spy
This is the worst that it could say
That being well I faine wold stay
And that I loue my heart and louer so
That I wold not from him wch hath them goe

Must busines thee from hence remoue
Oh thats the worst disease in→of loue
The poore the foole the false loue can
Admit but not the busied man
Hee that hath busines and makes loue doth doe
Suche wrong as if a maried man should woe

finis

II, 24. John Donne, The triple Foole

{24}

I am two fooles I know
for loving and for saying soe
    In whyneing poetrie
But wheeres that wyse man that wold not be I
    if shee wold not deny
Then as the earths inward crooked lanes
Doe purge sea waters fretfull salt away
    I thought if I could draw my pains
Through ~~rayes~~ rymes vexatioune I should then allay
Greefe brought to numbers cannot be so fierce
for hee teames itt that fetters it in verse

But when I have done soe
some man his art and voyce to show
    Did sitt and sing my paine
And by delighting many frees againe
    Greefe wch werse did restraine
To loue and greefe tribute of verse belongs
But not of such as pleases when t'is redd
    Both are encreased by such songs
For both there Triumphs soe are published
And I wch two foolles doe so growe three
Whoe are a littill wyse the best foolles bee

finis

John Donne, Loves diet

Loues Dyett

To whatt a cumbersome vnwildines
And burthenous corpulence my loue hade growne
    But that I did to mak it lesse
    And keep itt in proportionne
Giue it a dyett made it feed vponne
That wch loue woorst endures, discretione

Aboue one sigh a day I allowed him not
Of wch my fortune and my faults hade part
    And iff sometymes by stealth he gott
    A shee sighe from my mistres hart
And thoughe to feast on that I lett him see
T'wes not verie sound nor meant to me

If hee wrong from me a teare I brined too
With scorne or shame that him itt nourisht not
If hee suckd hers I lett him knowe
  T'wes not a teare wche hee hade gott
His drink wes counterfeit as wes his meat
for eyes wch roule towards all weepe not but sweat

II, 24v

Whatsoevir hee wold detaste I write that
And burnt my lr̄es when shee writt to me
  And that that favour made him fatt
  I said iff any title bee
Convoyed by this (ah) what dothe it availl
To bee the foreteethe name in an entayle

Thus I reclaimed my buzzard loue to flie
Att when and how and where I choose
  Now negligent of sport I lie
  And now as other falconers vse
I spring a mistris sweare writte sigh and weepe
And the game kild or lost goe talk and sleepe

finis

John Donne, A Valediction forbidding mourning

Elegie

As vertuous men pas mildlie away
And whisper, to their soules to goe
And some of there sadd freinds doe say
  The breath goes now and some sayes noe
So let vs melt and make no noyse
  No teare floudes nor sigh tempestes mooue
T'were prophanatione of our joyes
  To tell the laittie of our loue
Mooving of the earthe brings harmes and feares
  Men reckon what it did and meant
But tripidationne of the sphears
  Though greatter far is Innocent
Dull sublunarie lovers loue
  (Whose soule is sence) cannot admitt
Absence, becaus it doth remoue
  those things wch elemented ~~ed~~ itte
But wee by a loue so much refind
  that our selues know not what it is
+ I'hter→I'[c]ht[,]er assured of the mynd
  Careles eyes ~~and~~ lippes and hands to misse
Our two soules wch are therefore one
  though I must goe endure not yett
A breache but ane expansionne
  Lyk gold to ather thinnes beatt
If they be two they are two soe
  As stiff twine compasses ar two
Thy soule the fixed foott maketh noe showe
  to move, but doth if thother doe
And thoughe it in the center sitt
  Yett when the other far dothe come
IT leans and hearkens after itt
  And growes direct as it comes home
Such wilt thow bee to me who must
  Lyk thother foote obliquilly runne

{25}

Thy firmnes makes my circle just
And makes mee end where I begunne

finis

John Donne, Elegie: "Oh, let mee not serve so"

Elegie

Oh let ~~me~~ not mee serue so, as those men serue
Whom honour smoakis at once flatter and sterue
Poorelie enriched with gryt mens words and lookes
Nor soe wright my name in thy loving bookes
As those Idolatrous flatterers wch still
Their princes stylles with many realmes full fill
Whence they no tribute haue and where noe *sway*
Such ~~offices~~ services I offer as shall pay
Themselues, I hate dead names! O then let mee
ffavoritte in Ordinarie or ~~not~~ favorite bee
When my soule wes in myne owne bodie sheath[d]
Not yett by oathes betrothed nor kisses breath[d]
Into my purgatorie & faithlesse thee
Thy heart seemes waxe and steele thy constancie
Soe careles flowrs strow[d] in→[o]n the waters face
The curled whirlepoolles suck smak and embrace
Yett droune them, So the Tapers beamie eye
Amorouslie twinkling, beckons the giddie flie
Yett burnes his→hir winges, And such the devill is
Scarse visiting him who are entirlie his
When I beheld a streame wch from the spring
Dothe with doubtfull melodius murmuring
Or in a speechles slumber calmelie ryd
Her welled channells bosome and there chyd
And bend her browes and swell if any bough
Doe but stoope downe to kisse hir vpmost browe
Yett if her often gnawing kisses win
The Traiterous bank to gape and let her in
Shee rusheth violentlie, and doth divorce
Her from her natiuie and her long kept course
And roares and braues itt in a gallant skorne
In flattering Eddies promising returne
Shee floottes her channell who thencefurth is drie
Then say I that is shee, and this am I
Yett let ~~me~~ not this deep bitternes ~~forgett~~[begett]
Careles dispaire in mee for that will whett

II, 25v

My mynd to scorne and oh love dulld wth paine
Wes ne're so wise nor so well arriu'd as disdaine
Then wth new eyes I shall survey thee and spie
Death in thy cheekis and darknes in thyne eye
Though hope breed fayth and love thus taught I shall
(As nations doe from Rome) from thy loue fall
Mine heat shall outgrowe thyne and vtterlie
I will renunce thy dalliance and when I
Am ~~the~~ the recusant in that resolute state
What hurts it me to be excommunicate/

finis

John Donne, The Will

Loues Legacie

Before I sighe my last gaspe let me breath
(grytt loue) some legacies, heere I bequeath
Mine eyes to Argus, ~~e~~ if my eyes can sie
If they be blind, then loue I giue them thee
My toung to fame, To Ambassadors myne eares
    To women or the sea my teares
    Thou loue hast taught mee heertofore
By making mee serue who hade twentie more
That I should giue to none, but suche as hade too much before

My Constancie I to the planetts giue
My trueth to them who att the Court doe liue
Myne Ingenuitie and oppennesse
To Iesuits, To Buffones my Pensiuenes
My silence to any who abroad hath beene
    My money to a Capushin
Thou loue taught mee by appoynting mee
To love there where no loue received could bee
Onlie to giue such incapacitie

I giue my reputatione to those
Wch were my freinds myne Industrie to foes
To schoolmen I bequeath my doubtfulnes
My sicknes to Phisitians or excesse
To Nature all that I in Ryme haue wreatt
    And to my Companie my witt
    Thou loue by making mee adore

her

{26}

Her, who begott this loue in mee before
Taughst mee to make as thoughe I gaue when I did but restore

To him for whome the Passing bell nixt tolles
I giue my Physick bookes, my written Rolles
Of morall counsell I to Bedlame giue
My Brazen meddalls vnto them wch liue
In want of bread, To them wch passe among
All forrainners, myne English townge
Though loue by making me loue one
Who thinkes her freindship a fit portione
For yonnger lovers doest my gifts thus disproportione

Therefore I'le giue no more, But I'le vndoe
The world by dying, becaus loue dyes too
Then all yor beauties will be noe more worth
Then gold in Mines where none doe draw itt foorthe
And all yor graces no more vse shall haue
Then a Sun-diall in a graue
Thou loue taughst mee by making mee
Loue her who doth neglect both thee and mee
To Invent and practise this one way to adnihilate all three

finis

Francis Beaumont, To the Countesse of Rutland

To the Countesse of Rutland

Madame
So may my verses pleasing bee
So may yow laugh at them and not at mee
T'is something to yow I wold gladlie say
But how to doe it, cannot find the way
I would avoyd the Commone troden wayes
To ladies vsd wch be or loue or praise
As for the first the littill witt I have
Is not yett growne so neere vnto the grave
But that I can by that droune [dime] fading light
Perceiue of what and vnto whome I wright
Lett such as in a hopeles wittles rage
Can sighe a quier and reade it to a page
Such as can mak tenn sonnetts ere they rest
When each is but a great blott at the best
Suche as can backs of bookes and windowes fill
With there two furious diamond and quill

II, 26v

Suche as are mortified that they can liue
Laughe at by all the world and yet forgiue)
Writte loue to yow I wold not ~~w~~ willinglie
Be poynted at in everie Companie
As wes the littill Talyour who till death
Wes hott in loue wth *Queene Elizabeth*
And for the last in all my Idle dayes
I nevir did yet living woman praise
In verse or prose and when I doe begin
Ile pyke some woman out as full of sinne
As yow are full of vertue with a soule
As blak as yours is whyt, with a face as foule
As yours is beautifull, for itt shalbe
Out of the rules of *Phisiognomy*
So farr that I doe feare I must displace
The art a littill, to lett in the face
IT shall at least four places→faces be below
The diuelles, and her parched corps, shall show
In her loose skin as iff some spirit shee were
Kept in a bagg by some grytt *Conjurer*
Her breath shalbe as horrible and vyld
As everie word yow speak is sweet and mild *
IT shalbe such a one as will not be
Covered with any art or Policie
But let her tak all waters fumes and drink
Shee shall mak nothing but a dearer stink
Shee shall have such a foot and such a nose
As will not stand in any thing but prose
If I bestow my prayses vponne such
T'is charitie and I shall merit much
My prayse will come to her lyk a foult→full bowle
Bestow'd at most need on a thirstie soule
Where if I sing yor praises in my ryme
I loose my Inke my paper and my tyme
Adde nothing to yor overflowing store
And tell yow naught but what yow knew before
Nor doe the vertuous myndet (wth I sweare)
Madam I* think yow are) indure to heare
Theere→The[i]re owne perfections into questione
brought
But stoppe there eares at them for if I thought
Yow took a pride to have yor vertues knowen
(Pardone me *Madame*) I should think them none
But if your braue thoughtes (wch I must respect
Aboue yor glorious titles) shall accept
These harsh disordored lynes I shall ere long
Dresse vpp yor vertues new in a new song
yett

{27}

Yett far from all base prayse or flatterie
Althoughe I know what ere my verses bee
They will lyk the most seruile flatterie show
If I writte trueth and mak my subject yow

finis

John Donne, Elegie: The Expostulation

Elegie

To make the doubt more cleare that no [wo]∧man's true
Wes it my faute to prove it strong in yow
Thought I but one hade breathed purest ayre
And must shee needs be false becaus shees ~~i~~ faire
Is it your beauties mark or of your youthe
Or of your perfectione not to studie trueth
Or think yow heaven is deaf or hath noe eyes
Or those shee hath smile at your perjuries
Are vowes so cheap wch women of the mater
Whereof they are made, that they are write in water,
And blowne away with wind? or doth they breath
(both hott and Cold) at once mak life and death
Who could have thought so many accents sweet
formd into words so many sighes should meet
As from our hearts so many oathes ~~sighes~~ and teares
sprinkled among all sweeter by yor feares
And the divine Impressione of stolne kisses
That seald the rest, should now prove emptie blissis
Did yow draw bonds to forfeyt, signe to break
Or must wee read yow quit from what yow speak
And find the truth out the wrong way? or must
The first desyre yow false would wish yow just
O I prophane, Though most women bee
This kynd of beast, My thought shall accept the
My dearest loue, froward Iealousie
With circumstance might vrge thy Inconstancie
Sooner Ile think the Sunne will cease to cheare
The teeming earth and that forget to beare
Sooner that riuers will rune bak or Thames
With Ribbes of yce in Iuine would bind his streames
Or nature by whose strenthe the world endures
Would change her course, before yow alter yours
But O that treacherous breast to whome weak yow
Did trust our counselles and wee both may rue

II, 27v

Having his falsehood found too late T'wes hee
That made yow cast your guiltie and yow mee
Whilst hee blak wretch betrayed each simple woorde
Wee spake vnto the cuñing of a third
Curst may hee bee that so our loue hath slane
And wander on the earth wretched as Cayne
Wretched as hee and not deserue least pittie
In plagueing him let miserie bee wittie
Lett all eyes shune him and hee shun each eye
Till hee be noysume as his Infamie
May hee without remorse deny god thryce
And not be trusted more on his soules price
And after all self torment when hee dies
May volues teare out his heart, vulturs hes eyes
Swyne eat his bowelles and his falser tounge
That vttered all, be to some Raven flunge
And let his Carione Coarse bee a longer feast
To the kings dogs then any other beast
Now I have curst let vs our loue reviue
In mee the flame wes nevir more aliue
I could begin againe to court and prayse
And in that pleasure lenghten the short dayes
Of my lyues lace, lyk Painters that doe tak
Delight, not in the made work, but whilst they make
I could renewe these tymes when first I saw
Loue in yor eyes that gaue my tounge the law
To lyk what yow lik'^{d} and at masques and playes
Commend the selfe same actours the same wayes
Ask how yow did, and often with Intent
Off being officious being Impertinent
All wch were such soft pastimes as in these
Loue wes as subtile catcht as a disease
But being gott it is a treasure sweet
W^{ch} to defend is hard or→[-e]r then to gett
And ought not be prophan'^{d} ~~or~~ on eyther part
ffor thought is gott be chance, t'is kept by art

finis

II, 28. John Donne, Song: "Goe, and catche a falling starre"

{28}

A Song

Goe and catch a falling starr
  gett with chyld a mandrak roote
Tell mee where all past yeers are
  Or who cleft the diuelles foot
Teach mee to heere Marmaides singing
    Or to keep of envyes stinging
        And find
        What wind
Serues to advance ane honest mind

If thou beest borne to strange sights
  things Invisible see
Ride ten thousand dayes and nights
    Till age snow whyt haires on the
Then when thou returnst willt tell me
All strange wonders that befell the
        And swere
        No where
Liues a woman true and faire

If thou findst one let me know
  Such a Pilgrimage were sweet
Yett doe not, I would not goe
    Though at nixt doore wee might meet
Though shee were true when yow met her
    And last till yow writte your letter
        Yet shee
        Will be
False ere I come, to two or three

finis

II, 28v. John Donne, Loves Deitie

Loues dietie

I long to talk with some old louers ghost
Who died before the God of loue wes borne
I cannot think that hee who loued most
sunck→s[a]nck so low: as to loue one wch did skorne
But since this god produc'd a destinie
And that vice-nature Custome letts it bee
I must loue her that loues not mee

Sure they wch made him God meant not so much
Nor hee in his yonng godhead practisd itt
But when ane ever flame two harts did touche
his office wes Indulgentlie to fitt
Actiues to passives correspondencie
Onlie s his subject wes it cannot be
Loue till I loue her that loues mee

But everie Moderne God will now extend
his vast prerogatiue as farr as Ioue
To rage to lust to write to to commend
All is the peurlue of the God of loue
Oh were wee weakned by this Tyranny
To vngod this child againe it wold not bee
That I should loue, who loues not me

Rebell and Atheist too why murmure I
As though I felt the worst that loue can doe
Loue might mak mee leaue louing, or might trie
A deeper plague to mak ~~me~~ her loue ~~her~~ me too
W^{ch} since shee loues before I am loath to sie
ffalshood is worse then hate, and that must bee
If shee whome I loue should loue mee

finis

II, 29. John Donne, The Flea

{29}

Mark but this flea and mark in this
    How littill that wch thou deniest mee is
Mee it suckd first and now suckes thee
    And in this flea our two ~~mi~~ bloodes mingled be
Confesse itt this cannot be said
A sinne or shame or losse of Maydenhead
        Yett this enjoyes ~~itt~~ before itt woe
        and pamperd swelles with one blood made of two
        and this alasse is more then wee ~~cald~~ could doe

Oh, stay three liues in one flea spare
Where wee almost nay more then maried are
    This flea is yow and I and this
    Our mariage bed and maried temple is
Though parents grudge and yow wee are mett
And cloystered in these living walls of Iett
        Thoughe vse mak the apt to kill mee
        Lett not to thy self Murther added bee
        and Sacriledge, thrie sinnes in killing three

Cruell and suddaine hast thou since
Purpled thy naile in blood of Innocence
    In what could this flea guiltie bee
    Except in that drop wch shee suckt from thee
Yett thou triumphst and sayst that thou
Findst not thy self nor mee the weaker now
        T'is true then learne how fals feares bee
        Iust so much honour when thou yeeldest to mee
        Will wast as this fleas death tooke lyk from thee

finis

John Donne, Communitie

Good wee must loue and must hate ill
  ffor ill is ill, and good, good still
      But there are things Indifferent
  Wche wee may nayer hate nor loue
      But one and then another proue
      as wee shall find o^{r} fancie bent

If then at first wyse nature hadd
  Made women ather good or badd
      Then some wee might hate and some wee might choose
But since shee did them so create
That wee may nather loue nor hate
      Onlie this rests, all all may vse

II, 29v

If they were good it wold be seene
   Good is as visible as greene
         And to all eyes it self betrayes
If they wer badd they could not last
Badd doth it self and others wast
      Soe they deserue nor blame nor praise

But they are ours as fruits are oures
   hee that but tasts hee that devoures
         And hee wch leaues all doth aswell
Changd loues are but changd sorts of meat
And when hee hath the kernell eatt
      Who doth not fling away the shell

finis

John Donne, Womans constancy

Now thow hast lou'd mee one whole day
To morrow when thow leaust what wilt thow say
Wilt thow antidate some new made vow
            Or say that now
Wee are not just those persones wch wee were
Or that Oathes made in reverentiall feare
Of loue and his wrath any may for sweare
Or as true deaths true mariages vntie
Soe lover's contracts Images of those
Bind but till sleep? deathis Image thee vnloose
            Or your owne end to justifie
ffor having purposd change and falshood yow
Can have noe way but falshood to be true
Vaine lunatik, Against those scapes I could
            Dispute and conquere if I would
            Wch absteine to doe
ffor by too morrow I may think so too

finis

II, 30. Sir Walter Ralegh, The Lie

{30}

Goe soule the bodies guest
  Vpone a thankles errant
ffeare not to touch the best
    the trueth shalbe thy warrant
Goe since I needs must die
    And give them all the lie

Say to the Court it glowes
  and shynes lyk rotten wood
Say to the churche it shoes
  What's good but doth noe good
    If Court and church reply
      Giue Court and church the lie

Tell men of hie Conditione
  that rules affaires of state
There purpose is ambitione
  there practise onlie hate
      And if they doe reply
      Feare not to giue the lie

Tell Potentates they liue
  acting but others actions
Not lou'd vnles they giue
  not strong but by there factions
      If Potentates reply
      giuePotentates the lie

Tell those that braggs it most
  They begge for more by spending
And in there grytest cost
  seek nothing but commending

Tell witt how much it wrangles
  In tikill poyntes of *finnesse*
Tell wisdome shee Intangles
  In poyntes of overnycenes

Tell zeale it wants devotione
  Tell loue it is but lust
Tell tyme it is but motione
  Tell flesh it is but dust

Tell age it daylie wasteth
  Tell hono^{r} how it alters
Tell beautie that shee blasteth
  Tell favo^{r} that shee faulters

II, 30v

Tell Physick of her boldnes
  Tell skill it is preventione
Tell Charitie of coldnes
  Tell loue it is contentione

Tell fortune of her blindnes
  Tell nature of decay
Tell freindship of vnkyndnes
  Tell justice of delay

Tell Artes they haue noe scandalles
  But varie by esteeming
Tell schoolles they want profoundnes
  And stand too much on seeming

Tell faith ites fledd the Citie
  Tell how the Cuntrie erreth
Tell Man hee shakes of Pittie
  Say vertue least preferreth

Soe when thou hast as I
Commanded thee done babling
Although to giue the lie
Deserues noe lesse then stabbing
    Stabb at thy soule who will
    Noe stabb thy soule can kill

finis

Josuah Sylvester, The Fruites of a cleere Conscience

The fruites of a good Conscience

To shyne in silk and glister all in gold
To shew in wealth; and feed on daintie fare
To build vs houses statelie to behold
The Princes fauour and the peoples care
Although these gifts be gryt and verie rare
The groaning Gout the Collik and the stone
Will marre there mirth and turne it all to moane
But be it that the bodie subject bee
To no such siknes or the lyk annoy
Yett if the Conscience be not firme and free
Riches is Trash and hono^{r} but a Toy
The peace of Conscience is that perfect joy
Wherewith gods children in this lyf be blest
To want the w^{ch}, better want the rest
The want of this made Adam hide his head
The want of this made Cain vaile and weepe
The want of this maks manie goe to bedd
When they god wott haue littill lust to sleep
striue

II, 31

{31}

Striue Striue therefor to entertaine and keep
Soe rich a Iewell and so rare a guest
Wch being hade a Rash for all the rest

finis

John Donne, Elegie: The Anagram

Marie and loue thy flauia for shee
Hath all things whereby others bewties bee
for though her eyes be small, her mouth is greatt
Though they be Iuorie, yett her teeth be Iett
Though they bee dimme, yett shee is light
And though her harsh hare faile, her skinne is rough
What thought her cheeks be yeallow, her haire is read
Giue her thyne and shee hath then a maidenhead
These things are beauties eliments, where these
Meet in one that one must as perfyt pleis
If read and whytt and each good qualitie
Bee in the wench neere ask where it doth lye
In buying things perfumd, wee ask if there
Bee musk and Amber in it, but not where
Though all her pairtes bee not in the vsuall place
Shee hath the→ane *Anagram* of a good face
If wee might pairt the letters but one way
In that leane dearth of woords what could wee say
When by the Gam-vt, some musicians make
A Perfeyt sonng, others will vndertak
By the same Gam-vt changed to aequall it
Things simplie good can nevir be vnfit
Shee is fare as any if all be lyk her
And if none be, then is shee singular
All loue is wonder if wee justlie doe
Account her wonderfull why not louelie too
Loue built one beautie soone as beautie dyes
Chose this face charged wth no deformities
Women are lyk angells, then faire bee

II, 31v

Lyk those wch fell to worse, but such as shee
Lyk to good angelles nothing can Impare
T'is lesser greif to bee foule, then to have beene fare
ffor one night Revelles silk and gold wee chuse
But in long Iorneyes cloth and leather vse
Beautie is barren oft, best husbands say
Ther is best land, where is the foulest way
Oh what soveraigne plaster will shee bee
If thy past sinnes have taught the Iealousie
Here needs noe spyes, nor Eunuches her committ
Safe to thy foes yee to a marmasett
When Belgias Cities, the round Centries dround
That dirtie foulnes guards and arms the toune
Soe doth her face guard her, and soe for thee
Wch forced by busines oft must absent bee
Shee whose face lyk cloudes turnes day to night
Who mightier then the Sea maks mores seeme whyt
Whom though sevin yeeres shee in the stewes hade layed
A Nunnerye durst receave and think a mayde
And though in chyldbirth shee did lye
Midwyues wold sweare T'wes but a Tympanie
Whom if shee accause I credit lesse
Then witches wch Impossibles confes
Whome dildoes bedstaues and her velvet glas
Wold be as loth to sutch→[so]utch→[To]utch as Ioseph wes
One lyk none, and lyk't, of none fittest were
Things in fashione, everie man will weare

finis

Jonathan Richards, a songe: "I die when as I doe not see"

I die when as I doe not sie
her who is lyf and all to mee
and when I sie her yet I die
In seeing of her crueltie
So that to me lyk miserie is wrought
Both when I sie and whē I sie her not
Or shall I speak or silent greive
But how can silence then releive
And iff I speak I may offend
And speaking not my hart will rend
Soe that to me itis all one
Speak I or speak I not I am vndone

finis

II, 32. Anonymous, Once and no more soe sayd my loue

{32}

Once and no more soe sayd my loue
When in myne armes Inchand
Shee vnto me her lips did move
And so my hart shee gayned

Adew shee sayd begone I must
For feare of being missed
Your heart putts over, but in trust
and so againe shee kissed

II, 32v. William Herbert, When my Carliles Chamber was on fire

Hade shee a glase and feard the fyre
That tells hir that hir eyes
Can mak all hearts burnt offerings off desyre
And not become themselues a sacrifice
            fyre burnes not fyre
Naught can there force Impaire
But what is bred by there owne crueltie dispaire

Anonymous, My dead and buried loue is resin againe

    [My de]

My dead and buried loue is resin againe
A true type of our other day
And now doth in my thought remaine
Refin'^{d}, as then shalbe our fleshie clay

T'will bee a glorious garment of our soule
No burden then no whitt a bate
The soules powers wch without controule
Shall work more freelie then iff separat

So my loue now hath infinit desyre
As much delight, not built vpone
Sensuall touches no, no in spight
off those my sight is now fruitione

[my]
    [of those my siges]

Anonymous, Why doe yee giue mee leaue to sip

Why doe yee giue mee leaue to sip
And pull the Cupp from my soe thirstie lip
            Before I drink
Desyre hath left my heart to think
And is disperst in everie outward part
            As hands, lips, eyes,
That all restraint despise
While it wes in my hart
IT did your will in chains off slavish feares
        But these haue all noe eares

{33}

Carold for newe yeares day. 1624

Tymes haue there seasones and doe comprehend
Mens severall actions, and produce there end.
One day another telles, and everie yeare
Vers. 1. To'th mazed world strange thinges doe still appeare
The world turnes round, as whether Cock in wind
Man turnes as oft yett care and thought doth find
Still doe wee hope, a~~n~~ new yeare[~~s~~] bringes vs rest
And yet poore soules wee find our cares encreast

Gymill Is trueth and worth of thinges now wholie gone
Must all bee caryed by opinionne,
Can nothing pleis, but that wch shee esteemes
And nothing good but that ~~wh~~ wch onlie seemes

Chorus Flee→Fl[i]e soule on winges of faith to heaven aboue
Bidd wordlie Ioyes adew, there fixe thy lord→lo[ue]
Heere Pilgrim lyk thou liuest in wretched Case
Earth's but thy Inne, heaven is thy dwelling place

Tyme weares out all thinges with his Chariot wheele
The flint the Adamant, the twise heat steile
The statelie stagge, the Eagle and the Oake,
Vers. 2. All bend and bow, vnder tymes heavie yoak
All freindlie giftes and favoures of the yeare
Are cleane forgot, as tho they nevir were
There is no thing heere, but gods grace lasteth sure
And this in spyte→spyght of tyme shall still endure

[II, 33v blank] *II, 34. George Morley, On the Death of King James*

{34}

All that hath eyes, now wake and weepe
hee whose waking was our sleepe
Is fallen asleepe himselfe, and nevir
shall wake ~~noe~~ more, till wak'de for ever
Deathes Iron hand hath closd those eyes
That were at once three kingdomes spies→spyes
Both to forsee and to preuent
Dangers, assoone as they were ment
That head, whose working braine alone
Wrought all mens quiet, but itts owne
Now lyeth at rest, o lett him haue
The peace hee lent ~~him~~ vs to his graue
If noe Naboth all his raigne
Was for his fruitfull vineyard slaine
If noe Vriah lost his life
Because hee hade soe fare a wife
Then let not Shimeis curses wound
His honour or prophane this ground
Lett noe blak mouth'd rank breathed Curre
Pacefull Iames, his ashes sturre
Princes are godes; O doe not then
Rake in there graues to proue them men.
  For two an twentie yeares long care
  For prouiding such ane heire
  That to the peace wee hade before
  May adde thrice two an twentie more
  For his day trauels and night watches
  For his crasd sleepe stolne by snatches
  For two fierce kingdomes Ioyn'd in one
  For all hee did or meant to haue done
  Doe this for him wreat on his dust
  Iames the peacefull and the Iust

II, 34*v*. Anonymous, An Epitaph vpon the Duke off Buckinghame

An Epitaph vpon the
Duke off Buckinghame

Dearling off Kings, Patrone off armes,
Muses protector, who from harmes
Did sheild professores off them twaine,
Lyes heere by a base Soldier Slaine
And by poetasteres cankred breath
Dyes everie day a lingring death:

Be silent malice from henceforth,
And know detractione from his worth
(off Kings off Mars, off Muses lou'd)
Is onely from such spirits mou'd,
As loue not Kings and would advance
Base Cowardise and Ignorance

EXPLANATORY NOTES

The Explanatory Notes define all unusual words or usages at their first occurrence. Definitions of English words are from the *Oxford English Dictionary* unless otherwise stated. Persons, places, and allusions are identified at their first appearance or cross-referenced to a later, more appropriate identification. Problematical readings in the texts are noted, and the traditional readings given. Unique manuscript abbreviations in the texts are noted and expanded. Except for titles, passages annotated in the Explanatory Notes are given here in italics regardless of the type used in the transcription.

I, 1. Archbishop George Abbot, trial testimony

George Abbot (1562–1633), archbishop of Canterbury from 1611, presided over the commission of five bishops and six civil lawyers that ajudicated Lady Frances Howard's 16 May 1613 suit for divorce from Robert Devereux (1591–1646), Third Earl of Essex. Abbot opposed the suit; King James I favored it. On 25 September 1613 the suit succeeded, and on 26 December 1613 the divorced countess married Robert Carr (1587–1645), First Earl of Somerset.

23–24. *tyme . . . Remensis.* Archbishop Hincmar (806–882) of Reims, author of *De divortio Lotharii* (J. P. Migne, *Patrologiae Cursus Completus: Series Latina* [Paris, 1844–1882], 125:623–772).

35. *hoc . . . ieminiū.* Matt. 17:20.

36. *St. . . . fide.* 1 Pet. 5:9.

53. *Philippus . . . impotentia.* Philipp Melanchthon (1497–1560), *Loci Communes Theologici* (Basil, 1562), pp. 464–65, 468–69.

54. *Pezelius . . . melanchtonis.* Christoph Pezel (1539–1604), *Examen theologicum* (Neostadii, 1589).

56. *Hemmingius . . . diuorsio.* Niels Hemmingsen (1513–1610), *Libellvs de Coniugio, Repudio, & Diuortio* (Lipsiae, 1578).

57. *Polanus . . .* 94. Amandus Polanus von Polansdorf (1561–1610) allows only adultery and desertion as grounds for divorce in *Partitiones Theologicae* (Basil, 1599), p. 424.

64–66. *Doubdted . . . elapsū.* Polanus and Hemmingsen allow separation (not divorce) after three years for men gelded subsequent to marriage.

I, 2. King James I, trial testimony

24–26. *ratio . . . copula.* James is arguing that without consummation there is no "joining" in marriage. The phrasing in 1 Cor. 6:16, "duo in carne una," is the same used to describe marriage in Matt. 19:6 and Mark 10:9; however, Paul is lecturing against fornication.

33–34. *Amputatio . . . law.* William Stanford, *Plees de Coron* (London, 1560), f. 39.

47–49. *quos . . . only.* "Quos ergo Deus conjunxit" occurs in Matt. 19:6 and Mark 10:9, both times followed by "homo non separet."

59–61. *kinge . . . illam.* Gen. 20:2–6.

I, 5. Anonymous, Prayer

This prayer resembles various Roman missals; however, I have found no specific source.

7. *mulieri Cananee.* John 8:3–11.

8. *publicano, et latroni.* Matt. 21:32 and 27:38.

I, 10. Anonymous, "mr: Lamb: Cookes Epi: to his Bro: Hen:"

Possibly Lambard Cook (1582–?), B.A. Oxford, 8 July 1603 (Joseph Foster, *Alumni Oxonienses* [Nendeln, Liechtenstein: Kraus Reprint, 1968], 1:321).

I, 10v. Sir John Davies, "Unto that sparkling wit, that spirit of fire"

3. *audactie.* Audacity.

10. *tonge of angelles.* 1 Cor. 13:1.

36. *one.* On.

I, 15v. Sir Robert Ayton, "The Sheppherd Thirsis"

21. *retourd.* Returned to a place.

I, 16. John Donne, "Elegie: The Anagram"

19. *Gam. vt.* After Thomas Morley's usage of "*Gam ut*" in *Plaine and Easie Introduction to Practical Musicke* (London, 1597), "'gamut' came to be used, incorrectly, if conveniently as synonymous with 'gam' for 'scale'" (*Grove's Dictionary of Music*, 5th ed. [London: Macmillan, 1975], 3:560).

40. *marmasett.* Literally, the marmoset monkey; applied to a person, a term of contempt.

50. *Tympanie.* Morbid swelling or tumor.

54. *Ioseph.* Gen. 39:7–12.

I, 19. Anonymous, "a songe: 'When my hart seemes most ingaged'"

9. *coure.* Court.

I, 21. John Donne, "Satyre III"

17. *Mutinous Dutch.* The English had aided Dutch rebels against Spanish rule since 1568.

23–24. *deuine . . . Ouen.* Dan. 3:12–30.

24. *ffires of Spaine.* Burning of heretics during the Spanish Inquisition.

24. *line.* Equator.

30–31. *who . . . garison.* Job 7:1.

83–84. *age . . . night.* John 9:4.

91. *Blanck=charters.* Document given to agents of the crown in Richard II's reign, with the power to fill it out as they pleased.

96. *Phillipp.* Philip II of Spain (1527–1598).

96. *Gregorie.* Pope Gregory XIII (1502–1585).

97. *Harry.* Henry VIII (1491–1547).

97. *Martin.* Martin Luther (1483–1546).

I, 22. John Donne, "Satyre IV"

20. *posed Adam.* Adam named the beasts in Gen. 2:19–20.

22. *Guianaes rarities.* Perhaps as reported in Sir Walter Ralegh's *The Discovery of Guiana* (1596).

26. *pretences.* The apprentices revolted in 1517.

33. *Tufftaffata.* Taffeta with a pile or nap arranged in tufts.

34. *Rash.* Smooth fabric of silk or worsted.

48. *Iovius.* Paolo Giovio (1483–1552), author of several histories including *Dell'istorie del svo tempo* (Venice, 1556).

48. *Lurius.* Laurentius Surius (1522–1578), hagiographer and historian, whose works include *Histoire ov commentaires de tovtes choses memorables* (Paris, 1571).

54. *Calepines Dictionary.* Ambrose Calepine (1455–1511), compiler of the *Dictionarium octo linguarum* (Basel, 1584).

55. *Beza.* Theodore de Beze (1519–1605), French Calvinist quoted frequently in Donne's prose.

56–57. *twoo . . . Academies.* Shawcross notes (p. 398), "The Dobell MS names the reverend men as Lancelot Andrewes, Master of Pembroke College, Cambridge (1589–1605), and John Reynolds, president of Corpus Christi College, Oxford (1598–1607)."

59. *Panirge.* Ungentlemanly, multilingual, companion of Pantagruel in Rabelais's *Pantagruel* (2.9).

65. *Babells Brick Layers.* Gen. 11:3–9.

70. *Aretines pictures.* Pietro Aretino (1492–1556) wrote a set of licentious sonnets to accompany an equally immoral series of engravings by Marcantonio Raimondi from drawings by Giulio Romano (1499–1546).

79. *Kings street.* From Charing Cross to Westminster Palace.

85. *Grogaran.* Grogram: coarse fabric of silk or mohair and wool.

94. *Sembreefe.* Semibreve: longest musical note in ordinary use.

96. *Hollensheads or Hales or Stowes.* Raphael Holinshed (d. 1580), author of *The First and Second Volumes of Chronicles* [of England, Scotland, and Ireland] (London, 1587); Edward Halle (1499–1547), author of *The Union of the two noble and illustrate famelies of Lancastre & Yorke* (London, 1548); and John Stow (1525–1605), author of *A summarie of Englyshe chronicles* (London, 1565) and *The Annales of England* (London, 1584).

105. *Spanncounter or blewepoint.* In span-counter, one throws counters within a hand-span of the opponent's counters; blowpoint is played with darts blown through a tube.

111. *Gallobelgicus.* Michel van Isselt,

Mercvrivs Gallobelgicus: siue, Rervm in Gallia & Belgio potissimvm (Cologne, 1588–1603).

113. *Spaniards . . . Amyens.* Seized by the Spaniards from the French in 1597, Amiens was recaptured in September of 1598.

116. *Macron.* Macaronic: burlesque verse form mixing two or more languages.

125. *Dunkerkers.* Privateers belonging to Dunkirk in French Flanders.

156–57. *traunce . . . Hell.* Probably Dante Alighieri (1265–1321), author of *The Divine Comedy.*

174. *Mewes.* The royal stables at Charing Cross.

175. *Ballowne.* Game played with large inflated ball; also ball of pasteboard stuffed with combustibles that bursts into sparks when shot into the air.

175. *Diett.* Court session.

175. *stewes.* Brothels.

185. *Cheapside.* Merchant district of London.

188. *Cutchanell.* Cochineal: scarlet dye from dried bodies of the insect *Coccus cacti.*

191. *scarlett gownes.* Ceremonial dress for judges and cardinals.

196. *Macrine.* Invented name suggesting "macaronic," a confused heap or huddle of many things; cf. line 116.

197. *Hate.* Hat.

197. *sue.* Most texts read "shue."

198. *Att.* Most texts read "As if."

198. *Meschite.* Mosque.

203. *Dureus.* Albrect Dürer (1471–1528), German artist and author of *Treatise on Proportions* (Nuremberg, 1528).

215. *Purseuant.* A warrant officer employed to discover Roman Catholics; also a suitor for a lady's hand.

218. *Glorius.* Invented, suggestive name.

232. *Ascapartes.* Askapart: giant allegedly defeated by Sir Bevis of Southampton (circa 1320).

233. *Charingcrosse . . . Barr.* The last of twelve crosses erected by Edward I in memory of Eleanor (d. 1290). Bar: thick rod of iron or wood thrown in contests of strength.

234. *Queenes man.* The yeomen of the guard.

241. *Maccabees modestie.* 2 Macc. 15:38. The Books of the Maccabees are apocrypha and not canonical for Protestants.

I, 24v. John Donne, "Satyre V"

2. *He.* Possibly Baldassare Castiglione (1478–1525), author of *Il Cortegiano* (*The Courtier*, translated by Thomas Hoby in 1561).

23. *Wittolls.* Aware and complaisant cuckolds.

24. *Empresse.* Elizabeth I (1533–1603).

38. *Angellica.* Heroine of Ariosto's *Orlando Furioso* (Venice, 1516) who escapes various suitors and a dragon.

56–57. *Dominations Powres Cherubins.* Dominations rank fourth in the Dionysian celestial hierarchy and manifest the glory of God; Powers rank third in the second triad and stop the demons who would overthrow the world; Cherubim rank second and excel in knowledge (Gustav Davidson, *A Dictionary of Angels*, pp. 97, 227, and 86–87).

79. *Vrim and Thummim.* "Oracle and truth": Exod. 28:30.

81. *Caricke.* Carrack: ship of burden.

83. *Haman.* Esther 8.

85–87. *Esops . . . vanished.* Aesop (620–560 B.C.), "The Dog and the Shadow" in *The Fables of Aesop.*

I, 25v. John Donne, "Satyre II"

40. *Coscus.* According to Shawcross, a name associated in Renaissance poetry with court pleaders (p. 19n).

41. *poxe.* Syphilis.

48. *Pleas and Bench.* Court of Common Pleas and the King's (or Queen's) Bench, court over which the sovereign presided.

50. *Tricessimo of the Queene.* Thirtieth year (1588) of Queen Elizabeth's reign.

53. *Hillary terme.* Term or session beginning 23 January of the High Court of Justice.

55. *Remitter.* Principle by which one having two titles to an estate, and entering on it by the later or more defective of these, is adjudged to hold it by the earlier or more valid one.

59. *Sclauonians.* Slavs.

68. *Suertishipp.* Suretyship: position of liability for the default or miscarriage of another.

71. *wring.* Pressed, forced (to speak).

72. *Bearing like Asses.* 1 Sam. 16:1, 20.

86. *prime.* Hand in game of primero with a card from each of the four suits.

88. *Assurances.* Legal evidence of property conveyance.

88. *glosd Ciuill lawes.* The *Corpus Juris Civilis* with all its glosses.

94–95. *Pater . . . Beads.* The Catholic Rosary consists of fifteen decades of Aves, each decade being preceded by a Paternoster ["Our Father"] and followed by a Gloria: a string of 165 beads assists the memory in the recital.

96. *Christs . . . clawes.* Phrase added by Protestants to the Lord's Prayer: "For thine is the Kingdom, and the Power, and the Glory, for ever" (Matt. 6:13).

101. *vouchd texts.* Cited to support one's views.

105. *Haules.* Halls.

106. *Carthusian.* The Carthusians, a monastic order founded in 1084 by St. Bruno, practice silence and solitude.

108. *Hecatombs.* Large number of animals set aside for sacrifice.

I, 27. John Donne, "Elegie: The Bracelet"

42. *seauenteene headed Belgia.* Until 1609, "Belgia" (now Belgium and the Netherlands) consisted of seventeen independent provinces.

50. *loose . . . foot.* Matt. 18:5–10.

56. *groat.* English coin equal to four pence.

71–72. *first . . . knowledge.* Rev. 12:9.

77–78. *their dignities / Passe vertues powers and Principalities.* Vertues: "a high order of angels placed usually 2nd or 3rd in the 2nd triad of the 9 choirs in the Dionysian scheme"; Powers: "Dionysius placed the powers 3rd in the 2nd triad of the celestial hierarchy"; Principalities: ranked "1st in the 3rd triad" by Dionysius (Davidson, pp. 307, 227, 228).

101. *Interdicted.* Debarred from ecclesiastical use.

114. *Cordiall.* Medicine to invigorate the heart.

I, 28. Anonymous, "A Paradoxe of a Painted Face"

10. *St Georges day.* 23 April: St. George is the patron saint of England and of the Order of the Garter.

13. *Fucus and Cerusse.* Red and white facial coloring.

31. *Put case.* Perhaps.

34. *Candian.* From Candia, former capitol of Crete.

35. *Ciuett.* A yellowish or brownish unctuous substance having a strong musky smell, obtained from the sacs or glands in the anal pouch of the African civet cat.

49. *Cordiuant.* Cordwain: Spanish leather of tanned goat-skins.

55. *purles.* Embroiders with gold or silver thread (covers with makeup).

83. *Pigmalions painted statue.* Ovid's *Metamorphoses* (10.243).

I, 29. Sir Thomas Overbury, "A Very Very Woman"

1. *dowbakd.* Deficient, especially in intellect.

10. *voider.* A receptacle for removing dirty dishes.

14. *Mariageable and fourteene.* Paylor sees this "character" as an attack on Lady Frances Howard and notes that she married at fourteen (p. 110).

20. *knight of the Sunne.* Hero of a Spanish romance, *The Mirrour of Princely deedes and Knighthood*, translated by Margaret Tyler in 1578.

20–22. *She . . . toyes.* Toy: a close cap or headdress with flaps coming down to the shoulders.

45. *Salamons cruell creature.* Perhaps Pharaoh's daughter (1 Kings 11) or the wicked woman in Pro. 5:1–6.

I, 29v. Sir Thomas Overbury, "Her Next Part"

32. *fustian.* Coarse cloth made of cotton and flax.

I, 30v. John Donne, "Elegie: The Comparison"

10. *Sanserraes starued men.* The Catholics besieged the Protestants at Sancerre for five months in 1569 and for nine in 1573.

13. *vile . . . tinn.* Gemstones, probably fake, poorly set in tin colored yellow-orange.

16. *fatall . . . Ide.* Eris, goddess of discord and strife, rolled the Golden Apple among Hera, Athena, and Aphrodite; the resulting argument over who was fairest precipitated the Trojan War. Ide: Mount Ide, Greece.

22. *Cinthia.* Surname of Artemis, the moon goddess.

23. *Proserpines . . . chest.* The daughter of Zeus and wife of Pluto had her chest containing the ointment of beauty stolen by Psyche.

24. *Ioues best fortunes vrne.* Zeus had urns of good and ill fortune (*Iliad* 24.527).

31. *sunn . . . gate*. Persons hanged, drawn, and quartered.

I, 31. John Donne, "Elegie: The Perfume"
8. *Cocatrice*. Mythical serpent able to kill with a glance; also, a prostitute.
29. *ingled*. Fondled, cajoled.

I, 32. John Donne, "Elegie: Change"
19. *Danvoy*. "Danuby" or the Danube.

I, 32v. John Donne, "Elegie: Loves Warre"
6. *presse*. Oppress.

I, 33. John Donne, "Elegie: Going to Bed"
36. *Atlantaes . . . viewes*. Hippomenes cast three golden apples in the path of Atalanta, distracting her sufficiently to defeat her in a race.

I, 33v. John Donne, "The Autumnall"
16. *trench . . . Anchoritt*. Anchorits lived as hermits in caves.
29. *Zerzes . . . tree*. Herodotus 7.31.
46. *lation*. Motion of body from one place to another.

I, 34. Anonymous, "Libell agaynst Bashe"
Ruth Hughey, in *The Arundel Harington Manuscript of Tudor Poetry*, identifies "Mr Bash" as "Edward Bashe, or Baesh (d. 1587), who in 1559 was granted the Crown manor of Stansteed in Herts" (2:229) and the "Elliott" of lines 77 and 80 as John Ellyot, a fellow "victualler of the Navy" (2:300).
8. *Crash*. A short bout of revelry or amusement.
13. *Curtall Iade*. Horse having a docked tail; also, a rogue with a short cloak.
32. *Neates*. Oxes.
81. *Seigneur*. A feudal lord taking his designation from the name of his estate.
119. *bare the bell*. Took the prize.
159. *of*. Off.
170. *feltred*. Clogged with filth or maggots.
171. *dizard*. Fool.
172. *vizard*. Mask; also, a prostitute.
205. *Saracens head*. Head of Saracen, Arab, or Turk used as a charge in heraldry and as an inn sign.
218. *cogg*. Cheat.
236–70. Bash was granted the following coat of arms in 1550 and 1572: "*Arms,-Quarterly-1 and 4, Per chevron Argent and Gules, in chief two moor-hens Sable beaked and legged of the second, in base a saltire Or; 2 and 3, Per chevron Argent and Sable, three towers triple-towered counterchanged. Crest-A griffen segreant per pale Argent and Sable, holding in the beak a broken spear of the first*" (Hughey, 2:300).
238. *Clarentius*. Clarencieux, office of the second King-of-Arms.
262. *Cheuin*. A fish, the chub.

I, 36v. Anonymous, "Lenvoy"
5–14. For the defense of "decorum" in *The Canterbury Tales*, see "The Miller's Prologue" and "The Reeve's Prologue." In addition to the admitted debt to Chaucer, Hughey (2:300) notes a close parallel between lines 216–22 of the "Libell agaynst Bashe" and the beginning of *Colin Clout* (circa 1531) by John Skelton (1460–1529).

I, 37. Sir John Davies, "On Bp. Richard Fletcher, Feb. 1594–5"
A manuscript note following this poem and the next in British Library Additional MS. 5832 provides the relevant biographical details: "*BP. Fletcher*, as says Sir *Iohn Harrington p. 27*, of his *Brief View*, being a *Widower, married a gallant Lady, & a widow, Sister to Sir George Gifford, the Pensioner*: who was an *handsome Lady*, adds *Mr Masters* in his *History of Benet College*, & the *Widow of Sir John [Richard] Baker of Sisinghurst in Kent. p. 286*. . . . I suppose he married this *Lady* after he was *BP. of London . . . Richard Fletcher Dean of Peterborough* was made *BP. of Bristol* in *1589*, removed to *Worcester* in *1592*, & from thence translated to *London* in *1594*, & *died June 15 1596*."
1. *Tarquin*. Lucius Tarquinius, last of the legendary kings of Rome (traditionally 534–510 B.C.). His son, Sextus, raped Lucrece.
6. *Miter*. Headband worn by ancient Greek women, the wearing of which by men was regarded by the Romans as effeminacy.

I, 37v. Anonymous, "M^ris^ Attorney scorning long to brooke"
2. *master Cooke*. Possibly Robert Cook (d. 1593), M.A. St. John's College, Cambridge; the poem's details match some notorious aspects of his life (*DNB*, 12:73–74).
9–10. *Trumpettes . . . walles*. Joshua 6:4–20.
24. *Cuckoes nest*. The cuckoo traditionally lays its eggs in the nests of other birds.

I, 38. John Donne, "The Storme"
1. *Thou*. Many manuscript headings of "The Storme" indicate that the poem is addressed to Christopher Brooke (d. 1628) on the occasion of Donne's participation in the 1597 expedition to the Azores headed by the Second Earl of Essex, Lord Thomas Howard, and by Sir Walter Ralegh.
4. *Hilliard*. Nicholas Hilliard (1547–1619), English painter of portrait miniatures.
14. *ayers . . . roome*. Region of air between the clouds and the air near the ground.
22. *Sara*. Gen. 21:7.
33–34. *Ionas . . . then*. Jonah 1:4–6.
47–48. *sin . . . day*. John 5:28–29.
59. *Ordinance*. Military equipment, particularly cannon.
72. *Fiat*. "Fiat lux" (Gen. 1:3).

I, 39. John Donne, "The Calme"
3–4. *fable . . . before*. In the version of Aesop's fable of "The Frogges and Jupiter" in *The Fables of Esope in Englishe* (London, 1570), the frogs ask Jupiter for a king, receive a block of wood, ask for a new king, receive a heron, and are eaten (sig. F3).
16. *Frippery*. Old clothes.
23. *Calenture*. Disease incident to sailors in the tropics.
33. *Baiazet . . . scoffe*. In Christopher Marlowe's *Tamburlaine The Great, Part the First* (1590), Bajazeth, Emperor of the Turks, is imprisoned by Tamburlaine, a Scythian shepherd (4.2).
34. *Sampson*. Judges 16:19.
36. *Ants . . . snake*. Suetonius, "Tiberius" in *The Lives of the Caesars*, book 3, sec. 72.
37. *Galleyes*. Low, flat, seagoing vessels rowed by condemned criminals or slaves.
37. *ffinny*. Having fins; also, moldy.
37. *chippes*. Anything dried out or parched.
38. *Venices*. Anything made in Venice, a city famed for finely equipped ships; or, like Venice, rising from the sea.
46. *pray*. Prey.

I, 39v. John Donne, "To Mr. *Rowland Woodward*: 'Like one who'in her third widdowhood'"
11–12. *skales . . . sin*. Job 31:6.
26. *soule of simples*. Pure organic substances.
32–33. *stock . . . day*. Matt. 6:19–21 and Romans 2:5–6.

I, 40. John Donne, "To Sr. *Henry Wootton*: 'Here's no more newes'"
2. *Callis or St Michaells*. Expeditions to Cadiz (1596) and the Azores (1597).
24. *Chests*. Chess.

I, 40v. Sir John Roe, "Song. 'Deare Love, continue nice and chaste'"
4. *woe*. Woo.

I, 41v. Sir John Roe, "*To Ben. Iohnson*, 6 *Ian*. 1603"
16. *Pophans . . . Cookes tongue*. Sir John Popham (1531–1607) and Sir Edward Coke (1552–1634) earned their reputations for harsh sentences and vicious prosecution at the trials of the Second Earl of Essex and Sir Walter Ralegh.
21. *Serieant*. One charged with the arrest of offenders.
31. *bruised . . . flaxe*. Matt. 12:20.

I, 42. Sir John Roe, "*An Elegie to M^ris^ Boulstred*: 1602"
Cecilia, daughter of Edward Bulstrode, baptized 12 February 1584, died 4 August 1609.
24. *succuba*. A demon in female form, prostitute.

I, 42v. Sir John Roe, "*To Sr Tho. Roe* 1603"
Sir Thomas Roe (1581–1644), English diplomat and author.
15. *nenewe*. Usually, "renewe."

I, 43. Sir John Roe, "*An Elegie*. 'True Love findes witt, but he whose witt doth move'"
13. *And . . . lott*. In Grierson, the line, conjectured by a later copyist in the present text, reads "Whom dauncing measures tempted, not the Scott:" (1:412).

I, 43v. Sir John Roe, "An Elegie. *Reflecting on his passion for his mistrisse*"
27. *Diues*. The rich man in Luke 16:19–24.
52–54. *Queene . . . Actaeon*. Actaeon, having accidentally seen Diana bathing, was changed into a stag and killed by his hounds (Ovid, *Metamorphoses* 3.188–252).

I, 45. John Donne, "Twicknam garden"
Twickenham Park, twelve miles west-southwest of St. Paul's Cathedral, was the residence of Donne's patroness Lucy, Countess of Bedford, from 1608 to 1618.
17. *Mandrake*. Mandragora plant with

fancied human resemblance, fabled to give a fatal shriek when plucked up from the ground.

I, 45v. John Donne, "The good-morrow"
4. *seauen sleepers den.* During the persecution of Christians under emperor Decius (201–251), seven Christian youths of Ephesus concealed themselves in a cavern, fell into a slumber, and awakened in the reign of Theodosius II (401–450).
19. *mixt equallie.* Composed of a balanced mixture of the four elements.

I, 46. John Donne, "Loves Alchymie"
7. *Elixer.* The fifth element or "quintessence" for turning lead into gold.
8. *pregnant pott.* Limbeck.

I, 46v. John Donne, "The Sunne Rising"
17. *Indies . . . Myne.* India and the Americas.

I, 47v. John Donne, "Loves diet"
20. *lres.* Letters.

I, 48. John Donne, "A Valediction forbidding mourning"
11. *tripidation of the spheres.* Libration of the eighth (or ninth) sphere, added to the Ptolemic system to account for certain astronomical phenomena.

I, 48v. John Donne, "Elegie on the Lady Marckham"
Lady Bridget Markham, first cousin to Lucy, Countess of Bedford, died at her home at Twickenham on 4 May 1609.
12. *Godes Noe.* Gen. 6:5–9:17.
19. *imbrothered.* Embroidered.
22. *purslane.* Porcelain.
49–50. *Moses . . . wronged.* Exodus 25:18–20. Most texts read "winged" for "wronged."
52. *teares . . . men.* Hebrews 5:7.

I, 49v. John Donne, "Elegie to the Lady Bedford"
Lucy Harington Russell married Edward, Third Earl of Bedford, in 1594 and died 26 May 1627.
7. *Cusco.* Cuzco, Peru.
7. *Musco.* Moscow.
44. *Iudith.* Book of the Apocrypha.

I, 50. John Donne, "Elegie on Mris. Boulstred"
See note for I, 42.
20. *tenth . . . Hierarchie.* St. Ambrose, Gregory the Great, Pseudo-Dionysius, Isidore of Seville, John of Damascus, and Dante all allot nine orders to the celestial hierarchy, with the Angels as the ninth rank.
24. *fower Monarchies.* Dan. 2:36–45.
29. *bellowes were.* Lungs wear.
66. *had.* Most texts read "told" or "said."

I, 51. John Donne, "Elegie: Death"
10. *fift . . . Monarchie.* The millennial reign of Christ predicted in the apocalypse.
16. *race.* Raze.
30. *the.* Most texts read "she."
45–46. *Bush . . . inspire.* Exodus 3:2–4.
51–52. *Angells . . . fell.* The Seraphim are the highest order of angels and included Satan before he fell.
55–56. *lesse . . . Goddesses.* Acts 19:26–27.
58. *Lemnia. Lemnia sphrasis,* "Lemnian seal," the medicinal earth of the Greek island of Lemnos.

I, 51v. John Donne, "Elegie: 'Oh, let mee not serve so'"
10. *ffauorite in Ordinarie.* Belonging to the regular, permanent staff of the monarch.
38. *arriud.* Most texts read "armed."
45. *recusant.* Roman Catholic who refused to attend services of the Church of England.

I, 52. John Donne, "The Will"
This version lacks the third stanza as usually printed.
15. *Capuchin.* Order of mendicant friars dedicated to poverty.
30. *Bedlam.* St. Mary of Bethlehem, London hospital for the insane.

I, 52v. Francis Beaumont, "To the Countesse of Rutland"
Elizabeth (1585–1615), daughter of Sir Philip Sidney, married Roger Manners (1576–1612), First Earl of Rutland, in 1598.
15–16. *windowes . . . diamond.* See George R. Guffey's "Graffitti, Hurlo Thrumbo and the Other Samuel Johnson," *Forum: A Journal of the Humanities and Fine Arts* 17 (Winter 1979):36–47.
55. *question.* Discussion.

I, 53v. John Donne, "Elegie: The Expostulation"
45. *deny god thrice.* Peter in Matt. 26:69–74.

I, 55. John Donne, "Loves Usury"
14. *comfitures.* Preserved fruit; also, drugs.
15. *Quelque choses.* Kickshaw: dainty or elegant, yet unsubstantial, food.

I, 56v. Sir John Harington, "Of the commodities that men haue by their Marriage"
1. *frier ffrapper.* Harington's choice of name suggests that our priest belongs to a brotherhood of libertine and debauched monks: under "Frapart," the *OED* gives "[a. OF. *frapart.* f. *frapper* to strike.] Only in *friar frapart* [F. *frère frappart* 's'est dit d'un moine libertin et débauché (Littre)]."
5. *harriage.* Average: service done by tenants to a feudal superior.

I, 57. Sir John Harington, "Of a Precise Tayler"
10. *precisian.* Puritan.
11. *bible . . . translation.* Geneva Bible (1560).
28. *venetian hose.* Style of hose or breeches introduced from Venice by 1582.

I, 57. Anonymous, "The famous learned Tullie long agoe"
Marcus Tullius Cicero (106–43 B.C.), Roman statesman and orator.

I, 57v. Sir Walter Ralegh, "The Lie"
30. *tickle.* Difficult to deal with.

I, 58. Josuah Sylvester, "The Fruites of a cleere *Conscience*"
15. *Adam . . . head.* Gen. 3:8.
16. *Cain . . . weepe.* Gen. 4:13–14.

I, 58v. Sir Thomas Overbury, "The Remedy of Loue"
25–26. *Scylla . . . Nisus.* Scylla betrayed her father, King Nisus of Megara, by cutting off a golden lock of his hair out of her love for Minos (*Aeneid* 4.698).
69. *neare.* Never.
81. *Parthian . . . Runnaway.* During the reign of Augustus Caesar, the Parthians broke away once more from Roman rule, and Gaius Caesar led a campaign against Phraates, king of the Parthians in 4 B.C.
83. *Ægistus.* Aegistus became the lover of Clytemnestra, Agamemnon's wife, and after killing Agamemnon ruled as king of Mycenae.
140. *Pluto . . . loue.* According to Homer and Hesiod, Pluto abducted Persephone and married her.
141–42. *Circes . . . her.* Odysseus remained with Circe, a famous sorceress, for a year, but returned to Penelope, his faithful wife.

I, 60v. Sir Thomas Overbury, "The second part of the Remedy of Loue"
30. *Helen Paris lost Oenones loue.* After Paris seduced Helen, Oenone, his previous amour, refused to cure a wound he had received, and Paris died.
85. *Phillis.* In one version of the story of Phyllis, princess of Thrace, her ninth visit to an appointed spot for a sign of Demophoon's return from Troy prompted Athena, overcome with Phyllis's grief, to turn her into an almond tree.
150. *musicke . . . mollifie.* When Orpheus, the supreme minstrel of Greek mythology, played, the whole of nature listened entranced.
151–52. *fishes . . . Arions voyce.* Arion, 8th–7th century B.C., lyric poet rescued from drowning by a dolphin.
171–73. *Atrides . . . Paris.* Atrides: Menelaus, Helen's husband.

I, 62v. Thomas Campion, "A Ballad"
1–2. *Dido . . . knight.* For the love of Dido, legendary Queen of Carthage, for Aeneas, see book 4 of the *Aeneid.*

I, 63. Anonymous, "On a Cobler"
6. *nall.* Awl.

I, 64. Richard Corbett, "An *Elegie* on the late *Lord William Haward* Baron of Effingham, dead *the tenth of December.* 1615"
William Howard, Baron Howard of Effingham (17 December 1577–28 November 1615). Corbett probably knew Howard and the actual date of his death (J. A. W. Bennett and H. R. Trevor-Roper, *The Poems of Richard Corbett*, pp. xvii–xix, 115).
27. *russet.* Coarse homespun woolen cloth usually worn by peasants.
28. *satten.* Clothed in satin.
65. *water=men.* Boatmen, notorious for defamatory gossip and foul language.
78–83. *And . . . Admirall.* Howard's father, Charles Howard, Lord High Admiral, did not die until 14 December 1624.

I, 65v. Anonymous, "On the Duke of Richmonds fate an Elegie"

Lodovic Stewart (29 September 1574–16 February 1623/4) died suddenly in bed on the day fixed for the opening of Parliament, which was delayed.

5. *Herua.* Master of the house.

6. *minerua.* She issued directly from the head of Jupiter; her name has its roots in "mens," "mind."

11. *king.* James I (1566–1625).

16. *Buckingham.* See II, 34v.

21–22. *Thesus . . . Proserpines.* Theseus was trapped (along with Pirithous) in the Chairs of Forgetfulness in Hades until released by Hercules. Theseus then helped Pirithous abduct Proserpine.

27. *Neptune . . . maine.* Stewart was appointed Lord High Admiral of Scotland on 4 August 1591 by then King James VI of Scotland.

31. *Admirall.* Buckingham became Lord High Admiral on 19 January 1619.

32. *Castors . . . reuiues.* As Castor, a mortal, was dying, his twin, Pollux, pleaded successfully for his brother to share his immortality.

70. *Duke Humphryes' guest.* Humphrey (1391–1447), Duke of Gloucester. A Duke Humphrey's guest would be a loiterer about St. Paul's Cathedral seeking a dinner invitation (*DNB* 28:248).

72. *indigitate.* Point out.

75. *Cesars . . . feares.* Plutarch, *The Life of Caesar* 63.5.

124. *Gondamur.* Diego Sarmiento de Acuña (1567–1626), Count of Gondomar, Spanish ambassador to England, 1613–1618 and 1619–1622.

138–44. *affaires . . . negotiation.* "Up to the end of 1619, [Buckingham] appears as James's mouthpiece in advocating an understanding with Spain for the settlement of the Bohemian troubles" (*DNB* 58:329). On 17 February 1623, Prince Charles and Buckingham went to Spain to arrange a marriage with the Infanta of Spain; negotiations did not break off until 23 March 1624.

II, 1. Anonymous [Patrick Maule?], Notations

1. *kitching.* Children's.

II, 1v. Andrew Ramsay, Prayer

I find no record of an Andrew Ramsay; however, Peter Beal has suggested to me that Andrew may have died in childhood, and the brief prayer does allude to illness.

2. *guhen.* When.

4. *RAmsey.* Family name of the earls of Dalhousie.

II, 5. John Donne, "Elegie: Loves Progress"

52. *Canarie.* A light, sweet wine from the Canary Islands.

58. *Remora.* Marine fish noted for attaching itself to other fish and to boats.

60–63. *straight . . . sea.* Leander supposedly swam across the Hellespont (the Dardanelles, a narrow strait in northwest Turkey, linking the Aegean Sea with the Sea of Marmara) from the town of Abydos in Turkey to the town of Abydos in Asia Minor to meet his lover Hero.

96. *Clister.* Clyster: rectal enema.

II, 21v. Anonymous, "*Carold for new yeeres day 1624*"

9m. *Gymill.* Duet.

II, 32v. Anonymous, "My dead and buried loue is resin againe"

2. *type.* A person, object, or event of Old Testament history, prefiguring some person or thing revealed in the new dispensation.

II, 34. George Morley, "On the Death of King James"

James I (19 June 1566–5 March 1625).

13. *Naboth.* 1 Kings 21:1–16.

15. *Vriah.* 2 Sam. 11:3–27.

17. *Shimeis.* 2 Sam. 16:5–13.

II, 34v. Anonymous, "An Epitaph vpon the Duke off Buckinghame"

George Villiers (28 August 1592–23 August 1628) became Lord High Admiral on 19 January 1619 and First Duke of Buckingham on 18 May 1623. John Felton, a discharged naval lieutenant, assassinated the generally unpopular Buckingham.

SEVENTEENTH-CENTURY MANUSCRIPT LOCATIONS AND SIGLA

[AF] United States Air Force Academy, Colorado
1. John Donne, *Poems* (1633), emended by H. Mapletoft

[AU] Aberdeen University Library
1. Aberdeen MS. 29

[B] British Library
1. Additional MS. 5832
2. Additional MS. 5956
3. Additional MS. 10308
4. Additional MS. 10309
5. Additional MS. 10377
6. Additional MS. 11811
7. Additional MS. 12049
8. Additional MS. 15118
9. Additional MS. 15225
10. Additional MS. 15226
11. Additional MS. 15227
12. Additional MS. 17792
13. Additional MS. 17796
14. Additional MS. 18044
15. Additional MS. 18647
16. Additional MS. 19268
17. Additional MS. 21433
18. Additional MS. 22118
19. Additional MS. 22603
20. Additional MS. 23229
21. Additional MS. 24665
22. Additional MS. 25303
23. Additional MS. 25707
24. Additional MS. 27407
25. Additional MS. 27408
26. Additional MS. 27879
27. Additional MS. 28000
28. Additional MS. 29408
29. Additional MS. 29481
30. Additional MS. 29764
31. Additional MS. 29921
32. Additional MS. 30982
33. Additional MS. 32463
34. Additional MS. 34064
35. Additional MS. 34324
36. Additional MS. 34744
37. Additional MS. 36484
38. Additional MS. 44963
39. Additional MS. 52585
40. Additional MS. 53723
41. Cotton Caligula MS. B. V
42. Cotton Cleopatra MS. D. viii
43. Cotton Vitellius MS. E. X
44. Egerton MS. 923
45. Egerton MS. 1160
46. Egerton MS. 2009
47. Egerton MS. 2011
48. Egerton MS. 2012
49. Egerton MS. 2013
50. Egerton MS. 2026
51. Egerton MS. 2230
52. Egerton MS. 2421
53. Egerton MS. 2725
54. Harley MS. 791
55. Harley MS. 1221
56. Harley MS. 1576
57. Harley MS. 1836
58. Harley MS. 2127
59. Harley MS. 2296
60. Harley MS. 2311
61. Harley MS. 3511
62. Harley MS. 3889
63. Harley MS. 3910
64. Harley MS. 3991
65. Harley MS. 4064
66. Harley MS. 4888
67. Harley MS. 4955
68. Harley MS. 5110
69. Harley MS. 6038
70. Harley MS. 6057
71. Harley MS. 6383
72. Harley MS. 6910
73. Harley MS. 6917
74. Harley MS. 6931
75. Harley MS. 7392
76. Lansdowne MS. 98
77. Lansdowne MS. 696
78. Lansdowne MS. 740
79. Lansdowne MS. 777
80. Sloane MS. 542
81. Sloane MS. 1446
82. Sloane MS. 1489
83. Sloane MS. 1792
84. Sloane MS. 2497
85. Sloane MS. 3769
86. Stowe MS. 961
87. Stowe MS. 962
88. Stowe MS. 972
89. MS. 1019 (on permanent loan from St. Michaels College Library, Tenbury Wells)
90. William Byrd, *Psalmes, Sonets, & Songs of Sadnes and Pietie*, shelfmark D.101.d

[BA] Bradford District Archives
1. Hopkinson's MSS, vol. 17
2. Hopkinson's MSS, vol. 27
3. Hopkinson's MSS, vol. 34

[BN] Bibliothèque Nationale
1. Conservatoire MS. Res. 2489
2. MS. fonds anglais n° 149

[BR] Bedfordshire Record Office
1. MS. J1583, St. John MS

[C] Cambridge University Library
1. Additional MS. 29, Edward Smyth MS
2. Additional MS. 4138
3. Additional MS. 5778(c)
4. Additional MS. 7196G
5. Commonplace Book of Mary Browne. Sir Geoffrey Keynes, *Bibliotheca Bibliographici* (London: Trianon Press, 1964), 1301
6. Edward Hyde MS
7. MS. Ee.4.14
8. MS. Ee.5.23
9. John Donne, *Poems* (1639), emended by Giles Oldisworth
10. John Harington, *Orlando Fvrioso* (London, 1591)
11. Leconfield MS. Keynes, 1860
12. Narcissus Luttrell MS. Keynes, 1861

[CE] Cambridge University, Emmanuel College Library
1. MS. I.3.16

[CJ] Cambridge University, St. John's College Library
1. MS. S.32
2. MS. U.26

[CM] Cambridge University, Magdalene College, Pepys Library
1. MS. 2803

[CT] Cambridge University, Trinity College Library
1. MS. R.3.12

[DR] Derbyshire Record Office
1. MS. 258/31/16
2. MS. 258/60/26a

[DT] Trinity College Library, Dublin
1. MS. 408
2. MS. 412
3. MS. 690
4. MS. 877
5. MS. 877, second collection
6. MS. 1375

[EU] Edinburgh University Library
1. MS. D.c.1.69
2. MS. Laing III.436
3. MS. Laing III.493
4. MS. 401, Halliwell-Phillips Collection

[F] Folger Shakespeare Library
1. MS. D347
2. MS. V.a.96
3. MS. V.a.97
4. MS. V.a.103
5. MS. V.a.124
6. MS. V.a.125
7. MS. V.a.162
8. MS. V.a.170
9. MS. V.a.245
10. MS. V.a.262
11. MS. V.a.319
12. MS. V.a.322
13. MS. V.a.339
14. MS. V.a.345
15. MS. V.a.399
16. MS. V.b.43
17. MS. V.b.110
18. MS. V.b.198
19. MS. V.b.296
20. MS. W.a.118

[H] Harvard University Library
1. Eng. MS. 626
2. Eng. MS. 686
3. Eng. MS. 703
4. Eng. MS. 966.1, Norton MS. 4502, Carnaby MS

5. Eng. MS. 966.3, Norton MS. 4503
6. Eng. MS. 966.4, Norton MS. 4506, Dobell MS
7. Eng. MS. 966.5, Norton MS. 4504, O'Flahertie MS
8. Eng. MS. 966.6, Norton MS. 4500, Stephens MS
9. Eng. MS. 966.7, Norton MS. 4620, Utterson MS
10. Eng. MS. 1015
11. Eng. MS. 1035

[HH] Henry E. Huntington Library
1. MS. EL 6893
2. MS. HM 93
3. MS. HM 106
4. MS. HM 116
5. MS. HM 172
6. MS. HM 198, book I
7. MS. HM 198, book II
8. MS. HM 46323

[HR] Hertfordshire Record Office
1. MS. 19061
2. MS. D/ELW Z6, bundle 1.k

[IU] University of Illinois Library
1. MS. 821.08/C737/17–

[JR] John Rylands University Library
1. Rylands English MS. 410

[KU] University of Kansas Library
1. MS. 4A:1

[LA] Leeds Archives Department
1. MS. MX237

[LB] University of Leeds, Brotherton Collection
1. MS. Lt. 25
2. MS. Lt. 48

[LD] Dulwich College, London
1. Alleyn Papers, vol. 1, no. 136

[LI] Inner Temple, London
1. MS. Petyt 538.10

[LP] London Public Record Office
1. State Papers Miscellaneous S.P. 9/51

[LR] Leicestershire Record Office
1. MS. DG.7/Lit.2
2. MS. DG.9/2796

[LY] Leeds, Yorkshire Archaeological Society
1. MS. 329

[MC] Chetham's Library, Manchester
1. Farmer-Chetham MS. 8012, A.4.15
2. Halliwell-Phillips MS. no. 2757

[NP] University of Nottingham, Duke of Portland Library
1. MS. PwV 37
2. MS. PwV 191
3. MS. PwV 323
4. MS. PwV 1198

[NT] University of Newcastle upon Tyne Library
1. MS. Bell/White 25

[NY] New York Public Library
1. Arents Collection, cat. no. S191, John Cave MS
2. Arents Collection, cat. no. S288
3. Berg Collection, Westmoreland MS
4. Music Division, Drexel MS. 4175

[O] Bodleian Library
1. Additional MS. 2156
2. Additional MS. B.97
3. Additional MS. B.106
4. Ashmole MS. 36, 37
5. Ashmole MS. 38
6. Ashmole MS. 47
7. Ashmole MS. 51
8. MS. Aubrey 6
9. MS. Aubrey 8
10. MS. Broxbourne R. 359
11. MS. Cherry 35
12. MS. Don.b.9
13. MS. Don.c.54
14. MS. Don.c.57
15. MS. Don.d.58
16. MS. Douce f.5
17. MS. Douce I
18. MS. Eng. poet. c.50
19. MS. Eng. poet. c.53
20. MS. Eng. poet. d.3
21. MS. Eng. poet. e.14
22. MS. Eng. poet. e.37
23. MS. Eng. poet. e.97
24. MS. Eng. poet. e.99
25. MS. Eng. poet. e.122
26. MS. Eng. poet. f.9
27. MS. Eng. poet. f.10
28. MS. Eng. poet. f.25
29. MS. Eng. poet. f.27
30. MS. Firth d.7
31. MS. Firth e.4
32. Malone MS. 13
33. Malone MS. 19
34. Malone MS. 21
35. Malone MS. 23
36. Malone MS. 117
37. MS. Music f.20–4
38. Rawlinson MS. B.35
39. Rawlinson MS. D.1048
40. Rawlinson MS. D.1092
41. Rawlinson poet. MS. 26
42. Rawlinson poet. MS. 31
43. Rawlinson poet. MS. 66
44. Rawlinson poet. MS. 85
45. Rawlinson poet. MS. 116
46. Rawlinson poet. MS. 117
47. Rawlinson poet. MS. 142
48. Rawlinson poet. MS. 153
49. Rawlinson poet. MS. 160
50. Rawlinson poet. MS. 172
51. Rawlinson poet. MS. 173
52. Rawlinson poet. MS. 199
53. Rawlinson poet. MS. 208
54. Rawlinson poet. MS. 209
55. Rawlinson poet. MS. 212
56. Rawlinson poet. MS. 214
57. Tanner MS. 169
58. Tanner MS. 306
59. Tanner MS. 465

[OA] Oxford University, All Souls College Library
1. MS. 155

[OC] Oxford University, Corpus Christi College Library
1. MS. 176
2. MS. 309
3. MS. 317
4. MS. 318
5. MS. 327
6. MS. 328

[OJ] Oxford University, St. John's College Library
1. John Donne, *Poems* (1633), emended by Nathaniel Crynes

[OQ] Oxford University, Queen's College Library
1. MS. 216

[OX] Oxford University, Christ Church College Library
1. MS. 439
2. MS. 984
3. Evelyn MS. 254

[OW] Oxford University, Worcester College Library
1. MS. 4.29

[P] Private hands
1. MS. Beal Δ74
2. Bedford MS. 26, The Bedford Estates, London
3. Edwin Wolf, 2d MS
4. Harington MS, Arundel Castle
5. MS. LJ. II. 8, Helmington Hall
6. Heneage MS
7. MS. 261, Marquess of Bath, Longleat House
8. MS. Jones B.60, Dr. Williams's Library
9. Thomas Fraser Duff MS

[PM] Pierpont Morgan Library, New York
1. MS. MA 1057

[PT] Princeton University, Robert Taylor Collection
1. W. A. White MS

[R] Rosenbach Museum and Library, Philadelphia
1. MS. 239/16
2. MS. 239/18
3. MS. 239/22
4. MS. 239/27
5. MS. 240/2
6. MS. 243/4
7. MS. 1083/15
8. MS. 1083/16
9. MS. 1083/17

[RI] Rhode Island Historical Society
1. John Saffin Miscellany

[RU] Rutgers University Library
1. MS. FPR 2247, E37

[SA] South African Public Library, Capetown
1. MS. Grey 7 a 29

[SN] National Library of Scotland
1. Advocates' MS. 18.7.21
2. Advocates' MS. 19.3.4
3. MS. 2060, Hawthornden MS. VIII
4. MS. 2067, Hawthornden MS. XV
5. MS. 6504, Wedderburn MS

[SP] St. Paul's Cathedral Library
1. MS. 49.B.43
2. MS. 52.D.14

[TA] Texas A&M University Library
1. John Donne, *Poems* (1633), Henry White volume

[TM] Meisei University Library, Tokyo
1. Crewe MS (formerly Monckton-Milnes MS)

[TT] Texas Tech University Library
1. MS. PR 1171 D14, Dalhousie I

2. MS. PR 1171 S4, Dalhousie II
3. John Donne, *Poems* (1633), emended by John Brodrick

[TU] University of Texas at Austin Library
1. MS. File/(Herrick, R)/Works B

[U] Unlocated
1. Alice Law MS. Beal, vol. 1, pt. 1, p. 29
2. John Payne Collier, *Memoirs of Edward Alleyn* (London, 1841), p. 54
3. John Sparrow Miscellany. Beal, vol. 1, pt. 1, pp. 269, 538

[VA] Victoria and Albert Museum, Dyce Collection
1. Cat. no. 17, MS. 25.F.16
2. Cat. no. 18, MS. 25.F.17
3. Cat. no. 21, MS. 25.F.19
4. Cat. no. 44, MS. 25.F.39

[WA] Westminster Abbey Library
1. MS. 41

[WC] William Andrews Clark Memorial Library, Los Angeles
1. MS. S4975M1

[WN] National Library of Wales
1. Dolau Cothi MS. 6748
2. Peniarth MS. 500B
3. Sotheby MS. B2
4. MS. 5308E
5. MS. 5390D
6. MS. 12443A, part ii
7. MS. 16852D

[Y] Yale University Library, James Osborn Collection
1. MS. b62
2. MS. b114
3. MS. b148
4. MS. b197
5. MS. b200
6. MS. b205
7. MS. f b66
8. MS. f b88

MANUSCRIPT AND PRINT LOCATIONS OF THE POEMS

I, 6. Anonymous, "Arms of Christ"
First published: Thomas Wright and J. O. Halliwell-Phillips, *Reliquiae Antiquae* (London, 1841–1843), 2:18.
MSS: Carleton Brown and Rossell Hope Robbins, *The Index of Middle English Verse* (New York: Columbia University Press, 1943), item 91. B42 (f. 1v); O1 (f. 116); P5 (f. 3v); SN1 (f. 120v).

I, 9r–v. Edward de Vere, "My Mind to Me a Kingdom Is"
First published: Byrd, sig. D2v.
Modern edition: May (pp. 39–40).
MSS: Crum (M817). B8 (f. 3v); B9 (f. 43r–v); B12 (f. 62v); B13 (f. 62); B37 (f. 52v); B39 (f. 74); B46 (ff. 55v–56); B47 (f. 55v); B48 (f. 55v); B75 (ff. 73v–74); B79 (f. 277v); B84 (f. 27v); B90 (sig. D2v); F15 (f. 12); H10 (f. 14v); LI1 (f. 3v); O25 (ff. 22–23); O27 (f. 87r–v); O44 (f. 19r–v); OX1 (p. 102); OX2 (no. 118).

I, 10. Anonymous, "mr: Lamb: Cookes Epi: to his Bro: Hen:"
Unique.

I, 10v–11. Sir John Davies, "Unto that sparkling wit, that spirit of fire"
Modern edition: Robert Krueger, *The Poems of Sir John Davies*, pp. 194–95.
MSS: Beal (DaJ 3). B78 (f. 129r–v); TT2 (f. 10).

I, 11. Sir Henry Wotton, "The Character of a Happy Life"
First published: Overbury, *Wife*, 4th (sig. F2).
Modern editions of this version of the poem: Norman K. Farmer, Jr., "Poems from a Seventeenth-Century Manuscript with the Hand of Robert Herrick," *Texas Quarterly*, no. 4 (supp.) (Winter 1973):50–51, and Ted-Larry Pebworth, "New Light on Sir Henry Wotton's 'The Character of a Happy Life,'" *The Library*, 5th ser. 33 (1978):223–26.
MSS: Beal (WoH 1–48); Crum (H1407). B14 (ff. 147v–48v); B17 (ff. 115v–16); B22 (f. 121); B23 (f. 34v); B31 (f. 42r–v); B32 (f. 160 rev); B50 (f. 11v); B51 (f. 20v); B56 (f. 2); B65 (f. 234v); B70 (f. 18); B79 (f. 65); B85 (f. 2); B87 (f. 176r–v); B88 (f. 8); BA1 (f. 124); BA3 (p. 44); C5 (pp. 84–83 rev); C7 (f. 76); DT5 (ff. 165v–66, 261v–62); F1 (pp. 5–6 at end of volume); F4 (f. 77); F10 (pp. 89–90); F14 (p. 63); F19 (f. 332); H2 (ff. 15v–16); H9 (f. 17v); H11 (f. 10); HH2 (p. 183); HH3 (p. 89); LB1 (f. 7); LB2 (f. 48); LD1 (f. 259r–v); LR1 (f. 278); NP1 (p. 169); O6 (f. 29v); O10 (f. 40v); O14 (ff. 51v–52); O32 (p. 11); O33 (pp. 146–47); O39 (f. 58); O41 (f. 1v); O42 (f. 5r–v); O43 (ff. 55–56); O53 (f. 1); O55 (f. 150 rev); PM1 (p. 137); R1 (p. 18); R3 (f. 25v); RI1 (p. 86); SN5 (f. 85v); TU1 (pp. 78–79); U2 (np); Y4 (p. 49).

I, 15v. Sir Robert Ayton, "The Sheppherd Thirsis"
Modern edition: Charles B. Gullans, *The English and Latin Poems of Sir Robert Ayton*, The Scottish Text Society (Edinburgh and London: William Blackwood & Sons, 1963), p. 179.
MSS: B3 (f. 9); EU2 (p. 32).

I, 16r–v. John Donne, "Elegie: The Anagram"
First published: John Donne, *Poems* (London, 1633), pp. 45–47.
Modern editions: Gardner (pp. 21–22); Grierson (1:80–82); Shawcross (pp. 60–62).
MSS: Beal (DnJ 31–99); Crum (M207). AU1 (pp. 169–71); B15 (f. 1r–v); B18 (f. 7v); B23 (f. 12r–v); B32 (ff. 81–82); B52 (f. 35r–v); B67 (ff. 96v–97); B78 (f. 97r–v); B80 (ff. 53v–54); B83 (ff. 83–84); B86 (f. 53r–v); B87 (ff. 127v–28v); C1 (f. 39v rev); C3 (ff. 26–27); C6 (ff. 3v–4); C7 (f. 76v); C11 (ff. 23–24v); C12 (ff. 30v–31v); CE1 (f. 3v); CJ2 (pp. 92–94); CT1 (pp. 1–2); DR2 (ff. 35–36); DT4 (ff. 29v–30); F3 (pp. 42–43); F4 (f. 54r–v); F8 (pp. 57–59); F9 (f. 47r–v); F11 (ff. 44v–45); F12 (pp. 39–41); F16 (ff. 9v–10); H2 (ff. 61v, 78v); H4 (ff. 13v–14v); H5 (ff. 16v–17v); H6 (f. 145r–v); H7 (ff. 68–69); H8 (ff. 82v–84); H9 (ff. 6v–7, 89v–90); HH1 (ff. 60–61); MC1 (pp. 95–97); NP1 (pp. 112–13); NY1 (pp. 20–21); NY3 (ff. 21v–22); O2 (ff. 55v–56); O15 (f. 48r–v); O21 (ff. 29v–30); O22 (pp. 31–32); O24 (ff. 15v–16v); O26 (pp. 116–18); O29 (pp. 113–14); O46 (f. 224v–r rev); O49 (f. 104r–v); OJ1 (pp. 45–47); P2 (ff. 52v–53); PM1 (pp. 86–87); R3 (ff. 4v–5); SA1 (pp. 57–58); SN5 (ff. 18v–19v); SP1 (ff. [25–26]); SP2 (f. [180r–v]); TM1 (pp. 16–18, 67); TT2 (31r–v); U3 (np); VA2 (ff. 24–25); WA1 (f. 14r–v); WN1 (pp. 21–23); Y3 (pp. 115–16); Y6 (ff. 32v–33).

I, 17. John Donne, "The Curse"
First published: Donne (1633), pp. 231–32.
Modern editions: Gardner (pp. 40–41); Grierson (1:41–42); Shawcross (pp. 128–29).
MSS: Beal (DnJ 806–46); Crum (W2238). B15 (f. 17r–v); B23 (f. 28v); B51 (f. 22r–v); B64 (f. 113); B65 (ff. 277v–78); B67 (f. 124r–v); B78 (f. 108v); B87 (ff. 124v–25); C1 (f. 15); C3 (f. 65r–v); C7 (ff. 62v–63); C11 (ff. 94v–95); C12 (f. 115v); CE1 (f. 6); CT1 (pp. 37–38); DT4 (f. 45v); H5 (f. 32r–v); H6 (f. 199v); H7 (f. 142v); H8 (f. 158r–v); H9 (ff. 23v–24); HH1 (ff. 14v–15); HH6 (pp. 34–35); HH7 (ff. 30, 122r–v); NY1 (pp. 31–32); O5 (p. 39); O24 (f. 122r–v); O26 (pp. 118–19); O46 (f. 208 rev); OQ1 (f. 209r–v); SA1 (p. 65); SN3 (f. 247); SN5 (f. 45r–v); SP1 (f. [100r–v]); TM1 (pp. 10–11); TT2 (f. 11); VA2 (f. 27r–v); WN1 (pp. 77–78); Y2 (pp. 277–79); Y3 (pp. 116–17).

I, 17v. Josuah Sylvester, "A Caution for Courtly Damsels"
First published: William Corkine, *The Second Book of Ayres*, sig. C1v.
Modern edition: Grosart, *Sylvester* (2:341).
MSS: Crum (B357). B4 (f. 133v); B23 (f. 58); B44 (f. 16); B51 (f. 59v); B87 (ff. 64r–v, 229v); BA1 (f. 12v); C4 (ff. 9 rev, 19v rev); C8 (p. 8); DT5 (f. 168); O26 (p. 25); O28 (f. 69); O46 (f. 28v); O57 (f. 199v); TT2 (f. 13); WN6 (pp. 48–50).

I, 17v. Anonymous, "On a Maiden-head"
First published: John Gough, *The Academy of Complements* (London, 1640), p. 146.
MSS: Crum (J104). B52 (f. 16); B77 (f. 153v); C4 (f. 9v rev); O23 (p. 28); O29 (p. 123); O48 (f. 22); TT2 (f. 13).

I, 18. Sir John Harington, "Of a Lady that giues the cheek"
First published: John Harington, *Epigrams Both Pleasant and Seriovs* (1615), sig. B3r–v.
Modern edition: Norman Egbert McClure, *The Letters and Epigrams of Sir John Harington together with The Prayse of Private Life*, p. 230.
MSS: Beal (HrJ 102–24); Crum (I1783). B7 (p. 130); B21 (f. 49r–v); B29 (f. 12); B32 (f. 23); BA1 (f. 12v); BA3 (p. 33); F5 (f. 41v); F10 (p. 102); H2 (f. 54); HH4 (p. 53); MC1 (p. 75); NT1 (f. 44v); NY4 (no. xx); O21 (f. 81v rev); O42 (f. 4); O45 (f. 53); OC1 (f. 29v); OW1 (f. 14); P3 (p. 88); R3 (f. 7v); R4 (p. 202); R8 (p. 59); TT2 (f. 13); VA4 (f. 64v).

I, 18. Jonathan Richards, "a songe: 'I die when as I doe not see'"
First published: John Danyel, *Songs for the Lvte Viol and Voice* (London: T. E. for Thomas Adams, 1606), sig. I2.
MSS: Crum (I134). B32 (f. 36); DT2 (ff. 55v–56); NP1 (p. 68); O23 (p. 164); TT2 (ff. 13v, 31v).

I, 18. Anonymous, "Onste and no more, so sayd my love"
First published: John Cotsgrave, *Wits Interpreter* (London, 1655), sig. O5.
MSS: Crum (O1113). HH7 (f. 38); OC5 (f. 30v); TT2 (ff. 13v, 32).

I, 18v. Anonymous, "for a louinge constand harte"
MSS: DT1 (p. 51); TT2 (f. 13v).

I, 19. Anonymous, "a songe: 'When my hart seemes most ingaged'"
MS: TT2 (f. 14).

I, 19v–20. Anonymous, "Some who the speakinge sparke of my first loue did spie"
Unique.

I, 21–22. John Donne, "Satyre III"
First published: Donne (1633), pp. 333–36.
Modern editions: Grierson (1:154–58); W. Milgate, *John Donne: The Satires, Epigrams and Verse Letters*, pp. 10–14; Shawcross (pp. 22–26).
MSS: Beal (DnJ 2786–814); Crum (K32). B23 (ff. 52v–53v); B67 (ff. 90v–91v); B68 (ff. 99–100v); B78 (ff. 58–59); B87 (ff. 99–100v); C3 (ff. 18–19); C11 (ff. 6v–9); C12 (ff. 14–15v); DT4 (ff. 14v–16); H4 (ff. 12–13v); H5 (ff. 2v–4); H6 (ff. 128–29v); H7 (ff. 36–37v); H8 (ff. 46–48v); H9 (ff. 70–71v); HH1 (ff. 65–67); NY1 (pp. 9–12); NY3 (ff. 7–8); O24 (ff. 4v–6v); O26 (pp. 177–81); OJ1 (pp. 333–36); OQ1 (ff. 201–2v); OX3 (f. [43v]); P6 (ff. 7–8); SP1 (ff. [12–13v]); TT3 (pp. 333–36); VA1 (ff. 5–6v); VA2 (ff. 8–9); Y2 (pp. 17–25); Y3 (pp. 12–15).

I, 22–24. John Donne, "Satyre IV"
First published: Lines 18–23, Joseph Wybarne, *The New Age of Old Names* (London, 1609), p. 113; Donne (1633), pp. 337–45.
Modern editions: Grierson (1:158–68); Milgate, *Satires* (pp. 14–22); Shawcross (pp. 26–34).
MSS: Beal (DnJ 2815–49); Crum (W275). B20 (f. 95r–v); B23 (ff. 48–50); B67 (ff. 91v–94v); B78 (ff. 59v–62v); B86 (ff. 6–10v); B87 (ff. 100v–104v); C3 (ff. 19–22); C11 (ff. 9–15v); C12 (ff. 16–19v); DT4 (ff. 16–20); H4 (ff. 9–12); H5 (ff. 4–7v); H6 (ff. 122–27v); H7 (ff. 38–42); H8 (ff. 49–54v); H9 (ff. 72–75v); HH1 (ff. 67v–72); LR1 (ff. 283–85v); NP2 (ff. 1–4); NY1 (pp. 13–20); NY3 (ff. 8v–11v); O5 (pp. 40–43); O24 (ff. 6v–10v); O26 (pp. 184–93); OJ1 (pp. 337–45); OQ1 (ff. 202v–5v); P2 (f. 53v); P6 (ff. 8v–11); SN4 (ff. 15–20v); SN5 (ff. 3–8); SP1 (ff. [14–18]); TA1 (pp. 337–45); TT3 (pp. 337–45); VA1 (ff. 6v–10); VA2 (ff. 9v–12); Y2 (pp. 25–42); Y3 (pp. 17–22).

I, 24v–25. John Donne, "Satyre V"
First published: Lines 3–4 in William Basse, *A Helpe to Discovrse*, p. 116; Donne (1633), pp. 346–49.
Modern editions: Grierson (1:168–71); Milgate, *Satires* (pp. 22–25); Shawcross (pp. 34–37).
MSS: Beal (DnJ 2850–76); Crum (T2252). B20 (ff. 96–98); B23 (ff. 54–55v); B78 (ff. 63–64); B87 (ff. 105–6); C3 (ff. 22–23v); C11 (15v–17v); C12 (ff. 20–21v); DT4 (ff. 20–21v); H5 (ff. 7v–9); H6 (ff. 118–19); H7 (ff. 42–43v); H9 (ff. 76–77); HH1 (ff. 72–74); NY1 (pp. 21–24); NY3 (ff. 12–13); O24 (ff. 10v–12); O26 (pp. 181–84); OJ1 (pp. 346–49); OQ1 (ff. 206–7); P6 (ff. 11v–12v); SP1 (ff. [18–19v]); TT3 (pp. 346–49); VA1 (ff. 10–11v); VA2 (ff. 12v–13v); Y2 (pp. 43–50); Y3 (pp. 15–17).

I, 25v–26v. John Donne, "Satyre II"
First published: Donne (1633), pp. 329–32.
Modern editions: Grierson (1:149–54); Milgate, *Satires* (pp. 7–10); Shawcross (pp. 18–22).
MSS: Beal (DnJ 2753–85); Crum (S752). B23 (ff. 51v–52v); B67 (ff. 89–90v); B68 (ff. 97v–98v); B78 (ff. 64v–66); B86 (ff. 1–3); B87 (ff. 95–97); C3 (ff. 16v–18); C7 (ff. 69v–70v); C11 (ff. 3v–6v); C12 (ff. 10–11v); DT4 (ff. 23v–25v); H4 (ff. 7v–9); H5 (ff. 11–12v); H6 (ff. 126–27v); H7 (ff. 32–33v); H8 (ff. 43–45v); H9 (ff. 68–69v); HH1 (ff. 61–63); NY1 (pp. 5–8); NY3 (ff. 5v–6v); O24 (ff. 2v–4v); O26 (pp. 143–47); OJ1 (pp. 329–32); OQ1 (ff. 199v–200v); P2 (f. 53r–v); P6 (ff. 5v–6v); SN4 (ff. 21–23); SN5 (ff. 9–11); SP1 (ff. [10–11v]); VA1 (ff. 3–4v); VA2 (ff. 6v–7v); Y2 (pp. 9–16); Y3 (pp. 138–41).

I, 27r–v. John Donne, "Elegie: The Bracelet"
First published: John Donne, *Poems* (1635), pp. 89–93.
Modern editions: Gardner (pp. 1–4); Grierson (1:96–100); Shawcross (pp. 43–46).
MSS: Beal (DnJ 357–413); Crum (N397). AF1 (pp. [414–17]); B23 (ff. 5v–6v); B51 (ff. 15–16v); B64 (f. 114r–v); B67 (ff. 94–95v); B78 (ff. 66–67v); B83 (ff. 39v–41v); B86 (ff. 94v–96); B87 (ff. 214v–16v); C1 (ff. 1–2); C3 (ff. 23v–25); C6 (ff. 7–8); C7 (ff. 67–68); C11 (ff. 17v–20v); C12 (ff. 43–44v); CJ2 (pp. 94–98); DR2 (ff. 33v–35); DT4 (ff. 25v–27); EU3 (ff. 92v–94); F8 (pp. 200–203); F10 (pp. 12–15); H2 (f. 14); H4 (ff. 5–6); H5 (ff. 12v–14v); H6 (ff. 162–63v); H7 (ff. 80v–81v); H8 (ff. 79v–82v); H9 (ff. 61v–63); HH1 (ff. 76v–78v); HH6 (pp. 35–37); HH7 (ff. 112v–13v); LA1 (f. 6); NY1 (pp. 1–5); NY3 (ff. 14–15v); O4 (f. 61v); O13 (ff. 24v–25); O19 (ff. 30v–32); O24 (ff. 13–14v); O26 (pp. 44, 209–13); O33 (p. 150); O35 (p. 220); O46 (ff. 225v–24v rev); O49 (ff. 171v–72v); O55 (f. 152v rev); OC5 (f. 5); P1 (np); P2 (f. 54v); PM1 (pp. 125–27); R3 (ff. 44–45v); SN5 (ff. 40v–42v); SP1 (ff. [21–23]); TM1 (pp. 23–27); TT2 (ff. 9–10); VA2 (ff. 18v–19v); WA1 (ff. 30v–32); WN1 (pp. 32–35); WN5 (pp. 207, 444–42 rev); WN6 (p. 104); Y2 (pp. 98–105); Y3 (pp. 64–66).

I, 28r–v. Anonymous, "A Paradoxe of a Painted Face"
First published: Abraham Wright, *Parnassus Biceps* (London, 1656), pp. 97–100.
Modern edition: Grierson (1:456–59).
MSS: Crum (I372). B51 (f. 24); B63 (ff. 20v–21v); B86 (f. 70); B87 (ff. 49–50); BA3 (pp. 63–64); C7 (ff. 77–78v); DT5 (ff. 244–45v); H8 (pp. 326–30); O21 (ff. 83–82v rev); O34 (ff. 74–75); O36 (f. 29v); O46 (ff. 29v–30); OC5 (ff. 15v–16v); OC6 (ff. 32–33v); TT2 (f. 12r–v).

I, 29r–v. Sir Thomas Overbury, "A Very Very Woman"
First published: Sir Thomas Overbury, *A Wife*, 1st impression (London, 1614), sigs. C4v–D1v.
Modern edition: Paylor (pp. 4–5).
MSS: B78 (f. 80r–v); DT4 (f. 141r–v).

I, 29v. Sir Thomas Overbury, "Her Next Part"
First published: Overbury, *Wife* (sigs. D1v–2).
Modern edition: Paylor (pp. 5–6).
MSS: B78 (ff. 80v–81); DT4 (ff. 141v–42).

I, 30. Sir Thomas Overbury, "A Good Woman"
First published: Overbury, *Wife* (sig. C4r–v).
Modern edition: Paylor (pp. 3–4).
MSS: B78 (f. 81r–v); DT4 (f. 142r–v).

I, 30. Sir Thomas Overbury, "The Authours Epitaph. Written by Himselfe"
First published: Overbury, *Wife* (sig. C3).
Modern edition: Edward F. Rimbault, *The Miscellaneous Works in Prose and Verse of Sir Thomas Overbury, Knt*, p. 46.
MSS: B78 (f. 81v); DT4 (f. 142v).

I, 30v–31. John Donne, "Elegie: The Comparison"
First published: Donne (1633), pp. 149–50.
Modern editions: Gardner (pp. 5–6); Grierson (1:90–92); Shawcross (pp. 47–48).
MSS: Beal (DnJ 680–714); Crum (A1684). B15 (ff. 3v–4); B23 (f. 8); B78 (f. 82r–v); B86 (ff. 31v–32); B87 (ff. 130v–31v); BR1 (ff. 3v–4); C1 (f. 3); C7 (ff. 66v–67); CE1 (f. 6r–v); CT1 (pp. 6–7); DT4 (ff. 31v–32); F6 (f. 52); H4 (ff. 35v–36); H5 (ff. 18v–19); H6 (f. 143r–v); H7 (f. 60r–v); H8 (ff. 66–67); H9 (f. 83r–v); HH1 (ff. 35–36); HH6 (p. 64); IU1 (f. 49); NY1 (pp. 5–7); NY3 (f. 16r–v); O21 (ff. 60v–61); O26 (pp. 54–56); O46 (f. 206v–r rev); O47 (f. 18v); OC5 (ff. 28v–29); P9 (pp. 7–9); SA1 (pp. 58–59); TM1 (pp. 14–16); VA2 (ff. 19v–20); WA1 (ff. 67v–68); Y2 (pp. 113–17); Y3 (pp. 73–74).

I, 31r–v. John Donne, "Elegie: The Perfume"
First published: Donne (1633), pp. 49–51.
Modern editions: Gardner (pp. 7–9); Grierson (1:84–86); Shawcross (pp. 49–51).
MSS: Beal (DnJ 2537–83); Crum (O1112). AF1 (pp. 49–51); AU1 (pp. 63–65); B15 (ff. 4v–5v); B23 (ff. 8v–9); B64 (f. 114); B67 (ff. 97v–98v); B78 (f. 83r–v); B83 (ff. 38v–39v); B86 (ff. 28–29); B87 (ff. 128v–29v); C1 (f. 3r–v); C3 (ff. 27v–28v); C11 (ff. 25v–27); C12 (ff. 24–25); CE1 (ff. 5–6); CT1 (pp. 8–10); DT4 (ff. 32v–33v); F6 (ff. 32v–33v); H4 (ff. 17–18); H5 (ff. 19–20); H6 (ff. 146–47); H7 (ff. 61–62); H8 (ff. 94v–95v); H9 (ff. 84–85); HH1 (ff. 92–93); NY1 (pp. 7–10); NY3 (f. 17r–v); O21 (ff. 34v–35v); O24 (ff. 17v–18v); O26 (pp. 83–86); O33 (p. 81); O46 (ff. 212–11v rev); OC6 (ff. 2–3); OJ1 (pp. 49–51); PM1 (pp. 66–68); R3 (ff. 51v–52v); R8 (pp. 303–4); R9 (ff. 136v–38); SN4 (ff. 30–31v); SN5 (ff. 39–40); SP1 (ff. [26v–28]); TM1 (pp. 18–21); TT2 (f. 15r–v); VA2 (ff. 20v–21); WA1 (ff. 32v–33); WN1 (pp. 28–31); WN2 (pp. 20–24); Y3 (pp. 95–96).

I, 32. John Donne, "Elegie: Change"
First published: Donne (1633), pp. 47–48.
Modern editions: Gardner (pp. 19–20); Grierson (1:82–83); Shawcross (pp. 59–60).
MSS: Beal (DnJ 607–44); Crum (A1119). AF1 (pp. 47–48); B15 (ff. 5v–6); B23 (f.

12); B44 (f. 20); B67 (f. 97r–v); B78 (f. 84); B86 (f. 25r–v); B87 (f. 133r–v); C3 (f. 27r–v); C7 (f. 64v); C11 (ff. 24v–25); C12 (ff. 28v–29); CT1 (pp. 10–12); DT4 (ff. 33v–34); F4 (f. 55v); H4 (ff. 21v–22); H5 (ff. 20v–21); H6 (f. 147r–v); H7 (f. 66r–v); H8 (ff. 75–76); H9 (f. 88r–v); HH1 (f. 96r–v); HH7 (ff. 2v–3); NP1 (pp. 115–16); NY1 (pp. 18–19); NY3 (f. 21); O24 (ff. 16v–17); O26 (pp. 62–63); O46 (ff. 201v rev, 248 rev); P9 (p. 20); SN3 (f. 247v); SP1 (ff. [26r–v]); TT2 (f. 16); VA2 (f. 24); WN1 (pp. 24–25); WN6 (pp. 66–69); Y2 (pp. 75–78); Y3 (pp. 78–79).

I, 32v. John Donne, "Elegie: Loves Warre"
First published: Lines 29–46, *Harmony* (pp. 6–7); Waldron, *Collection* (pp. 1–5) and *Shakespeare* (pp. 1–5).
Modern editions: Gardner (pp. 13–14); Grierson (1:122–23); Shawcross (pp. 55–57).
MSS: Beal (DnJ 2184–226); Crum (T2681). B15 (ff. 15–16); B23 (ff. 10v–11); B32 (f. 142v–r rev); B67 (ff. 99v–100); B78 (ff. 84v–85); B86 (ff. 29v–30); B87 (ff. 133v–34v); C1 (f. 39 rev); C3 (f. 30r–v); C6 (f. 30r–v); C11 (ff. 29v–30v); C12 (ff. 64–65); CT1 (pp. 33–34); DT4 (f. 42r–v); F4 (ff. 76v–77); F14 (pp. 81–82); H4 (f. 27r–v); H5 (f. 29r–v); H6 (f. 148r–v); H7 (ff. 64–65); H8 (ff. 78v–79v); H9 (f. 95r–v); HH1 (f. 85r–v); HH7 (f. 126r–v); HH8 (f. 1r–v); NY1 (pp. 14–16); NY3 (ff. 19v–20); O21 (ff. 33v–34); O23 (pp. 101–2); O24 (ff. 20v–21); O26 (pp. 218–20); O46 (ff. 209–8v rev); OC5 (f. 3r–v); P1 (np); P2 (f. 52v); SA1 (pp. 52–53); SP1 (ff. [30v–31v]); TT2 (f. 16v); VA2 (ff. 22v–23); WN1 (pp. 37–38); Y2 (pp. 79–82); Y3 (pp. 84–85); Y6 (f. 82r–v).

I, 33. John Donne, "Elegie: Going to Bed"
First published: *Harmony* (pp. 2–3); John Donne, *Poems* (1669), pp. 97–99.
Modern editions: Gardner (pp. 14–16); Grierson (1:119–21); Shawcross (pp. 57–58).
MSS: Beal (DnJ 3155–218); Crum (C543 and C546). AU1 (pp. 173–75); B15 (f. 28r–v); B16 (f. 24r–v); B23 (f. 11r–v); B32 (f. 46r–v); B67 (ff. 95v–96); B74 (ff. 7v–8); B78 (f. 85r–v); B80 (f. 11r–v); B83 (ff. 27–28); B86 (f. 24r–v); B87 (ff. 82v–83); BA1 (ff. 19v–20); C3 (f. 25r–v); C7 (f. 78); C11 (ff. 20v–22); C12 (f. 28r–v); CJ1 (ff. 37v–38); CT1 (pp. 63–64); DT4 (ff. 56v–57v); F3 (pp. 68–70); F4 (ff. 40–41); F5 (ff. 24–25); F6 (f. 31); F8 (p. 89); F10 (p. 73); F11 (ff. 24v–25); F14 (pp. 80–81); H2 (ff. 35v–36v); H4 (f. 18r–v); H5 (ff. 43v–44); H6 (f. 144r–v); H7 (ff. 65–66); H8 (ff. 84–85); HH1 (f. 106r–v); HH6 (pp. 43–44); LA1 (ff. 59v–60v); LR1 (f. 281); NY1 (pp. 16–18); NY3 (f. 20r–v); O5 (p. 63); O12 (ff. 57v–58v); O18 (f. 42v); O23 (pp. 103–4); O24 (ff. 14v–15); O26 (pp. 64–66); O28 (f. 17); O29 (pp. 116–17); O46 (ff. 222v–21 rev); O49 (f. 171r–v); O52 (p. 14); P1 (np); P2 (ff. 53v–54); PM1 (p. 5); R3 (ff. 52v–53); R4 (pp. 47–48); SA1 (pp. 48–49); SP1 (ff. [23–24]); TT2 (f. 17); VA2 (f. 23r–v); WA1 (ff. 14v–15); WC1 (p. 10); Y1 (pp. 97–98); Y2 (pp. 69–71); Y3 (pp. 79–81); Y5 (pp. 208–9).

I, 33v. John Donne, "The Autumnall"
First published: Donne (1633), pp. 151–52.
Modern editions: Gardner (pp. 27–28); Grierson (1:92–94); Shawcross (pp. 113–15).
MSS: Beal (DnJ 240–84); Crum (N267). B15 (ff. 6v–7v); B23 (f. 22v); B53 (ff. 63v–64); B64 (f. 114); B65 (ff. 271–72); B67 (ff. 119v–20); B78 (f. 86r–v); B86 (f. 37); B87 (ff. 112v–13); C3 (ff. 59v–60v); C6 (f. 6r–v); C11 (ff. 85v–86v); C12 (ff. 31v–32v); CE1 (f. 3r–v); CT1 (pp. 13–15); DT4 (ff. 34v–35); DT5 (ff. 201v–2); F3 (pp. 34–35); F4 (f. 56r–v); H5 (ff. 21v–22); H6 (f. 141r–v); H7 (ff. 69–70); H8 (ff. 93–94v); H9 (ff. 5v–6); HH1 (ff. 90–91); LR2 (pp. 12–14); NP1 (pp. 116–17); NY1 (pp. 74–75); O21 (f. 38r–v); O24 (ff. 114v–15); O26 (pp. 38–39); O46 (f. 220v–r rev); O49 (ff. 103v–4); P2 (f. 50); P9 (pp. 11–12); SA1 (pp. 56–57); SN5 (f. 23r–v); SP1 (ff. [91–92]); TM1 (pp. 1–2); TT2 (f. 17v); VA2 (f. 40r–v); WN1 (pp. 19–21); WN4 (f. 6); Y2 (pp. 238–51); Y3 (pp. 57–58).

I, 34–36v. Anonymous, "Libell agaynst Bashe"
First published: Hughey, (1:225–32).
MSS: B20 (f. 30r–v [lines 1–4 only]); B34 (ff. 36–40v); B78 (ff. 87–90v); O44 (ff. 66–72); P4 (ff. 137v–39); R7 (ff. 34–37).

I, 36v. Anonymous, "Lenvoy"
First published: Hughey (1:232–33).
MSS: Crum (M812). B78 (ff. 90v–91); O44 (f. 72); P4 (f. 139).

I, 37. Sir John Davies, "On Bp. Richard Fletcher, Feb. 1594–5"
First published: Samuel H. Tannenbaum, "Unfamiliar Versions of Some Elizabethan Poems," p. 819.
Modern edition: Krueger (pp. 178–79).
MSS: Beal (DaJ 86–91, 93–99); Crum (I667). B1 (f. 205); B58 (f. 29); B72 (f. 141); B78 (f. 94); BA3 (p. 12); O23 (f. 20v); O55 (ff. 100v–101); O58 (ff. 189, 190); OA1 (f. 108a); OC5 (f. 29v); R7 (f. 39); VA4 (f. 79).

I, 37. Sir John Davies, "In Londenensem Episcopum iampridem Dominae et scortae nuptias 1595"
First published: Tannenbaum (p. 819).
Modern edition: Krueger (p. 178).
MSS: Beal (DaJ 86–91, 93–99); Crum (I1812). B1 (f. 205r–v); B58 (f. 29); B72 (f. 141); B78 (f. 94); BA3 (p. 12); O23 (f. 20v); O55 (f. 100v); O58 (ff. 188v, 189); OA1 (f. 108v); OC5 (f. 29v); R7 (ff. 38v–39); VA4 (f. 79).

I, 37v. Anonymous, "M[ris] Attorney scorning long to brooke"
MS: B78 (f. 94v).

I, 38r–v. John Donne, "The Storme"
First published: Lines 71–72, Thomas Dekker, *A Knights Coniuring* (London, 1607), sig. B2; Donne (1633), pp. 56–59.
Modern editions: Grierson (1:175–77); Milgate, *Satires* (pp. 55–57); Shawcross (pp. 189–91).
MSS: Beal (DnJ 3047–87); Crum (T2295). AF1 (pp. 56–59); B23 (f. 55r–v); B61 (ff. 19v–20); B67 (ff. 102–3); B71 (ff. 41–42); B78 (ff. 95–96); B87 (ff. 55v–56v); C3 (ff. 33–34); C7 (ff. 72v–73v); C11 (ff. 35v–37); C12 (ff. 79–80); DT4 (ff. 27v–28v); EU3 (ff. 108–9); H4 (ff. 24v–25v); H5 (ff. 14v–15v); H6 (ff. 172–73); H7 (ff. 118–19v); H8 (ff. 105v–7); H9 (ff. 13v–14v); HH1 (ff. 103–4); HH7 (f. 12r–v); NY1 (pp. 38–40); NY3 (f. 26r–v); O21 (ff. 41–42); O24 (ff. 30v–31v); O26 (pp. 41, 213–15); O46 (ff. 26–27); OJ1 (pp. 56–59); OQ1 (ff. 207–8); P2 (ff. 50v–51); P6 (f. 13r–v); PM1 (pp. 98–99); SN4 (ff. 23v–25); SN5 (ff. 12–13); SP1 (ff. [41v–43]); TT2 (f. 18r–v); VA1 (ff. 12–13); VA2 (ff. 16v–17); WN1 (pp. 38–41); WN4 (ff. 8v–9); WN6 (pp. 105–10); Y2 (pp. 221–26); Y3 (pp. 59–60).

I, 39r–v. John Donne, "The Calme"
First published: Donne (1633), pp. 59–61.
Modern editions: Grierson (1:178–80); Milgate, *Satires* (pp. 57–59); Shawcross (pp. 191–93).
MSS: Beal (DnJ 534–71); Crum (O1339). B23 (ff. 55v–56); B61 (f. 20r–v); B67 (f. 103r–v); B71 (ff. 42v–43); B78 (f. 96r–v); B87 (ff. 156–57); C3 (ff. 34–35); C7 (ff. 73v–74); C11 (ff. 37v–38v); C12 (ff. 80–81); DT4 (ff. 28v–29v); H4 (ff. 25v–26v); H5 (ff. 15v–16v); H6 (ff. 173v–74); H7 (ff. 119v–20v); H8 (ff. 107–8); H9 (f. 15r–v); HH1 (ff. 104–5v); HH7 (f. 15r–v); NY1 (pp. 41–42); O13 (ff. 9av–9b); O24 (ff. 31v–32v); O26 (pp. 215–18); O46 (ff. 27–28); OJ1 (pp. 59–61); OQ1 (ff. 208–9); P2 (f. 51); P6 (f. 14r–v); SN4 (ff. 25–26v); SN5 (ff. 13v–14v); SP1 (ff. [43–44v]); TT2 (f. 19); VA1 (ff. 13–14); VA2 (ff. 17v–18); WN1 (pp. 41–42); WN4 (f. 9v); WN6 (pp. 111–15); Y2 (pp. 226–30); Y3 (pp. 60–61).

I, 39v–40. John Donne, "To Mr. *Rowland Woodward*: 'Like one who'in her third widdowhood'"
First published: Donne (1633), pp. 74–75.
Modern editions: Grierson (1:185–86); Milgate, *Satires* (pp. 69–70); Shawcross (pp. 197–98).
MSS: Beal (DnJ 3270–99); Crum (L401). AF1 (pp. 74–75); B15 (f. 2r–v); B67 (f. 107v); B78 (f. 98r–v); B86 (ff. 63v–64); C3 (ff. 39v–40); C11 (ff. 46–47); C12 (f. 63r–v); CT1 (pp. 3–4); DT4 (ff. 30v–31); F4 (f. 76r–v); H4 (ff. 40v–41); H5 (ff. 17v–18); H6 (ff. 174v–75); H7 (f. 101r–v); H8 (ff. 103v–4); H9 (ff. 58v–59v); HH1 (f. 82r–v); NY1 (pp. 88–89); NY3 (ff. 28v–29); O24 (f. 33r–v); O26 (pp. 82–83); OJ1 (pp. 74–75); OX3 (f. [44]); SN5 (ff. 16v–17); SP1 (ff. [44v–45v]); TM1 (pp. 30–31); TT2 (f. 19v); VA2 (ff. 44v–45); WN1 (pp. 131–33); Y2 (p. 217); Y3 (pp. 94–95).

I, 40. John Donne, "To Sr. *Henry Wootton*: 'Here's no more newes'"
First published: Donne (1633), pp. 76–77.
Modern editions: Grierson (1:187–88); Milgate, *Satires* (pp. 73–74); Shawcross (p. 194).
MSS: Beal (DnJ 3442–73); Crum (H1158). B15 (ff. 2v–3); B67 (f. 108); B78 (ff. 98v–99); B86 (f. 66r–v); B87 (ff. 209v–

10); C3 (f. 40r–v); C7 (f. 61v); C11 (f. 47r–v); C12 (ff. 63v–64); CT1 (pp. 4–5); DT4 (f. 31r–v); H4 (f. 37); H5 (f. 18r–v); H6 (f. 169v); H7 (ff. 101v–2); H8 (ff. 102v–3); HH1 (ff. 33v–34); HH6 (p. 65); NY1 (pp. 89–90); NY3 (f. 27); O13 (f. 8); O24 (ff. 33v–34); O26 (pp. 50–51); OX3 (f. [44]); SN4 (f. 29r–v); SN5 (ff. 17v–18); SP1 (ff. [45v–46]); TM1 (pp. 31–32); TT2 (f. 20); VA2 (f. 45r–v); WN1 (pp. 136–37); Y2 (pp. 215–20); Y3 (p. 71).

I, 40v. Sir John Roe, "Song. 'Deare Love, continue nice and chaste'"
First published: Donne (1635), pp. 65–66.
Modern edition: Grierson (1:412–13).
MSS: Crum (D107). AF1 (pp. [443–44]); B4 (f. 65v); B65 (f. 292v); B78 (ff. 99v–100); B86 (f. 58v); B87 (ff. 202–3); BA1 (f. 16r–v); C12 (f. 123v); DT4 (ff. 143v–44); H6 (ff. 213v–14); H7 (ff. 157v–58); HH1 (f. 95r–v); NP1 (p. 77); O26 (pp. 137–38); O42 (ff. 48v–49); O46 (ff. 205–4v rev); OC5 (f. 30v); SN4 (pp. 6–7); SN5 (f. 85r–v); TT2 (f. 20v); VA2 (f. 34r–v).

I, 41. Anonymous, "Wonder of Beautie, Goddesse of my sense"
Modern edition: Grierson (1:447).
MSS: B51 (ff. 13v, 22v); B78 (f. 101); TT2 (f. 21).

I, 41. Anonymous, "Faire eies do not think scorne to read of Love"
Modern edition: Grierson (1:447).
MSS: B78 (f. 101); B86 (p. 113); B87 (f. 81); H6 (f. 196v); H7 (f. 77v); HH1 (f. 23v); TT2 (f. 21).

I, 41v. Sir John Roe, "*To Ben. Iohnson*, 6 *Ian.* 1603"
First published: Donne (1635), pp. 207–8.
Modern edition: Grierson (1:414–15).
MSS: Crum (T1376). AF1 (p. [433]); B43 (f. 24r–v); B65 (ff. 247v–48); B78 (f. 102); C12 (f. 61r–v); H7 (f. 101v); H8 (pp. 216–17); HH1 (f. 31r–v); HH7 (ff. 1v, 126v–27).

I, 42. Sir John Roe, "*To Ben. Iohnson*, 9. *Novembris*, 1603"
First published: Donne (1635), pp. 208–9.
Modern edition: Grierson (1:415–16).
MSS: Crum (I782). AF1 (p. [434]); B65 (f. 248); B78 (f. 102v); C12 (f. 62); H7 (f. 102); H8 (pp. 217–18); HH1 (f. 33); HH7 (f. 2); O42 (f. 25r–v).

I, 42r–v. Sir John Roe, "*An Elegie to M*[ris] *Boulstred*: 1602"
First published: Sir Benjamin Rudyerd, *Le Prince d'Amour* (London, 1660), pp. 109–10.
Modern edition: Grierson (1:410–11).
MSS: Crum (S337). B4 (f. 66v); B78 (f. 103r–v); B87 (f. 113r–v); DT4 (ff. 142v–43); HH6 (p. 169); O42 (f. 26r–v); SN4 (pp. 4–5); SN5 (f. 83r–v).

I, 42v–43. Sir John Roe, "*To S*[r] *Tho. Roe* 1603"
First published: Donne (1635), pp. 209–10.
Modern edition: Grierson (1:416–17).
MSS: AF1 (pp. [434–35]); B4 (f. 62); B78 (f. 104r–v); B87 (f. 210r–v); C12 (ff. 68v–69); H7 (ff. 110v–11); H8 (pp. 191–92); HH1 (ff. 36v–37); HH6 (pp. 168–69).

I, 43. Sir John Roe, "*An Elegie*. 'True Love findes witt, but he whose witt doth move'"
First published: Grosart, *Donne* (1:247–48).
Modern edition: Grierson (1:412).
MSS: Crum (T3336 and T3339). B4 (f. 64v); B78 (f. 104v); C12 (f. 38); H4 (f. 28); H6 (f. 180v); H7 (f. 75); H8 (pp. 148–49); HH1 (f. 32v); HH6 (p. 165); O26 (pp. 86–87); O42 (f. 25v).

I, 43v–44. Sir John Roe, "An Elegie. *Reflecting on his passion for his mistrisse*"
First published: Donne (1635), pp. 93–95.
Modern edition: Grierson (1:407–10).
MSS: Crum (C450). AF1 (pp. [417–19]); B4 (f. 96v); B63 (ff. 17v–18v); B65 (f. 248v); B78 (f. 105r–v); H4 (ff. 36–37); HH6 (p. 172); O26 (pp. 56–58); O42 (f. 26v).

I, 44. John Donne, "The Legacie"
First published: Donne (1633), pp. 208–9.
Modern editions: Gardner (p. 50); Grierson (1:20); Shawcross (pp. 102–3).
MSS: Beal (DnJ 1816–57); Crum (W1165). B15 (ff. 10v–11); B51 (f. 17v); B65 (f. 272r–v); B67 (f. 117); B78 (f. 106); B86 (f. 78v); B87 (f. 122r–v); C3 (ff. 56v–57); C6 (ff. 30v–31); C11 (ff. 80v–81); C12 (f. 105v); CE1 (ff. 4v–5); CT1 (pp. 22–23); DT4 (f. 37v); DT5 (f. 202v); EU3 (f. 89v); F14 (p. 74); H5 (f. 25); H6 (f. 209); H7 (f. 132); H8 (f. 132v); H9 (f. 4); HH1 (f. 58v); HH7 (ff. 28v–29); O24 (ff. 109v–10); O26 (pp. 63–64); O45 (f. 52v); O46 (ff. 65v–66); OJ1 (pp. 208–9); PM1 (pp. 65–66); R8 (pp. 204–5); SA1 (pp. 66–67); SN5 (f. 21); SP1 (f. [86r–v]); TT2 (f. 22v); WN1 (p. 76); WN4 (f. 4); Y2 (pp. 285–87); Y3 (p. 79).

I, 44v. John Donne, "The broken heart"
First published: Lines 1–16, William Basse, *A Helpe to Memory and Discovrse*, pp. 45–46; Donne (1633), pp. 192–93.
Modern editions: Gardner (pp. 51–52); Grierson (1:48–49); Shawcross (pp. 85–86).
MSS: Beal (DnJ 472–520); Crum (H369). B4 (f. 127r–v); B15 (f. 14r–v); B23 (f. 15); B32 (f. 159v rev); B51 (f. 18r–v); B65 (f. 277r–v); B67 (f. 112r–v); B78 (f. 106v); B86 (ff. 76v–77); B87 (f. 124r–v); C1 (f. 4); C3 (ff. 50v–51, 85v); C7 (f. 62v); C11 (ff. 70v–71v); C12 (f. 106); CT1 (pp. 30–31); DT4 (f. 41); EU3 (f. 107r–v); F4 (f. 68v); F14 (p. 75); H1 (f. 77r–v); H4 (f. 125r–v); H5 (f. 28r–v); H6 (f. 208v); H7 (f. 132v); H9 (ff. 4v–5); HH1 (f. 89r–v); HH7 (f. 29r–v); NY1 (pp. 40–41); O21 (f. 40); O24 (ff. 101v–2); O26 (pp. 42–43); O46 (f. 205v rev); OJ1 (pp. 192–93); P9 (pp. 30–31); R8 (pp. 205–6); SA1 (p. 60); SN5 (f. 21v); SP1 (ff. [77v–78]); TM1 (p. 43); TT2 (f. 23); VA2 (ff. 29v–30); WN1 (pp. 58–59); WN4 (f. 4v); Y2 (pp. 303–5); Y3 (p. 62); Y6 (f. 26r–v).

I, 45. John Hoskyns, "A Poem upon Absence"
First published: Francis Davison, *A Poetical Rapsody* (London, 1602), sig. L2.
Modern edition: Osborn (pp. 192–93).
MSS: Crum (A621). B78 (f. 107); B86 (f. 80v); B87 (f. 50v); H4 (f. 33r–v); H6 (f. 213); H7 (f. 155); H8 (f. 118v); HH1 (f. 36); HH7 (f. 34r–v); O21 (ff. 39v–40); O26 (p. 43); SN4 (ff. 65–66); SN5 (f. 86v).

I, 45r–v. John Donne, "Twicknam garden"
First published: Donne (1633), pp. 218–19.
Modern editions: Gardner (pp. 83–84); Grierson (1:28–29); Shawcross (pp. 115–16).
MSS: Beal (DnJ 3639–84); Crum (B392). B15 (ff. 14v–15); B23 (f. 32); B61 (f. 40r–v); B64 (f. 113); B65 (f. 259r–v); B67 (f. 120r–v); B78 (f. 107v); B86 (f. 87); B87 (ff. 91v–92); C1 (f. 16v); C3 (f. 60); C7 (f. 64); C8 (p. 1); C11 (ff. 86v–87); C12 (f. 102v); CE1 (f. 6); CT1 (p. 32); DT4 (f. 41v); DT5 (f. 246r–v); EU3 (f. 88); F4 (ff. 39v–40); H4 (ff. 20v–21); H5 (ff. 28v–29); H6 (f. 183v); H7 (f. 128v); H8 (f. 160r–v); HH1 (ff. 89v–90); HH7 (f. 28v); LA1 (ff. 66v–67); NP1 (p. 73); NY1 (pp. 54–55); O18 (f. 64r–v); O24 (f. 115r–v); O26 (p. 37); O46 (f. 66r–v); OJ1 (pp. 218–19); PM1 (p. 61); SA1 (pp. 90–91); SN5 (ff. 24v, 31); SP1 (f. [92r–v]); VA2 (ff. 33v–34); WN1 (pp. 83–84); Y2 (p. 258); Y3 (pp. 56–60).

I, 45v. John Donne, "The good-morrow"
First published: Donne (1633), p. 165 [195].
Modern editions: Gardner (pp. 70–71); Grierson (1:7–8); Shawcross (p. 89).
MSS: Beal (DnJ 1432–71); Crum (I613). B15 (ff. 13v–14); B23 (f. 32v); B51 (f. 14); B65 (f. 274r–v); B67 (f. 113r–v); B78 (f. 108); B86 (f. 54); B87 (ff. 157v–58); C1 (f. 17); C3 (f. 52r–v); C11 (f. 73r–v); C12 (f. 118); CE1 (f. 4); CT1 (pp. 29–30); DT4 (f. 40v); DT5 (f. 201); F4 (ff. 36v–37); H5 (ff. 27v–28); H7 (f. 147); H8 (f. 127v); H9 (f. 38v); HH1 (f. 99); HH7 (f. 27v); NY1 (p. 94); O24 (f. 103v); O26 (p. 100); OJ1 (p. 165 [195]); R8 (pp. 202–3); SA1 (p. 98); SN3 (f. 246v); SN5 (ff. 35v–36); SP1 (f. [79v]); TT2 (f. 23v); VA2 (ff. 47v–48); WN1 (p. 62); WN4 (f. 5); Y2 (pp. 276–77); Y3 (p. 105).

I, 46. John Donne, "Loves Alchymie"
First published: Donne (1633), pp. 229–30.
Modern editions: Gardner (p. 81); Grierson (1:39–40); Shawcross (pp. 126–27).
MSS: Beal (DnJ 1947–84); Crum (S1001). B15 (f. 17v); B23 (f. 33v); B51 (f. 20); B65 (f. 291); B67 (f. 123v); B78 (f. 109); B86 (f. 58); B87 (ff. 126v–27); BR1 (f. 6v); C3 (ff. 64v–65); C7 (ff. 75v–76); C11 (f. 93r–v); C12 (f. 102); CE1 (f. 4v); CT1 (pp. 38–39); DT4 (f. 46); F7 (f. 66v); H4 (f. 33); H5 (ff. 32v–33); H6 (f. 198v); H7 (f. 128); H8 (f. 159r–v); HH1 (ff. 22v–23); HH6 (p. 65); HH7 (f. 25); NY1 (p. 76); O24 (f. 121r–v); O26 (pp. 13–14); OJ1 (pp. 229–30); P2 (f. 50v); R8 (pp. 201–2); SA1 (p. 66); SN5 (f. 26); SP1 (ff. [98v–99]); VA2 (ff. 40v–41); WN1 (pp. 82–83); Y2 (pp. 267–68); Y3 (pp. 62–63).

I, 46. John Donne, "Breake of day"

First published: Corkine (sig. B1v); Donne (1633), p. 212.
Modern editions: Gardner (pp. 35–36); Grierson (1:23); Shawcross (p. 106).
MSS: Beal (DnJ 414–71); Crum (T2871). AU1 (pp. 184–85); B4 (f. 48v); B11 (f. 75); B15 (f. 8r–v); B16 (f. 19); B23 (f. 18v); B32 (f. 52v); B51 (f. 13); B61 (ff. 39v–40); B65 (f. 262v); B66 (f. 253); B67 (f. 118); B78 (f. 109v); B80 (ff. 11v–12); B83 (ff. 11v–12); B86 (f. 71v); B87 (f. 130v); BA3 (p. 26); C1 (f. 6); C3 (ff. 57v–58); C7 (f. 64); C11 (ff. 82v–83); C12 (f. 104); CT1 (pp. 16–17); DT4 (f. 36); F3 (p. 70); F4 (f. 74); F10 (p. 102); F11 (f. 31v); F12 (p. 55); H2 (f. 94v); H5 (f. 22v); H6 (f. 203v); H7 (f. 130v); H8 (f. 134); HH1 (f. 91v); HH7 (ff. 22v–23, 120r–v); HH8 (p. 7); HR1 (single leaf); LA1 (f. 66v); NP1 (p. 76); NY1 (p. 48); O6 (f. 73r–v); O15 (f. 27); O24 (f. 111v); O26 (pp. 208–9); O28 (f. 11); O46 (f. 220v rev); O56 (f. 81v rev); OC6 (f. 47v); OJ1 (p. 212); P2 (f. 51v); PM1 (p. 140); R4 (pp. 51–52); R6 (p. 73); R9 (f. 135); SA1 (p. 74); SN2 (f. 9v); SN5 (f. 46r–v); SP1 (f. [88r–v]); TM1 (p. 64); TT2 (f. 23v); VA2 (ff. 31v–32); VA4 (f. 78); WN1 (p. 61); Y6 (f. 25); Y8 (f. 120).

Also as "Song. 'Stay, O sweet, and do not rise.'"
First published: In two stanza version, John Dowland, *A Pilgrames Solace* (London, 1612), sig. B2v; and in Orlando Gibbons, *The First Set of Madrigals and Mottets* (London, 1612), sig. C2; printed as the first stanza of "Breake of day" in Donne (1669), p. 17.
Modern editions: Gardner (p. 108); Grierson (1:432).
MSS: Beal (DnJ 2942–83); Crum (S1149 and A762). AU1 (pp. 185–86); B5 (ff. 20v–21); B16 (f. 19); B23 (f. 18v); B29 (f. 9); B40 (f. 10v); B54 (f. 55); B80 (ff. 11v–12); B83 (f. 12); B86 (f. 71v); BN1 (p. 269); C4 (f. 18v rev); C12 (f. 117v); F3 (p. 70); F10 (p. 102); F11 (f. 31v); F12 (p. 55); F14 (p. 237); H2 (f. 94v); H7 (f. 146v); HH7 (f. 42v); HR1 (single leaf); LA1 (f. 66v); LR2 (p. 56); NY2 (p. 48); NY4 (no. vi); O6 (f. 73r–v); O14 (f. 29v); O26 (p. 19); O28 (f. 11); O37 (f.20, f. 56v); O46 (f. 220v rev); O56 (f. 81v rev); OC6 (f. 47v); OW1 (f. 16v); PM1 (p. 137); R2 (p. 106); R4 (pp. 51–52); R6 (p. 73); R9 (f. 135r–v); SN2 (f. 9v); Y3 (p. 5); Y8 (f. 120).

I, 46v. John Donne, "The Sunne Rising"
First published: Donne (1633), pp. 169 [199]–200.
Modern editions: Gardner (pp. 72–73); Grierson (1:11–12); Shawcross (pp. 93–94).
MSS: Beal (DnJ 3088–123); Crum (B626). B15 (ff. 8v–9); B23 (f. 20); B67 (f. 114v); B78 (f. 110); B86 (f. 82r–v); B87 (ff. 121v–22); C1 (f. 8); C3 (ff. 53v–54); C11 (ff. 75v–76); C12 (f. 105r–v); CT1 (pp. 17–18); DT4 (f. 36r–v); F4 (f. 31v); H4 (ff. 38v–39); H5 (ff. 22v–23); H6 (f. 204v); H7 (f. 131v); H8 (ff. 165v–66); HH1 (f. 10v); HH7 (f. 22); HH8 (p. 5); NP1 (p. 64); NY1 (pp. 80–81); O24 (ff. 105–6); O26 (pp. 70–71); OJ1 (pp. 169 [199]–200); SA1 (p. 68); SN5 (f. 33r–v); SP1 (ff. [81v–82]); VA2 (f. 42); VA4 (f. 77r–v); WA1 (ff. 72v–73); WN1 (pp. 68–69); Y2 (pp. 312–14); Y3 (pp. 85–86).

I, 46v–47. John Donne, "Lecture upon the Shadow"
First published: Donne (1635), pp. 66–67.
Modern editions: Gardner (pp. 78–79); Grierson (1:71–72); Shawcross (pp. 86–87).
MSS: Beal (DnJ 1784–815.5); Crum (S1119). AF1 (pp. [444–45]); B15 (f. 9r–v); B23 (f. 33); B51 (f. 23); B65 (f. 256r–v); B67 (f. 112v); B78 (f. 110v); B86 (f. 79); B87 (f. 120); C1 (f. 17); C3 (f. 51r–v); C11 (ff. 71v–72); C12 (f. 111v); CT1 (pp. 18–19); DT4 (ff. 36v, 47); EU3 (f. 92); H5 (f. 23r–v); H6 (f. 192); H7 (f. 138); H8 (f. 153r–v); HH1 (f. 5r–v); HH6 (p. 167); HH7 (ff. 27v–28); NY1 (pp. 82–83); O24 (f. 102r–v); O26 (pp. 103–4); P1 (np); SN5 (ff. 30v–31); SP1 (f. [78r–v]); TM1 (p. 60); VA2 (ff. 42v–43); WN1 (p. 60); Y2 (pp. 287–90); Y3 (pp. 107–8).

I, 47. John Donne, "The triple Foole"
First published: Donne (1633), pp. 204–5.
Modern editions: Gardner (p. 52); Grierson (1:16); Shawcross (pp. 98–99).
MSS: Beal (DnJ 3603–38); Crum (I50). B15 (f. 11r–v); B64 (f. 113); B65 (ff. 270v–71); B66 (f. 253); B67 (f. 116); B78 (f. 111); B86 (f. 76); B87 (f. 121v); C3 (f. 55r–v); C7 (f. 75); C11 (ff. 78v–79); C12 (f. 103); CT1 (pp. 23–24); DT4 (f. 38); F4 (f. 69); H4 (ff. 37v–38); H5 (f. 25v); H6 (f. 205); H7 (f. 129); H8 (f. 124v); H9 (f. 2); HH1 (f. 105v); HH7 (f. 29); NY1 (pp. 84–85); O24 (f. 108r–v); O26 (pp. 67–68); SA1 (pp. 99–100); SN4 (f. 32r–v); SN5 (f. 24); SP1 (f. [84r–v]); TT2 (f. 24); VA2 (f. 43v); WN1 (pp. 63–64); Y2 (pp. 305–7); Y3 (pp. 81–82).

I, 47v. John Donne, "Image of her whom I love"
First published: Donne (1633), p. 153.
Modern editions: Gardner (p. 58); Grierson (1:95); Shawcross (pp. 92–93).
MSS: Beal (DnJ 943–72); Crum (I1177). B15 (ff. 7v–8); B64 (f. 114); B65 (f. 267); B67 (f. 114); B78 (f. 111v); B86 (f. 84); B87 (f. 187r–v); C3 (f. 53r–v); C11 (f. 75r–v); C12 (f. 107); CT1 (pp. 15–16); DT4 (f. 35v); H5 (f. 22r–v); H6 (f. 209v); H7 (f. 133v); H8 (f. 74r–v); H9 (f. 1v); HH1 (f. 10); HH6 (p. 67); HH7 (f. 3r–v); NY1 (p. 58); O24 (ff. 104v–5); O26 (pp. 113–14); SN3 (f. 247v); SN5 (f. 20v); SP1 (ff. [80v–81]); VA2 (ff. 34v–35); WN1 (pp. 18–19); Y3 (p. 113).

I, 47v–48. John Donne, "Loves diet"
First published: Donne (1633), pp. 281–82.
Modern editions: Gardner (pp. 45–46); Grierson (1:55–56); Shawcross (pp. 135–36).
MSS: Beal (DnJ 2023–69); Crum (T3201). B15 (ff. 18v–19); B23 (f. 20v); B64 (f. 113); B65 (ff. 296v–97); B67 (f. 126v); B78 (f. 112); B86 (f. 83r–v); B87 (ff. 87–88); BR1 (f. 2); C1 (f. 8v); C3 (ff. 67v–68); C7 (f. 63v); C11 (ff. 98v–99); C12 (f. 107v); CE1 (f. 6); CT1 (pp. 41–42); EU3 (ff. 106v–7); F2 (f. 50v); F6 (f. 32); F14 (pp. 146–47); H1 (ff. 77v–78); H4 (f. 23r–v); H5 (ff. 33v–34); H6 (f. 193r–v); H7 (f. 134); H8 (ff. 152v–53); H9 (ff. 7v–8); HH1 (f. 20r–v); HH5 (f. 32v); HH6 (p. 64); HH7 (ff. 32v–33); O9 (f. 21); O18 (ff. 117v–18); O19 (f. 9v); O24 (ff. 125v–26v); O26 (pp. 9–10); O46 (f. 204v–r rev); OC5 (f. 29); R8 (pp. 200–201); SA1 (p. 64); SN3 (f. 246v); SP1 (ff. [103v–4v]); TM1 (pp. 58–59); TT2 (f. 24r–v); WN1 (pp. 53–54); WN4 (f. 1r–v); Y2 (p. 264); Y3 (pp. 53–54).

I, 48r–v. John Donne, "A Valediction forbidding mourning"
First published: Donne (1633), pp. 193–94.
Modern editions: Gardner (pp. 62–64); Grierson (1:49–51); Shawcross (pp. 87–88).
MSS: Beal (DnJ 3710–63); Crum (A1711). AU1 (pp. 28–29); B4 (ff. 126–27); B15 (ff. 9v–10); B23 (f. 19); B51 (f. 3r–v); B61 (f. 37r–v); B65 (f. 270r–v); B66 (f. 254); B67 (ff. 112v–13v); B78 (f. 112v); B83 (ff. 58v–59); B86 (ff. 84v–85); B87 (ff. 90v–91); BR1 (f. 4r–v); C1 (f. 7); C3 (ff. 51v–52); C6 (ff. 6v–7); C11 (ff. 72–73); C12 (f. 99r–v); CE1 (ff. 3v–4); CT1 (pp. 19–20); DR2 (ff. 39v–40); DT4 (f. 47r–v); EU3 (f. 91r–v); F8 (pp. 241–42); H4 (ff. 4v–5); H5 (ff. 23v–24); H6 (ff. 186v–87); H7 (f. 124r–v); H8 (ff. 162v–63v); HH1 (f. 11r–v); HH6 (p. 165); LA1 (ff. 10v–11); MC1 (pp. 101–2); NY1 (pp. 27–28); O5 (p. 121); O7 (f. 7); O21 (f. 39r–v); O22 (pp. 33–34); O24 (ff. 102v–3); O26 (pp. 39–41); O47 (f. 18v); OJ1 (pp. 193–94); OX3 (f. [43v]); R6 (pp. 130–31); SA1 (p. 71); SN5 (f. 25r–v); SP1 (ff. [78v–79v]); TT2 (ff. 24v–25); U3 (np); VA2 (f. 26v); WA1 (f. 69r–v); WN1 (pp. 98–99); Y3 (p. 58).

I, 48v–49. John Donne, "Elegie on the Lady Marckham"
First published: Donne (1633), pp. 66–68.
Modern editions: Grierson (1:279–81); Milgate, *Epithalamions* (pp. 57–59); Shawcross (pp. 250–52).
MSS: Beal (DnJ 1050–89); Crum (M106). AF1 (pp. 66–68); B15 (ff. 11v–12v); B16 (f. 36v); B23 (f. 29r–v); B32 (ff. 47v–48v); B65 (ff. 264v–65v); B67 (f. 105r–v); B78 (f. 113r–v); B86 (ff. 20v–21v); B87 (ff. 48–49); C1 (ff. 15v–16); C3 (ff. 37–38); C11 (ff. 41v–43); C12 (ff. 45v–46); CT1 (pp. 24–26); DT4 (ff. 38–39); DT5 (ff. 258v–60); EU3 (ff. 94v–95v); EU4 (f. 70v); H4 (f. 45r–v); H5 (ff. 25v–26v); H6 (ff. 140–41); H7 (ff. 82v–83); H9 (ff. 93–94); HH1 (ff. 100–101); NP1 (pp. 23–24); NY1 (pp. 96–97); NY2 (pp. 104–6); O24 (ff. 24v–26); O26 (pp. 124–26); OJ1 (pp. 66–68); P2 (f. 51); PM1 (pp. 103–4); SA1 (pp. 54–55); SN3 (f. 247v); SN5 (ff. 26v–27v); SP1 (ff. [35v–37]); VA2 (ff. 48–49); WN1 (p. 109); Y2 (pp. 129–34); Y3 (pp. 119–21).

I, 49v. John Donne, "Elegie to the Lady Bedford"
First published: Donne (1633), pp. 298–99.
Modern editions: Grierson (1:227–28); Milgate, *Satires* (pp. 94–95); Shawcross (pp. 249–50).

MSS: Beal (DnJ 3586–602); Crum (Y366). B32 (ff. 46v–47); B63 (f. 22r–v); B65 (ff. 285v–86v); B78 (f. 114r–v); C12 (ff. 66v–67v); DT4 (ff. 43v–44); H4 (ff. 42v–43); H5 (ff. 30v–31); H7 (ff. 105v–6v); H8 (ff. 68v–69v); H9 (f. 90r–v); HH6 (pp. 79–80); O12 (f. 56r–v); O26 (pp. 58–60); O42 (ff. 46v–47); Y3 (pp. 75–76).

I, 50r–v. John Donne, "Elegie on Mris. Boulstred"
First published: Donne (1633), pp. 69–71.
Modern editions: Grierson (1:282–84); Milgate, *Epithalamions* (pp. 59–61); Shawcross (pp. 252–54).
MSS: Beal (DnJ 994–1027); Crum (D187). B15 (ff. 12v–13v); B16 (f. 37); B23 (f. 14r–v); B32 (ff. 48v–49v); B65 (ff. 260–61); B67 (f. 106r–v); B78 (ff. 115v–16v); B86 (ff. 35v–36v); B87 (ff. 93–94); C1 (f. 40v rev); C3 (ff. 38–39); C11 (ff. 43–44v); C12 (ff. 47–48); CT1 (pp. 27–29); DT4 (ff. 39–40v); EU3 (ff. 95v–96v); H4 (ff. 43–44v); H5 (ff. 26v–27v); H6 (ff. 138v–39v); H7 (ff. 84–85); H8 (ff. 87–88v); HH1 (ff. 101v–2v); NP1 (pp. 24–25); O24 (ff. 26–27v); O26 (pp. 119–22); OJ1 (pp. 69–71); OX3 (f. [44]); SN3 (f. 165v); SN4 (ff. 13–14v); SN5 (ff. 28–29); SP1 (ff. [37–38v]); WN1 (pp. 109–12); Y2 (pp. 134–39); Y3 (pp. 117–19).

I, 51r–v. John Donne, "Elegie: Death"
First published: Donne (1633), pp. 296–98.
Modern editions: Grierson (1:284–86); Milgate, *Epithalamions* (pp. 61–63); Shawcross (pp. 254–56).
MSS: Beal (DnJ 1090–1115); Crum (L43). B15 (ff. 16–17); B16 (ff. 36v–37); B65 (ff. 284–85v); B78 (f. 117r–v); B86 (ff. 34–35); B87 (ff. 92–93); C12 (ff. 48v–49v); CT1 (pp. 35–37); DT4 (ff. 42v–43v); F7 (f. 90); H4 (f. 42r–v); H5 (ff. 29v–30v); H7 (f. 86r–v); H8 (ff. 85v–86v); HH1 (ff. 26v–27v); HH6 (p. 169); O26 (pp. 60–62); O42 (ff. 45–46v); OJ1 (pp. 296–98); SA1 (pp. 46–47); SN3 (ff. 165v–66v); SN4 (ff. 10v–12); SN5 (ff. 91v–92v); Y2 (pp. 140–44); Y3 (pp. 77–78).

I, 51v–52. John Donne, "Elegie: 'Oh, let mee not serve so'"
First published: Donne (1633), pp. 53–55.
Modern editions: Gardner (pp. 10–11); Grierson (1:87–89); Shawcross (pp. 52–54).
MSS: Beal (DnJ 2431–71); Crum (O557). B15 (f. 10r–v); B23 (f. 10); B61 (f. 41r–v); B64 (f. 114); B67 (f. 99r–v); B78 (f. 118r–v); B86 (f. 26r–v); B87 (ff. 211–12); C1 (f. 38v rev); C3 (ff. 29–30); C6 (ff. 2v–3); C7 (f. 66r–v); C9 (p. 79); C11 (ff. 28v–29v); C12 (ff. 25v–26v); CT1 (pp. 21–22); DT4 (ff. 47v, 37r–v); DT5 (ff. 170v–71); H4 (f. 21r–v); H5 (ff. 24–25); H6 (f. 149r–v); H7 (ff. 62v–63v); H8 (ff. 71–72); H9 (ff. 86–87); HH1 (ff. 7v–8v); NY1 (pp. 11–13); NY3 (ff. 18v–19); O24 (ff. 19v–20); O26 (pp. 46–47); O46 (ff. 213–12v rev); OJ1 (pp. 53–55); P2 (f. 53v); SA1 (pp. 98–99); SN3 (f. 246r–v); SN5 (f. 22r–v); SP1 (ff. [29v–30v]); TT2 (f. 25r–v); VA2 (ff. 21v–22); WN1 (pp. 35–37); Y2 (pp. 87–90); Y3 (pp. 67–68).

I, 52r–v. John Donne, "The Will"
First published: Donne (1633), pp. 283–85.
Modern editions: Gardner (pp. 54–55); Grierson (1:56–58); Shawcross (pp. 136–38).
MSS: Beal (DnJ 3885–930); Crum (B143). B4 (ff. 50v–51); B15 (ff. 19v–20); B23 (f. 19v); B24 (f. 125r–v); B51 (f. 12r–v); B53 (ff. 104v–5); B65 (ff. 297–98); B67 (f. 127r–v); B78 (f. 119r–v); B86 (ff. 67v–68); B87 (ff. 80–81); C1 (f. 7v); C3 (ff. 68v–69); C7 (f. 62); C11 (ff. 99–100); C12 (ff. 108v–9); CJ2 (pp. 112–14); CT1 (pp. 43–44); EU3 (ff. 105v–6); F6 (f. 30v); H4 (f. 19r–v); H5 (f. 34r–v); H6 (ff. 190v–91); H7 (f. 135r–v); H8 (ff. 154–55); H9 (ff. 47v–48v); HH1 (ff. 18v–19v); HH6 (p. 68); HH7 (ff. 33v–34); NY1 (pp. 62–63); O24 (ff. 126v–27v); O26 (pp. 31–33); O33 (p. 83); O46 (ff. 215–14v rev); OC5 (ff. 5v–6); SA1 (pp. 71–72); SN3 (f. 246v); SN5 (f. 41r–v); SP1 (ff. [104v–5v]); TM1 (pp. 50–51); TT2 (ff. 25v–26); VA2 (f. 36r–v); WN1 (pp. 54–56); Y2 (pp. 200–205); Y3 (pp. 52–53).

I, 52v–53. Francis Beaumont, "To the Countesse of Rutland"
First published: *Certain Elegies, Done by Sundrie Excellent Wits* (London, 1618), sigs. A2–3.
Modern edition: Rev. Alexander Dyce, *The Works of Beaumont & Fletcher*, 11 vols. (1843–1846; rpt. Freeport, N.Y.: Books for Libraries Press, 1970), 11:505–7.
MSS: Beal (BmF 1–26); Crum (M37). B22 (ff. 102v–3v); B23 (f. 31r–v); B51 (ff. 8v–9v); B55 (ff. 79v–80); B63 (ff. 15v–16v); B65 (ff. 268–69); B69 (ff. 24–25); B78 (f. 120r–v); B81 (ff. 73v–74); B87 (ff. 88–89); DR2 (ff. 40v–41v); DT4 (ff. 44–45); EU3 (ff. 98–99); H5 (ff. 31–32); H9 (f. 63v); HH6 (pp. 205–6); HH7 (f. 114r–v); KU1 (pp. 56–57); LA1 (f. 9r–v); LR2 (pp. 24–28); O12 (ff. 56v–57v); O19 (f. 13r–v); O42 (ff. 37v–39); PM1 (pp. 105–6); TT2 (ff. 26–27); VA3 (ff. 3–4).

I, 53v–54. John Donne, "Elegie: The Expostulation"
First published: Donne (1633), pp. 300–302.
Modern editions: Gardner (pp. 94–96); Grierson (1:108–10); Shawcross (pp. 71–72).
MSS: Beal (DnJ 1215–42); Crum (T3023). B27 (f. 368); B65 (ff. 246–47); B78 (f. 121r–v); B86 (ff. 32v–33v); B87 (ff. 212v–14); C6 (ff. 4–5); C12 (ff. 38v–39v); DT4 (f. 48r–v); F7 (ff. 20v–21); H4 (ff. 22–23); H5 (ff. 35–36); H6 (ff. 150v–51v); H7 (ff. 75v–76v); H8 (ff. 76v–78v); H9 (ff. 91–92); HH1 (ff. 38v–39v); HH6 (pp. 85–86); SN4 (ff. 33–34v); SN5 (ff. 48v–49v); O26 (pp. 75–77); O42 (ff. 22–23v); OC5 (ff. 3v–4v); R9 (ff. 103–4); TM1 (pp. 4–5); TT2 (f. 27r–v); TT3 (pp. 300–302); Y3 (pp. 90–91); Y4 (pp. 31–32).

I, 54. John Donne, "Song: 'Goe, and catche a falling starre'"
First published: Lines 1–4, 10–18, Basse, *Memory* (p. 143); Donne (1633), pp. 196–97.
Modern editions: Gardner (pp. 29–30); Grierson (1:8–9); Shawcross (p. 90).
MSS: Beal (DnJ 2897–941); Crum (G118). B2 (f. 37v); B15 (f. 21); B23 (f. 61); B49 (f. 58v); B65 (ff. 286v–87); B67 (f. 113v); B78 (f. 122); B86 (f. 75v); B87 (f. 65r–v); C1 (f. 19); C3 (ff. 52v–53); C7 (f. 61); C11 (ff. 73v–74v); C12 (f. 120); CT1 (pp. 46–47); DT4 (f. 49r–v); F4 (f. 74r–v); F7 (f. 25v); F17 (p. 43); H4 (f. 33v); H5 (ff. 36v–37); H6 (f. 203); H7 (f. 149v); H8 (f. 124); HH1 (f. 21r–v); HH7 (f. 21v); NY1 (p. 51); O22 (p. 58); O24 (ff. 103v–4); O26 (pp. 44–45); O46 (f. 217 rev); P9 (pp. 20–21); PM1 (p. 101); R5 (p. 78); R6 (p. 21); SA1 (p. 145); SN5 (f. 43); SP1 (f. [80r–v]); TM1 (p. 52); TT2 (f. 28); VA2 (f. 32v–33); WA1 (f. 70); WN1 (pp. 104–5); WN5 (pp. 6–7); Y3 (pp. 66–67); Y5 (p. 92).

I, 54v. John Donne, "Loves Deitie"
First published: Donne (1633), pp. 280–81.
Modern editions: Gardner (pp. 47–48); Grierson (1:54); Shawcross (pp. 134–35).
MSS: Beal (DnJ 1985–2022); Crum (I298). B15 (f. 24v); B23 (f. 21); B65 (ff. 295v–96); B67 (f. 126r–v); B78 (f. 122v); B86 (f. 55r–v); B87 (f. 111r–v); BR1 (f. 1v); C1 (f. 9); C3 (f. 67v); C11 (ff. 97v–98v); C12 (f. 108); CT1 (p. 54); DT4 (f. 52); DT5 (ff. 238v–39); F4 (f. 37); F14 (p. 146); H4 (f. 34r–v); H5 (f. 39r–v); H6 (f. 192v); H7 (f. 134v); H8 (f. 152r–v); H9 (ff. 8v–9); HH1 (ff. 99v–100); HH7 (f. 32v); NY1 (pp. 81–82); O24 (f. 125r–v); O26 (pp. 47–48); R8 (pp. 199–200); SN5 (ff. 46v–47); SP1 (f. [103r–v]); TT2 (f. 28v); VA2 (f. 42v); WN1 (pp. 52–53); WN4 (f. 2); Y2 (pp. 262–63); Y3 (p. 69).

I, 54v–55. John Donne, "The Funerall"
First published: Donne (1633), pp. 285–86.
Modern editions: Gardner (pp. 90–91); Grierson (1:58–59); Shawcross (pp. 138–39).
MSS: Beal (DnJ 1383–407); Crum (W2236). B15 (f. 25); B67 (f. 127v); B78 (f. 123); B86 (f. 57); B87 (f. 127r–v); C3 (f. 69r–v); C11 (f. 100r–v); C12 (f. 114v); CJ2 (pp. 114–15); CT1 (p. 55); DT4 (f. 52v); H4 (ff. 19v–20); H5 (ff. 39v–40); H6 (f. 191v); H7 (f. 141v); H8 (f. 169r–v); H9 (f. 44); HH1 (ff. 19v–20); O24 (ff. 127v–28); O26 (pp. 30–31); SA1 (p. 73); SP1 (ff. [105v–6]); TA1 (pp. 285–86); TT3 (pp. 285–86); WN1 (pp. 56–57); Y3 (p. 51).

I, 55. John Donne, "Loves Usury"
First published: Donne (1633), pp. 201–2.
Modern editions: Gardner (p. 44); Grierson (1:13–14); Shawcross (pp. 95–96).
MSS: Beal (DnJ 2159–83); Crum (F444). B65 (ff. 278v–79); B67 (f. 115); B78 (f. 123v); B86 (f. 56); B87 (f. 208v); C3 (f. 54r–v); C11 (f. 77r–v); C12 (f. 119v); H4 (f. 39v); H6 (f. 208); H7 (f. 148v); H8 (ff. 121v–22); H9 (f. 37v); HH1 (ff. 15v–16); HH6 (pp. 69–70); HH7 (ff. 29v–30); LP1 (single leaf); O24 (ff. 106v–7); O26 (pp. 74–75); OJ1 (pp. 201–2); SN5 (f. 38v); SP1

(ff. [82v–83]); WN1 (pp. 57–58); Y2 (p. 259); Y3 (pp. 89–90).

I, 55v. John Donne, "The Flea"
First published: Donne (1633), pp. 230–31.
Modern editions: Gardner (p. 53); Grierson (1:40–41); Shawcross (pp. 127–28).
MSS: Beal (DnJ 1340–82); Crum (M181). B15 (f. 22v); B23 (f. 15v); B51 (f. 11); B65 (f. 289v); B67 (f. 124); B78 (f. 124); B86 (f. 57v); B87 (ff. 110v–11); C1 (f. 4r–v); C3 (f. 65); C7 (f. 75v); C11 (f. 94r–v); C12 (f. 111); CT1 (p. 50); DT4 (f. 50r–v); F4 (f. 38); F8 (pp. 214–15); H4 (f. 20); H5 (ff. 37v–38); H6 (f. 199); H7 (f. 137v); H8 (ff. 156v–57); HH1 (f. 98v); HH7 (ff. 30v–31); NY2 (pp. 114–15); O24 (ff. 121v–22); O26 (pp. 29–30); O33 (p. 57); O46 (ff. 218–17v rev); O50 (f. 74v); OC5 (f. 21v); OJ1 (pp. 230–31); R6 (p. 42); SA1 (p. 96); SN5 (f. 47); SP1 (ff. [99–100]); TM1 (p. 65); TT2 (f. 29); WN1 (pp. 85–86); Y2 (pp. 282–84); Y3 (pp. 50–51); Y7 (item 38); Y8 (f. 120).

I, 55v–56. John Donne, "Communitie"
First published: Donne (1633), p. 222.
Modern editions: Gardner (pp. 33–34); Grierson (1:32–33); Shawcross (pp. 119–20).
MSS: Beal (DnJ 645–79); Crum (G420). AF1 (p. 222); B15 (f. 21v); B51 (f. 17); B65 (f. 287r–v); B67 (f. 121v); B78 (f. 124v); B86 (f. 85v); B87 (f. 158v); C3 (ff. 61v–62); C11 (ff. 64r–v, 89r–v); C12 (f. 121v); CT1 (p. 48); DT4 (ff. 49v–50); DT5 (ff. 200v–201); H4 (f. 16r–v); H5 (f. 37r–v); H6 (f. 201v); H7 (f. 151v); H8 (f. 120r–v); H9 (f. 23); HH1 (ff. 21v–22); HH6 (p. 69); HH7 (f. 27r–v); NY1 (p. 65); O24 (ff. 117v–18); O26 (pp. 102–3); OJ1 (p. 222); SN5 (f. 47v); SP1 (f. [95r–v]); TT2 (f. 29r–v); VA2 (f. 37); WN1 (p. 102); Y2 (pp. 254–57); Y3 (pp. 106–7).

I, 56. John Donne, "Womans constancy"
First published: Donne (1633), pp. 197–98.
Modern editions: Gardner (pp. 42–43); Grierson (1:9); Shawcross (pp. 91–92).
MSS: Beal (DnJ 3969–97); Crum (N577). B15 (f. 22); B64 (f. 113); B65 (f. 288v); B67 (f. 114); B78 (f. 125); B87 (f. 159); C3 (f. 53); C11 (f. 74v); C12 (f. 103v); CT1 (p. 49); DT4 (f. 49v); DT5 (f. 203); H5 (f. 37); H6 (f. 207); H7 (f. 130); H8 (f. 131); HH1 (f. 22r–v); HH7 (ff. 19v–20); O24 (f. 104v); O26 (pp. 105–6); OC5 (ff. 7v–8); PM1 (pp. 61–62); SA1 (p. 67); SN5 (f. 48); SP1 (f. [80v]); TT2 (f. 29v); WN1 (p. 70); Y3 (pp. 108–9).

I, 56v. Sir John Harington, "Of the commodities that men haue by their Marriage"
First published: John Harington, *The Most Elegant and Witty Epigrams of Sir Iohn Harrington, Knight, Digested into Fovre Bookes*, sigs. G1v–2.
Modern edition: McClure (pp. 213–14).
MSS: Beal (HrJ 253–55); Crum (A129). B7 (pp. 90–91); B23 (f. 128); B78 (f. 128); O2 (f. 38v).

I, 57. Sir John Harington, "Of a Precise Tayler"
First published: Harington (1618), sigs. B5v–6.
Modern edition: McClure (pp. 156–57).
MSS: Beal (HrJ 167–86); Crum (A485). B7 (pp. 17–18); B11 (f. 14); B19 (ff. 52v–53); B23 (f. 120v); B65 (f. 233v); B78 (f. 128v); BA3 (p. 92); CJ2 (pp. 22–23); HH6 (pp. 27–28); LA1 (f. 18v); LR1 (f. 322); O5 (p. 85); O41 (f. 3v); O42 (ff. 4–5); O50 (f. 12); O55 (f. 101r–v); R4 (pp. 170–71); R8 (pp. 186–87); VA4 (f. 84); Y1 (pp. 94–95); Y4 (p. 99); Y6 (ff. 47v–48).

I, 57. Anonymous, "The famous learned Tullie long agoe"
Unique.

I, 57. Sir John Harington, "Of Women learned in the tongues"
First published: Harington (1615), sig. B1.
Modern edition: McClure (pp. 255–56).
MSS: Beal (HrJ 273–89.5); Crum (Y396). B7 (p. 4); B32 (f. 20v); B58 (f. 16v); BA3 (p. 83); C6 (f. 8v); C10 (p. 14); DT3 (f. 140v); F7 (f. 32v); F10 (p. 69); H2 (f. 85); HH4 (p. 13); LB1 (f. 7v); O6 (f. 48); O21 (f. 87 rev); O29 (p. 133); OC6 (f. 47v); R4 (p. 187); R8 (p. 20); Y6 (f. 40v).

I, 57. John Donne, "Faustus"
First published and attributed to Donne: Shawcross, "Drummond."
Modern edition: Shawcross (p. 165).
MSS: Beal (DnJ 1302–4). SN4 (f. 32v); SN5 (f. 48).

I, 57v–58. Sir Walter Ralegh, "The Lie"
First published: Francis Davison, *A Poetical Rapsodie* (London, 1608), pp. 17–19.
Modern edition: Agnes M. C. Latham, *The Poems of Sir Walter Ralegh* (Cambridge: Harvard University Press, 1962), pp. 45–47.
MSS: Beal (RaW 147–77); Crum (G205). B1 (ff. 218–19); B30 (ff. 9–10v); B59 (f. 135); B72 (ff. 141v–42); BA3 (pp. 9–11); BN2 (f. 73); C2 (f. 46r–v); CJ2 (p. 43); DT5 (ff. 216–17v); F4 (f. 67r–v); F14 (pp. 176–77); F18 (f. 2); HH6 (f. 1); MC1 (pp. 103–6); NP1 (pp. 138–39); O7 (f. 6); O16 (ff. 11–12); O20 (f. 2v); O30 (ff. 146–50); O31 (pp. 3–5); O50 (f. 12v); O55 (ff. 88–90); O58 (f. 188r–v); OA1 (ff. 18v–19v); P8 (pp. 257–60); PM1 (p. 42); PT1 (single leaf); R4 (pp. 175–77); R7 (ff. 16v–17); TT2 (f. 30r–v); WN3 (ff. 66–67, 131–33).

I, 58. Anonymous, "*Emelia* embraceing many guifts and loues"
Unique.

I, 58. Josuah Sylvester, "The Fruites of a cleere *Conscience*"
First published: Josuah Sylvester, *Du Bartas His Diuine Weekes and Workes* (London: Robert Young, 1633), p. 651.
Modern edition: Grosart, *Sylvester* (2:340–41).
MSS: B41 (f. 271); B43 (f. 78); B76 (f. 204r–v); TT2 (ff. 30v–31).

I, 58v–60v. Sir Thomas Overbury, "The Remedy of Loue"
First published: Sir Thomas Overbury, *The First and Second part of The Remedy of Loue*, sigs. A4–B1.
Modern edition: Rimbault (pp. 205–12).
MSS: B78 (ff. 131–33v); B87 (ff. 194–97v).

I, 60v–62. Sir Thomas Overbury, "The second part of the Remedy of Loue"
First published: Overbury, *Remedy* (sigs. B2–7).
Modern edition: Rimbault (pp. 212–19).
MSS: B78 (ff. 134–36v); B87 (ff. 198–201v).

I, 62v. Thomas Campion, "A Ballad"
First published: Mason and Earsden (sig. C1).
Modern edition: Walter R. Davis, *The Works of Thomas Campion* (Garden City, N.Y.: Doubleday & Co., 1967), p. 467.
MSS: Beal (CmT 187–91). B26 (f. 220v); EU2 (pp. 75–76); EU4 (f. 84v); R6 (pp. 16–17).

I, 62v. Anonymous answer to Thomas Campion, "A Ballad"
Unique.

I, 63. Anonymous, "On a Cobler"
First published: Sir John Mennes, *Wits Recreations* (London, 1641), sig. R2v.
MSS: Crum (H774 and H825). B11 (f. 5); B19 (f. 32v); B82 (f. 38); C6 (f. 4); DT5 (f. 257v); NT1 (f. 30v); O5 (pp. 166, 199); O29 (p. 128); O40 (f. 268); O59 (f. 65); OC2 (f. 49); OC6 (ff. 43, 61).

I, 64–65. Richard Corbett, "An *Elegie* on the late *Lord William Haward* Baron of Effingham, dead *the tenth of December*. 1615"
First published: *Sir Thomas Ouerbury His Wife. With Addition of many new Elegies vpon his vntimely and much lamented death. The ninth impression* (London, 1616), pp. 32–35.
Modern edition: Bennett and Trevor-Roper (pp. 20–23).
MSS: B25 (f. 162r–v); BA3 (pp. 27–28); DT4 (ff. 59–60); DT5 (ff. 251v–53); H5 (ff. 45v–46v); H9 (ff. 98–99v).

I, 65v–67. Anonymous, "On the Duke of Richmonds fate an Elegie"
MSS: B17 (f. 181); B22 (f. 124); B80 (f. 48).

II, 3. Anonymous, "My deare and onelie loue tak heede"
First published: Sir John Mennes, *Wit and Drollery* (London, 1656), sig. D1r–v.
Modern edition: *Ancient and Modern Scottish Songs* (Edinburgh, 1776), 1:237–41.
MSS: Crum (M620 and M621). B28 (f. 177v); B58 (ff. 5, 8); B62 (ff. 3–4); O17 (f. 101v); O38 (ff. 46 rev, 58 rev).

II, 4. Anonymous, "My deere and onlie loue tak heed"
Another version of previous item.

II, 4v. Anonymous, "My deere and onlie loue tak heed"
Another version of the two previous items.

II, 5–6. John Donne, "Elegie: Loves Progress"
First published: *Harmony* (pp. 36–39); Donne (1669), pp. 94–97.
Modern editions: Gardner (pp. 16–19);

Grierson (1:116–19); Shawcross (pp. 65–68).
MSS: Beal (DnJ 2123–58); Crum (W2241). AF1 (pp. [425–27]); B15 (ff. 25v–27); B23 (ff. 27–28); B67 (ff. 101–2); B86 (ff. 48–49v); C1 (f. 14r–v); C3 (ff. 32–33); C11 (ff. 33–35v); C12 (ff. 32v–34); CE1 (f. 5); CT1 (pp. 56–60); DT4 (ff. 54v–56); F9 (ff. 12–13v); F10 (p. 17); F12 (pp. 149–53); H4 (ff. 29–30v); H5 (ff. 41v–43); H7 (ff. 70–71v); H8 (ff. 72–74); H9 (ff. 33v–35); HH1 (ff. 93–95); HH6 (pp. 193–94); LR2 (pp. 68–72); NY1 (pp. 35–38); O24 (ff. 22v–24v); O26 (pp. 89–92); O45 (f. 51); O46 (ff. 211–9v rev); P1 (np); R2 (pp. 78–79); R4 (pp. 49–50); RU1 (single leaf); SA1 (pp. 50–52); SP1 (ff. [33v–35v]); VA2 (ff. 28–29); WN7 (ff. 150–51); Y2 (pp. 106–13); Y3 (pp. 98–100).

II, 7–8. Anonymous, "If kinges did heretofore there loues indite"
Unique.

II, 9–10. John Donne, "Elegie: The Bracelet." See I, 27r–v.

II, 10. Sir John Davies, "Unto that sparkling wit, that spirit of fire." See I, 10v–11.

II, 11. John Donne, "The Curse." See I, 17.

II, 11v. John Donne, "The Message"
First published: Donne (1633), p. 186.
Modern editions: Gardner (pp. 30–31); Grierson (1:43); Shawcross (p. 80).
MSS: Beal (DnJ 2274–321); Crum (S295). AF1 (p. 186); B4 (f. 132r–v); B15 (f. 56v); B16 (f. 10); B23 (f. 61); B52 (f. 25); B67 (f. 111r–v); B86 (f. 74); B87 (f. 110v); B89 (f. 1v); BA3 (p. 40); C3 (ff. 49v–50, 87); C6 (f. 6v); C7 (f. 75); C8 (p. 3); C11 (f. 69r–v); C12 (f. 106v); CE1 (f. 4r–v); CT1 (p. 122); DT4 (ff. 90v–91); EU3 (f. 90); F4 (f. 38r–v); F13 (f. 195); H4 (f. 16); H5 (f. 73r–v); H6 (f. 213v); H7 (f. 133); H8 (f. 126v); H9 (f. 1); HH1 (ff. 96v–97); HH7 (ff. 24r–v, 112r–v); LA1 (f. 13); NP1 (p. 78); NY1 (p. 45); O22 (p. 59); O24 (f. 100); O26 (pp. 49–50); O46 (f. 217v rev); OC6 (f. 74v); R6 (p. 72); SP1 (f. [76]); TT3 (p. 186); VA2 (f. 31); WN1 (p. 100); WN4 (f. 3); Y2 (pp. 314–16); Y3 (p. 70).

II, 12r–v. Anonymous, "A Paradoxe of a Painted Face." See I, 28r–v.

II, 13. Josuah Sylvester, "A Caution for Courtly Damsels." See I, 17v.

II, 13. Anonymous, "On a Maiden-head." See I, 17v.

II, 13. Sir John Harington, "Of a Lady that giues the cheek." See I, 18.

II, 13v. Jonathan Richards, "a songe: 'I die when as I doe not see.'" See I, 18 and II, 31v.

II, 13v. Anonymous, "Onste and no more, so sayd my loue." See I, 18 and II, 32.

II, 13v. Anonymous, "ffor a louinge constant hart." See I, 18v.

II, 14. Anonymous, "a songe: 'when my hart seemes moste ingaged.'" See I, 19.

II, 15r–v. John Donne, "Elegie: The Perfume." See I, 31r–v.

II, 16. John Donne, "Elegie: Change." See I, 32.

II, 16v. John Donne, "Elegie: Loves Warre." See I, 32v.

II, 17. John Donne, "Elegie: Going to Bed." See I, 33.

II, 17v. John Donne, "The Autumnall." See I, 33v.

II, 18r–v. John Donne, "The Storme." See I, 38r–v.

II, 19. John Donne, "The Calme." See I, 39r–v.

II, 19v. John Donne, "To Mr. *Rowland Woodward*: 'Like one who'in her third widdowhood.'" See I, 39v–40.

II, 20. John Donne, "To Sr. *Henry Wootton*: 'Here's no more newes.'" See I, 40.

II, 20v. Sir John Roe, "Song. 'Deare Love, continue nice and chaste.'" See I, 40v.

II, 21. Anonymous, "Wonder of Beautie, Goddesse of my sense." See I, 41.

II, 21. Anonymous, "Faire eies do not think scorne to read of Love." See I, 41.

II, 21v. Anonymous, "*Carold for new yeeres day* 1624"
Unique to TT2. See also II, 33.

II, 22. Francis Bacon, "The worlds a bubble, and the life of man"
First published: Thomas Farnaby, *Florilegium Epigrammatvm Graecorum* (London, 1629), pp. 8–10.
Modern edition: Alexander B. Grosart, *Miscellanies of The Fuller Worthies' Library*, 4 vols. (1870–1876; rpt. New York: AMS Press, 1970), 1:49–51.
MSS: Beal (BcF 1–53); Crum (T1591). B11 (f. 91); B14 (ff. 153v–54); B17 (ff. 87–88); B22 (ff. 74v–75); B53 (f. 60r–v); B60 (ff. 24v–25); B61 (ff. 73v–74); B70 (f. 17); B87 (f. 169r–v); C3 (f. 81); CE1 (f. 148v); CJ1 (f. 42); CM1 (ff. 95–97v); DR1 (pp. 8–9); DT5 (f. 164r–v); DT6 (pp. 160–61); EU3 (f. 116); EU4 (f. 62); F1 (pp. 8–9); F2 (f. 6r–v); F7 (ff. 5v–6); F10 (p. 99); F12 (pp. 96–97); F14 (pp. 143–44); H3 (f. 16r–v); H11 (ff. 12v–13v); HH2 (p. 56); HH5 (f. 4r–v); HR2 (f. 48v); JR1 (ff. 32v–33); LY1 (pp. 13–14); MC2 (single leaf); NP1 (p. 196); NP4 (p. 3); O3 (ff. 13v, 14v); O5 (p. 2); O8 (f. 71v); O11 (f. 7); O15 (f. 8v); O18 (ff. 60v–61); O27 (ff. 16v, 117); O29 (pp. 76–77); O46 (ff. 173–72v rev); O47 (f. 20v); O49 (f. 33r–v); O51 (f. 162r–v); O54 (f. 23); O58 (f. 188r–v); OC4 (f. 40v); P7 (p. 9); R1 (pp. 6–7); R4 (pp. 168–69); R5 (p. 91); R8 (p. 149); SA1 (p. 111); U1 (np); WN5 (pp. 534–33 rev); Y1 (pp. 134–35).

II, 22v. John Donne, "The Legacie." See I, 44.

II, 23. John Donne, "The broken heart." See I, 44v.

II, 23v. John Donne, "The good-morrow." See I, 45v.

II, 23v. John Donne, "Breake of day." See I, 46.

II, 24. John Donne, "The triple Foole." See I, 47.

II, 24r–v. John Donne, "Loves diet." See I, 47v–48.

II, 24v–25. John Donne, "A Valediction forbidding mourning." See I, 48r–v.

II, 25r–v. John Donne, "Elegie: 'Oh, let mee not serve so.'" See I, 51v–52.

II, 25v–26. John Donne, "The Will." See I, 52r–v.

II, 26–27. Francis Beaumont, "To the Countesse of Rutland." See I, 52v–53.

II, 27r–v. John Donne, "Elegie: The Expostulation." See I, 53v–54.

II, 28. John Donne, "Song. 'Goe, and catche a falling starre.'" See I, 54.

II, 28v. John Donne, "Loves Deitie." See I, 54v.

II, 29. John Donne, "The Flea." See I, 55v.

II, 29r–v. John Donne, "Communitie." See I, 55v–56.

II, 29v. John Donne, "Womans constancy." See I, 56.

II, 30r–v. Sir Walter Ralegh, "The Lie." See I, 57v–58.

II, 30v–31. Josuah Sylvester, "The Fruites of a cleere *Conscience*." See I, 58.

II, 31r–v. John Donne, "Elegie: The Anagram." See I, 16r–v.

II, 31v. Jonathan Richards, "a songe: 'I die when as I doe not see.'" See I, 18 and II, 13v.

II, 32. Anonymous, "Once and no more soe sayd my loue." See I, 18 and II, 13v.

II, 32v. William Herbert, "When my Carliles Chamber was on fire"
MSS: Crum (H29). B15 (f. 109v); C2 (f. 49v); DT5 (f. 189v); O45 (f. 49v).

II, 32v. Anonymous, "My dead and buried loue is resin againe"
MS: B15 (f. 109v).

II, 32v. Anonymous, "Why doe yee giue mee leaue to sip"
Unique

II, 33. Anonymous, "Carold for newe yeares day. 1624." See II, 21v.

II, 34. George Morley, "On the Death of King James"
First published: William Camden, *Remaines Concerning Britaine* (London: Thomas Harper, 1636), pp. 398–99.
MSS: Crum (A1016 and H421). B6 (f. 29v); B10 (f. 26); B11 (f. 91v); B23 (f. 79); B24 (f. 126); B32 (f. 59); B45 (f. 89v); B73 (f. 72v); B83 (f. 44); B87 (f. 165r–v); BA2 (p. 150); BA3 (f. 24); C5 (pp. 46–47); DT5 (f. 184r–v); EU2 (pp. 25–26); MC1 (p. 165); NP1 (p. 27); NP5 (f. 1); O5 (p. 186); O18 (f. 23v); O21 (f. 10); O23 (p. 10); O52 (pp. 61–62); OC6 (f. 7); WA1 (f. 48v).

II, 34v. Anonymous, "An Epitaph vpon the Duke off Buckinghame"
Unique.

TEXTUAL APPARATUS

The apparatus below lists substantive variants among the texts of the John Donne poems in the two Dalhousie manuscripts; the seven seventeenth-century editions/issues of Donne's collected *Poems*; and selected, modern critical editions. The following sigla represent these artifacts:

TT1 Texas Tech University MS. PR 1171 D14. Formerly, MS. Dalhousie I (Scottish Record Office GD 45/26/95/1)

TT2 Texas Tech University MS. PR 1171 S4. Formerly, MS. Dalhousie II (Scottish Record Office GD 45/26/95/2)

D33 Donne, John. *John Donne Poems 1633*. Menston, Eng.: The Scolar Press, 1970 [facsimile of British Library copy]

D35 ———. *Poems*. London: M.F. for John Marriot, 1635 [Microfilm of Harvard University Library copy]

D39 ———. *Poems*. London: M.F. for John Marriot, 1639 [Texas Tech University Library copy]

D49 ———. *Poems*. London: M.F. for John Marriot, 1649 [microfilm of Yale University Library copy]

D50 ———. *Poems*. London: John Marriot, 1650 [microfilm of Yale University Library copy]

D54 ———. *Poems*. London: J. Flesher, 1654 [microfilm of Yale University Library copy]

D69 ———. *Poems*. London: T.N. for Henry Herringman, 1669 [Texas Tech University Library copy]

Gr12 Grierson, Herbert J. C., ed. *The Poems of John Donne*. London: Oxford University Press, 1912. Vol. 1.

Ga65 Gardner, Helen, ed. *John Donne: The Elegies and the Songs and Sonnets*. Oxford: Clarendon Press, 1965.

M67 Milgate, W., ed. *John Donne: The Satires, Epigrams and Verse Letters*. Oxford: Clarendon Press, 1967.

S67 Shawcross, John T., ed. *The Complete Poetry of John Donne*. Garden City, N.Y.: Doubleday & Co., 1967.

M78 Milgate, W., ed. *John Donne: The Epithalamions, Anniversaries and Epicedes*. Oxford: Clarendon Press, 1978.

The headnote for each poem gives the title, the sigla for the artifacts in which the poem occurs, and the location(s) in the Dalhousie manuscripts. For brevity, sequences of more than three artifacts appear as "initial siglum-last siglum," with the hyphen representing all sigla in the chronological sequence between the initial and last sigla. For example, the listing for "The Storme" reads "'The Storme.' Texts: TT1 (38r–v), TT2 (18r–v), D33–Gr12, M67, S67" to indicate that "The Storme" occurs on folio 38r–v in TT1, on folio 18r–v in TT2, in D33, D35, D39, D49, D50, D54, D69, Gr12, M67, and S67, but not in Ga65 or M78.

For each entry recording a substantive variant, the line numbers are those of the complete poems in modern critical editions; the reading left of the bracket is that of TT1 (TT2 if the poem does not occur in TT1) and all subsequent artifacts with the same reading; readings in parentheses immediately to the right of the bracket are additional substantive variations among readings of the artifacts that agree in a general way with the reading left of the bracket; readings not in parentheses immediately right of the bracket are in chronological order followed by the appropriate sigla and separated by semicolons; readings in parentheses following the sigla for readings right of the bracket are additional substantive variants within readings that agree in a general way with the listed variant reading. These entries record only the substantive difference(s) among the readings and not differing accidentals, with the actual entry being the reading of the earliest artifact in the sequence; thus, the entry for line 49 of "Elegie: Loves Progress" (TT2, 5–6) reads "49 *Hemispheare*] a rosie *Hemispheare* D69–S67" even though D69, Gr12, and S67 literally read "a rosie Hemisphere," and Ga65 reads "a rosy hemispheare." When multiple substantive differences occur in a single entry and writing them out individually would involve substantial repetition, these substantive variants are recorded in parentheses in the entry: for example, the entry for line 70 of "Satyre II" (TT1, 25v–26v) reads "70 Like a Kinges *fauourite* yea like a kinge] (or like D35, D69; kinge. D35–D69; kinge; Gr12–S67); ______ D33" because D35 through S67 generally agree with TT1, even though D35 and D69 have substantive verbal variants and D35–D69 as well as Gr12–S67 have substantive punctuation variants. When the variant(s) involve punctuation only, a "~" replaces the reading to the left of the bracket in the remainder of the entry, and a "^" indicates omitted punctuation. Omitted words are represented by "*om.*" For brevity, sequences of three or more sigla with the same reading appear as "initial siglum-last siglum," with the hyphen representing only the artifacts containing the poem; for example, the entry for line 60 of "The Storme" reads "60 thence] ~. D33–D39, Gr12–S67" to indicate the period in artifacts D33, D35, D39, Gr12, M67, and S67 but not in Ga65, which does not contain the poem. Bracketed readings are in a hand other than that of the original copyist or are emendations created by Donne's modern editors. "HE" indicates title or heading.

"Elegie: The Anagram." Texts: TT1 (16r–v), TT2 (31r–v), D33–Ga65, S67.

HE *om*] *Elegie* II. D33, Gr12; Eleg. II. *The Anagram*. D35–D69 (ELEGIE D69); The Anagram Ga65; *Elegie: The Anagram*. S67.

1 Marrye:] ~^ TT2; ~, D33–S67.

2 bewtious] bewties TT2. bee] ~, D33–D49, Gr12–S67; ~; D50–D69.

4 they] theirs D69. bee Iett] bee Iett, D33, D49–S67 (are Iett Ga65); bee Iett. D35, D39.

5 donne] dimme D33–S67. enowghe] *om* TT2.

6 fale] faile TT2; foul D69. rowghe:] ~^ TT2; ~; D33, D69–S67; tough; D35–D54.

7 thowghe] thought TT2.

8 hath then] hath D33–S67. mayden head,] maydenhead^ TT2; maydenhead. D33–S67.

9 elamentes:/] ~,^ TT2–S67.

10 please.] ~^ TT2.

12 the] thy D33–S67. wentch;] ~^ TT2, S67; ~, D33–Ga65. lye.] ~^ TT2.

13 aske] ~; D33–D39, Gr12–S67; ~, D49–D69.

14 where.] ~^ TT2.

16 hath] hath yet D33–S67. an] the→ane TT2; the D69. *Anagram*] *Anagrams* D69. face] ~. D33–S67.

17 pte] put D33–S67.

18 that] the D33, Gr12–S67. saye] ~? D33–S67.

19 Gam. vt;] Gam-vt, TT2; Gamut^ D33–D54, Gr12–S67; Gamuth^ D69.

20 sonnge] ~, TT2–D54, Gr12–S67; ~; D69.

21 gam, vt;] gam-vt^ TT2; gamut^ D33–D54, Gr12–S67; gamuth^ D69. it] ~. D33–S67.

22 vnfitt.] ~^ TT2; ~; D33–D69, S67.

23 any;] ~^ TT2; ~, D33–S67. albe] al be TT2–S67. her.] ~^ TT2; ~, D33–S67.

24 bee.] ~, TT2–S67. is she] she is D33–S67. singular.] ~^ TT2.

25 wonder;] ~^ TT2.

26 he] her TT2–S67. wonderfull;] ~^ TT2; ~, D33–S67. too.] ~^ TT2; ~? D33–S67.

27 one] on D33–S67.

28 Chose] Chuse D33–S67. charged] changed D33–S67. w^th^] by D33–S67. deformityes] ~; D33, S67; ~. D35–Ga65.

29 like] all like D33–S67. angells,] ~; D33–S67. they] then TT2; the D33–S67.

30 worse:] ~, TT2; ~; D33–D39, Gr12–S67; ~: D49–D69.

31 impare.] ~^ TT2; ~: D33–S67.

32 lesser] lesse D33–S67.

33 nights reuelles] nightReuelles TT2.

34 vse:] ~^ TT2; ~. D33–S67.

35 oft;/] ~,^ TT2; ~;^ D33–S67.

36 is the] there is D33–S67. waye.] ~^ TT2.

37 what] what a D33–S67.

38 Ielowsye] ~! D33–S67.

39 Eweunches;] ~^ TT2, D49–D54; ~, D69.

40 fooes,] ~^ TT2; ~; D33–D39, Gr12–S67. yee] yea D33–S67. marmasett,] ~^ TT2; ~. D33–S67.

41 When] Like D69. the round] when the D69. Centryes] Countries D33–D54, Gr12–S67; Country D69. drownd] drowne D33–D54, Gr12–S67.

42 towne,] ~^ TT2; ~: D33–D54, Gr12–S67; towns; D69.

43 her,] ~; D33–S67.

44 ofte must absent] absent oft must D33–S67.

45 day] the day D33–S67.

46 then] than D35–D69. Sea;] ~^ TT2; ~, D33–S67. mores] Moores D33–S67.

47 vii] sevin TT2–S67.

49 childbearth] childbeds D33–D54, Gr12, S67; childbirths D69, Ga65. labor] *om* TT2.

50 twere] T'wes TT2.
51 accuse] accuse her selfe D33–S67.
52 then] than D35–D69. confesse] ~. D33–D69; ~, Gr12–S67.
53 Whom dildoes, beadstaves and her veluet glase] (or her D69); *om* D33–D54.
54 would be as loth to tutch as Ioseph was] (sutch→[so]utch→ [To]utch TT2; was. D69; was: Gr12–S67); *om* D33–D54.
55 none;] ~, TT2–S67. were.] ~^ TT2; ~, D33–S67.
56 ffor] *om* TT2. fassion;] ~, TT2; ~^ D33–S67. weare:/] ~^^ TT2; ~.^ D33–S67.

"The Curse." Texts: TT1 (17), TT2 (11), D33–Ga65, S67.
HE *A*] *The* TT2–S67.
1 Whoeve^r:] Who ever^ TT2–S67.
2 mistris;] M^rs, TT2; ~, D33–S67. wither] whither TT2. curse.] ~^ TT2; ~; D33–D54, Gr12–S67; course; D69.
3 only;] ~^ TT2, D69; ~, D33–D54, Gr12–S67. purse] purpose→[purs] TT2.
4 harte;] ~^ TT2–D54, Gr12–S67; whore^ D69.
5 she] then D69. then to] unto D69. fooes;] ~^ TT2–S67.
6 scorned;] ~^ TT2–S67. men] ~~else~~[men] TT2; else D33–S67.
8 ffor feare] forsweare TT2; With feare D33–S67. missinge;] ~, TT2–S67. torne:/] ~^^ TT2; ~;^ D33–D54; ~.^ D69; ~:^ Gr12– S67.
9 crampes;] crampe^ TT2; crampe, D33–D54, Gr12, S67; ~^ D69; ~, Ga65.
10 make;] ~, D33–D54, Gr12–S67; ~^ D69. him] them D69. sutch] ~: D33–S67.
12 conscience] contyence→con[c]yence TT2. fame;] ~, TT2–S67.
13 shee] ~: D33–S67.
14 Or maye he, for her vertue reuerence] in earely scarcenesse, and longe may he rott TT2; In early and long scarcenesse may he rot D33, Gr12–S67.
15 Her y^t hates him, only for impotence] for land, wch had been his, if he had not TT2, D33, Gr12–S67.
16 And equall traytors be she; and his senc,] (she^ D35–D69; senc. D35–D69); himselfe incestuouslie an heire begott TT2, D33, Gr12–S67 (begott: D33, Gr12–S67).
19 why,] ~^ TT2; ~: D33–S67.
20 sonnes;] ~^ TT2; ~, D33–S67.
21 infamye,] ~^ TT2; ~: D33–S67.
23 theres] theires TT2–S67.
24 be] he→[b]e TT2. bread.] ~^ TT2; ~: D33–D39, Gr12–S67.
25 all] owld TT2.
26 there] their D33–S67.
27 hearbs] ~~plantes,~~[hearbs] TT2; Plants D33–S67. mynes] myne[s] TT2; myne D33–D69.
28 and all] all ill TT2–S67.
29 poets or pphetts] prophets, or poets TT2–S67. spoke,] speake^ TT2; spake; D33–S67.
30 me] [the]~~ty~~^me TT2.
31 man:] ~, TT2; ~; D33–S67.
32 Nature] nature TT2. before hand] beforehand D49–D69. oute cursed] oute-cursed D33–S67. mee:/] ~^^ TT2; ~.^ D33–S67.

"Satyre III." Texts: TT1 (21–22), D33–Gr12, M67, S67.
HE *Satire*] *Satyre III.* D33–S67.
1 spleene] ~; D33–S67.
2 eielidds] eie-lidds, D33–D39, S67; eie-lidds D49–D69; eie-lidds; Gr12, M67.
3 Surs] sinnes D33–S67. and] but D69.
4 Maladies] ~? D33–S67.
7 to] in D33. age] ~? D33–S67.
9 them] ~? D33–S67.
11 end] ~, D33, Gr12–S67; ~? D35–D69.
13 heere] heare D33–S67.
15 Or] O D33–S67. this] ~. D33; ~: D35–D69; ~; Gr12, M67; ~, S67.
16 is] ~; D33, S67; ~. D35–M67.
17 *Dutch*] ~, D33, Gr12–S67; ~? D35–D69.
19 death] dearth? D33–S67.
20 earth] ~? D33–S67.
22 discoueries] ~, D33–D69; ~? Gr12–S67.
23 then] than D39–D69. *Salamanders*] ~? D33–D69; ~, Gr12–S67.
24 line] ~, D33, D35, Gr12–S67; ~. D39.
27 goddesse] Goddesse D33–S67.
28 woords] ~, D33; ~? D35–S67. strawe] ~! D33–S67.
30 stand] to stand D33–S67.
31 his] this D69. garison] ~) D33–S67.
32 forbidden] forbid D35–D69. *field*] ~? D33–S67.
33 foe] ~, D33; foes; D35–D54; foes: D69–M67; foes, S67. is whom] h'is, whom D33, S67; he, whom D35–D54; (he, whom D69; (whom Gr12; whom M67.
34 please] ~: D33, S67; ~, D35–D54, M67; ~) D69, Gr12.
35 quitt] ~; D33–S67.
39 strumpett] ~; D33–S67.
40 selfes] selfe D33.
41 louest] ~; D33–S67.
42 loth] ~; D33, S67; ~. D35–D54, Gr12, M67; ~, D69.
43 *Religion*;] ~. D33, Gr12–S67; ~, D35–D69. where] ~? D33–D54, Gr12–S67; ~: D69.
44 here] her D33. vs] ~, D33–D54, Gr12–S67; ~; D69.
45 *Roome*,] ~; Gr12, M67. she] he D33–S67.
47 He] And D35–D54. the] her Gr12–S67.
48 *statecloth*] *state-cloth* D69. yesterday] ~. D33–S67.
49 *Grants*] *Crants* D33–D54, Gr12–S67. to] to such D33–S67. loue] Loues D33–S67.
52 vnhandsome] ~. D33–D69, S67; ~; Gr12, M67.
53 humours] ~, D33, D39–S67; ~. D35.
54 course] coarse D35–D69. drudges] ~: D33–D69; ~. Gr12–S67.
56 (vile] ~^ D33–S67.
57 fashions)] ~, D33–S67. biddes] bidd Gr12–S67.
60 tender.] ~, D33, Gr12–S67; ~; D35–D69.
63 good] ~, D33, Gr12–S67; ~; D35–D69.
64 none] ~. D33–S67.
67 kind] ~; D33–D69, S67; ~, Gr12, M67.
68 *Religion*] ~; D33–S67. blindnes] blind- D33–S67.
69 Too] nes too D33–S67 (to D49–D54). breedes] ~; D33, Gr12– S67; ~. D35–D69. then] thou D33–S67.
70 alowe] ~; D33–S67.
71 right,] ~; D33–S67. father] Father D35–D69.
72 his] ~; D33, Gr12–S67; ~. D35–D69.
73 is] ~; D33, Gr12–S67; ~. D35–D69.
74 her] ~, D33, Gr12–S67; ~; D35–D69.
75 w^ch] that D33–S67. best] ~. D33–S67.
76 to] or D33–S67.
77 badd;] ~. D35–D69. wiselie] ~, D33–Gr12, S67; ~; M67.
78 stray] ~; D33–S67.
79 is:] ~. D35–M67.
80 truth] Truth D33–S67.
81 must about] about must D33–S67. goe] must goe; D33–D39, Gr12–S67; must goe: D49–D54; it goe: D69.
82 soe] ~; D33, Gr12–S67; ~. D35, D39; ~, D49–D69.
84 that] the D35–D54. night] ~, D33; ~. D35–S67.
85 doe] ~. D33–D54, S67; ~: D69–M67.
86 paines] ~; D33–S67. too] to D33–D69.
87 reach.] ~, D33, Gr12–S67; ~; D35–D69.
88 sunne] Sunne D33–S67. eies] ~; D33, S67; ~. D35–M67.
89 found] ~; D33–S67.
90 here] *om* D33–D69, S67.
92 fate] Fate. D33–S67.
94 not] *om* D35–D54.
95 day] ~? D33–S67. will] Or will D35–D69; Oh, will Gr12, S67.
97 or] or a D33–S67. thee] me D69. this] ~? D33–S67.
99 stronger?] strong^ D33; strong; D35–D69; strong? Gr12–S67. so] ~? D33–S67.
100 know] to know; D33–D54, M67, S67; ~; D69, Gr12.
101 changd] ~; D33–S67.
102 Idolatry] ~; D33, M67, S67; ~. D35–Gr12.
103 is] ~, D33; ~; D35–S67.
104 proove] do D33–Gr12, S67.
108 lost] ~: D33–S67.
110 god] God D33–S67. truste] ~. D33–S67.

"Satyre IV." Texts: TT1 (22–24), D33–Gr12, M67, S67.
HE *om*] *Satyre IIII.* D33–S67 (*IV* D35–D69, M67, S67).
1 Well] ~; D33–S67. die] ~; D33, Gr12–S67; ~. D35–D69.
2 I] yet I D35–D69.
4 and] to, and Gr12; to, 'and M67. scant] scarse Gr12. this] ~. D33–S67.
6 seene /] ~, D33–S67.
8 Court] ~; D33–S67. *Glare*] *Glaze* D33, Gr12–S67.
9 a] *om* D33–D69.
10 curse] ~; D33–D39, Gr12–S67; ~, D49–D69.
11 scapd.] ~, D33–S67.
12 Guiltie] (~ D33–S67.
13 forgettfull] forget- D33–S67.
14 As] full, as D33–S67. lustfull] as lustfull D33, Gr12–S67.
15 and wittlesse] as wittlesse D33–S67.
16 att] in D33–D69. way] ~. D33–S67.
17 this,] ~; D33–S67.
18 then] than D35–D69.
19 bredd,] ~; Gr12, M67. came] ~: D33–D69, S67; ~; Gr12, M67.
20 name] ~, D33, S67; ~: D35–D69; ~; Gr12, M67.
21 then] than D39–D69.
22 Then] Than D39–D69. rarities] ~, D33–D69, S67; ~. Gr12, M67.
23 then] than D39–D69. strangers] ~; D33–D54, Gr12–S67; ~: D69.
25 then] ~; D33–S67. dies] ~, D33, D35, D49–S67; ~. D39.
26 pretences] the prentises D33–S67. rise] ~. D33–S67.
27 by] ~, D33–D39, Gr12–S67; ~; D69.
29 *Sir*] '~ M67. are] ~. D33–Gr12, S67; ~.' M67.

30 course] coarse; D33–S67. though] (~ D35–D54. bare] ~; D33, D35, Gr12–S67; ~) D39–D54.
32 so] (~ D33–S67. seene] ~) D33–S67.
33 *Tufftaffata*] ~; D33–S67.
34 a while] awhile D33–D39, Gr12–S67.
35 This] The D35–D69. trauelld] trauaild D33–S67. saith] faith D69.
36 states] States D33–S67. belonges] ~, D33; ~. D35–Gr12, S67; ~; M67.
37 these] ~, D33–D54, Gr12–S67; ~. D69.
38 strange] one D33–D69, M67; no Gr12, S67. language] ~; D33, Gr12–S67; ~. D35–D54; ~, D69. displease] ~, D33–D54, Gr12–S67; ~. D69.
41 drugg tonge] druggtonge D33–D54, Gr12–S67; drugg-tonge D69.
43 beare] heare D69. this] ~, D33–D69, S67; ~: Gr12, M67.
44 tonge in] tonge: in D33–D54, S67; tonge, in D69–M67. complement] ~: D33–S67.
47 Out flatter] Out-flatter D33, Gr12–S67. either] ~: D69.
48 *Lurius*] *Surius* D33–S67. together] ~. D33–S67.
49 to mee] to mee; D33–S67. *God*] ~! D33–D39, Gr12, S67; '~! M67.
51 mee] ~? D33, D35, Gr12, S67; ~; D39–D69; ~?' M67. saieth.] ~, D33–S67. *Sir*] '~ M67.
52 iudgement] ~; D33–D39, Gr12–S67; ~, D49–D69.
53 Linguists?] Linguist? D33–Gr12, S67; Linguist?' M67.
54 *Dictionary*] ~; D33, Gr12–S67; ~. D35–D69.
55 Nay] '~ M67. *Sir.*] ~; Gr12; ~?' M67.
56 *Iesuitts*] other *Iesuitts* Gr12. reuerent] reuerend D33–S67.
57 there] here D35–D69.
58 said] ~; D33, Gr12–S67; ~: D35–D69. nay] '~ M67.
59 Linguists] ~, D33, D39–S67; ~; D35. and] *om* D69. *Panirge*] *Panurge* D35–D54, Gr12–S67; *Panurgus* D69. was] ~; D33–S67.
60 gentleman] ~; D33–D69, S67; ~, M67. passe] ~. D69.
61 By] But D69. trauaile] ~. D33–D54, Gr12, S67; ~.' M67.
62 woordes] wonders D35–M67.
63 If] '~ M67.
64 be] have beene D33–S67.
65 *Brick Layers*] *bricklayers* D33–S67. stood] ~. D33, D35, D49–Gr12, S67; ~, D39; ~.' M67.
66 if] '~ M67. knowe] knewe D33–S67.
67 lonelines] ~; D33; lonenes. D35–Gr12; lonenes.' M67; lonenes; S67. not] '~ M67.
68 lonelinesse] lonenesse D35–S67. is] ~, D33–Gr12, S67; ~. M67. fashion] ~, D33, Gr12–S67; ~. D35–D69.
69 tast] last D33, D69, Gr12, S67.
70 Now] ~; D33–D54, Gr12–S67. chast] ~; D33–S67.
72 the] *om* D33–S67. vertue] ~; D33, Gr12, S67; ~. D35–D69; ~.' M67.
73 high streatcht] high-streatcht D35–D69. *Lutestring*] *Lute string* D33, Gr12–S67; *Lute-string* D35–D69. O] '~ M67.
74 Kinges] ~. D33–Gr12, S67; ~.' M67. *Att*] '~ M67. *Westminster*] ~' M67.
75 the] 'the M67.
77 *Sir*] our D33–S67. *Sir*] our D33–S67.
78 naught but *kings* you^{r} eies meet./] and all their kin can walke: D33–S67.
79 *om*] Your eares shall heare nought, but Kings; your eyes meet D33–S67.
80 only] ~; D33–S67. *Kings street*] *Kingstreet.* D33–D39, Gr12, S67; *Kings street.* D49–D69; *Kingstreet.*' M67.
81 hees] '~ M67. *coarse*] *course* D69.
82 *Englishmen*] *English men* D69. discourse] ~. D33–S67.
83 french men] frenchmen D33–S67. neat] ~? D33–Gr12, S67; ~?' M67. fine] ~, D33; mine? D35–D54; mine, D69, Gr12; mine? M67, S67.
84 *Frenchman*] Sir D35–D69. mee] ~. D33–D39, D69, Gr12, S67; ~, D49–D54; ~.' M67.
85 Certes] '~ M67. clothd.] ~; Gr12, M67.
86 y^{e}] your D33–S67. *Grogaran*] ~; D33; ~, D35–D69; ~. Gr12, S67; ~.' M67.
87 Not] '~ M67. more] ~. D33–Gr12, S67; ~.' M67.
88 flie] ~; D33–S67. him] ~; D33, Gr12–S67; ~. D35–D49; ~: D50–D69. Itch] as Itch D33–S67.
89 ground] grownd D33–D69.
90 woorse] ~: D33–D69. (so] ^~ D33–S67. foole)] ~^ D33; (~) D35–S67.
91 me] ~; D33, Gr12–S67; ~. D35–D69.
92 dresse] addresse. D33; ~. D35, D39; ~; D49–D69; addresse, Gr12–S67.
93 what] '~ M67. newes] ~? D33–D54, Gr12, S67; ~; D69; ~?' M67. plaies] ~. D33–D39, Gr12–S67; ~, D49–D69.
96 mee] ~, D33, D39–S67; ~. D35.
97 then] than D49–D54.
98 trash he knowes] trash; he knowes; D33–S67 (trash. D35, D39; trash, D49–D69; trash^ Gr12–S67).
100 states man] States-man D33–S67. that] ~; D33–S67.
101 loues] ~; D33–D54, Gr12–S67; ~; D69. whom] ~; D33, D69–S67; ~, D35–D54.
102 *Reuersion*] ~; D33–S67.
104 Eggeshells] egge- D33–S67.
105 To] shels to D33–S67. transport] ~; D33–S67.
106 Spanncounter] Spann-counter D33–D54, Gr12–S67; Spann counter D69. blewepoint] blowe-point D33–S67. shall] they Gr12–S67.
107 Courtie^{r}] ~; D33–S67.
108 *painted,*] ~; D33, Gr12–S67; ~. D35–D69.
109 home meates] home-meates D33, Gr12–S67. tryes] cloyes D35– D69. mee] ~; D33, Gr12–S67; ~. D35–D69.
110 *Patient,*] ~; D33, D35, Gr12–S67.
111 me] on D33–Gr12, S67; men M67. more] ~; D33–S67. vndertooke] had vndertooke D35–D69.
112 *Gallobelgicus*] *Gallo-Belgicus* D33–S67.
114 *Amyens*] ~. D33–S67.
115 to] *om* D33–S67.
116 trauell] trauaile: D33–S67.
117 his] this D33–S67. *Macron*] *Makeron* D33, Gr12–S67; *Makaron* D35–D69. talke] ~, D35–D69, S67; ~: Gr12, M67. vayne] ~: D33–D69, S67; ~; Gr12, M67.
120 man] ~. D33–S67.
121 paid] ~; D33–S67.
122 delayd] ~; D33–S67.
123 that] *om* D35–D54.
125 day] ~; D33–S67.
126 *Dunkerkers*] ~. D33–S67.
127 notes] ~; D33–S67.
128 goates] ~. D33–S67.
129 then] than D35–D69.
131 me thought] methought D69.
132 *Statues*] *Statutes* D33–S67.
133 in.] ~; D33, D69–S67; ~, D35–D54. him] ~. D33, D35; ~, D39–S67.
134 That as burnt venomd *Leachers* doe growe sound] (venome D35–D54, Gr12, S67; venomous D69); *om* D33.
135 By giuing others their sores I might growe] *om* D33.
136 Guiltie and he free, therefore I did showe] (free: D35–S67; shewe D35–S67); *om* D33.
137 loathing] ~; D33–S67.
139 farthinge] ~; D33, Gr12–S67; ~. D35–D69.
140 the] this D33–S67. Crosse] crosse; But the houre D33–S67.
141 But the houre of] Of D33–S67. come] ~; D33, D35, Gr12–S67; ~: D39–D69.
143 Sir] '~ M67. mee] ~; D33, Gr12, S67; ~? D35–D69; ~?' M67. willinglie] ~; D33–Gr12, S67; '~.' M67.
144 Nay] '~ M67. Crowne] ~? D33–Gr12, S67; ~?' M67.
145 *Ransome*] ~; D33–S67.
146 Though] Thou D35.
147 ligge more] more ligge D33–S67. yow] ~: D33–S67.
148 mee] ~. D33–D54, Gr12–S67; ~: D69.
150 *Purgatorie*] *Prerogative* D33–S67. Crowne] ~: D33–S67.
151 w^{ch}] (~ D33–S67.
152 more] such D69. then] than D35–D54; as D69. hee] ~) D33– S67.
153 them] thence D33–S67. then] than D35–D69.
154 make] hast D33–D69. prison] ~; D33, S67; ~. D35–M67.
156 pretious] piteous D35–D69.
159 on] o'r D35–D69. mee] ~, D33, Gr12, S67; ~: D35–D69; ~; M67. and] *om* D33–S67.
160 more] ~; D33–D54, Gr12–S67; ~. D69.
161 accuser,] ~; D33–D54, Gr12–S67; ~: D69.
162 nones] none D69.
163 frownes?] ~; D69. truth] Truth D33–S67.
164 *Nobilitie*] ~. D33; ~? D35–S67.
165 No!] ~, D33–S67.
167 Iorney] ~, D33, D35, D49–S67; ~. D39.
168 Court] ~? D33–S67.
169 I] *om* D33–S67.
171 presence] Courtiers D35–S67.
173 are ours] ours are, D33–S67 (are^ D39–M67).
174 all] ~. D33–S67.
175 past] ~; D33–S67.
178 are] were D35–D54.
179 mee] ~.) D33–D39, Gr12–S67; ~^) D49–D69.
180 the] their D33–S67.
181 them] ~; D33, Gr12–S67; ~. D35–D69. for] '~ M67.
182 Those] Those hose D33–S67. are] ~' M67. cries] cry D33–D54, Gr12–S67. the] his D35–D54. flatterer] flatterers; D33–D54, Gr12–S67; ~; D69.
183 sell] ~; D33, Gr12–S67; ~. D35–D69.
184 states] ~; D33, Gr12–S67; ~. D35–D69.
185 Court] ~; D33–S67. players] ~, D33, Gr12–S67; ~; D35–D69, M67.
187 Inventory.] ~; D33, S67.
188 come] ~; D33, Gr12–S67; ~. D35–D69.
190 them] ~; D33–S67. as] (~ D69. I] they D33–S67. thinke] ~) D69.

191 beauties] ˜; D33–S67. wittes] ˜; D33–S67. bought] ˜. D33–S67.
194 scarlett] scarlets D33–S67. die] ˜. D33–S67.
195 Nett] ˜. D33, S67; ˜: D35–D69; ˜; Gr12, M67.
196 sett] ˜; D33, S67; ˜. D35–M67.
198 Hate] hat D33–S67. sue] shooe D33–S67.
199 Att] As if D33–S67. weare] were D33–S67. *Meschite*] ˜, D33, Gr12–S67; ˜: D35–D69.
200 calls] call D33–S67. stifte] shrift D33–S67.
202 them] ˜; D33, Gr12–S67; ˜, D35–D69. also] *om* D33–S67.
203 fornicate] ˜. D33; ˜: D35–Gr12, S67; ˜; M67.
205 tryes] trye Gr12, S67.
206 so] *om* D33–S67. his] *om* D33–S67. thighes] ˜. D33–D69, M67; thighe. Gr12, S67.
209 (As] ˆ˜ D33–S67.
210 preach)] ˜ˆ D33–S67.
211 goodwill] good will D33–S67.
213 haue serud] serue D33–S67.
214 Cardynall] Cardynalls D33–S67. *Inquisicon*] ˜; D33–D39, D69–S67; ˜, D49–D54.
215 whispered] whispers D35–D69. by] ʼ˜ M67. Iesu] ˜ʼ M67.
217 *Psalter*] ˜; D33, Gr12–S67; ˜. D35–D69.
218 itt] ˜. D33–S67.
221 fashion] ˜; D33–S67.
222 teare] ˜; D33–S67. whom] or whom D35–D69.
223 not] ˜, D33, Gr12, S67; not hee. D35–D69; ˜; M67.
224 him] ˜; D33, D35, Gr12–S67; ˜, D39–D69. rusheth] rushes D39–D69. *Arme*] ʼ˜ M67. *Arme*] ˜ʼ M67.
226 whipt] whip D33–S67. yett] *om* D35–Gr12, S67.
227 woorse] D33, D49–S67; ˜; D35, D39. awe] ˜; D33–S67.
228 Liciencd] *om* D33–S67. a] a licenc'd D33–S67. law] ˜. D33–S67.
229 be] *om* D33–S67.
230 w^{ch}] *om* D33–D69.
231 Soe] Goe D33–S67. why] (˜ D33–S67. it is] is it D33–S67.
232 sinnes] ˜) D33–D39; ˜?) D49–D69, S67; ˜?). Gr12; ˜?); M67.
234 *Charingcrosse*] *Charing Crosse* D33–S67.
235 *Queenes*] ʼ˜ M67. *man*] ˜ʼ M67. find] fine D33–S67.
236 Liuing] ˜, D69–S67. *flaggons*] and *flaggons* D69. wine] ˜. D33–D69, S67; ˜; Gr12, M67.
237 spie] ˜; D33, S67; ˜. D35–M67.
238 *Witt*] *Witts* D33–D54, S67.
240 scarse] scant D35–D69.
241 those] the D33–S67. away] ˜; D33, D35, Gr12–S67; ˜: D39–D69. though] although D35–Gr12.
242 With] (˜ D69. modestie] ˜) D69. the] the knowne D33–S67.
243 lessen] ˜: D33–S67. men] man D33–D39, Gr12–S67.
244 *Canonicall*] ˜. D33–S67.

"Satyre V." Texts: TT1 (24v–25), D33–Gr12, M67, S67.
HE *A Satire 3*] *Satyre* V. D33–S67.
1 shalt] shal D69.
2 warnes] warmes; D33, Gr12–S67; ˜. D35–D69.
3 (Hee] ˆ˜ D69.
4 good] ˜?) D33–D54, Gr12–S67; ˜?ˆ D69.
5 stings] sting D33–S67.
6 wicked] ˜: D33–D54, Gr12–S67; ˜, D69.
7 mee!] ˜. D33–S67.
9 and] in D69. Iest] ˜? D33–S67.
10 thinke] ˜, D33–D39, D69–S67; ˜. D49–D54.
11 Elementes] ˜: D33–S67.
12 imployes] implyes D35–S67. representes] ˜, D33; ˜. D35–S67.
13 world] ˜; D33–S67.
14 *om*] Are the vast ravishing seas; and Suiters, D33–S67.
15 *om*] Springs; now full, now shallow, now drye; which to D33–S67 (Springs, D69; dryeˆ D39; drye, D49–D69).
16 *om*] That which drownes them, run: These self reasons do D33– S67.
17 *om*] Prove the world a man, in which, officers D33–S67.
19 void.] ˜; D33–D54. dust] ˜, D33–D69; ˜; Gr12–S67.
21 prayes] ˜. D33–D54, S67; ˜? D69–M67. then] than D35–D69.
22 eat] ˜. D33–S67.
24 them] ˜; D33–S67.
25 itt!] ˜; D33–S67.
26 the] their D33–S67.
27 *Wittolls*] ˜, D33–D69, S67; ˜; Gr12, M67. is] ˜; D33, S67; ˜. D35–M67.
28 this] ˜? D33–S67.
29 then] than D35–D69.
30 drownes] drowne D33–S67. o^{r}eflow] ˜, D35; ˜. D39–D54; ore-flow. D69; ˜: Gr12–S67.
34 sinne] ˜. D33–S67.
35 age] Age D33–S67. Iron] ˜! D33–S67. some] (˜ D35–D54.
36 itt] ˜; D33, Gr12–S67; ˜) D35–D54; ˜. D69.
37 age *Age*] Age D33–S67. that] *om* D69. sould!] ˜, D33–D69, S67; ˜; Gr12, M67. now] (˜ D35–D54.
38 dearer] ˜) D35–D54. farr!] ˜; D33, S67; ˜ˆ D35–D54; ˜, D69; ˜. Gr12, M67. Allowe] did allowe D35–D54.
39 Demaundes] claim'd D35–D69. duties] ˜; D33, M67, S67; ˜. D35–D54; ˜, D69, Gr12.
41 others] other D33–S67. handes] ˜: D33–S67.
42 handes] ˜. D33–S67.
44 nor] no D33–S67.
46 thee] *om* D33–S67.
47 (If] Thee, if D33–S67. thee)] ˜ˆ D33–S67. into] in, to D33–S67.
48 Halters] ˜; D33, Gr12–S67; ˜. D35–D69.
49 complaine] ˜; D33; ˜, D35–S67.
50 when] *om* D69. vppwardes] vppwardes: when D33–S67 (vppwardes, D69).
51 faint] ˜; D33–S67.
52 Gainst] ʼ˜ D35–S67. bee] will D33–S67. thy] the D33, Gr12–S67.
55 before] ˜; D33, Gr12–S67; ˜. D35–D69.
56 likes] like D33–S67. more] ˜. D33–S67.
57 *Gods*] ˜; D33–S67. he] and he D69. said] *om* D69.
58 not] not that D33–D54, Gr12–S67.
59 Angells] ˜; D33, Gr12–S67; ˜. D35–D69. *Supplications*] *Supplication* D35–D69.
61 and] and all D33–S67. Courts] Court D33.
62 here!] ˜, D33–S67.
63 Kinges] ˜; D33–S67. it is] 'tis, D33; 'tis; D35–D54; 'tis. D69–S67.
64 stone] Stoicke D33–S67.
66 Copes] ˜; D33–S67. Primmers] ˜; D33–S67.
67 *Chalices*] ˜; D33–D39, Gr12–S67; ˜, D49–D69.
68 aske] lack D33–D54. comminge] ˜; D33; ˜? D35–S67. Oh] ˜, D33, Gr12–S67; ˜; D35–D69. neare] ne'r D33–S67.
69 reuerent] reuerend D33–S67.
70 *Theftes*] ˜: D33–S67.
71 destinie] Destinie D33–S67.
72 fates] Fates D33–S67. and] and but Gr12–S67. tells] tells us who must bee D33–S67 (tells who D33–D69).
73 Who] Rich, who D33–S67. must be rich] *om* D33–S67. Iayles] ˜: D33–S67.
74 nayles] ˜, D33, D35, D49–S67; ˜. D39.
75 suitors] ˜; D33, Gr12–S67; ˜: D35–D54; ˜. D69. of men] *om* D33–S67.
76 men] ˜; D33; ˜, D35–S67. the] *om* D33–D69. Extremities] ˜, D33, Gr12–S67; ˜. D35–D69.
77 then] than D35–D69.
78 too] to. D33–S67.
79 Officer.] ˜? D33–S67.
80 men erst] men D33; erst men D35–S67. thee] ˜? D33–S67.
82 right] ˜; D33, D35, Gr12–S67; ˜, D39–D69. die] ˜. D33–D39, D69–S67.
84 more] ˜; D33–S67.
85 *Caricke*] Carricks D33–S67. pepper] ˜. D33–S67.
87 when] if D35–D54. Antiquities] ˜. D33–S67.
89 prophesies] ˜. D33–S67.
90 cossened] cosseneth D69.
91 And] Which D35–D69. vanished] vanisheth D69.

"Satyre II." Texts: TT1 (25v–26v), D33–Gr12, M67, S67.
HE *om*] *Satyre* II. D33–S67.
1 Sir] ˜; D33–S67. god] God D33–S67. itt] ˜) D33–S67.
4 towardes] toward D33–D54, Gr12, S67. toward] towards D33, D69–S67. rest] ˜; D33, S67; ˜. D35–M67.
6 dearths] dearth D33–D69. in] ˜, D33, Gr12–S67; ˜: D35–D69.
8 men] ˜; D33, Gr12–S67; ˜, D35–D69.
9 out!] ˜; D33–D54, Gr12–S67; ˜. D69.
10 hate] ˜: D33–D69, S67; ˜. Gr12, M67.
11 wretch)] ˜, D33–S67.
13 life] ˜) D33–S67.
14 Steruing] (˜ D33, D69–S67. himselfe)] ˜ˆ D35–D54. *Sceanes*] ˜. D33–D69, S67; ˜; Gr12, M67.
15 Organ] Organs D69.
16 mooue] ˜. D33–S67.
17 loue] Loue D33–D39, Gr12–S67. *Rimes*] *Rithmes*; D33–Gr12, S67; ˜; M67.
18 harmes.] ˜, D49–D54; ˜: Gr12, M67.
20 thee] the D33–S67. *Artillery*] ˜. D33–S67.
21 that] who D33–S67.
22 meat] ˜? D33–S67.
23 that] who D33–S67.
24 ill] ˜; D33, Gr12, S67; ˜. D35–D69, M67.
25 beggarlie] (˜) D33–S67.
27 these] those D33–S67. out spue] out-spue D33–S67.
28 thinges] ˜; D33–S67.
29 my] eate my D33–S67.
30 owne] ˜: D33–Gr12, S67; ˜. M67.
31 those] these D33–S67. those] they D33–S67.
32 out doe] out-doe D33–S67. Dilldoes] ————; D33; ˜, D35–S67. out vsure] out-

vsure D33–S67. Iewes] D33, Gr12–S67; ˜, D35–D69.
33 out drinke] out-drinke D33–S67. Letany] ———— D33; *om* D35, D39; gallant, he D49–D54; ˜, D69; ˜; Gr12–S67.
34 of] *om* D35–S67. kind] kinds D33–S67.
35 *Confessours*] ˜; D33, Gr12–S67; ˜, D35–D69.
36 make] ˜: D33–S67.
38 commandementes] Commandementes D33–S67. dwell] ˜. D33–D54, Gr12–S67; ˜, D69.
39 ffor] But D33–S67. those] these D33–S67. themselues] ˜; D33, Gr12–S67; ˜. D35–D69.
42 Oxe] an Oxe D35.
43 Lawyer] ˜; D33–D69, S67; ˜, Gr12, M67. alas] (˜) D35–M67.
44 a scarce] scarce a D33–D69. Poett] ˜, D33–D69, S67; ˜; Gr12, M67. sollicitor] jollier D33–S67.
46 limetwigges] lime-twigges D33, D69–S67.
48 woes] wooes D33–S67. *Bench*] ˜: D33, Gr12–S67; ˜. D35–D69.
49 A] '˜ M67. Lady] ˜, D33; ˜. D35, D39, S67; ˜: D49–D69; ˜; Gr12; ˜,' M67. (speake] ˜˜ D33–Gr12, S67; '˜˜ M67. *Coscus*)] ˜; D33, Gr12, S67; ˜. D35–D69; ˜.' M67. I] '˜ M67.
50 *Queene*] ˜, D33–D39, Gr12–S67; ˜. D49–D69.
52 proceed] *om* D33–S67.
53 Spare] Proceed, spare D33–D54; Proceed; spare D69, Gr12, S67; Proceed.' 'Spare M67. me] ˜; D33–D54, Gr12, S67; ˜, D69; ˜.' M67. in] 'In M67.
54 returne] returned D35–Gr12, S67. *Assize*] size D33–S67.
55 grace] ˜; D33–S67.
57 *Affidauitts*] ˜: D33, Gr12, S67; ˜. D35–D69; ˜—': M67.
58 soft maides] maides soft D69. eare] ˜. D33–D54; ˜, Gr12–S67.
59 then] than D35–D54. scolding] scolding's D69.
60 Then] Than D39–D69. rore] ˜; D33, S67; ˜. D35–M67.
61 When] Which S67. Muse] muse D33–S67.
62 hop't] ˜; D33–S67.
63 gaynes] gayne; D33–D69; gayne, Gr12–S67.
64 then] than D39–D69. prostitute] ˜. D33–S67.
65 Owlelike] Owle-like D49–D69.
68 there] ˜, D33, D39–S67; ˜. D35.
69 And to euery Suitor lie in euery thinge] ———— D33.
70 Like a Kinges *favourite* yea like a kinge] (or like D35, D69; kinge. D35–D69; kinge; Gr12–S67); ———— D33.
72 Bearing like] Bearing-like Gr12. harmelesse] shamelesse D33–S67.
73 Lye] Then carted whores, lye, D33–S67 (Than D35–D69). *Graue.*] graue^ D33–S67. Bastardy aboundes] *om* D33–S67.
74 Not in Kings titles nor] ———— D33; Bastardy abounds not in Kings titles D35–S67.
75 *Symony or Sodomy* in Churchmens liues] (*Symony and* D35–S67; Church-mens D69); ———— D33.
76 him] ˜; D33–S67. thriues] ˜. D33–S67.
77 as] (˜ D33–S67. Sea] ˜) D33–S67. ou^r^] the D33–D69. Land] ˜; D33–S67.
78 *Wight*] ˜; D33–D54, Gr12–S67; ˜, D69. strand] ˜. D33–S67.
80 his] their D33–S67. he] ˜. D33–D54, Gr12–S67; ˜, D69.
81 as] (˜ D69. kitchin stuffe] kitching-stuffe D33–S67.
84 *Relique like*] (*Reliquely* D33–D69; (*Relique-like* Gr12–S67. kept] ˜) D33–S67. geare] ˜; D33–D54, Gr12–S67; chear) D69.
86 men] Maids D69. *prime*] ˜. D33–S67.
87 Parchment] Parchments Gr12–S67. his] the D69.
89 forwardnes] ˜) D33–S67.
90 fathers] Fathers D33–S67. lesse] ˜. D33–S67.
91 not] ˜; D33–S67.
92 length] ˜; D33–D54, Gr12–S67; ˜, D69. as] (˜ D35–D69.
93 When] Where D35–D54.
96 clawes] clause. D33, Gr12–S67; clause.) D35–D69.
98 wrighting] writings D33–S67. vnmatchd] (vnwatchd) D33–S67. his] *ses* D33–S67.
99 As] And D69.
102 Shewd] Shrewd D33–S67. doubt] ˜: D33, S67; ˜. D35–M67.
104 doore] ˜. D33–S67.
105 Where's] Where D35–D69. *Almes*] ˜, D33; ˜? D35–S67. *Haules*] great hals? D33, Gr12–S67 (hals^ Gr12–S67); hals D35–D69.
107 hate] ˜, D33, S67; ˜. D35–D69; ˜; Gr12, M67. meanes] meane's D35–D69. blesse] ˜; D33, Gr12–S67; blest. D35–D69. *Ritchmens*] rich mens D33–S67.
109 so] ˜; D33, Gr12–S67; ˜. D35–D69. Oh] (˜) D33–S67.
110 are] as D33–S67.
111 *wardroabes*] D33, Gr12–S67; ˜; D35–D69. drawes] none drawes D33–S67.
112 None] *om* D33–S67. huge] th'huge D33–S67. statute] statutes D69. lawes] ˜. D33–D54, Gr12–S67; Jawes. D69.

"Elegie: The Bracelet." Texts: TT1 (27r-v), TT2 (9–10), D35–Ga65, S67.
HE *Elegia.* 1.] *om* TT2; Eleg. XII. *The Bracelet. Vpon the losse of his Mistresses Chaine, for which he made satisfaction.* D35–D54, Gr12–S67 (XII. *Vpon* D39; Eleg. IV. *Vpon* D49–D54; ELEGIE XI Gr12; *The* Ga65; *Elegie: The* S67); Elegie XII D69.
2 *Arme letts*] *armletts* TT2–S67. weare] ˜: D35–S67.
4 miste] ˜: D35–Gr12, S67; ˜; Ga65.
6 those] these D35–Gr12, S67. were] are Ga65, S67. tied] knit D35–Gr12. bee] ˜: D35–Gr12, S67; ˜; Ga65.
7 seauen fold] seauenfold D35–S67. chaine] chine TT2. lost] ˜; D35, D39, Gr12, S67; ˜: D49–D69; ˜, Ga65.
8 lucke sake] ˜; D35–S67 (lucke-sake D69). bigger] bitter D35–S67. cost] ˜. D35–S67.
10 admitt] ˜; D35, D39, Gr12, S67; ˜: D49–D69; ˜, Ga65.
11 fault] way D35–Gr12.
12 their] there TT2. *Creation*] ˜; D35, D39, Gr12, S67; ˜: D49–D69; ˜, Ga65.
14 guide] ˜; D35, D39, Gr12, S67; ˜: D49–D69; ˜, Ga65.
15 enimies] ˜; D35, D39, Gr12, S67; ˜: D49–D69; ˜, Ga65.
16 rise] ˜. D35–D69, S67; ˜; Gr12, Ga65.
18 dread] (˜ D35–S67. Iudge] ˜) D35–S67. beare] ˜? D35–S67.
20 their] there TT2. owne] ˜? D35–S67.
22 chaynes] ˜: D35–D69, S67; ˜. Gr12, Ga65.
23 Were] where→w[a]ere TT2.
24 them] these D35–D54, Gr12. their] there TT2. Country] Countrys D35–D54, Gr12, S67.
25 possesseth!] ˜, D35–Gr12, S67; ˜; Ga65. here] [t]here TT2.
26 ruinous] [r]*[u]ainous TT2; ˜. D35–D54, Gr12, S67; ˜, D69; ˜; Ga65.
27 how so ere] howsoever TT2; howsoe'r D35–S67.
28 Their] There TT2. Iewishly] ˜; D35–D69, S67; ˜. Gr12, Ga65.
29 trauailing] trauelling D35–Gr12, S67.
30 their] there TT2.
31 *Bearewhelpes*] *Bare whelps* TT2; *Beare-whelpes* D35–S67.
32 more] (˜ D35–Gr12, S67. then] than D35–D54, Gr12, S67. cannon shott] cannon shott) D35–Gr12, S67; cannon-shott, Ga65.
34 many Angled] many-Angled Ga65.
35 great] dread D69. which] that D35–Gr12. inforce] insorce TT2.
36 those] these TT2–S67. their] there TT2; her D35–S67. course] ˜. D35–D69; ˜; Gr12–S67.
37 quickens] quickes TT2.
38 Of] As D35–S67. runnes] run D35–S67. thorough] through TT2–S67. earthes] earth TT2.
40 ruind] ˜: D35–D54; ˜, D69–S67. ragged] rugged TT2. decayd] ˜, D39–D54, Ga65; ˜; D69, Gr12, S67.
41 state] State D35–Gr12, S67. day] ˜: D35–Gr12, S67; ˜, Ga65.
42 seauenteene headed] seauenteene-headed D35–S67. *Belgia*] ˜: D35–D69, S67; ˜. Gr12, Ga65.
43 where withall] we[a]re withall TT2; wherewithall D35–S67.
45 out pulld] out-pulld; D35–Gr12, S67; out-pulld Ga65.
46 gulld] ˜: D35–Gr12, S67; ˜; Ga65.
47 were] are D35–Gr12, S67.
48 sinne] ˜. D35–S67.
49 *Angells*] angells D35–Gr12, S67.
50 loose] lose D35–S67. head] ease D35–S67. foot] food D35–S67.
51 wilbe] will be TT2–S67. dead] ˜. D35–D69, S67; ˜, Gr12, Ga65.
52 *Lustiehead*] *Lustie head* TT2–D69.
53 vanish] ˜, D35–Gr12; ˜; Ga65, S67. loue] Loue D49–D69.
54 gone] ˜, D35–D69, S67; ˜; Gr12; ˜. Ga65.
55 Oh] And D35–Gr12.
56 Well pleasd] Well-pleasd D35, D39, Gr12, S67. thredd bare] thredd-bare D35–D54, Gr12–S67. groat] goat D39.
57 thorough] through TT2–S67. street] ˜; D35–Gr12, S67; ˜, Ga65.
58 conscience] ˜; D35; ˜, D39–Gr12, S67. he] they D69–S67. meet] ˜. D35–S67.
59 meet with] creepe to D35–S67. Coniurer] ˜, D35–D54, Gr12–S67; ˜; D69.
60 W^ch^] That D35–Gr12. *Sceanes*] scheames Ga65, S67. filles full] fullfills Ga65. paper] ˜; D35, D39, Gr12, S67; ˜: D49–D69; ˜, Ga65.
61 haue] hath D35–S67.
63 passe] place D69.
64 in] ˜. D35–S67.
65 And] But D35–Gr12.
66 neere] ne'r D35–S67. found] ˜; D35–S67. (Oh] yet D35–Gr12; ˜˜ Ga65, S67. content] ˜; D35–Gr12, S67; ˜. Ga65.
67 the] that D35–D54, Gr12, S67.
68 Destinye] destinye TT2; destinye. D35–Gr12, S67; ˜. Ga65.

69 alas] (˜) D35–S67.
70 chayne] ˜, D35–D69, S67; ˜; Gr12; ˜. Ga65.
71 *Angells*] *angells* D35–D54, Gr12, S67.
72 knowledge] ˜; D35, D39, Gr12, S67; ˜: D49–D54; ˜, D69, Ga65. ill] ˜: D35–Gr12, S67; ˜; Ga65.
73 woorkes] ˜; D35, D39, Gr12, S67; ˜: D49–D69; ˜, Ga65.
74 Necessities] ˜; D35, D39, Gr12, S67; ˜: D49–D54; ˜, D69, Ga65. pride] ˜, D35–D69, S67; ˜; Gr12, Ga65.
75 they] they are D35–S67. Angelles] ˜; D35, D39, Gr12, S67; ˜: D49–D69; ˜, Ga65. none] ˜; D35, D39, Gr12, S67; ˜: D49–D69; ˜. Ga65.
76 their] there TT2. gone] ˜: D35–Gr12, S67; ˜. Ga65.
77 *Angells* yett] *Angells* yett; D35–D69, Ga65, S67 (yett: D49–D69); *Angells*; yett Ga65. their] there TT2.
78 vertues] Vertues D35–S67. powers] Powers D35–S67. Principalities] principalities TT2; ˜. D35–S67.
79 resolute] D35, D39, Gr12–S67; ˜: D49–D69. done] ˜; D35, D39, S67; ˜: D49–D54; ˜? D69; ˜! Gr12; ˜. Ga65.
80 *Sonne*] *sonne* D35–S67.
81 mother] Mother TT2–Gr12, S67.
82 fire] frier TT2. betray] ˜. D35–S67.
83 for] (˜ D35–Gr12, S67. life] lite→li[f]e TT2. thinge] ˜) D35–Gr12, S67; ˜, Ga65.
84 for] (˜ D35–Gr12, S67. bring] ˜) D35–Gr12, S67; ˜, Ga65.
85 Destind] desdaind→des[t]ind TT2. a] an D35–Gr12.
86 alone] ˜: D35–Gr12, S67; ˜, Ga65.
87 w^{ch}] that D35–Gr12.
88 lesse] ˜. D35–Gr12, S67; ˜; Ga65.
89 But I am guiltye of your sad decay] (decay; D35, D39, Gr12, S67; decay: D49–D69; decay, Ga65); [but I am guiltie of your sade decay,] TT2.
90 fellowes] few fellowes D35, Gr12–S67; few-fellowes D39–D69. with mee longer] longer with mee D35–S67. stay] ˜. D35–S67.
92 So much] So D35–Gr12, S67. state] estate TT2; estate: D35, Gr12, S67; ˜. D39; ˜, D49–D69; ˜; Ga65.
93 *Mettall* amongst] amongst *Mettall* D69. all] ˜, D35, D69–S67; ˜; D39; ˜: D49–D54.
94 curse] course TT2. thee] the TT2. fall] ˜: D35–Gr12, S67; ˜. Ga65.
96 bee] ˜; D35–Gr12, S67; ˜, Ga65. paynes] ˜; D35, D39, Gr12–S67; ˜: D49–D69.
98 that] it D35–D69. thy] *om* D69. pay] ˜. D35–S67.
100 brayne] ˜; D35, D39, Gr12, S67; ˜: D69; ˜, Ga65.
102 bringe] ˜. D35–S67.
103 Lust breed] Lust breedes TT2; Lust-bred D35–S67. the] ˜, TT2; thee; D35, D39, D69, Gr12, S67; thee: D49–D54; theeˆ Ga65.
104 *Itchy*] If→I[tchie]~~thy~~ TT2; Itching D35–Gr12, S67. *Abilitie*] ˜. D35–S67.
105 hurt] evils D35–Gr12. that] which Ga65, S67. euer gold] gold euer D35–Gr12. hath] hat[h] TT2; *om* D35–Gr12, S67. wrought] wrongt TT2; ˜; D35–Gr12, S67; ˜, Ga65.
106 mischiefes] mischiefe D35–D69. w^{ch}] that D35–Gr12. diuelles] duells→d[i]u[i]lls TT2. thought] ˜; D35, D39, Gr12, S67; ˜: D49–D69; ˜, Ga65.
107 plentie] ˜; D35, D39, Gr12, S67; ˜: D49–D69; ˜, Ga65. age] ˜; D35, D39, Gr12, S67; ˜: D49–D69; ˜, Ga65.
108 Plagues] Plague D69. Trauailers] Trauellers TT2; Trauellers; D35, D39, Gr12, S67; Trauellers: D49–D69; Trauellers, Ga65. loue] ˜; D35, D39, Gr12, S67; ˜: D49–D54. and] *om* D35–D54, Gr12, S67.
109 thee] ˜, TT2–D54, Gr12, S67; ˜; D69, Ga65. att] that D69. liues] lifes Ga65. last] latest Ga65.
110 thee] the TT2. present] ˜. D35, D39, D69–S67; ˜: D49–D54.
111 forgiue] ˜; D35, D39, Gr12, S67; ˜: D49–D69; ˜. Ga65. thou] thee D35–D54, Gr12, S67. man] ˜: D35–Gr12, S67; ˜. Ga65.
112 restoratiue] ˜, D35–Gr12, S67; ˜; Ga65. then] ˜: D35, D39, Gr12, S67; than: D49–D69; ˜. Ga65.
113 Or] But D35–Gr12. with] from D35–D54, Gr12; that from D69. depart] part D69.
114 hart] ˜. D35–S67.

"Elegie: The Comparison." Texts: TT1 (30v–31), D33–Ga65, S67.
HE *Eligia* 2] *Elegie* D33; *Eleg.* VIII. *The Comparison.* D35–D54, Gr12; *Elegie.* VIII D69; Comparison Ga65; *Elegie: The Comparison.* S67.
2 Muskattes] Muskets D69.
4 on] of D33–Gr12, S67.
5 necke] [brow] Gr12.
6 Coronetts] ˜. D33–Gr12; carcanetts. Ga65, S67.
7 Mistres] Mistresse's D33–Gr12, S67.
8 monstrous] menstruous D33–S67. biles] boiles. D33, D69; boiles, D35–D54, Gr12–S67.
9 that] the D33–D54, Gr12, S67.
10 Enforcd] ˜, D33–D54, Gr12–S67.
13 liyng stones] stones lying D33, D69.
14 they] it D33–D69. hung] hangs D33–D69; hang Gr12–S67. skinn] ˜. D33–S67.
15 World's] Worlds D69.
16 that] the D33–Gr12, S67. *Ide*] ˜, D33, D49–S67; ˜. D35, D39.
18 die] ˜. D33–S67.
19 a] *om* D39. rough] rough-hewne D33–S67.
20 yett] *om* Ga65, S67. sett] ˜; D33–D39, Gr12–S67; ˜: D49–D69.
22 embrace] ˜. D33–S67.
23 beautie keeping] beautie-keeping D33–S67.
24 brest] ˜. D33–S67.
25 worme eaten] worme-eaten D35–D69. skinns] skin D33–S67.
26 durt] dust D33–Gr12, S67. stinch] stinke D33–S67. within] ˜. D33–S67.
28 Woodbine] Wood-bine D33–S67. handes] ˜, D33–D69; ˜. Gr12–S67.
30 sinn] ˜, D33–D39, Gr12–S67; ˜; D49–D69.
31 sunn parchd] sunn-parchd D33–S67.
32 state] ˜. D33, Gr12–S67; ˜, D35, D39; ˜: D49–D69.
34 thy] her D33. gowtie] mistress D69. hand] ˜; D33–D69; ˜. Gr12–S67.
37 durt] part D33.
38 hold] ˜. D33–S67.
41 that] to that D33–S67.
42 round about] round-about D35–D54. burnd] burnt D33–S67. away] ˜. D33–S67.
44 sore] ˜? D33–S67.
46 feard] feares D33–Gr12, S67.
48 when] where D33. rent] ˜? D33–S67.
50 Are] A D69. Priests] Priest D69. in] is in his D69. reuerent] *om* D69.
51 such] nice D33–D69.
52 kisse] ˜. D33–D39, Gr12–S67; ˜, D49–D69.
54 odious] ˜. D33–S67.

"Elegie: The Perfume." Texts: TT1 (31r–v), TT2 (15r–v), D33–Ga65, S67.
HE *Elegia* 3.] *Elegie* IV. D33, D69; *Eleg.* IV. *The Perfume.* D35–D54, Gr12; The Perfume Ga65; *Elegie: The Perfume.* S67.
2 escapes] scapes D69. mee] ˜; D33–S67.
6 catechisde] ˜. D33–S67.
7 Though he had woont to search wth glazed eies] *om* D33.
8 As though he came to kill a *Cocatrice*] *om* D33.
9 haue] hath D33–D69, Ga65, S67.
10 of ou^{r}] [of] o^{r} TT2.
11 goodes;] ˜, D33–S67.
12 beene] ˜. D33–S67.
15 Take] Takes D33–D69, Ga65, S67. day light] day-light D33–D54, Gr12–S67.
20 least] lest D35–D69. embrace] ˜; D33–D54, Gr12–S67; ˜, D69.
21 And] *om* D33, Ga65, S67. meates] ˜. D33; ˜, D35–S67.
22 blushinges] blushing D33–D54, Ga65, S67; blushes D69. sweats] ˜; D33–S67.
23 vnto] to D33–S67.
24 lustinesse] ˜; D33–S67.
25 sorceries] sorcerers TT2.
26 thy] thine owne D33–S67. Loue] ˜. D33–S67.
27 spirittes] sprights D33–S67.
29 ingled] dandled D69.
30 day] ˜, D33–D54, Gr12–S67; ˜; D69. see] ˜. D33–D54, Gr12–S67; ˜: D69.
31 grim eight=foot=high Ironbound=seruing-man] grim-eight-foot-high-iron-bound seruing-man D33–D69; grim eight-foot-high iron-bound seruing-man Gr12–S67.
32 god] God D33–S67. then] than D33–S67.
36 there] ˜: D33–S67.
37 for] to D33–Gr12, S67.
38 kisse] ˜; D33, S67; ˜. D35–Ga65.
39 of] Oh D33–S67. twoo] too D33–S67. Ill:] ˜, D33–S67.
40 mine] my D33–D39, Gr12, S67. enimie] ˜: D33–S67.
41 mine] my D33–S67.
42 spide] ˜. D33–S67.
44 Smelt] Smells D69. shiuered] ˜; D33–D69, S67; ˜. Gr12, Ga65.
46 that] the D69. wrought] ˜. D33–S67.
50 good] sweet D69. all] ˜. D33–S67.
51 their] there TT2. whistling] whistlinges TT2. forbeare] ˜, D33, D49–S67; ˜. D35, D39.
53 bitter sweet] bitter-sweet D49–D69.
55 hast] haste TT2.
56 mee] ˜. D33–S67.
58 sound] ˜; D33–S67.
60 breath] ˜, D33–D69; ˜; Gr12–S67.
62 ffall's] ffalls TT2–S67. effeminate] ˜; D33–S67.
63 thou] you D33–S67.
64 substantiall] ˜. D33–D69, S67; ˜; Gr12, Ga65.
66 smell] ˜, D33–D39, D69; ˜; Gr12–S67.
67 loath some] loathsome D33–S67.
68 all] ill D33–S67. one] ˜? D33–S67.
69 decay] ˜; D33–S67.
70 away] ˜. D33–S67.
72 coarse!] ˜; D33–S67. what] What? D33–

D54, Gr12–S67. die /] ˜^ TT2; ˜? D33–S67.

"Elegie: Change." Texts: TT1 (32), TT2 (16), D33–Ga65, S67.

HE *Elegia 4.*] *Elegie* III. D33, D69; *Eleg.* III. *Change.* D35–D54, Gr12; Change Ga65; *Elegie: Change* S67.

1 woorkes] word D69.

2 vndoe] ˜, D33–D54, Gr12–S67; ˜. D69.

3 that] thatst TT2. *Apostasie*] *postasie* TT2.

4 Confirmes] Confirme D33–D54, Gr12–S67. loue] ˜; D33, D35, Gr12–S67; ˜, D39–D69. much in much] much, much D33–S67. thee] ˜. D33–S67.

5 Arts] ˜. TT2; ˜, D33–S67.

6 vnknowne] ˜. D33–S67.

8 fowler] fouler, D33, Gr12–S67; Fouler D35–D69. seeing] using D33–S67.

9 bird] ˜; D33–S67. those] these D33–S67.

10 man] men D33–S67. mee] ˜. D33–S67.

11 *goates*] ˜; D33–S67. all] and all D69. please] ˜, D33–D54, Gr12–S67; ˜; D69.

12 women] ˜, D33–D54, Gr12–S67; ˜; D69. then] than D35–D69.

13 man?] ˜^ TT2; ˜, D33–S67. nature] Nature D33–S67.

14 then] than D35–D69. men] ˜? D33–D54, Gr12–S67; ˜; D69.

15 not] and D69. their] there TT2. owne] ˜; D33–S67.

16 free] ˜; D33, Gr12–S67; ˜. D35–D69.

17 plowd land] plow-land D33–S67. seed corne] seed-corne D69.

18 beare] ˜; D33–S67.

19 *Danvoy*] *Danrvy* TT2; *Danuby* D33–S67.

20 *Rhene*] the *Rhene* D33–S67. *Poe*] ˜. D33, Gr12–S67; ˜, D35–D69.

21 libertie] ˜. D35–D69.

22 oh] Oh! D33–S67 (oh D69). mee] ˜? D33–S67.

23 Loue] ˜: D33–D54, Gr12–S67; ˜; D69. then] and D33–Gr12. so thou] that thou so D33–Gr12.

24 too.] ˜? D33–S67.

25 then] than D69.

26 charge] change TT2–S67. then] than D69. oftner then] as oft as D33–S67.

28 one] ˜. D33–S67.

30 *Roguery*] ˜; D33–S67.

31 stinke] stinkes TT2. bide] abide D69.

32 woorse] more D33–D54. putrifide] ˜: D33–D39, Gr12–S67; purifide: D49–D69.

34 *om*] Never looke backe, but the next banke doe kisse, D33–S67.

35 purest] ˜; D33–S67. ioy &] *om* D33–S67. nursery] misery TT2.

36 life ioy] ioy life D33–S67. eternitie] ˜. D33–S67.

"Elegie: Loues Warre." Texts: TT1 (32v), TT2 (16v), Gr12, Ga65, S67.

HE *Eligia 5*] *ELEGIE XX. Loves Warre.* Gr12; Loves Warre Ga65; *Elegie: Loves Warre.* S67.

1 When] Till Gr12–S67.

2 then] ˜? Gr12–S67.

3 scrupulous] ˜; Gr12–S67.

5 anyone] any one TT2–S67 (one: Gr12, S67).

6 Whether] Whither TT2. presse] ˜; Gr12; ˜, Ga65. rebell] ˜? Gr12–S67.

7 not] that Gr12–S67.

8 that] which Gr12–S67. come] comes TT2. fray] ˜. Gr12–S67.

10 and] yea and Gr12–S67. late] ˜; Gr12; ˜, Ga65; ˜. S67.

11 our] [our] TT2. *Angell*] *Angells* Gr12–S67.

12 returne] ˜; Gr12–S67. fell] ˜. Gr12–S67.

13 strong] strange Gr12–S67.

14 *Ague*] ˜; Gr12, S67; ˜, Ga65. rest] ˜; Gr12, S67; ˜, Ga65.

15 cure] ˜: Gr12, S67; ˜; Ga65.

16 head vayne] head-vayne Ga65. blood] ˜. Gr12–S67.

17 giue] giues TT2.

18 liue] ˜. Gr12, S67; ˜; Ga65.

19 that] the Gr12.

20 time] ˜. Gr12–S67.

22 prison] a prison Gr12–S67. were] weare Gr12, S67. fall] ˜; Gr12–S67.

23 *Cloyster*] ˜; Gr12, S67; ˜, Ga65.

24 *Hell*] ˜. Gr12–S67.

26 Executions] ˜. Gr12, S67; ˜, Ga65.

27 deaths] ˜; Gr12–S67.

28 another] an other Gr12, S67. die?] ˜^ TT2.

29 warr] ˜; Gr12–S67. lie] ˜; Gr12–S67.

30 parlee] ˜. TT2; ˜, Gr12–S67. batter] better TT2. die] ˜. Gr12–S67.

31 Thine] Thy S67. mine] my TT2. thee] ˜; Gr12, Ga65; ˜, S67.

32 is] ˜, TT2, S67; ˜; Gr12, Ga65. from] for Gr12–S67. mee] ˜. Gr12–S67.

33 their] there TT2. gaine] ˜; Gr12, S67; ˜, Ga65.

34 againe] ˜. Gr12–S67.

35 experienc'd] experience TT2. loue] ˜, Gr12, S67; ˜; Ga65.

36 That] There Gr12–S67. her] here Gr12–S67. aboue] ˜. Gr12– S67.

37 Their] There TT2–S67. of] off Gr12–S67.

38 ene] *om* Gr12–S67. no] not Gr12–S67. neere] here. Gr12–S67.

39 Their] There Gr12–S67. wronges] ˜; Gr12, S67; ˜, Ga65. lie] ˜; Gr12–S67.

40 men!] ˜, Gr12–S67. *second* by] ˜. Gr12–S67.

41 nothing] ˜; Gr12–S67.

42 those] these Gr12–S67. those] they Gr12–S67.

43 springe!] ˜. Gr12–S67. see] see which Gr12–S67.

44 warrs] ˜; Gr12, S67; ˜, Ga65.

45 home] ˜; Gr12, S67; ˜: Ga65.

46 staying] *om* TT2. men] ˜? Gr12–S67.

"Elegie: Going to Bed." Texts: TT1 (33), TT2 (17), D69–Ga65, S67.

HE *Elegia 6*] *To his Mistress going to bed.* D69; *ELEGIE XIX. Going to Bed.* Gr12; To his Mistris Going to Bed Ga65; *Elegie: Going to Bed.* S67.

2 lie] ˜. D69–S67.

3 ofttymes] oft-tymes D69–S67.

4 they] he D69, Gr12, S67. fight] ˜. D69–S67.

5 *zones*] *zone* D69–S67. glisteringe] glittering D69, Gr12, S67.

6 encompassinge] ˜. D69–S67.

7 brest plate] brestplate TT2, D69, Gr12, S67; brest-plate Ga65.

8 th eies] thee eies TT2; th'eyes D69–S67. fooles] fobles TT2. there] ˜. D69, Gr12, S67; ˜: Ga65.

10 is] it is D69, Gr12, S67; 'tis Ga65. your] *om* D69, Gr12, S67. time] ˜. D69–S67.

11 Of] Off D69–S67. whom] which D69, Gr12, S67.

12 nigh] ˜. D69–S67.

13 Gownes] gown D69, Gr12, S67. of] off D69–S67.

14 from] through D69. the *Hill*] th'hills D69–S67. shadowe] shadowes D69. steales] ˜. D69–S67.

15 Of] Off D69–S67. you[r] that D69, Gr12, S67. wiery] wearie TT2. showe] shewe D69, Gr12, S67.

16 yow] your head D69. growe] ˜: D69, Gr12, S67; ˜. Ga65.

17 Now off] Now of TT2; Off Ga65. shoes] ˜, D69, Gr12, S67; ˜: Ga65. softly] safely Gr12, Ga65.

18 *Temple*] *temple* D69–S67. bedd] ˜. D69–S67.

19 vse] vs'd D69–S67.

20 Receiued] Reveal'd D69. by] to D69. *Angells*] *Angell* D69–S67.

21 paradise] Paradise, D69, S67; Paradise; Gr12, Ga65.

22 white] ˜; D69; ˜, Gr12–S67.

23 those] these D69–S67. spiright] sprite, D69, Gr12, S67; sprite: Ga65.

24 They] Those D69, Gr12, S67. the] our D69, Gr12, S67. vpright] ˜. D69–S67.

26 Behind] ˜. TT2; Before, D69, Gr12; ˜, Ga65, S67. before] ˜. TT2; behind, D69, Gr12; ˜, Ga65, S67. betweene] ˜. TT2; ˜, D69, Gr12; aboue, Ga65, S67. aboue] ˜, TT2, D69, Gr12; between, Ga65, S67. belowe] ˜: TT2; ˜, D69; ˜. Gr12–S67.

27 *America*] ˜! D69, Gr12, S67; ˜, Ga65. new found land] new-found-land D69, Gr12, S67.

28 *Kingdome*] *Kingdom's* D69. safe] safest D69; safeliest Gr12–S67. mand] ˜. D69; ˜, Gr12–S67.

29 stones] ˜: D69, S67; ˜, Gr12, Ga65.

30 blest am I] am I blest D69. thus] this Gr12–S67. thee] ˜? D69; ˜! Gr12, S67; ˜. Ga65.

31 those] these TT2–S67. free] ˜; D69, Gr12, S67; ˜, Ga65.

32 where] were→[wher]e TT2. bee] ˜, D69; ˜. Gr12–S67.

33 *Nakednes*] ˜. TT2; ˜! D69, Gr12, S67; ˜, Ga65. thee] ˜, D69, Gr12, S67; ˜. Ga65.

34 vncloathd] vncloathe TT2–S67.

35 Ioyes] ˜. TT2–S67.

36 as] like D69, Gr12, S67. *Balles*] *ball*: D69; ˜, Gr12–S67.

37 soules] fooles D69–S67.

38 them] ˜: D69, S67; ˜. Gr12, Ga65.

40 lay men] lay-men D69, Gr12, S67; laymen Ga65. arayed] ˜. D69, S67; ˜; Gr12, Ga65.

41 are] are only D69. onlie] *om* D69.

42 Whom] (˜ D69, Gr12, S67. imputed] impa[r]ted TT2. dignifie] ˜) D69, Gr12, S67.

43 reueald.] ˜^ TT2. since] since that D69, Gr12, S67. know] ˜; D69, Gr12, S67; ˜, Ga65.

44 liberallie] ˜: TT2; ˜, D69, Gr12, S67. a] thy D69. showe] shewe D69, Gr12, S67.

45 selfe] ˜: D69, Gr12, S67; ˜; Ga65. hence] ˜, Gr12, S67; ˜. Ga65.

46 Here] There D69, Gr12, S67. much lesse] due to D69, Gr12, S67. Innocence] ˜: D69, S67; ˜. Gr12, Ga65.

47 first] ˜, D69; ˜; Gr12, S67; ˜: Ga65. then] than D69–S67.

48 then] than Ga65. man /] ˜./ TT2; ˜. D69–Ga65; ˜? S67.

"The Autumnall." Texts: TT1 (33v), TT2 (17v), D33–Ga65, S67.
HE *om*] *Elegie. The Autumnall.* D33–Gr12 (*Elegie.* IX. D35–Gr12); The Autumnall Ga65, S67.
1 summer] summers D35–D69. beautie] Beautie D33–D54, Gr12–S67.
2 face] ˜, D33–D69, S67; ˜. Gr12, Ga65.
3 your] our D33, Gr12, S67. loue] loues D69.
4 councell] counsaile D33–S67. scape] ˜. D33–S67.
5 it were] t'were D33–D39, Gr12, S67; twere D49–D69, Ga65.
6 Affection] Affections D33–D69. takes] take D33–D69. reuerence his] Reuerences D33–S67. name] ˜. D33–S67.
7 Wher] Were D33–S67. golden] Golden D33–S67. age?] Age; D33–S67 (age D69). true] ˜, D33–D54, Gr12–S67; ˜. D69.
8 shees] they are D33. but neuer] and euer D33–S67. new] ˜. D33–S67.
10 habitable] tolerable D33, Gr12–S67. clyme] ˜. D33–S67.
11 then] than D35–D69.
12 pestilence] ˜. D33–S67.
13 those] these D33–S67. graues;] ˜, TT2; ˜: D49–D69.
14 loues] Loues D33–S67. graues] ˜; D33–D39, Gr12–S67; ˜: D49–D69. for els] forels TT2; or else D39–D69. where] ˜. D33–S67.
15 loue] Loue D35–S67.
16 Anchoritt] ˜. D33–S67.
18 Tombe] ˜. D33–S67.
19 he] *om* TT2.
20 progresse] Progresse D33–S67. heere] ˜. D33–S67.
21 euening] Euening D33–S67. is] ˜; D33, Gr12–S67; ˜, D35–D69. night] ˜; D33–S67.
22 but] yet D33–S67. delight] ˜. D33–S67.
24 yea] you D33–S67. Councell] Counsaile D33–D54, Gr12–S67; Counsails D69. sitt] ˜. D33–S67.
25 Tymber] ˜, D33, D35, Gr12–S67; ˜; D39–D69. vnderwood] vnder-wood; D33–S67.
28 past] ˜; D33; ˜. D35–S67.
30 large] old D35–D69.
31 Or] Or else D33–S67.
32 *Barenesse*] ˜. D33–S67.
34 compassinge] ˜. D33, D35, D49–S67; ˜, D39.
35 *om*] If transitory things, which soone decay, D33–S67.
36 day] ˜. D33–S67.
37 winter faces] winter-faces D33–Gr12, S67. slack] ˜; D33–D39, D69–S67; ˜, D49–D54.
38 purse] ˜; D33–S67. soules] fooles D35–D54. sack] ˜; D33–S67.
39 shade] ˜; D33–D39, D50–S67; ˜, D49.
40 then] than D39–D69. made] ˜; D69–S67.
42 their] there TT2. att the] att D33–S67. Resurrectyon] ˜; D33, Gr12–S67; ˜, D35–D69.
43 deaths heades] Deaths-heades D33, Gr12–S67; Death-heades D35–D69.
44 ancient] ancients D35–D54. Antiques] Antique D33, D69, Gr12, S67. bee] ˜; D33, S67; ˜. D35, Gr12, Ga65; ˜, D39; ˜: D49–D69.
47 naturall lation] motion naturall D33; naturall station D35–D69.
49 groning] growing D33–S67. soe] foe TT2.
50 on] out D33, Gr12, S67. that] who D33–S67. homeward] home-ward D33, Gr12–S67. goe] ˜. D33–S67.

"The Storme." Texts: TT1 (38r–v), TT2 (18r–v), D33–Gr12, M67, S67.
HE *A Storme*] *The Storme. To Mr Christopher Brooke.* D33, Gr12–S67; *The Storme. To Mr. Christopher Brooke, from the Island voyage with the Earle of Essex.* D35–D69.
1 soe] ˜) D33–S67.
2 art] art still D33–S67. these] this D35–D69.
3 passage] ˜; D33–S67.
4 an] a D35–D69.
5 without] (˜ D33–S67. pride] ˜) D33–S67.
7 such] ˜. D33–D69, S67; ˜; Gr12, M67.
8 Excellence] ˜. D33–S67.
10 Sadd] *om* TT2. should] did D33–S67.
11 (ffor] ˆ˜ TT2. fates] Fates D33–S67. *fortunes*] *Fortunes* D33–S67. sooth say] South-say D33–D39; soothsay D49–D54, Gr12–S67; gain-say D69.
12 and way)] and wayˆ TT2; and way.) D33, Gr12–S67; one way. D35–D69.
14 middle=marble-roome] middle marble roome D33–S67.
16 againe] ˜; D33–S67.
17 leese] lease TT2.
20 meete] meetes TT2.
21 came,] ˜; D33–S67.
22 see] ˜. D33–S67.
23 *Contrymen*] *contry men* D39–D69.
24 then] ˜. D33–D39, Gr12–S67; ˜, D49–D54; ˜; D69.
26 asunder;] a sunder, TT2; ˜, D33–D54, Gr12–S67; ˜ˆ D69.
27 *West windes*] *Westwindes* D69.
28 Waues] Wayues→[Wa]ues TT2. threwe] ˜. D33–S67.
29 then] than D39–D69.
30 assaile] ˜; D33–S67.
32 name] ˜. D33–S67.
34 thee] the TT2. then] ˜; D33, Gr12–S67; ˜. D35; ˜: D49–D69.
35 easiest] easie D49–D54.
36 kill] ˜. D33–S67.
37 saw] ˜: TT2; ˜, D33–S67. not] ˜. D33–D69, S67; ˜; Gr12, M67.
38 sunne] Sunne D33–S67.
39 *Night*] ˜, D33, Gr12–S67; ˜; D35–D69. but] onely D33–Gr12, S67.
40 now] yet D35–D54. day] ˜. D33–S67.
41 neere] weer TT2; were D33–S67.
42 his] this D69. call] ˜: D33–S67.
44 Then] Than D39–D54. druncke] dranck TT2. before] ˜; D33, S67; ˜. D35, D49–M67; ˜, D39.
45 lie!] ˜, D33–D54, Gr12–S67; ˜ˆ D69.
46 die] ˜. D33–D54, S67; ˜: D69; ˜; Gr12, M67.
47 sin burthened] sin-burd'ned D33, D49–S67; sinburd'ned D35, D39. graues] graue D35–D54.
48 their] there TT2. peepe] ˜: D33–S67.
49 newes] what newes D33–S67.
50 Like] As D35–D69. knowe] ˜. D33–S67.
52 *second* feare] ˜. D33–S67.
53 There] Then D33–D54, Gr12, S67.
54 *Wast*] *Waste* D35–D69.
56 to high stretchd] too-high-stretchd D33–D54, Gr12–S67; to too-high-stretchd D69. stringes] ˜. D33–S67.
57 Tatterd] Totterd D33–S67.
58 agoe] a goe TT2; ˜. D33–S67.
59 Euen] Yea euen D35–D69. placd] place TT2.
60 Striue] Striues D35–D69. thence] ˜. D33–D39, Gr12–S67.
61 gaine] ˜? D33–S67.
62 againe] ˜; D33–D39, Gr12–S67; ˜: D49–D69.
63 sailours] ˜; D33, Gr12–S67; ˜, D35–D69.
64 knewe] knowes D33–S67. say] ˜. D33–S67.
65 death] Death TT2.
66 *Bermuda*] *Bermudas* D35–D54; *Bermuda's* D69. *calme*] *calmes* TT2; ˜. D33–S67.
67 elder] eldest D33–D69. birthright] birth-right D33–S67.
68 Claymes] Claym'd D33. this] the D35–D69. light] ˜. D33–S67.
69 are one] ˜ ˜. D33–D39, Gr12–S67; ˜ ˜: D49–D69.
71 couer.] ˜, TT2, D33, Gr12–S67; ˜; D35–D69. god] God D33–S67.
72 day] ˜. D33–D54, Gr12–S67; ˜, D69.
73 furies] faries TT2.
74 thee] ˜. D33–S67.

"The Calme." Texts: TT1 (39r-v), TT2 (19), D33–Gr12, M67, S67.
HE *A*] *The* D33–S67.
2 swage] ˜. D33–S67.
4 storke] stock TT2; stroke D39.
5 were] weare D33–S67. vs] ˜; D33–S67.
6 thvs] ˜. D33–S67.
7 can] could D35–D69. that] *om* D35–D69.
8 there] ˜, D33–D54, Gr12–S67; ˜; D69.
9 nowe] ˜. D33, Gr12–S67; ˜, D35–D69. wee] you→[wee] TT2.
10 bee] ˜. D33–S67.
11 stormes] ˜, D33–D39, Gr12, S67; ˜; D49–D69, M67. out] ˜: D35–Gr12, S67; ˜, M67.
12 lead] ˜, D33, D39–S67; ˜; D35. spout] ˜. D33–S67.
13 trime] traine TT2.
14 ended] ending D69. playes] ˜. D33–S67.
15 *fightings*] fightinge TT2–S67. ragges] rage D69.
16 but] a D33–S67. *Frippery*] ˜. D33–S67.
17 No] Now D69. Lanthornes] ˜; D33, Gr12–S67; ˜: D69.
18 today] to day TT2–S67. yesterday] ˜. D33–S67.
19 hollownesses] hollownes TT2.
20 then] than D35, D39. thayre] th'ayre TT2; aire. D33, Gr12–S67; ayre. D35–D69.
21 left] lost D33–Gr12, S67. recouer] ˜, D33–D39, D69–S67; ˜. D49–D54.
22 *Meteorlike*] *Meteor-like* D35–D69. houer] honer TT2; ˜. D33–S67.
24 iawes] ˜: D33, Gr12–S67; mawes, D35–D69.
26 sacrifice] ˜. D33–S67.
28 lie] dye. D33–S67.
29 this] these D33–S67.
30 then] than D39–D69. the] our D33, Gr12–S67; a D35–D69. *Bath*] ˜, D33–D39, Gr12–S67; ˜; D49–D69.
32 burne] ˜. D33–S67.
33 scoffe] ˜, D33–D39, Gr12–S67; ˜; D49–D69.
34 slack sinewed] slack-sinewed D35–D54.
35 shippes] ˜. D33–S67.
36 invade] ˜, D33, Gr12–S67; ˜: D35–D69.
37 sea *Gaoles*] sea goates TT2; sea-goales D33,

D69, Gr12; sea gulls D35–D54; sea-gaoles M67, S67.
38 our] with D69. *Venices*] Pinnaces D35–D54, Gr12, S67; Vinice D69.
39 and] or TT2.
40 diffuse] dessuse TT2; disuse D33–S67.
41 louing;] ˜, TT2, D33, Gr12–S67; ˜: D35–D69.
42 out pushd] out past→p[u]s[h'd] TT2; out-pushd D35–D69.
43 loose] lose D33–S67. end] ˜: D33–S67.
44 a] *om* D35–D69. die] ˜. D33–S67.
46 dies] ˜. D33–D54, Gr12–S67; ˜: D69.
47 grudgeth] grudges D33–S67.
48 forgett] forgott D69. pray] ˜, D33, Gr12–S67; ˜. D35–D69; ˜; M67.
49 may] *om* D33–S67.
50 *Poles*] *Poles* may D33–S67. or] *om* D33–S67. *Hell*] ˜. D33–S67.
51 then] ˜, TT2; ˜? D33–S67.
52 was] ˜? D33, Gr12–S67; ˜, D35–D69. was] ˜? D35–D69.
53 Nothing] ˜; D33–D54, Gr12–S67. fitt] ˜; D33–S67.
54 ou^{r}] ~~ever~~[our] TT2. itt] ˜. D33–D39, Gr12–S67; ˜; D49–D69.
55 will] power D33–Gr12, S67. power] will D33–Gr12, S67. sence!] ˜; TT2–S67.
56 misery] ˜. / TT2; ˜; D33–S67.

"To Mr. *Rowland Woodward*: 'Like one who'in her third widdowhood.'" Texts: TT1 (39v–40), TT2 (19v), D33–Gr12, M67, S67.
HE *om*] To Mr. *Rowland Woodward.* D33–S67.
2 tir'd] tyed D33–S67. a] *om* D33–S67.
3 fallownesse] ˜. D33–D69, S67; ˜; Gr12, M67.
4 showne] flowne D35–D69.
5 loue song] loue-song D33, D69–S67; long loues D35–D54. woordes weedes] weedes D33–S67.
6 sowne] ˜. D33, Gr12, M67; ˜? D35–D69, S67.
8 Bethrothd] Bethrothe TT2. Adultery] ˜; D33–S67.
9 bee] ˜. D33–S67.
10 and] but D35–D69. be light] de-light→[b]elight TT2; light D35–D69.
11 god] God D33–S67. throwes] thrownes→throw[s] TT2.
12 sin] ˜. D33–S67.
14 cloath] cloth D33, Gr12, M67.
15 god] God D33–S67. Natiue] Nature→Natiue TT2. puritie] ˜, D33; ˜. D35–S67.
16 Religion] ˜, D33; ˜. D35–D54; ˜: D69–S67.
18 discretion] ˜. D33–S67.
19 selues] ˜; D33–S67. as] als TT2.
20 sunne] Sunne D33–S67. wth] wch TT2.
21 glasse] ˜; D33, D39–D69, Gr12–S67; ˜: D35.
22 if] (˜ D35–D69.
23 the] our D33–S67. vertue] ˜) D35–D69. outburne] out-burne D35–D69.
24 soiourne] ˜. D33–S67.
26 soule] soules D33–S67.
27 chuse] ˜. D33, D49–S67; ˜: D35, D39.
28 vs] ˜: D33–S67.
29 and to] and D33–S67.
30 become] ˜. D33–S67.
31 farmers] termers D33.
32 our] out D49–D54. vpp lay] and thrive, up-lay D33–S67.
33 deare] good D35–D69. day] ˜. D33–S67.
34 Manure] Nature TT2–S67.
36 thee] ˜, D49, D50, D69; ˜; D54. beloued] be lou'd. D33–S67.

"To Sr. *Henry Wootton*: 'Here's no more newes.'" Texts: TT1 (40), TT2 (20), D33–Gr12, M67, S67.
HE *om*] To Sr. *Henry Wootton.* D33–S67.
1 then] than D35–D54.
2 tale] Mount D69.
3 dwell] ˜./ TT2; ˜. D33–S67.
5 sweeter] sweeten D33–S67. god] God D33–S67.
6 or] and→or TT2; and D69. Towne] ˜. D33–S67.
7 here] where TT2. no one] none TT2. free] *om* D33–S67.
9 then] than D35–D54. hee] ˜. D33–S67.
10 Ragged] Rugged D33–S67. fate] Fate D33–S67.
11 (Godes] ˜˜ TT2. Commissary)] ˜˜ TT2. thoroughly] throughly D33–S67.
12 their] there TT2. state] estate TT2; ˜: D35–S67.
14 wishing] wishes D35–D54.
15 bee] ˜. D33–S67.
16 Suspicious] Suspitions TT2.
17 tonges] tongues; D33–S67.
18 loath] though D33–S67. wronges] ˜. D33–S67.
20 plaies] players D39–D69.
21 are] *om* D35–D69. plaies] ˜. D33–S67.
22 *Antique*] antiques D33–S67.
23 gests] guests D69.
24 Are] And D69. *Chests*] ˜. D33–S67.
25 t'is] t'is an D69.
26 end] ˜; D33–S67.
27 *Court*] ˜, D33, D69; ˜: D35–D54; ˜; Gr12–S67. stile] ˜. D33–S67.

"The Legacie." Texts: TT1 (44), TT2 (22v), D33–Ga65, S67.
HE *Elegie*] *The Legacie.* D33–Gr12, S67; The Legacie Ga65.
2 thee] the TT2.
3 *om*] Though it be but an houre agoe, D33–S67 (be an Ga65).
6 bestowe] ˜; D33–S67.
7 sent] meant D35–D54.
8 Legacy] ˜. D33–S67.
10 (thats] ˜˜ D33–D69, Ga65, S67. I)] ˜˜ D33–D69, Ga65, S67.
12 gone] ˜, D33–Gr12, S67; ˜; Ga65.
14 bee] lye, D33–D39; lye D49–D69; lye; Gr12–S67.
16 yow] ˜. D33–S67.
20 part] ˜. D33–D39, Gr12–S67; ˜; D49; ˜: D50–D69.
22 losses] loss D69. sadd] be sadd D69.
23 thought] meant D33–Gr12, S67. that] this D33, Gr12, S67.
24 thine] ˜. D33–S67.

"The broken heart." Texts: TT1 (44v), TT2 (23), D33–Ga65, S67.
HE *Eligie*] *The broken heart.* D33–Gr12, S67; The Broken Heart Ga65.
2 one] an D33–S67.
4 deuoure] ˜; D33–S67.
6 yeare] ˜? D33–S67.
7 mee] ~~once~~[mee] TT2.
8 flash] flask D33, Gr12–S67. day] ˜? D33–S67.
10 come] ˜? D33–D69; ˜! Gr12–S67.
12 some] ˜, D33–D69; ˜; Gr12–S67.
13 loues] loue D33–S67 (Loue D33, Gr12–S67).
14 chawes] ˜: D33–S67.
15 chaind shott] chain-shott Ga65.
16 our] and D69. hartes] we D69. frie] ˜. D33–S67.
17 could] did D33–S67.
18 thee] ˜? D33–S67.
20 and] But D33–S67. mee] ˜; D33–D39, Gr12–S67; ˜: D49–D69.
21 thine] thee D33–S67.
22 thy] thine D33–Gr12, S67.
23 mee] ˜, TT2; ˜: D33–S67. loue] Loue D33–S67.
24 doth] did D33–S67. like] as D33–S67. glasse] ˜. D33–S67.
28 vnite] ˜; D33–D39, Gr12–S67; ˜: D49–D69.
30 thousand] hundred D33–S67.
32 more] ˜. D33–S67.

"Twicknam garden." Texts: TT1 (45r-v), D33–Ga65, S67.
HE *Twittnam Garden*] *Twicknam garden.* D33–Gr12, S67 (*Garden* D35–D69); Twicknam Garden Ga65.
2 came] come D33–S67.
3 eares] ˜, D33–D39, Gr12–S67; ˜. D49–D54; years, D69.
4 balmes] balme D35–D69. cures] cure D33, Gr12–S67. thinge] ˜, D33, S67; ˜: D35–D69; ˜; Gr12, Ga65.
5 selfe traitor] selfe-traitor D35–D69.
6 spider] spiders D69.
8 thoroughlie] throughlie D49–D69.
9 paradise] Paradise D33–S67. serpent] Serpent D39–D69. brought] ˜. D33–S67.
12 would] did D33–S67.
13 in] to D33–S67. face] ˜; D33–S67.
14 But] But that D33–D54, Gr12–S67; But since D69. may] *om* D69. not] cannot D69.
15 nor] nor yet D33, Gr12. the garden] loving D33, Gr12; this garden D35–D69, Ga65, S67. loue] Loue D33–S67.
16 part] peece D33–S67. bee] ˜; D33–S67.
17 grone] grow D33–D69, Ga65.
18 the] my D33, D69–S67. yeare/] ˜. D33–S67.
20 Loues] loues D33, D35, D49–S67; louers D39.
22 w^{ch}] that D33–S67. mine] ˜; D33–S67.
24 womans] womens D35–D69.
25 then] than D39. weares] ˜. D33–S67.
26 *Sexe*] *sexe* D33–S67.
27 mee /] ˜. D33–S67.

"The good-morrow." Texts: TT1 (45v), TT2 (23v), D33–Ga65, S67.
HE *om*] *The good-morrow.* D33–Gr12, S67 (*Good-morrow* D69); The Good-morrow Ga65.
2 lov'd] ˜, TT2–D35; ˜? D39–S67. then] ˜? D33–D54, Gr12–S67; ˜, D69.
3 suck'd] suck TT2. childish] countrey D33–D54, Gr12–S67. seelilie] ˜? D69; childishly? D33–D54, Gr12–S67.
4 slumbred] snorted D33–D54, Gr12–S67. seauen sleepers] seauen-sleepers D35–D69. den] ˜? D33–S67.
5 so] ˜; D33–S67. as] this D33–D54, Gr12–S67. bee] ˜. D33, D35, Gr12–S67; ˜, D39–D69.

7 thee/] theˆ TT2; ˜. D33–S67.
8 good morrow] good-morrow D35–D69.
9 feare] ˜; D33–S67.
10 But] For D33–S67. loue;] ˜ˆ TT2, D69; ˜, D33–D54, Gr12–S67.
11 a] one D33–S67. where] ˜. D33–S67.
12 sea discoverours] sea-discoverours D33–S67.
13 one] on D33–D54, Gr12–S67; our D69. worldes] world D69.
14 our] one D33–Gr12, S67. *second* one] ˜. D33–S67.
16 plaine true] true plaine D33–S67. rest] ˜, D33–D39, Gr12–S67; ˜. D49–D54; ˜; D69.
17 fitter] better D33, Gr12–S67.
18 West] ˜? D33–S67.
19 is] was D33–D54, Gr12–S67. equallie] ˜; D33–S67.
20 both our] our two D33–S67. or] both D35–D69.
21 iust] so D33, Gr12–S67. in all] that D33, Gr12–S67. of] doe D33, Gr12–S67. these] slacken D33, Gr12–S67. loues] none D33, Gr12–S67. die] ˜. D33–S67.

"Loves Alchymie." Texts: TT1 (46), D33–Ga65, S67.
HE *Mummy*] *Loves Alchymie*. D33–S67.
1 Loues] loues D33–D39, Gr12–S67. then] than D35–D69.
2 lie] ˜: D33–S67.
4 gett;] ˜, D33–S67. olde] ˜, D33, Gr12–S67; ˜; D35–D69.
5 mistery] ˜; D33–S67.
6 all] ˜: D33–S67.
12 winter seeming sommers] winter-seeming sommers D33–D54, Gr12–S67; winter-seeming-sommers D69. night] ˜. D33–S67.
13 and thrift] our thrift D33–S67.
14 pay] ˜? D33–S67.
15 this?] ˜, D33–S67.
16 can?] ˜; D33–S67.
17 play] ˜? D33–S67.
22 Spheares] ˜. D33–S67.
23 woman] women; D33–S67 (womenˆ D69).
24 possest] ˜. D33–S67.

"Breake of day." Texts: TT1 (46), TT2 (23v), D33–Ga65, S67. Both TT1 and TT2 omit the initial stanza first published as Donne's in D69.
HE *om*] *Breake of day*. D33–S67.
1 day] ˜, D33, Ga65, S67; ˜; D35–Gr12. bee] ˜? D33–S67.
2 Wilt] O wilt D33–S67. mee] ˜? D33–S67.
3 light?] ˜ˆ TT2.
4 night] ˜? D33–S67.
5 that] which D33–S67. despite] spight D33–D39, D69–S67.
6 despight] spight D35, D39. hold] keepe D33–S67. together] ˜. D33–S67.
7 eie] ˜; D33–D39, Gr12–S67; ˜, D49–D69.
9 is] were D33–S67.
11 loue] lov'd D33–S67. louer] honor D33–S67.
12 him] her D69. w^{ch}] that D33–S67. hath] had D33–S67. goe] ˜? D33–S67.
13 remooue] ˜? D33–S67.
15 foole] foule D33–S67.
16 man] ˜. D33–S67.
17 that] which D33–S67.
18 if] when D33–S67. should] doth D33, D69–S67. woe] wooe. D33–S67.

"The Sunne Rising." Texts: TT1 (46v), D33–Ga65, S67.
HE *om*] *The Sunne Rising*. D33–S67.
2 dost] dust D49–D54.
3 thorough] through D33–S67. call] look D69. vs] ˜? D33–S67.
4 runn] ˜? D33–S67.
6 schoole boyes] schoole-boyes D35–D69. and] or D69. soure prentises] soure-prentises D35–D54.
7 court huntsmen] Court-huntsmen D33–S67. doth] will D33–S67.
8 Offices] ˜, D33, D35; ˜; D39–S67.
10 tyme] ˜. D33–S67.
11 reverenc'd] reverend D33–S67.
12 Whie shouldst thou] Dost thou not D35–D69. thincke] ˜? D33, Gr12–S67.
14 loose] lose D33–S67. long] ˜: D33, Gr12–S67; ˜? D35–D69.
17 Whither] Whether D33–S67. Indies] the'India's D33–S67.
18 there] where D33–S67. lefts] leftst D33, Gr12–S67; left D35–D69. mee] ˜. D33–D54, Gr12–S67; ˜, D69.
20 lay] ˜. D33–S67.
21 states] States D33–S67.
22 is] ˜. D33–S67.
23 vs] ˜, D33; ˜; D35–S67.
24 *Mimique*] ˜; D33–S67. *Alchymy*] ˜; D33–D69, S67; ˜. Gr12, Ga65.
25 sunn] Sunn D35–D69.
26 worlds] world's D33–S67. thus] ˜. D33–D69, S67; ˜; Gr12, Ga65.
28 vs] ˜. D33–D54, Gr12–S67; ˜, D69.
29 where] ˜; D33, Gr12–S67; ˜, D35–D69.
30 sphere] ˜. D33–S67.

"Lecture upon the Shadow." TT1 (46v–47), D35–Ga65, S67.
HE *om*] *Song*. D35, D39; *A Lecture upon the shadow*. D49–Ga65; *Lecture upon the Shadow*. S67.
2 loue] Loue D35–S67. Philosophy] ˜. D35–S67.
4 heere] ˜; D35, D39; ˜: D49–D69; ˜, Gr12–S67.
5 produc'd] ˜; D35, D39, Gr12–S67; ˜. D49–D69.
6 sunn] Sunn D35–S67.
7 these] those D35–S67. tred] ˜; D35, D39, Gr12–S67; ˜: D49–D69.
8 reduc'd] ˜. D35–S67.
11 cares] ˜; D35, D39, Gr12–S67; ˜: D49–D69. soe] ˜. D35–S67.
13 see] ˜: D35; ˜. D39–D54, Gr12–S67; ˜, D69.
15 way] ˜. D35–S67.
17 others] ˜; D35–S67.
18 eyes] ˜. D35–S67.
19 decline /] ˜; D35–S67.
21 thee to] thee D35–S67. disguise] ˜. D35–S67.
24 (oh)] ˆ˜ˆ D35–S67. decay] ˜. D35–S67.
25 light] ˜; D35, D39, Gr12–S67; ˜: D49–D69.
26 first] short D39–D69. night] ˜. D35–S67.

"The triple Foole." Texts: TT1 (47), TT2 (24), D33–Ga65, S67.
HE *om*] *The triple Foole*. D33–S67.
3 Poetry] ˜; D33–D39, Gr12–S67; ˜, D49–D69.
4 that] the D69. wise man] wiseman D33, Gr12–S67; wiser man D69.
5 deny] ˜? D33–S67.
6 narrow] *om* TT2.
9 then] them D33–S67.
10 Numbers] Number D69.
11 tames] teames TT2. verse] ˜. D33–S67.
13 Act] art TT2–S67. and] or D69.
14 doth] Did TT2. sitt] set D33–S67.
16 restrayne] ˜. D33–S67.
18 red] read D33–S67.
19 songes] ˜: D33–S67.
20 their] there TT2.
21 w^{ch}] wch was D33–S67. three] ˜; D33–D39, Gr12–S67; ˜, D49–D69.
22 bee /] ˜ˆ TT2; ˜. D33–S67.

"Image of her whom I love." Texts: TT1 (47v), D33–Ga65, S67.
HE *Elegie*] ELEG. X. *The Dreame*. D35–D54, Gr12; ELEGIE. X. D69; [Image and Dreame] Ga65; "Image of her whom I love." S67.
1 then] than D35–D69.
3 Mettall] Medall D33–S67.
5 valewe,] ˜: D33–S67.
6 *om*] Which now is growne too great and good for me. D33–S67 (me: D35–S67).
8 dull] ˜, D33; ˜; D35–S67. see] ˜. D33–S67.
10 fantasie] *Fantasie* D33–S67 (Fantasie Ga65). all] ˜; D33–S67.
11 then] than D35–D69. doe] ˜: D33–S67.
12 proportionall] ˜. D33–S67.
13 *second* yow] ˜, D33–D39, Gr12–S67; ˜: D49–D69.
14 Phantasticall] ˜. D33–S67.
15 true] ˜; D33–S67.
16 all] ˜. D33–S67.
17 a such] such a D69.
18 repent] ˜; D33–S67.
20 spent] ˜. D33–S67.
21 stay] ˜; D33, Gr12–S67; ˜, D35–D69.
22 inough] ˜; D33–S67.
23 away] ˜: D33–S67.
24 snuffe] ˜. D33–S67.
26 none] ˜. D33–S67.

"Loves diet." Texts: TT1 (47v–48), TT2 (24r–v), D33–Ga65, S67.
2 growne] ˜, D33–D54, Gr12–S67; ˜; D69.
6 discretion/] ˜ˆ TT2; ˜. D33–S67.
8 part] ˜; D33–S67.
11 though] thought D33–S67.
12 neither] not TT2. mee] ˜; D33, D35, S67; ˜: D39–D69; ˜. Gr12, Ga65.
13 wrung] wrong TT2–D39, Gr12–S67. itt] *om* TT2. too] so D33–S67.
14 not] ˜; D33–S67.
16 gott] ˜, D33, Gr12–S67; ˜. D35–D69.
17 meat] ˜; D33–S67.
18 sweat] ˜. D33–S67.
19 Whatsoever] What ever D33–D39, D69–S67; What e'r D49–D54. he would] might him D49–D54. I] I still D49–D54.
20 and] But D33–S67. my] her D35–D54. t̄r̄ēs̄] ˜; D33, Gr12–S67. when] which D69. mee] ˜, D33, D35, Gr12–S67; ˜; D39–D69.
21 that that] if that D35–D69.
23 (ah)] ˆ˜ˆ D33–S67.
24 name] man D69. entayle] ˜? D33–S67.
25 reclaimd] redeemd D33.
26 att what and when] Att when TT2. choose] ˜; D33–S67.
27 sport] sports D33.
29 weepe] ˜: D33–S67.
30 *second* and] or D35–D69. sleepe] ˜. D33–S67.

"A Valediction forbidding mourning." Texts:

TT1 (48r-v), TT2 (24v–25), D33–Ga65, S67.
HE *Elegie*] *A Valediction forbidding mourning.* D33–S67 (*Valediction:* Gr12, Ga65).
3 And] Whilst D33–S67. their] there TT2.
4 the] Now his D69. now] *om* D69. sayes] say D33–S67. no] ˜. D33–D54, S67; ˜; D69; ˜: Gr12, Ga65.
6 teare floudes] teare-floudes D33–S67. sigh tempestes] sigh-tempestes D33–S67.
8 of] *om* D33–S67. Loue] ˜. D33–S67.
12 Innocent] ˜. D33–S67.
15 Absence] Of absence D69. because] cause D69.
16 those] The D69. thinges] thing D69. itte] ˜. D33–S67.
17 much] far D69.
19 Itter→Inter→In['o]t[h]er assured] I'hter→I'[c]ht[,]er assured TT2; Inter-assured D33–S67.
20 careles] care les D33, D35, D69–S67. and] *om* D33–S67. misse] ˜. D33–S67.
21 therefore wch are] wch are therefore TT2.
24 ayerie] ather TT2. beat] ˜. D33–S67.
26 twin=compasses] twin compasses TT2–S67.
27 maketh] makes D33–S67.
28 doe] ˜. D33–S67.
30 come] rome D33–S67.
32 direct] erect D33–S67. itt] that D33–Gr12, S67. home] ˜. D33–S67.
34 runne] ˜. D33–D69, S67; ˜; Gr12, Ga65.
35 circle] circles D39–D54.
36 begunn .] ˜^ TT2.

"Elegie on the Lady Marckham." Texts: TT1 (48v–49), D33–Gr12, S67, M78.
HE *An Eligie vpon the death of the La: Markham*] *Elegie on the Lady* Marckham. D33–M78 (*An Elegie* D69; *on Lady* M78).
2 god] God D33–M78. man] ˜. D33–M78.
3 The] This D33–M78.
4 god] God D33–M78.
6 and] To D69. breake] breaks D33–D54, Gr12–M78. banck] bancks Gr12, M78. freind] ˜. D33–M78.
7 vent] ˜; D33–M78.
8 firmament] ˜. D33, Gr12; ˜, D35–D69, S67, M78.
9 Teares] (˜ D33–M78. sinne] sinnes D33–S67. fall] ˜) D33–M78.
10 funerall] ˜. D33–D69; ˜, Gr12–M78.
11 those] these Gr12, S67. sinne] ˜. D33–M78.
12 Godes] God D69. *Noe*] new D69. the] our D69–M78. againe] ˜. D33–M78.
14 itt] itselfe D33, D35, Gr12–M78; it selfe D39–D69. w^{th}in borne] with inborne D33–M78. stinges] ˜. D33–M78.
15 spectacles:] ˜, D33–M78.
16 thorough] through D33–M78. mistes] mist D33–M78. nor] or D33–M78. shee] ˜. D33–M78.
20 hand] ˜. D33–M78.
22 clay] ˜; D33, Gr12–M78; ˜: D35–D69.
23 w^{ch}] (˜ D35–D69.
25 (Of] ˜^ D33–M78. was)] ˜^ D33–M78.
27 the] this D33–M78.
28 then] them D49–D69. all] ˜. D33–M78.
29 when the Sea gaines itt] the Sea when itt gaines D33–M78. too] ˜; D33, D69–M78; ˜, D35–D54.
30 death] Death D33–M78. the] (˜ D33–M78. brother] ˜) D33–M78.
31 bodie] ˜, D33, Gr12–M78; ˜; D35–D69.
32 sinne] ˜, D33, D49–M78; ˜: D35, D39. this] ˜; D33–M78.
33 lust] ˜; D33–M78.
34 Dust] ˜. D33–M78.
35 both] ˜; D33–M78.
36 w^{ch}] that D33–M78. are] is D33–M78. loth] ˜. D33–D69, S67; ˜, Gr12, M78.
37 die] ˜, D33–D69, S67; ˜; Gr12, M78.
38 shee hath] hath shee D33–M78. *Virginitie*] ˜. D33–M78.
40 repent] ˜. D33–M78.
42 breakes] cracks D33–Gr12. glasse] ˜? D33–D69; ˜! Gr12–M78.
44 That Godes Woord must bee true. All sinners bee] (woord Gr12, S67; true, D35–M78; bee. D35–M78); *om* D33.
45 So much did zeale her conscience rarifie] *om* D33.
46 lie] ˜, D33–D39, Gr12–M78; ˜; D49–D69.
47 Actes,] ˜; D33–M78.
48 w^{ch}] that D33–M78. sometimes] sometime D35–D69. such] ˜. D33–M78.
50 too] ˜: D33–M78.
52 men] ˜. D33–M78.
53 god] God D33–M78.
54 death] Death Gr12, M78. repent] ˜. D33–M78.
56 meet!] ˜, D33–M78.
58 women] woman D33. not] no D33–M78. bee] ˜; D33–M78.
60 thinck] thincks D39. old] ˜. D35–D69; ˜: Gr12, S67; ˜, M78.
61 deaths] Deaths D33, Gr12–M78.
62 adde] ˜. D33–M78.

"Elegie to the Lady Bedford." Texts: TT1 (49v), D33–Gr12, M67, S67.
HE *An Elegie to the La: Bedford*] *To the Lady Bedford.* D35–M67 (*Countess of* D69); *Elegie to the Lady Bedford* S67.
1 that] that are D33–S67. shee] ˜, D33, Gr12–S67; ˜; D35–D69.
2 see] ˜; D33–S67.
4 twoo] ˜; D33–S67.
5 but that] that but D33–S67.
6 yett] ˜. D49–D69; ˜; Gr12, M67.
7 birth:] ˜^ D33–S67.
8 make] ˜, D33–D69, S67; ˜; Gr12, M67.
10 and] one D33–S67. goe] ˜; D33–D69, S67; ˜. Gr12, M67.
11 beene] ˜; D33–S67.
12 seene] ˜; D33–S67.
14 frend] ˜; D33, Gr12–S67; ˜, D35–D69. clay] ˜; D33–D69, S67; ˜. Gr12, M67.
16 there] ˜; D33–D69, S67; ˜, Gr12, M67.
17 honour] ˜: D33; ˜, M67. due] ˜; D33.
18 yow] ˜; D33–S67.
20 was] were D35–Gr12, S67.
22 that] as all D33–S67 (as M67). all] *om* D35–Gr12, S67. is] ˜; D33–D69, S67; ˜. Gr12, M67.
23 all] ˜, D33–S67.
24 stay] ˜; D33–S67.
26 all] All D33–S67. vnite] ˜: D33–S67.
28 a] the D33–Gr12, S67. bedd] ˜; D33–S67.
29 due] do D33–S67.
30 yow] they D33–S67. were] ˜; D33, S67; ˜. D35, D39; ˜: D49–M67.
32 whose] whence D33–S67. are/] ˜; D33, S67; ˜. D35–M67.
33 *Mettalls*] ˜; D33–S67.
34 knowe] ˜; D33, S67; ˜. D35–M67.
36 last] ˜, D33–D54, Gr12–S67; ˜; D69.
38 impaire] ˜; D33–S67.
40 make] ˜. D33–M67; ˜, S67.
41 doubt] ˜, D33–D39, Gr12–S67; ˜; D49–D69.
42 w^{th}out] ˜; D33–S67.
44 shee] ˜. D33–S67.

"Elegie on Mris. Boulstred." Texts: TT1 (50r-v), D33–Gr12, S67, M78.
HE *An Eligie vpon the death of M^{ris} Boulstredd*] *Elegie on Mris. Boulstred.* D33–M78 (*Mistris* D35–D69).
2 may] might D33–M78. thee] ˜. D33–M78.
4 disobey] ˜. D33–M78.
5 table] ˜; D33–M78. and thy meat] there are set D33–M78.
6 dished] dishes D33, D49–M78. death] Death D33–M78. eat] ˜. D33–M78.
8 iawes] ˜. D33–M78.
10 tast] last. D33–M78.
12 rott] ˜. D33–M78.
13 the] this D33–M78. him] ˜; D33–M78.
14 keepe] ˜. D33, D49–D69; ˜, D35, D39, Gr12–M78.
15 were] (˜ D33–M78. (death] ˜Death D33–M78. by] the D35–D69. Rowes] Roes D33–M78.
16 Land] ˜. D33–M78.
18 *Heauens*] (˜ Gr12. *Quiristers*] ˜) Gr12.
19 if] (˜ D33–M78. die] ˜) D33–M78.
20 *Hierarchie*] ˜. D33–M78.
21 long liu'd] long-liu'd D33–D39, D69–M78. death] Death D49–D69.
22 creation] Creation D33–M78. beginn] ˜? D33–M78.
24 *Antichrist*] ˜. D33–M78.
26 *second* all] All D33–M78. tis] is D33–M78. thou] ˜. D33–D39, Gr12–M78; ˜? D49–D69.
27 lifes] life D33, M78.
28 thee] ˜. D33–M78.
30 death] ˜. D33–Gr12, M78; ˜, S67.
31 (O] ˜^ D33–D39, Gr12–M78. pray] ˜) D49–D69.
32 of] by D33–M78. god] God D33–M78. maist] must D33–M78.
34 to] for D35–D69. thee] ˜. D33–M78.
35 hast] has Gr12, M78.
36 owne] ˜. D33–D39, Gr12–M78; ˜; D35–D69.
37 hie!] ˜: D33–M78.
38 Roome] ˜. D33–M78.
39 Court] ˜: D33–M78.
40 fort] ˜. D33–M78.
41 king] Kings D35–D69.
42 rests] rest D33–M78. aboue] ˜. D33–M78.
45 woorkes] woorke D33–M78. diuorce] ˜. D33–D54, Gr12–M78; ˜, D69.
46 the] her D33–M78.
47 shalbe] shall be D33–M78.
48 then] than D69. heere] ˜. D33–M78.
50 yeares.] ˜, D33–M78. Ô emulous death wouldst thou] wouldst thou O emulous death D33–M78 (Death M78). doe] doe so? D33–M78 (so, D35–D69).
52 lost] ˜? D33–M78.
53 youth] ˜? D33–M78.
54 On] Oh D33–M78. pursueth] ˜. D33–M78.
56 ambitious] ˜, D33; ˜: D35–D54; ˜; D69–M78.
57 prou'd] ˜: D33–M78.
58 superstīcon] ˜. D33–M78.
60 delight] ˜. D33–M78.

62 what] that D33–M78. *second* sinn] ˜. D33–S67; ˜; M78.

64 prophane] ˜. D33; ˜, D35–D54, S67; ˜; D69, Gr12, M78.

66 had] told D33–M78. whatt] ˜. D33–M78.

67 might] might'st D33, Gr12–M78; mightst D35–D69.

68 thy] thine D33–M78. lost] ˜. D33–M78.

70 gon] ˜. D33–D54, Gr12, M78; ˜: D69; ˜, S67.

72 such] ˜. D33–M78.

74 though] but D33. lost] ˜. D33–M78.

"Elegie: Death." Texts: TT1 (51r-v), D33–Gr12, S67, M78.

HE *Another Eligie vpon the death of M^{ris} Boulstred*] (*Mistress* M78); *Elegie*. D33; ELEG. XI. *Death* D35–D54; ELEGIE XI. D69; ELEGIE. *Death*. Gr12; *Elegie: Death*. S67.

2 now] ˜; D33–D39, Gr12–M78; ˜, D49–D69. sorrowe] sorrowes D35–D69. speake] ˜; D33–D39, Gr12–M78; ˜. D49–D69.

3 our] out D33–M78.

4 affoordes] ˜. D33, Gr12–M78; ˜, D35–D69.

5 doe] they D33–M78.

8 desperate] ˜; D33–D69, S67; ˜. Gr12, M78.

9 bee] ˜; D33–S67; ˜, M78.

12 thine] thy D33–M78. more] ˜? D33–M78.

14 Innocent] ˜? D33–M78.

16 race] raze D33–M78. vndon] ˜? D33–M78.

19 then] than D35–D69.

20 they] the D33–M78. begin] ˜; D33–D69, S67; ˜. Gr12, M78.

21 for] to D33. thee] ˜; D33–M78.

22 bee] ˜; D33–M78.

23 weake] ˜; D33–M78.

24 breake] ˜? D33–M78.

26 for] *om* D35–D69. her] her we D35–D69. all] ˜; D33–D39, Gr12–M78; ˜: D49–D69.

28 that] who D35–D69. well] ˜; D33, S67; ˜. D35–Gr12, M78.

29 or] and D33–M78. or] and D33–M78. die] ˜; D33–M78.

30 the] shee D33–M78. misery] ˜; D33–D39, S67; ˜: D49–D69; ˜. Gr12, M78.

32 and] and and D49–D54. oppression] ˜; D33–D39, Gr12–M78; ˜: D49–D69.

34 the] that D35–D69. *Cardinall*] ˜; D33–D39, S67; ˜: D49–D69; ˜. Gr12, M78.

35 *Paradice*] ˜; D33–D39, Gr12–M78; ˜: D49–D69.

36 grace] Grace D35, D39. sin] ˜; D33–D39, S67, M78; ˜: D49–D69; ˜. Gr12.

37 more] ˜; D69. that] then D33, D69–M78; than D35–D54.

38 tree] ˜; D33–D39, S67, M78; ˜: D49–D69; ˜. Gr12.

39 least] lest D33–M78.

40 the] that D33–M78. aboue] ˜, D33–D39, Gr12–M78; ˜: D49–D69.

42 is] ˜; D33–D39, Gr12–M78; ˜: D49–D69.

43 Where] Who D33–M78.

44 now] have now D33–M78. holliday] ˜; D33, S67; ˜. D35–Gr12, M78.

45 Bush] bush D33–M78.

47 godes] Godes D33–M78.

48 w^{ch}] what D33–M78. turnd] turne D33–M78. feasts] feast D33–M78. wee] she D33–M78.

50 her] her high D33–M78. last] ˜; D33, S67; ˜. D35–Gr12, M78.

52 fell] ˜) D33–M78.

53 bodie] bodie's D35–D69. least] lest D33–M78.

54 dead] ˜; D33–M78.

56 *Goddesses*] ˜. D33–D54, Gr12–M78; ˜, D69.

57 woes] wooes D33–M78.

58 wilbe] will be a D33–S67; will be M78. *Lemnia*] ˜; D33–M78.

59 wrappr] wraps D33–M78.

60 shalbe] shall be D33–M78. Diamond] ˜; D33–D39, Gr12–M78; ˜: D49–D69.

61 here] her D33–M78. gladd sadd] sadd gladd D33–M78.

62 wast] breake D35–D69. *stoicks*] Stoicks D33–M78. *hart*] ˜. D33–M78.

"Elegie: 'Oh, let mee not serve so.'" Texts: TT1 (51v–52), TT2 (25r-v), D33–Ga65, S67.

HE *Elegie*] *Elegie* VII. D33; *Elegie* VI. D35–Gr12; Recusancy Ga65.

1 not mee] mee not D33–S67.

2 honours] honour TT2. flatter] fatten D33–D54, Gr12–S67. sterue] ˜; D33–D39, Gr12–S67; ˜: D49–D69.

3 &] or D33–S67. lookes] ˜; D33–D39, Gr12–S67; ˜: D49–D69.

4 bookes] ˜: D69.

6 wth] which D33–D69. *Realmes*] names D69. full fill] fulfill D33–S67.

7 sway] ˜. D33–S67.

9 Themselues;] ˜, TT2–S67. names!] ˜: D33–S67.

10 bee] ˜. D33–S67.

11 mine] her D33–S67. sheathd] ˜, D33, Gr12–S67; ˜; D35–D69.

13 Purgatorie] Purgatorie & TT2. (faithlesse] ^˜ TT2–S67.

14 seem'd] seemes TT2. constancy] ˜. D33, Ga65, S67; ˜: D35–Gr12.

17 them.] ˜, TT2; ˜; D33–S67.

19 his] his→hir TT2. winges] ˜, TT2; ˜; D33–S67.

20 him] them D33–S67. his] ˜. D33, D49–S67; ˜, D35, D39.

21 beheld] behold D33–S67.

24 wedded] welled TT2. there] then D33, Gr12–S67.

26 to] or D33, Gr12. vppmost] utmost D35–D69. browe] ˜: D33–D69, Ga65, S67; ˜; Gr12.

28 banck] bancks D33–D69, S67.

30 long kept] long-kept D33–S67.

31 and in] in a TT2.

33 her] the D33, Gr12–S67. who] which D35–D69. drie] ˜; D33–S67.

34 I] ˜; D33–S67. I] ˜. D33–S67.

35 mee] ~~mee~~ TT2; *om* D33–S67. this] thy D33–S67. forgett] ~~forgett~~[begett] TT2; beget D33–S67.

37 scorne] ˜; D33–S67. (oh)] ^˜^ D33–D54, Gr12–S67; ^ah^ D69.

38 so] *om* D33–S67. arriud] arm'd D33–S67. disdaine] ˜. D33–S67.

39 thee] *om* D69.

40 eie] ˜; D33–D54, S67; ˜: D69; ˜. Gr12, Ga65.

41 Though] Through D69. breed] bred D33, Gr12–S67. loue:] ˜^ TT2, D49–D69; ˜; D33, Gr12–S67.

42 (As] ^˜ D33–S67. *Rome*)] ˜^ D33–S67. fall] ˜. D33, D35, Gr12–S67; ˜, D39–D69.

43 Mine] My D33–S67. hate] heat TT2.

44 dalliance] ˜: D33–S67.

45 recusant] Recusant D33–S67.

46 excommunicate] ˜/ TT2; ˜? D33–S67.

"The Will." Texts: TT1 (52r-v), TT2 (25v–26), D33–Ga65, S67. TT1 and TT2 omit the third stanza of the printed versions.

HE *Loues Legacie*] *The Will* D33–S67.

2 (great] ^˜ D33–S67. Loue)] ˜^ D33–S67. Legacies] ˜, TT2; ˜; D33–S67.

3 mine] my TT2.

4 thee] ˜; D33–S67.

5 fame.] ˜, TT2; ˜; D33–S67. eares] ˜; D33–S67.

6 teares] ˜; D33–D69; ˜. Gr12–S67.

8 serue] serue her D33–D54, Gr12–S67; love her D69.

9 before] ˜. D33–S67.

10 giue] ˜, D33–D69, S67; ˜; Gr12, Ga65.

11 liue] ˜; D33–S67.

13 Iesuites,] ˜; D33–S67. pensiuenes] ˜; D33–S67.

14 beene] ˜; D33–S67.

15 *Capuchin*] ˜. D33–S67.

17 could] can D33–S67.

18 giue] giue to D33–S67. an Incapacitie] Incapacitie TT2; as have an Incapacitie D33–D54, Gr12–S67; as have no good Capacity. D69.

19 *om*] My faith I give to Roman Catholiques; D33–S67.

20 *om*] All my good works unto the Schismaticks D33–S67.

21 *om*] Of Amsterdam; my best civility D33–S67.

22 *om*] And Courtship, to an Universitie; D33–S67.

23 *om*] My modesty I give to souldiers bare; D33–S67 (bare: D49–D54; bare. D69).

24 *om*] My patience let gamesters share. D33–S67.

25 *om*] Thou Love taughtst mee, by making mee D33–S67.

26 *om*] Love her that holds my love disparity, D33–S67.

27 *om*] Onely to give to those that count my gifts indignity. D33–S67.

29 frendes] ˜; D33–D39, Gr12–S67; ˜: D49–D69. foes] ˜; D33–D39, Gr12–S67; ˜: D49–D69.

30 doubtfullnes] ˜; D33–D39, Gr12–S67; ˜: D49–D69.

31 excesse] ˜; D33–D39, Gr12–S67; ˜: D49–D69.

32 nature] Nature TT2–S67. writt] ˜; D33–D39, Gr12–S67; ˜: D49–D69.

33 witt] ˜; D33–D39; ˜: D49–D69; ˜. Gr12–S67.

35 her:] ˜, TT2–D39, Gr12–S67; ˜^ D49–D69.

36 restore] ˜. D33–S67.

37 passing bell] passing-bell D35–D69.

38 bookes] ˜, TT2; ˜; D33–D39, Gr12–S67; ˜: D49–D69.

39 counsell] counsells D33–S67. giue] ˜; D33–D39, Gr12–S67; ˜: D49–D69.

41 bread;] ˜, TT2; ˜: D49–D69.

42 forrainers:] ˜, TT2–S67. tongue] ˜. D33–S67.

43 Though] Thou D33–S67.

44 portion] ˜. D69.

45 disproportion] ˜. D33–S67.

46 more] ˜, TT2, D35–D69; ˜; D33, Gr12–S67.

47 dying] ~, TT2; ~; D33–D39, Gr12–S67; ~: D49–D69. too] ~. D33–S67.
49 doe] doth D33–S67. foorth] ~. D33–D39, ~; D69–S67.
51 Then] Than D69. *Sun=Diall*] Sun Diall D33–D54, Gr12–S67. graue] ~, D33–D39; ~. D49–S67.
53 thee & mee] mee & thee D33–S67.
54 all] ~. D49–D54; *om* D69. three] ~. D33–D39, Gr12–S67; thee. D69.

"Elegie: The Expostulation." Texts: TT1 (53v–54), TT2 (27r-v), D33–Ga65, S67.
HE *Elegie*] ELEG. XVII. *The Expostulation.* D35–D54; ELEGIE. XVII. D69; ELEGIE XV. *The Expostulation* Gr12; The Expostulation Ga65; *Elegie: The Expostulation* S67.
1 more] *om* D33–S67.
2 you] ~? D33–S67.
4 faire] ~? D33–S67.
6 of] *om* D33–S67. truth] ~? D33–S67.
7 eies] ~? D33, Gr12–S67; ~, D35–D69.
8 she] it D33–S67. periuries] ~? D33–S67.
9 wth] wch TT2. or] of TT2.
11 they] their D33–S67.
12 cold)] ~^ Gr12, Ga65. once] ~) Gr12, Ga65. death] ~? D33–S67.
16 (among] ^~ TT2–S67. all] (~ D33–S67. sweeter] sweetend D35–D69. your] our D33–S67. feares] ~) D39–D69.
18 (that] ^~ TT2–S67. rest)] ~, TT2, D35–D69. blisses] ~? D33–S67.
19 forfeyt] ~, TT2; ~? D33–S67. breake] ~? D33–S67.
22 The] Hee D33–S67. lust] ~? D33–S67.
23 prophane] ~, TT2, D33, Gr12–S67; ~; D35–D69. most] most of D33–S67.
24 beast;] ~, TT2–S67. thought] thoughts D35–D69. accept] except D33–S67. thee] ~; D33, D35, Gr12–S67; ~, D39.
25 loue.] ~, TT2; loue, though D33, Gr12–S67; loue; though D35–D69.
28 earth!] ~^ TT2; ~, D33–S67. beare] ~, D33, Gr12–S67; ~: D35–D69.
30 would] will D35–D69. streames] ~; D33–D69, S67; ~, Gr12, Ga65.
32 yours] ~; D33, S67; ~. D35–Ga65.
36 yow] me D33–S67. you^{r}] you D33–S67.
37 black] (~ D69. wretch] ~) D69.
38 third] ~; D33–D54, S67; ~, D69; ~. Gr12, Ga65.
41 pittie] ~; D33–S67.
42 wittie] ~; D33–D39, Gr12–S67; ~. D49–D69.
44 infamy] ~; D33–S67.
45 god] God D33–S67.
46 price] ~; D33–S67.
47 selfe torment] selfe-torment D35–D69.
51 carion coarse] carion-coarse D69.
52 dogges] ~; D33; ~, D35–S67. beast] ~; D33, S67; ~. D35, D69–Ga65; ~, D39.
53 I haue] haue I D33–D54, Gr12, S67. reuiue] ~; D33–S67.
54 aliue] ~; D33–S67.
57 lease] lace, TT2; ~; D33–S67.
58 the] *om* D33–S67. whilst] whiles D33–S67. make] ~; D33, Gr12–S67; ~. D35–D69.
59 these] those D33–S67.
61 lik'd] ~; D33–S67.
62 selfe same] selfe-same D35–D69. wayes] ~; D33–S67.
64 be] being TT2. impertinent] ~; D33–S67.
66 subtle] subtilly D33–S67. disease] ~; D33–S67.
68 then] than D39–D54. gett] ~: D33–S67.
70 though t'is] thought is TT2. art] ~. D33–S67.

"Song: 'Goe, and catche a falling starre.'" Texts: TT1 (54), TT2 (28), D33–Ga65, S67.
HE *A*] *om* D33–S67.
3 past yeares] times past D69.
9 mind] ~. D33–S67.
11 see] to see D33–D54, Gr12–S67; go see D69.
14 Then] Thou D33–S67.
18 faire] ~. D33–S67.
20 sweet] ~, D33–D54, Ga65, S67; ~; D69, Gr12.
27 I] she D69. three] ~. D33–S67.

"Loves Deitie." Texts: TT1 (54v), TT2 (28v), D33–Ga65, S67.
2 God] god D33–S67. borne] ~: D33–S67.
3 then] *om* TT2.
4 lowe] ~: TT2; ~; D33–S67. skorne] ~. D33–S67.
5 God] god TT2–S67.
6 bee] ~; D33–S67.
7 mee] ~. D33–S67.
8 God] god D33–S67. much] ~: D33, Ga65, S67; ~? D35; ~, D39–Gr12.
9 itt] ~. D33–D69, Ga65, S67; ~; Gr12.
10 ever] even D33–S67.
12 Passiues:] ~^ TT2; ~. D33–D54, Gr12, Ga65; ~, D69.
13 was] ~; D33–Gr12, S67; ~. Ga65.
14 till] if D35–D54. her] who D35–D54. that] *om* D35–D54. loues] loues not D35–D54. mee] ~. D33–S67.
15 God] god D33–S67.
16 *loue*] ~. D33–D39, Gr12–S67; ~, D49–D69.
18 loue] ~. D33–S67.
19 Oh] *om* D69. wee] wee not D69. weakned] wak'ned D33–D54, Gr12–S67.
20 would] could D33–S67.
21 that] *om* D33–Gr12. loue] loue her D33–Gr12. mee] ~. D33–S67.
23 can] could D33–S67. doe] ~? D33–S67.
24 might] may D33–D69.
26 see] ~: D33–S67.
27 then] than D35, D39, D69. hate] ~, TT2; ~; D33–S67.
28 mee] ~. D33–S67.

"The Funerall." Texts: TT1 (54v–55), D33–Ga65, S67.
3 wch crownes] about D69. mine] my D33–D54, Gr12, S67. arme] ~; D33–S67.
6 then to] unto D33–D69.
8 dissolution] ~. D33–S67.
11 all] ~; D33–S67.
12 These] Those D33–D69.
20 anothers] others D33–S67. came] ~; D33–D54, Gr12–S67; ~. D69.
21 and] As D33–S67.
22 itt] to itt D33–S67. w^{ch}] that D33–S67.
24 saue] have D33–S67. you] ~. D33–S67.

"Loves Usury." Texts: TT1 (55), D33–Ga65, S67.
HE *om*] *Loves Vsury* D33–S67.
3 (Vsurious] ^~ D33–S67. thee)] ~^ D33–S67.
4 bee] ~; D33–S67.
5 raigne] range D35–D69.
6 trauaile] travell D33–S67. snatch] match D35–D54.
7 Relique.] relict: D33–D54, Gr12–S67; ~: D69.
8 mett] ~. D33–S67.
9 my] any D33–S67.
10 att att] And at D33–S67.
11 promise] ~; D33–S67.
12 that] her D69. delay] ~; D33–S67.
13 sport] ~; D69–S67.
14 att] of D33–S67.
15 report] not report D35–D54.
16 transport] ~. D33–S67.
17 *om*] This bargaine's good; if when I'am old, I bee D33–S67 (I'm D35–D54).
18 *om*] Inflam'd by thee, D33–S67.
19 or] and D35–D54.
20 couett] ~, Ga65, S67. most] ~, D33, D69, Gr12. gaine] ~. D33–D39, Gr12–S67; ~, D49–D54; ~; D69.
21 degree] ~, D33–D39, Gr12–S67; ~. D49–D54.
24 loues] loue D35, D39.

"The Flea." Texts: TT1 (55v), TT2 (29), D33–Ga65, S67.
HE *om*] *The Flea.* D33–S67.
2 is] ~; D33–S67.
3 Mee it] It mee D33–D54, Gr12, S67. now] now it D69.
4 bee] ~; D33–S67.
5 Confesse itt] Thou know'st that D33–D54, Gr12, S67.
6 or] nor D33–D54, Gr12, S67. or] nor D33–D54, Gr12, S67.
9 then] than D35, D39. could] would D33–D54, Gr12, S67. doe] ~. D33–S67.
11 nay] yea D33–D54, Gr12, S67. then] than D35. are] ~. D33–Gr12, S67; ~: Ga65.
13 is] ~; D33–S67.
15 lett] ~. D33–S67.
16 thee] you D33–Gr12, S67.
17 thy] that D33–Gr12, S67; this Ga65.
18 *second* three] ~. D33–S67.
20 Innocence] ~? D33–S67.
21 In what] Wherein D33–Gr12, S67.
22 dropp] bloud D69. itt] shee TT2. thee] ~? D33–S67.
24 now] ~; D33–S67.
25 bee] ~; D33–S67.
27 life] lyk TT2. thee] ~. D33–S67.

"Communitie." Texts: TT1 (55v–56), TT2 (29r-v), D33–Ga65, S67.
HE *om*] *Communitie.* D35–S67.
3 there] these D33.
6 bent] ~. D33–S67.
9 wee might chuse] chuse D33–S67.
12 vse] ~. D33–S67.
15 betrayes] ~, D33–D39; ~: D49–S67.
18 praise] ~. D33–S67.
21 w^{ch}] that D33–Gr12, S67. well] ~, D33–D69; ~: Gr12–S67.
22 meat] ~, D33, Gr12–S67; ~; D35–D69.
24 shell] ~? D33–S67.

"Womans constancy." Texts: TT1 (56), TT2 (29v), D33–Ga65, S67.
HE *om*] *Womans constancy.* D33–S67.
2 say] ~? D33–S67.
3 antidate] then antidate D33–S67. vowe] ~? D33–S67.
5 were] ~? D33–S67.
7 forsweare] ~? D33–S67.
8 Or] (For D35–D54.
10 sleepe?] ~, D33–S67. thee] them D33–S67. vnlose] ~? D33, D69–S67; ~?) D35–D54.

12 falshood] ˜; D33–S67.
13 true] ˜? D33–S67.
14 those] these D33–S67.
16 Which] Which I D33–S67.
17 too.] ˜^ TT2.

"Faustus." Texts: TT1 (57), S67.
HE *om*] *Faustus.* S67.
1 *faustinus*] Faustus S67.
2 *faustinus*] Faustus S67. more /] ˜. S67.

"Elegie: Loves Progress." Texts: TT2 (5–6), D69–Ga65, S67.
HE *om*] ELEGIE. XVIII. D69; ELEGIE XVIII. *Loves Progress.* Gr12; Loves Progress Ga65; *Elegie: Loves Progress.* S67.
2 endes] end D69–S67. w[ch]] that D69, Gr12, S67.
3 sick] ˜: D69, Gr12, S67; ˜. Ga65.
4 And loues] Love is D69, Gr12, S67.
5 force] force it D69–S67. strange] strong D69.
6 loue] a lump D69–S67. make] ˜. D69–S67.
8 then] than Ga65.
10 her] ˜. D69–S67.
16 *Naturs*] Nature D69–S67.
17 this] these D69–S67.
18 one] ˜. D69–S67.
19 then] than Ga65.
22 good] ˜? D69–S67.
23 soe:] ˜. D69, Gr12, S67.
24 woman] ˜; D69, Gr12, S67; ˜, Ga65. shee] ˜: D69, Gr12, S67; ˜, Ga65.
25 welth:] ˜. Ga65. strange→stryes] strayes D69–S67.
26 noe] is D69–S67.
27 Then] Than Ga65.
28 there:] ˜. Ga65.
29 Godes] God D69–S67.
30 aboundes] abound; D69, S67; abound: Gr12; abound. Ga65.
32 hoales] ˜: D69, S67, ˜. Gr12, Ga65.
36 part] ˜. D69–S67.
38 then] than Ga65. Infinit] infinit D69–S67.
39 desert] desired D69–S67.
40 stray] erre D69, Gr12, S67. face] the face? D69–S67 (face. Ga65; face! S67).
41 forrgst] forrest D69–S67.
42 Mannackles.] ˜: D69, Gr12, S67.
43 againe] ˜. D69, Gr12, S67; ˜; Ga65.
46 is] 'tis D69–S67.
47 first] sweet D69. Meridian] Meridian) runs D69–S67 (Meridian^ Ga65).
48 sonnes.] suns; D69–S67 (suns. Ga65).
49 rosie] *om* D69–S67. *Hemispheare*] a rosie *Hemispheare* D69–S67.
50 direct] directs D69–S67.
52 (Not] ^˜ D69, Ga65. *Canarie*] *Canaries* D69, Gr12, S67. *Ambrosiall*)] ˜. D69; ˜), Ga65; ˜^, S67.
53 Her] Unto her D69. lippes:] ˜^ D69.
54 thinkes] think D69–S67.
55 siren] Syrens D69–S67. songe] songs D69–S67.
56 Oracles] Oracles do fill the ear; D69–S67.
57 Then] There Gr12–S67.
58 dwell] ˜. D69–S67.
59 the] (˜ D69, S67. *Promontory*] ˜) D69, S67. her] her Chin D69–S67.
60 Orepast: and] Being past D69. straight] straits of D69.
61 sestos] *Sestos* D69, Gr12, S67; Sestos Ga65.
62 Not] (˜ D69, Gr12, S67. y[r]] the D69–S67. nestes] ˜) D69, Gr12, S67.
63 that] yet D69, Gr12, S67.
64 scatteredes] scattered D69–S67. discry] ˜; D69–S67.
65 way.] ˜^ D69–S67.
66 *Nauell*] Naval D69, S67. stay.] ˜; D69–S67.
67 thence] there D69. be] by Gr12, Ga65.
70 some] many D69, Gr12, S67. doe] *om* D69, Gr12, S67. further] farther Ga65. gett] ˜. D69–S67.
72 ffacce] ˜. D69–S67.
73 belowe,] ˜; D69–S67. Arte:] ˜, D69, Gr12, S67; ˜. Ga65.
76 at] ˜: D69, Gr12, S67; ˜; Ga65.
77 Eeach] Least D69–S67. is] ˜; D69, Gr12, S67; ˜, Ga65.
78 his] ˜. D69–S67.
79 w[ch]] that D69–S67.
80 the] the the D69. be|d|] bed. D69–S67.
81 soe] see D69–S67. refindes,] refin'd: D69–S67 (refin'd^ Ga65).
84 be:] ˜. Ga65.
86 kisse] Rise D69–S67. too.] ˜; Gr12.
87 then] than Ga65.
90 Then] Than Ga65. Elem[tes]] enemies D69. stay] ˜. D69–S67.
91 woman] women D69, Gr12, S67.
92 there] their D69–S67.
93 lover] lower D69–S67.
94 goe:] ˜. Ga65.
96 *Clister*] glister D69. gave] gives D69.

"The Message." Texts: TT2 (11v), D33–Ga65, S67.
HE Song] *om* D33; *The Message* D35–S67.
2 oh!] (˜) D33–S67.
3 since] if D69. there they] they there D69.
8 still] ˜. D33–S67.
11 w[ch]] But D35–Gr12.
14 crosse] breake D33–D69.
16 for then] still D69.
19 when] and D33–S67.
24 now[e]] ˜. D33, D39–S67, ˜, D35.

SELECTED BIBLIOGRAPHY

The following list includes works cited more than once in the preceding pages; the abbreviated forms used after the initial citation appear in brackets preceding the full bibliographical entry.

[Basse, *Memory*] Basse, William. *A Helpe to Memory and Discovrse*. London: T. B. for Leonard Becket, 1630.

[Beal] Beal, Peter. *Index of English Literary Manuscripts*. Vol. 1, pts. 1, 2. London and New York: Mansell Publishing, 1980.

[Bennett and Trevor-Roper] Bennett, J. A. W., and H. R. Trevor-Roper. *The Poems of Richard Corbett*. Oxford: Clarendon Press, 1955.

[Briquet] Briquet, C. M. *Les filigranes dictionnaire historique des marques du papier*. 2d ed. Leipzig: Karl W. Hiersemann, 1923.

[Byrd] Byrd, William. *Psalmes, Sonets, & Songs of Sadnes and Pietie*. London: Thomas East, 1588.

[Churchill] Churchill, W. A. *Watermarks in Paper in Holland, England, France, etc., in the XVII and XVIII Centuries and Their Interconnection*. Amsterdam: Menno Hertzberger & Co., 1935.

[Corkine] Corkine, William. *The Second Book of Ayres*. London: Printed for M. L. I. B. and T. S., 1612.

[Crum] Margaret Crum, *First-Line Index of English Poetry 1500–1800 in Manuscripts of the Bodleian Library Oxford*. Index Committee of the Modern Language Association of America, 1969.

[Davidson] Davidson, Gustav. *A Dictionary of Angels*. New York: The Free Press, 1967.

[Donne (1633)] Donne, John. *Poems*. London: Printed by M. F. for Iohn Marriot, 1633.

[Donne (1635)] ———. *Poems*. London: Printed by M. F. for Iohn Marriot, 1635.

[Donne (1669)] ———. *Poems*. London: Printed by T. N. for Henry Herringman, 1669.

[Gardner] Gardner, Helen. *John Donne: The Elegies and the Songs and Sonnets*. Oxford: Clarendon Press, 1965.

[Grierson] Grierson, Sir Herbert J. C. *The Poems of John Donne*. 2 vols. Oxford: Oxford University Press, 1912.

[Grosart, *Donne*] Grosart, Rev. Alexander B. *The Complete Poems of John Donne*. London: Robson and Sons, 1872–1873.

[Grosart, *Sylvester*] ———. *The Complete Works of Joshuah Sylvester*. Chertsey Worthies' Library. 2 vols. London: Printed for private circulation, 1880.

[Harington (1615)] Harington, John. *Epigrams Both Pleasant and Seriovs*. London: For Iohn Budge, 1615.

[Harington (1618)] ———. *The Most Elegant and Witty Epigrams of Sir Iohn Harrington, Knight, Digested into Fovre Bookes*. London: Printed by G. P. for Iohn Budge, 1618.

[*Harmony*] *The Harmony of the Muses*. London: Printed by T. W. for William Gilbertson, 1654.

[Howell] Howell, T. B. *A Complete Collection of State Trials*. 21 vols. London: T. C. Hansard, 1816.

[Hughey] Hughey, Ruth. *The Arundel Harington Manuscript of Tudor Poetry*. 2 vols. Columbus: Ohio State University Press, 1960.

[Krueger] Krueger, Robert. *The Poems of Sir John Davies*. Oxford: Clarendon Press, 1975.

[Keynes] Keynes, Sir Geoffrey. *Bibliotheca Bibliographici*. London: Trianon Press, 1964.

[McClure] McClure, Norman Egbert. *The Letters and Epigrams of Sir John Harington together with The Prayse of Private Life*. 1930; rpt. New York: Octagon Books, 1977.

[Marotti] Marotti, Arthur F. *John Donne, Coterie Poet*. Madison: University of Wisconsin Press, 1986.

[Mason and Earsden] Mason, George, and John Earsden. *The Ayres That Were Svng and Played, at Brougham Castle in Westmerland, in the Kings Entertainment*. London: Thomas Snodham, 1618.

[May] May, Steven W. "The Poems of Edward De Vere, Seventeenth Earl of Oxford and of Robert Devereux, Second Earl of Essex." "Texts and Studies." *Studies in Philology* 77 (1980).

[Milgate, *Epithalamions*] Milgate, W. *John Donne: The Epithalamions, Anniversaries and Epicedes*. Oxford: Clarendon Press, 1978.

[Milgate, *Satires*] ———. *John Donne: The Satires, Epigrams and Verse Letters*. Oxford: Clarendon Press, 1967.

[Osborn] Osborn, Louise Brown. *The Life, Letters, and Writings of John Hoskyns 1566–1638*. New Haven: Yale University Press, 1937.

[Overbury, *Remedy*] Overbury, Sir Thomas. *The First and Second part of The Remedy of Loue*. London: Nicholas Okes, 1620.

[Overbury, *Wife*] ———. *A Wife*, 1st impression. London: Printed for Lawrence Lisle, 1614.

[Overbury, *Wife*, 4th] ———. *A Wife*, 4th impression. London: Printed for Lawrence Lisle, 1614.

[Paylor] Paylor, W. J. *The Overburian Characters*. Oxford: Basil Blackwell, 1936.

[Rimbault] Rimbault, Edward F. *The Miscellaneous Works in Prose and Verse of Sir Thomas Overbury, Knt*. London: John Russell Smith, 1856.

[Shawcross] Shawcross, John T. *The Complete Poetry of John Donne*. Garden City, N.Y.: Doubleday & Co., 1967.

[Shawcross, "Drummond"] ———. "John Donne and Drummond's Manuscripts." *American Notes & Queries* 5 (March 1967):104–5.

[Tannenbaum] Tannenbaum, Samuel H. "Unfamiliar Versions of Some Elizabethan Poems." *PMLA* 45 (1930):809–21.

[Waldron, *Collection*] Waldron, F. G. *A Collection of Miscellaneous Poetry*. London: Knight and Compton, 1802.

[Waldron, *Shakespeare*] Waldron, F. G. *The Shakespeare Miscellany*. London: Knight and Compton, 1802.

INDEX

Anonymous poems and those by John Donne are indexed as separate entries by title; other poems are indexed by author and listed alphabetically within the entry. Titles are indexed by initial word. Poems within the Dalhousie text are indexed in the Title and First Line Index, which follows.

TITLE AND FIRST LINE INDEX

Poem titles are in italics, and poem first lines are in roman regardless of their font in the text. The titles of John Donne poems are as in Shawcross; other titles are as they appear in their respective modern printings. Titles and first lines are indexed by initial word and spelling on first occurrence.